D0935846

MAKING THE News

MAKING THE News

Modernity *&* the Mass Press in Nineteenth-Century France

Edited by Dean de la Motte *&* Jeannene M. Przyblyski

UNIVERSITY OF MASSACHUSETTS PRESS   *Amherst*

Copyright © 1999 by

The University of Massachusetts Press

All rights reserved

Printed in the United States of America

LC 98-38552

ISBN 1-55849-176-7 (cloth); 177-5 (pbk.)

Designed by Richard Hendel

Set in Monotype Garamond by Keystone Typesetting, Inc.

Printed and bound by BookCrafters

Library of Congress Cataloging-in-Publication Data

Making the news : modernity and the mass press in
nineteenth-century France / edited by Dean de la Motte
and Jeannene M. Przyblyski.

    p.   cm. — (Studies in print culture and the history of
the book)

Includes bibliographical references.

ISBN 1-55849-176-7 (cloth : alk. paper). —

ISBN 1-55849-177-5 (pbk. : alk. paper)

1. Press—France—History—19th century.   2. Popular
culture—France—History—19th century.   3. Mass media
and culture—France.   4. Women and journalism—
France.   5. Women in journalism—France.

I. De la Motte, Dean, 1961–   .   II. Przyblyski,
Jeannene M.   III. Series.

PN5177.M35   1999

074'.09034—dc21   98-38552

             CIP

British Library Cataloguing in Publication data are
available.

This book is published with the support and cooperation
of the University of Massachusetts Boston.

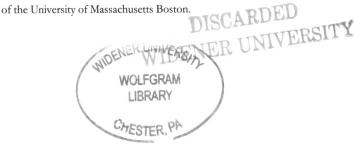

Contents

Acknowledgments

To its editors, trained as a literature scholar and an art historian respectively, the interdisciplinarity of this project has remained one of its most appealing aspects. It would be disingenuous, however, to pretend that our attempt to bring together and publish work from a variety of academic disciplines has not also been a source of considerable frustration, primarily because—despite much lip-service to the contrary—true interdisciplinarity continues to provoke considerable resistance from the academic establishment.

It is thus especially gratifying to be able to thank the following colleagues for their advice and support in the development of this volume: Jim Allen, whose initial enthusiasm as a contributor widened into boundless encouragement and wise counsel; Rich Hendel, whose experience in academic publishing helped us define our project and its public and whose friendship supplied still more encouragement; Gerry Prince, who read an early version of the manuscript and made many helpful suggestions, both scholarly and practical; Vanessa Schwartz, who was an endless source of suggestions for possible contributors and publishers; Patrick Leary, who suggested the University of Massachusetts Press; the two anonymous readers who recommended publication and made many helpful suggestions; Paul Wright, our editor at the press, for his unflagging support of the project and exemplary patience with the contributors and editors; Pam Wilkinson and Catlin Murphy at the University of Massachusetts Press, for keeping us on track through the production process. We also want to express our gratitude to the staff of the Correspondence Center of Guilford College, as well as to Miriam Collins, for their clerical and technical support throughout the development of *Making the News*. Finally, we wish to thank our families for their support and affection, but especially their forbearance, when this project occasionally threatened to swallow us whole.

MAKING THE News

Dean de la Motte & Jeannene M. Przyblyski

Introduction

*Modernity and history seem condemned to being linked together
in a self-destroying union that threatens the survival of both.*
—*Paul de Man,* Blindness and Insight

We cannot display the content of such a diffuse formation.
—*Richard Terdiman,* Discourse/Counter-Discourse

I n recent studies of early mass culture in nineteenth-century France by
literary scholars, art historians, historians, and others in the emerging
field of cultural studies, the mass press has received surprisingly little
systematic scrutiny. Other now canonical sites of modernity—panoramas, department stores, cinema and fashion, the boulevards and their
habitual denizens, the flâneur and the prostitute, to name only a few—
continue to hold sway, even as their elaboration often depends upon reconstructing their effects through their appearance in the mass press.[1] One
suspects that this is largely due to the view expressed by Richard Terdiman in
*Discourse/Counter-Discourse: The Theory and Practice of Symbolic Resistance in
Nineteenth-Century France* (1985) and shared by many, that the mass press
represents a stable, dominant discourse against which subversive counter-
discursive tactics are deployed, both from within (caricature in the early July
Monarchy) and from without (literary texts, like those of Flaubert and
Baudelaire).[2] Today the press, along with several other hegemonic systems
like objectivity and progress have ironically achieved—or recovered—an
invisibility we tend to associate with ideological efficacy. In short, it may well
be that the press has not been examined in greater detail precisely because it
is *taken for granted as dominant.* Certainly the press is increasingly ubiquitous as
the century unfolds: it serves not only as a source of documentation in
secondary literature, but is constituted as a recurrent motif of modernity in
primary texts from Balzac to Maupassant, as well as canonical works of
modern painting from Monet, Degas, and Cézanne to, most notoriously
perhaps, the cubist collages of Picasso and Braque (not to mention the work
of middlebrow genre painters like James Tissot).

The contributors to *Making the News* have taken as a broad, largely unspoken goal the task of restoring to the early mass press much of the heterogeneity that has been obscured or sacrificed in the interest of an admittedly compelling analysis of modernity. Jeremy Popkin, for example, notes in his essay that the "identification of the newspaper press with a stifling and corrupt dominant culture overlooks the fact that France was also the country where the modern revolutionary newspaper first appeared." The extent to which a revolutionary politics—of the masses—is possible in this earliest of mass media is a question that enters, directly or surreptitiously, into practically every essay in *Making the News*. Whether it be of class or gender, the self-conscious representation of the other (we might call it oppositional or counter-discursive) is both framed and ultimately neutralized by the increasingly commercial logic of the press. In this regard, and perhaps in spite of themselves, the contributors ultimately ratify Terdiman's argument, suggesting—as he himself does in his afterword—the uncanny ability of commercialized journalism to co-opt any counter-discursive irritants.

Be that as it may, the picture of the press fashioned in *Making the News* is decidedly more complex than we are accustomed to seeing in cultural histories. By considering not only the *content* of the press as the empirical raw material for whatever topic might be under consideration, but also the *forms* of the mass press as themselves important and eloquent, the contributors to *Making the News* are able to show the relevance of such innovations as the *roman-feuilleton,* the illustrated weekly, and the oppositional interventions of the satirical and caricatural press to the consolidation—if painfully protracted—of a bourgeois, democratic, consumer-based capitalist society in France in the years between 1830 and 1900. Certainly these years saw significant developments in the press as an instrument of modernity. Technological advances and changes in the laws governing the publication and distribution of printed materials made possible the emergence of the mass press in the early years of the July Monarchy.[3] Following the initial appearances in 1836 of the commercial dailies, *La Presse* and *Le Siècle,* by 1858 the Parisian dailies could claim sales of 235,000 copies. By 1870, those sales had expanded to one million, and by 1880 they had reached two million.[4] From the "penny papers" to the flourishing popularity of the satirical press (at one point or another, nearly every political faction had its own "funny paper"), the mass press changed the way topical narratives were organized and information was consumed.[5] These new discursive spaces betokened a shift from subscription-based periodicals to those founded upon the sale of commercial advertisements, a dramatic broadening of readership and circulation, and a sea change from an emphasis on subjective, partisan analysis to an investment in the objective reportage of the *actualité.* Through these changes, the mass press operated to form a common culture—urban and insistently up to the minute, with a specific emphasis on the inventions and events of modern life. Not only did the press have an impact on the reception of new discoveries and current happenings, it was also implicated in the formation of modern identity—that is, the process by which individuals were *typed into* the social order by their public construction in gray print and black-and-white images.

From as early as the 1830s, this modern identity was imagined by the creators of the new press—most obviously by Emile de Girardin—as an autonomous subject cut loose from the moorings of historical and political prejudice. Both newspaper and reader, splendidly apolitical, would nevertheless participate reciprocally in the heroic march of progress. How Girardin's innovations—themselves ostensibly inspired by the utopian socialism so influential in the 1830s—are simultaneously mocked and unconsciously mimicked in the rhetoric and practice of *l'art pour l'art* is the subject of Dean de la Motte's essay, but the triumph of the commercial over the political is treated, explicitly or implicitly, in nearly all of the essays collected here. This entails what Neil Postman has called the systematic decontextualization of news, which will be further accelerated by telegraphy, railroads, and then of course photography, cinema, radio and television.[6]

Clearly, the development of the news into an "item," "article," or commodity—the latest thing or "fad"—associates it unmistakably with an aesthetics of modernity, with what Paul de Man called "the ability to *forget* whatever precedes a present situation."[7] Modernity's act of *forgetting*—in itself clearly a historically conditioned idealization—is the radical decontextualization central to several influential "stories" of modernity, from Baudelaire to Rancière, by way of Benjamin, Kracauer, and de Man.[8] Both modernist aesthetics and the mass press, ostensibly antagonistic, have as their primordial constitutive element an objectifying ahistoricism and an obsession with inhabiting a continuously renewed present that, despite their pretenses toward autonomy, would render them much closer in sensibility than is often acknowledged. Certainly this is nowhere more apparent than in the fascination each has demonstrated with both the reality effects and cut-and-paste possibilities of photography. Jeannene Przyblyski, in her case study of Appert's photomontaged *Crimes de la Commune,* points out that "[e]ven before the mass press could accommodate photographs in its pages, it invoked photography as the mode (and model) of objectivity most well-suited, ideologically if not yet technologically, to the requirements of a modern, information-based society." While Benjamin would celebrate the liberating potential of the disjunctive effects of cinematic photomontage because they would seem to require an actively engaged viewer/reader, more often than not these same effects of incongruous juxtaposition, spatial and temporal displacement, and the cohabitation on the same page of the fantastic and the mundane were the stock-in-trade of a commercial press that seemed to rob its increasingly passive consumers of their connection to the past.[9] Kracauer writes that "[p]hotography is bound to time in precisely the same way as *fashion*,"[10] and his comparison underscores the frustrating degree to which the texts of the mass press, like fashion *and* photography, *were never meant to have lasting significance* and yet have tended to repeat themselves in ever-tightening circles. After all, wasn't it Girardin who said, "Le vrai nom de la presse, c'est l'oubli" [The true name of the press is oblivion]?[11] (Unless otherwise noted, all translations in the introduction are our own.)

Making the News is thus not a history of the press in nineteenth-century France, but rather, we hope, a point of departure for new considerations of its central role in the construction of the cultural landscape of modernity. We have chosen 1830 as our beginning, for when in that year the fiercely reactionary Bourbon Restoration gave way to the Orleanist July Monarchy of the "Citizen King" Louis-Philippe, the press was directly implicated. The crisis was provoked by the infamous *ordonnances* of 25 July 1830, in which Charles X's minister Polignac accused the press of being "an instrument of disorder and sedition."[12] The 1830s were years particularly rich in new ideas and techniques, and they witnessed the arrival of several developments crucial to the evolution of the mass press. Educational reforms, especially the Guizot Law of 1833, would lead to a dramatically larger and obviously more diverse public of information consumers. At the same time, the introduction of the so-called *presse à bon marché* in 1836—which cut subscriptions in half, turned to advertising as the primary source of revenue, and sold itself as information-based and politically neutral—would have a lasting effect on the public perception of news. The engineers of this *révolution de la presse périodique,* Girardin and Armand Dutacque, were also the first to introduce the serialized novel in the daily paper, the *roman-feuilleton,* which evolved from the earlier *feuilleton* devoted to art and literary criticism, travel narratives, society gossip, or social and political commentary.[13] As Elizabeth Childs points out in her study of Daumier and press censorship, this was also the golden age of caricature, which became particularly inventive during periods of extreme repression, especially under the July Monarchy after 1835 and in the early years of the Second Empire. Moreover, the ancestor of today's *Agence France Presse,* the *Agence Havas,* which began as a translation service in 1832, dates from 1835.[14] Finally, the late 1830s saw the first experiments in France with passenger rail (1837) and photography (1839), both of which would come to have an enormous impact on the gathering and dissemination of information, on perceptions of space, time and everyday reality, and on the relationship of the individual to the public sphere—and all this as early as the first decade of the Second Empire (1851–60).

The 1840s mark the last gasp of the *ancien régime,* and it coincided with an acceleration of industrialization, a population shift toward urban centers, and increasing rates of literacy among the middle and lower-middle classes. As the revolutionary year 1848 approached, the socialist heirs to Saint-Simon and Fourier, and with them a generation of idealistic young writers and artists shaped primarily by Romanticism, had hopes of witnessing at last the realization of the egalitarian promise of 1789. When the short-lived Second Republic gave way to the Second Empire of Louis-Napoléon in 1851, the repressive censorship laws and shattered political ideals combined with the industrialization of the press and a lowering of common denominators among readers to create a distinct, if problematic, rift between perceptions of so-called serious and mass cultures, which—for better or for worse—is still with us today. For example, Maria Adamowicz-Hariasz notes that even from its beginnings under the July Monarchy, the *roman-feuilleton* was believed not to "require any serious intellectual effort" but rather "sought an immediate satisfaction of a popular demand." Of course, those same serialized novels, most notably those of Balzac, Dumas, Zola, and even Flaubert, are now consumed in book form as canonical works of nineteenth-century French literature. It was also during the Second Empire that the inexpensive daily had its first phenomenal successes: between July 1863 and 1869, for example, daily circulation of *Le Petit Journal* rose from 38,000 to over 300,000. By 1880 it had reached nearly 600,000.[15]

It was during the Second Empire, too, that the visual culture of the mass press began to take on some of the contours we recognize today, with the content of images divided between the editorial and the illustrational, and the form of images divided as well between the sharp, improvisational inventiveness of the lithographic crayon and the "colorless" documentary quality of the woodcut engraving, precursor to the photographs that would not themselves appear in the pages of the illustrated weeklies until 1891.[16] Nevertheless, when *L'Illustration* first appeared in 1843, it claimed that its pages constituted "un miroir fidèle où viendra se réfléchir . . . la vie de la société au XIXe siècle" [a faithful mirror in which the social life of the nineteenth century would come to be reflected], going on to differentiate its product from the largely unillustrated daily press with the following assertion: "Combien les descriptions écrites, même les meilleures, sont pâles, inanimées, toujours incomplètes et difficiles à comprendre, en comparaison de la représentation même des choses!" [How pale written descriptions seem, even the best of them, how inanimate, always incomplete and hard to understand, in comparison to the representation of such things!] While contemporary nineteenth-century writers from Stendhal to Balzac would claim for their texts a mirrorlike propensity to reflect the social nuances and observational detail of their time, clearly *L'Illustration* hoped to raise the stakes.[17] Such a widespread, ideological investment in the persuasive power of the literal *visual* transcription meant that photography would find a receptive field in the mass press; certainly discussions of its journalistic potential and inadequacies were already taking place at midcentury.[18] In turn, it should come as no surprise that, even though they do not mention photography explicitly, the same repressive, regulatory laws imposed upon journalists by the *"Décret organique sur la presse"* of 17 February 1852, which Bellanger's *Histoire générale de la presse française* characterizes as the "true charter of the press," were invoked to suppress the work of photographers, most notably during the political instability of the late 1860s and then again immediately following the fall of the Paris Commune of 1871.[19]

As Childs points out, "In a society where not even all of the middle class was literate, the democratic allure of images was great." Perhaps all the more reason to subject them to strict regulatory oversight. Moreover, such visual innovations were central to the elaboration of the *faits divers,* or sensational news item, as a staple of both the daily news and the weekly illustrated.[20] Indeed, the very repetitious dailiness of the *fait divers* (murders, kidnappings, love affairs gone awry—in short, the lowest common denominator of our collective imaginary) demanded that the paper develop some other means than the simple appearance of the story in order to one-up the competition with a journalistic "exclusive." "Nothing resembles a crime of passion of a thousand years ago as much as a crime of passion read in this morning's newspaper," observes George Auclair in his fundamental study of the *fait divers.*[21] An image that might be promoted as emanating directly from the scene of the crime might serve to render such a crime unique—at least for the moment. By 1890, even dailies like *Le Petit Journal* would also publish an illustrated Sunday supplement.[22]

Under constant negotiation throughout the century, as Mary Louise Roberts reminds us, by 1900 the journalistic conventions of the mass press might be best understood as a fully formed system of representation: "Delivered from the threat of government censorship in 1881, bolstered by technological innovations and a burgeoning literacy rate, the Parisian mass press almost tripled its circulation between 1880 and 1914. . . . The results were spectacular. The fin de siècle became the 'golden age' or the 'apogee' of the French press due to both its prevalence and its influence." But as Roberts also points out, it was the very stability and recognizability of these conventions by the century's end that allowed their manipulation to productive effect by such challengers to the hegemony of the mainstream press as *La Fronde*. Indeed, in such a field of fixed rules of engagement, what Robert terms "cultural illegibility"—the positive decision to "fly in the face of" received ideas concerning female identity and feminine propriety—could be a powerful mode of contestation.

The scholars whose original work is collected in this volume have immersed themselves in primary sources, under the assumption that although one cannot hope to display in its totality the mass press of any historical period,[23] a selective, case-study approach might well shed light on questions of its structure that remain of immense importance to us today. The press *does* develop into the dominant discourse of the age, but it also fosters a latent subversiveness, an instability that manifests itself most clearly in the continual redefinition of political discourse, in the elaboration under constant pressure of the cult of objectivity (and its relation both to new techniques of news gathering and representation, especially photography and *reportage,* and to the development of the news *as object* or *commodity*), in the ongoing, pungent efficacy of satirical critique (especially, as Howard Lay reminds us, in persistently scatological forms), and in the contested construction of gendered writers and readers. As the essays by Morgan and Roberts ably demonstrate, female writers and readers could embrace publics that were both feminine *and* feminist. But as James Smith Allen notes, the mass press could be addressed not only by other publics (women, workers, etc.) but by private personages as well. In his study of the papers of the Belgian intellectual Céline Renooz, he traces the ways in which "by contrast, but also by example, the press provided Renooz the material she needed to 'construct' her subjectivity, her agency, in effect her identity, in writing the memoirs that she saw neither to completion nor to publication." Surely despite and perhaps because of Renooz's irredeemably outsider status, there could be no greater and more poignant proof of the interpenetration of institutional forms and individual identity.

Moreover, the democratizing tendencies of the mass press and the satirical interventions of caricature, particularly as they bridged the gap between the textual and the visual, could also harbor their own exclusions, most notably, as Childs points out, in the deployment of racial stereotypes used both to critique and to build consensus among the majority population. Thus, the discourse of objectivity, designed to persuade by appealing to all on an ostensibly nonpartisan basis and no less reliant on the mutually reinforcing proof of visual "document" and on-the-spot, textual *reportage,* also had its blind spots. Certainly, its apparent omnipotence remains in urgent need of consideration. By focusing on a test case of the functional limits of the discourse of photographic objectivity employed at its most repressive, Przyblyski's essay on Commune photography formulates its critique from within the dominant discourse in formation, rather than out of the comparison between dominant and oppositional narratives. Such methodological narrowness not only directs itself to the question of the press's apparently hegemonic totality; it is particularly required in cases such as accounts of women's involvement in the Commune, where "dominant" and "oppositional" points of view often boiled down to much the same thing.

The contributors implicitly hold that the archives are capable of speaking with an eloquence and complexity equal to the ostensibly resistant or counter-discursive texts of the literary or art-historical canon, and this return to noncanonical primary sources is, of course, one of the defining characteristics of recent work in cultural history, whether "New Historicism," "New Cultural History," or "Cultural Studies."[24] Clearly such scholarship strives toward a critical synthesis of materialist and formalist modes of cultural analysis. Such a fusion was long ago called for in literary studies by Hans Robert Jauss in his "Literary History as a Challenge to Literary Theory" (1970).[25] While the authors of the various pieces of *Making the News* can hardly be described as latter-day practitioners of *Rezeptionsästhetik,* they do attend assiduously to the issues that arise as a result of the changing conditions of the production and consumption of texts and images, as when John Barberet explores how Balzac "proposed adapting and applying the dynamics of the periodic press to the distribution of the novel." Circulating between close readings and broader considerations of the theory, context, and practices at work in the elaboration of modernity and the mass press, the contributors offer convincing proof of the richness that can result from combining the aims, methods, and procedures of disciplines traditionally walled off from one another.

The interdisciplinary approach of this collection and indeed of many of the individual essays thus demands an especially inclusive definition of intertextuality, one that accommodates the dizzying proliferation and diversification of periodical publications in France after 1830. The texts and contexts in question include not only newspapers, but legal documents, prospectuses, caricatures, sketches, paintings, photographs and photomontages, advertisements, personal letters and memoirs, poems, novels and essays—in short, fragments from the daunting body of texts and images that constitute and frame the mass press in nineteenth-century France. Across the range of work presented in this volume, we read the mass press textually, contextually, and visually—in content and format as a framing space for representations of how the world is known and how the self is understood. We focus on the intersection of nascent discourses of nineteenth-century objectivity and new and declining forms of literature and art, most particularly as this intersection engages the discursive formations of the mass press and aesthetic and ideological constructions of knowledge and subjectivity. The essays of *Making the News* attend closely to decisive cases of intertextuality and self-consciously seek out sites of contested meaning, broadening the usual concerns of our disciplines beyond the modernist polarity between mainstream culture and the canonical avant-garde, and asking how such discursive formations inflected the pursuit of scientific inquiry, evolving forms of political representation, the construction of gendered identity, and the practice of canon formation in general.

The prospect of placing their work on shared interests in dialogue with scholars in different disciplines, whose theoretical assumptions and influences, analytical procedures and frames of reference, and even critical vocabulary might at times be identical, but at others radically different, was a source of considerable excitement for the contributors and editors. We have not been disappointed, for historians, art historians, and literary scholars have approached the crucial questions with illuminating complementarity. Although we might have used chronology as an organizing principle, we chose instead to use category. Or, more accurately, three categories suggested themselves as the project took shape: "The Press and the Politics of Knowledge," "Readers and Consumers," and "Engendering the News." The division of the volume suggests not only the fundamental ideological and epistemological struggles waged in the nineteenth-century French press and society at large as we have sketched them here, but it also reflects preoccupations central to the work of today's cultural historians. The permeability or fluidity of these three groupings, however, is immediately apparent as one reads through the volume: for example, Lay's essay on Pouget's *Le Père Peinard* is in dialogue not only with Popkin's work on the oppositional press of the early July Monarchy; it also shares many of the central concerns of the work presented in "Readers and Consumers." Similarly, Morgan's analysis of the transformation of the *Journal des femmes* from "feminist" to "feminine" between 1832 and 1836 speaks not only to questions of gender, but also to the "politics of knowledge" and to a central topos of "Readers and Consumers," the neutralization of the political by the commercial. Examples of similar interrelations or interpenetrations could be multiplied indefinitely, but this is undoubtedly work better left to our readers.

Notes

1. For two early examples, see Rosalind H. Williams, *Dream Worlds: Mass Consumption in Late Nineteenth-Century France* (Berkeley: University of California Press, 1982) and Charles Rearick, *Pleasures of the Belle Epoque: Entertainment and Festivity in Turn-of-the-Century France* (New Haven: Yale University Press, 1985). Panoramas, the department store, the boulevard, etc. (not to mention the mass press) began to crystallize as key methodological motifs of the study of modernity in the work of Walter Benjamin. See Walter Benjamin, *Charles Baudelaire: A Lyric Poet in the Era of High Capitalism,* Harry Zohn, trans. (New York: Verso, 1983), and Benjamin's monumental, unfinished *Passagen-Werk* (soon to appear in English translation from Harvard University Press), from which his work on Baudelaire stems. For a sampling of current work on these themes, see the following important anthologies: Keith Tester, ed., *The Flâneur* (London and New York: Routledge, 1994); Margaret Cohen and Christopher Prendergast, eds., *Spectacles of Realism: Gender, Body, Genre* (Minneapolis: Minnesota University Press, 1995); Leo Charney and Vanessa R. Schwartz, eds., *Cinema and the Invention of Modern Life* (Berkeley: University of California Press, 1995). For three related works by literary scholars, see Christopher Prendergast, *Paris and the Nineteenth Century* (London: Blackwell, 1994); Philippe Hamon, *Expositions: Literature and Architecture in Nineteenth-Century France* (Berkeley: University of California Press, 1992); Priscilla Parkhurst Ferguson, *Paris as Revolution: Writing the Nineteenth-Century City* (Berkeley: University of California Press, 1994).

2. It is no exaggeration to claim that Terdiman's seminal work is the theoretical point of departure for *Making the News,* or that it represents one of the *dominant* critical discourses against which—or in dialogue with which—important new work on the mass press is being elaborated today. In his "Afterword: Reading the News," Professor Terdiman again takes up the question of the press, this time in the form of an extended meditation on the research printed here for the first time.

3. The authoritative account remains that of Claude Bellanger et al., *Histoire générale de la presse française* (Paris: Presses universitaires de France, 1969); see vol. 2: *De 1815 à 1871,* 11–26 (on the evolution of printing techniques) and 114–24 (on the *presse à bon marché*). For succinct overviews of the essentials, see Pierre Albert's *Histoire de la presse* (Paris: Presses universitaires de France, 8eme édition, 1996) and Jacques Wolgensinger's *La grande aventure de la presse* (Paris: Gallimard [Découvertes], 1989). This last is richly illustrated and has particularly useful appendices. From the perspective of literary history, see the excellent section on "La Vie culturelle" in Max Milner and Claude Pichois, *Histoire de la littérature française: de Chateaubriand à Baudelaire* (Paris: Flammarion, 1996), 30–77.

4. See Theodore Zeldin, *France 1848–1945,* 4 vols. (Oxford: Oxford University Press, 1980), 2:192. See also Richard Terdiman, *Discourse / Counter-Discourse: The Theory and*

Practice of Symbolic Resistance in Nineteenth-Century France (Ithaca, N.Y.: Cornell University Press, 1985), 122.

5. Zeldin, *France:* 2: 369.

6. Neil Postman, *Amusing Ourselves to Death: Public Discourse in the Age of Show Business* (New York: Viking Press: 1985), 66.

7. Ibid. 146. See also Terdiman, *Discourse / Counter-Discourse,* 122.

8. See Charles Baudelaire, "Le Peintre de la vie moderne" (1863), in *Ecrits sur l'art* (Paris: Livre de poche classique, 1992), 369–414, in English in *The Painter of Modern Life and Other Essays,* Jonathan Mayne, trans. (New York: Da Capo, 1964), 1–40; Walter Benjamin, *Charles Baudelaire: A Lyric Poet in the Era of High Capitalism,* Harry Zohn, trans. (New York: Verso, 1983); Siegfried Kracauer, *The Mass Ornament: Weimar Essays,* Thomas Y. Levin, trans. (Cambridge: Harvard University Press, 1995); Paul de Man, "Literary History and Literary Modernity," *Blindness and Insight,* 2d ed. (Minneapolis: University of Minnesota Press, 1983), 142–65; Jacques Rancière, "The Archeomodern Turn," in *Walter Benjamin and the Demands of History,* Michael P. Steinberg, ed. (Ithaca, N.Y.: Cornell University Press, 1996), 24–40.

9. See Benjamin's classic essay, "The Work of Art in the Age of Mechanical Reproduction," in *Illuminations: Essays and Reflections,* Hannah Arendt, ed. (New York: Schocken, 1969), 219–20.

10. Kracauer, *Mass Ornament,* 55.

11. Quoted in Jean Morienval, *Les Créateurs de la grande presse* (Paris: Editions Specs, 1934), 86.

12. Quoted in Pierre Albert, *Histoire de la presse,* 39.

13. Although Daniel Defoe's *Robinson Crusoe* (1719) was the first serialized novel, the golden age of the *roman-feuilleton*—in which the literary product was consciously used to boost sales and in which marketing clearly determined narrative structure—began in 1836. This was equally true in England: Dickens's *Pickwick Papers* dates from the same year.

14. Wolgensinger, *Aventure,* 53–54.

15. Bellanger, *Histoire générale de la presse française,* 2:327–28. Cited in Terdiman, *Discourse / Counter-Discourse,* 133.

16. Terdiman, *Discourse / Counter-Discourse,* 152. On the first appearance of photographs in *L'Illustration,* see Anne-Claude Ambroise-Rendu, "Du dessin de presse à la photographie (1878–1914); Histoire d'une mutation technique et culturelle," *Revue d'histoire moderne et contemporaine* 39 (January–March 1992): 6.

17. One thinks immediately of the canonical statements of protorealism, notably Stendhal's "un roman est un miroir qui se promène sur une grande route" [a novel is a mirror moving along a highway] in *Le Rouge et le noir* (Paris: Garnier-Flammarion, [1830] 1996), 398, and Balzac's "sachez-le: ce drame n'est ni une fiction, ni un roman: *All is true*" [rest assured: this drama is neither a fiction or a novel: *All is true*] in *Le Père*

Goriot (Paris: Livre de poche, [1836] 1983). Suggestive, too, is his epigrammatic remark in the "Avant-propos" to the *Comédie humaine* (1842): "La Société française allait être l'historien, je ne devais être que le sécretaire" [French society would be the historian and I simply the secretary], quoted in *Idées sur le roman: Textes critiques sur le roman français: XIIe–XXe siècle* (Paris: Larousse, 1992). This objective *reportage,* in which the author "simply" takes dictation from *actualité* clearly shares the strategy of the mass *presse d'information* that was just beginning to develop in the July Monarchy.

18. See, for example, the section on "Photographie historique" in Ernest Lacan, *Esquisses photographiques à propos de l'exposition universelle et de la guerre d'orient* (Paris, Grassart, 1856), 155ff.

19. Bellanger, *Histoire générale de la presse française,* 2:249. For the text of the *décret,* see *Gazette des tribunaux* (19 February 1852): 1. In the wake of the execution of the Emperor Maximilian of Mexico in 1867, Alphonse Liébert was fined and imprisoned under the *décret* for selling images of the Emperor and the two generals executed alongside him. See "Chronique," *Gazette des tribunaux* (27 October 1867): 1035. The *décret* was again invoked in the aftermath of the Commune. See "No. 882: Instructions relatives à la publication et à la vente des gravures, estampes, emblèmes, etc., Paris le 25 novembre 1872" in *Recueil officiel de circulaires émanées de la préfecture de police, 1849–1880,* 2 vols. (Paris: Chaix, 1883), 2: 289–92.

20. See the two important catalogues on the *fait divers:* Jean-Pierre Séguin, *Les Canards illustrés du 19e siècle: fascination du fait divers* (Paris: Musée-gallerie de la seita, 1982) and Musée national des arts et traditions populaires, *Le Fait divers* (Paris: Editions de la réunion des musées nationaux, 1982).

21. Georges Auclair, *Le Mana quotidien. Structures et fonctions de la chronique des faits divers* (Paris: Anthropos, 1970).

22. Michelle Perrot, "Note critique: Fait divers et histoire au XIXe siècle," *Annales ESC,* 38 (July–August, 1983): 913.

23. This has in fact been attempted by Marc Angenot, in his monumental study of all of the Parisian dailies of 1889, *1889: Un état du discours social* (Montréal: Editions du Préambule, 1989).

24. See, for example, H. Aram Veeser, ed., *The New Historicism* (New York: Routledge, 1989), and Lynn Hunt, ed., *The New Cultural History* (Berkeley: University of California Press, 1989).

25. See his *Toward an Aesthetic of Reception,* trans. Timothy Bahti (Minneapolis: University of Minnesota Press, 1982), 3–45.

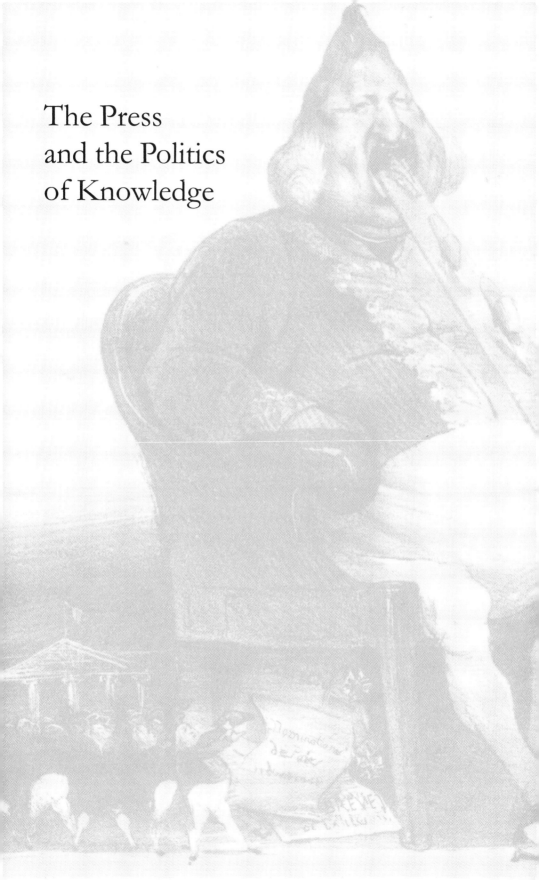

The Press
and the Politics
of Knowledge

1 Press and "Counter-Discourse" in the Early July Monarchy

From their own day onward, nineteenth-century French newspapers have had a bad press. As early as the 1830s, Balzac, in *Illusions perdues,* made the disillusionment of an idealistic young writer caught in the toils of Parisian journalism, where words were mere commodities to be bought and sold, into an emblem of the degradation of bourgeois society. Modern analyses of the press, such as Richard Terdiman's, continue this tradition. Terdiman reads nineteenth-century newspapers as vehicles of a "dominant discourse" that literary texts must play against in order to subvert hegemonic cultural messages. According to Terdiman, newspapers, in "their ubiquity, their very banality, stand as signs of dominant discourse self-confidently bodied forth. . . . In its routinized, quotidian recurrence, in its quintessential prosaicism, in its unrepentant commercialism, the newspaper almost seems to have been devised to represent the pattern of variation without change, the repetitiveness, autonomization, and commodification which, since the twin revolutions of the nineteenth century, have marked fundamental patterns of our social existence."[1] In Terdiman's interpretation, the press thus appears as the discreditable Other of literature, whose more complex structures allow subversive counter-discourses a precarious existence. Sterile and flattening, journalistic texts have no countercultural potential of their own. Historians' views have been no kinder. Most recently, William Reddy has argued that nineteenth-century journalists themselves were acutely uncomfortable with what they perceived as the dishonorable conduct imposed on them by the necessity of writing for money.[2]

But this identification of the newspaper press with a stifling and corrupt dominant culture overlooks the fact that France was also the country where the modern revolutionary newspaper first appeared.[3] The memory of journals such as Jean-Paul Marat's *Ami du peuple* and the *Père Duchesne* remained alive throughout the nineteenth century and into the twentieth, as the appearance of periodicals with those titles during the crises of 1848, 1871, and the German occupation in the 1940s attests. Modern French intellectuals, who were in many cases also at some point in their lives contributors to the daily press, have never entirely lost their faith that the newspaper, if properly employed, could be an effective weapon for the transformation of society. Every great crisis in French national life has been accompanied by a "press revolution" intended to transform this medium of communication into both a symbol of and a means for the construction of a regenerated society.[4] The appearance of publications claiming to represent new groups and new forms of journalism is part of that "representational enactment" of revolutionary change without which, as Sandy Petrey has argued, even participants may not recognize that they are participating in a revolution.[5]

This faith in the transforming possibilities of a transformed press may well have reached its peak in the first years of the July Monarchy. The Revolution of 1830 highlighted the role of newspapers more than any of modern France's subsequent political crises. The conservative Restoration ministers who set off the chain of events that culminated in the *Trois Glorieuses* defined the newspaper press as their main enemy. Their "Report to the King" of 25 July 1830, the manifesto of the attempted coup d'état, stated unequivocally that "the periodical press has been, as is its nature to be, only an instrument of disorder and sedition. . . . The press has thus disseminated disorder into the most upright minds, shaken the firmest convictions, and produced in the midst of society, a confusion of principles that yields to the most sinister attempts. Thus by anarchy of doctrines, it prepares anarchy in the state."[6] The first of the four July Ordinances specifically aimed to muzzle the opposition newspapers. The role of the Parisian press, and especially Adolphe Thiers's *National,* in promoting opposition to the Polignac ministry is well known and cited in every account of the crisis. Equally well known is the way in which newspaper printing-shop workers, whose jobs were put in jeopardy by the ordinances, helped swell the crowds in the Paris streets on 26 July 1830 and set the revolutionary process in motion.[7]

The importance attached to the press in the early July Monarchy went beyond the celebration of its instrumental role in the events of 1830, however. Proponents of journalism exalted the medium as being uniquely suited to promoting progress under the conditions of nineteenth-century society. "Elle s'est élevée à la hauteur d'un pouvoir nouveau, qui n'a pas de modèle dans le passé" [It has elevated itself to the status of a new power, without precedent in the past], the journalist Alexandre Saint-Cheron wrote in the *Revue encyclopédique* in 1832.

"Cette puissance d'universalité qui caractérise en tout l'époque moderne devait se créer un organe spécial. . . . Le journalisme, expression de l'opinion de tous, s'adresse à tous: il est la voix du peuple; car par lui le peuple parle, condamne ou acclame: il est le pouvoir du peuple; car, par lui, le peuple manifeste sa souveraineté. . . . Le journalisme est aujourd'hui la seule autorité légitime, la seule constituée et reconnue, la seule qui ne soit pas niée et combattue.[8]

[The aspiration to universality that characterizes every aspect of the modern era was bound to create a special means of expression. . . . Journalism, the expression of the opinion of all, addresses itself to all. It is the voice of the people, because through it the people speaks, condemns, or acclaims. It is the power of the people, because, through it, the people expresses its sovereignty. . . . Journalism is today the only legitimate authority, the only one legally constituted and recognized, the only one that is not denied and combatted.] (Unless otherwise noted, all translations in this chapter are my own.)

Nowhere, Saint-Cheron claimed, was the importance of the press more evident than in France.

Le Français est éminemment journaliste; son esprit social, sa faculté d'embrasser les intérêts généraux et de son pays, et des autres nations, cette facilité d'improviser sur tout, cette verve dans la polémique, toute cette nature privilégiée d'un peuple appelé à exercer une influence civilisatrice sur le monde, se prêtaient merveilleusement à l'institution du journalisme.

[The Frenchman is especially given to journalism. His concern with society, his faculty of taking into consideration the general interests of both his own country and other nations, his facility at improvising, his verve at polemics, the whole special nature of a people called to exercise a civilizing influence on the world, accommodated itself marvellously to the institution of journalism.]

Hence French politics had become a conflict of journalistic discourses:

Tous les hommes politiques, tous les chefs de parti, écrivent dans les journaux; par eux ils font leur popularité, par eux ils attaquent le ministère. . . . nulle part le combat n'est aussi directement engagé entre le gouvernement et le journalisme, parce que nulle part le journalisme n'est arrivé à devenir ainsi le représentant de la société entière.

[All politicians, all party leaders write for the papers. That is how they achieve popularity, how they attack the ministry. . . . Nowhere else have government and the press come into such open conflict, because no-where else has journalism managed to become so completely the repre-sentative of the entire society.]

Saint-Cheron reiterated the commonplace that the press had in effect caused the change of regime in 1830 and determined its outcome. In so doing, however, "le journalisme a achevé une mission, il doit en commencer une autre" [journalism has completed one mission; it should take up another]. Specifically, it was now the duty of the press to turn the public's attention to social issues. Journalists should "[e]mbrassez la grande question du pro-létariat, celle qui enveloppe toutes les autres, . . . de la solution de laquelle dépend le sort de l'humanité toute entière" [take up the great question of the proletariat, on the solution of which the fate of all humanity depends].[9]

Saint-Cheron's article posited that, under the restrictive conditions of the Restoration, the press had represented a unified public opinion determined to assert its sovereignty. Now that a government dependent on public opin-ion for its legitimacy had replaced the Bourbon monarchy, he called on the press to represent the needs of workers, who were still excluded from the officially recognized "public." More generally, his appeal suggested a faith in the potential power of print journalism to speak for all those groups outside the bounds of the legally defined political nation. His optimism reflected the wave of journalistic experimentation that had followed the overthrow of Charles X, not only in Paris but throughout the nation. This movement was noticeable in the capital, and Saint-Cheron in fact assumed that "il est dans la destinée de la presse de Paris de marcher à la tête de l'opinion publique, et de prendre toujours l'initiative dans l'oeuvre de réorganisation sociale" [It is the nature of the Paris press to march at the head of public opinion, and to always take the initiative in the work of social reorganization]. But his article recognized that one crucial aspect of the transformation wrought in 1830 was the impulse given to the provincial press. "La presse des départemens, dégagée de l'esprit de coterie et d'intrigue, en dehors de toutes ces questions de personne si arides et si hostiles, a su se placer sur un terrain plus large et plus réel. . . . elle est plus vivement frappée des désordres de la société" [The press of the departments, freed from the spirit of coterie and intrigue, mov-ing beyond questions of persons, which are always uninteresting and gener-ate hostilities, has placed itself in a larger and more significant frame-work. . . . It is more concerned with social problems].[10]

It is indeed true that the 1830 Revolution provided a stimulus to the development of politically significant newspapers in the French provinces. Nowhere was this development more marked than in Lyon, the country's "second city" and the location where the aftershocks of 1830 were most strongly felt. Lyon, which had its own bloodless insurrection in July 1830, experienced a massive workers' uprising in November 1831, during which the army had to evacuate the city, and it remained in a state of revolutionary crisis until the crushing of the republican insurrection of April 1834.[11] Aside from Paris, Lyon was the only city in which the number of papers was large enough that every significant political and social movement of the period had journalistic representation. The Lyon papers were no mere echoes of the press of the capital. Published in a great manufacturing center, they had to confront the social conflicts of France's developing class society more directly than the Parisian journals. "Ce n'est qu'à Lyon qu'on peut écrire ce que vous écrivez avec l'espoir d'être compris par les masses" [Only in Lyon can one write as you do with the hope of being understood by the masses], the leading Parisian republican journalist of the early 1830s, Armand Carrel, told his Lyon colleague Anselme Petetin.[12]

The aspect of the revolutionary crisis of 1830 in Lyon that has most attracted historians' attention is the surfacing of the social issues that the author of the *Revue encyclopédique*'s encomium to the press—which was re-printed in Lyon's leading paper[13]—urged the press to attend to. The silk-workers' revolt of November 1831 drew attention all over Europe. Their movement seemed to herald a new era of violent class conflict. The insur-rection of April 1834 appeared to signal an even more dangerous develop-ment: an alliance between workers and the republican movement. But the ferment in Lyon after July 1830 was not limited to the working-class popula-tion. Lyon's revolutionary crisis during the early 1830s also affected the middle classes, and the local press occupied a central position in the process by which new groups defined themselves and claimed a place in the arena of public discourse. Lyon's main daily newspaper, the *Précurseur*, had taken the lead in organizing resistance to the July Ordinances in 1830. It openly de-clared itself republican in mid-1832, and it was in Lyon that critics of the regime first decided to use the issue of press freedom as the symbolic theme around which to organize generalized resistance to the new government. The Association pour la liberté de la presse patriote, founded in Lyon in August 1832, served as a model for what became one of the most important national republican groups in the early years of the July Monarchy.[14]

The importance of the press in Lyon was closely connected to the re-definition of the "public space" in which the city's citizens met to discuss political issues. As used by historians, the term "public space," taken from Jürgen Habermas's seminal work,[15] often has a rather abstract quality. In Lyon in the years surrounding the Revolution of 1830, however, the term can be applied with considerable precision, both in social and in spatial terms, to refer to certain members of the city's population who regularly gathered in specific locations to engage in the social practice of newspaper reading and discussion. Through this shared ritual, they constituted themselves as the Lyonnais public.

Up to the early 1830s, newspaper reading was an activity carried on essentially in the central city, the peninsula or *presqu'ile* between the Place des Terreaux and the Place Bellecour. Even in this area, it was concentrated in particular places. In good weather, newspaper readers could be found at the fashionable promenade in the Place Bellecour, then near the southern edge of the built-up area on the city's central peninsula, where a canvas-covered open-air *cabinet de lecture* set out its wares on a rough wooden table that reminded one observer of the crude popular cabarets in the city's working-class suburbs. A contemporary engraving (fig. 1-1) shows readers, most dressed in the bourgeois uniform of frock coat and top hat, scrutinizing their papers under the square's celebrated linden trees. The article accompanying this depiction explained,

> Ce kiosque, c'est l'antre du démon lui-même, c'est le foyer de tous les journaux. Autour de lui s'éparpillent toutes les opinions, promeneuses ou stationnaires, assises ou adossées contre un arbre. Chacune y satisfait ses goûts et ses sympathies; chacune y trouve au même prix de quoi penser, et surtout de quoi parler tout le reste de la journée.[16]

> [This kiosk is the devil's own lair, the home of all the newspapers. Around it are scattered all the opinions, ambulatory or stationary, seated or leaning against a tree. There, each one finds satisfaction according to his tastes and his sympathies. For the same price, each one finds out what to think, and above all what to talk about for the rest of the day.]

Newspaper readers also clustered in certain indoor spaces, particularly newspaper reading rooms and cafés. These were well-known gathering places, familiar to all residents of the city. One could, for example, tell a friend to meet one at Madame Durval's *cabinet de lecture* on the Place des Célestins, "là où qu'il y a des caricatures collées sur les carreaux" [the one with the caricatures pasted up on the windows].[17] Already in 1820, the busiest of the city's cafés, Casati's, drew three to four hundred customers a day eager for news. "On y lit tous les journaux des deux partis à l'heure qu'ils sont reçus, on en fait la lecture à haute voix et une cinquantaine de personnes sont à écouter le *Constitutionnel*. C'est dans ce café où toutes les nouvelles d'un côté comme de l'autre se communiquent et de là ensuite se répandent

FIGURE 1-1: Anonymous, "Lyon vu de Fourvières" (Lyon, 1833).

dans la ville" [The newspapers of both parties are read as soon as they arrive, they are read aloud and fifty people come to hear the *Constitutionnel*. It is in this café where all reports from both sides are exchanged, and from there they spread to the rest of the city], a police commissioner reported.[18] In addition to the reading rooms and cafés, newspapers were distributed on a regular basis in the city's theaters. There, however, they had to be purchased individually, and a paper seeking a clientele in such a place had to emphasize amusing anecdotes and gossipy articles rather than serious political discourse.

The accounts we have of newspaper reading in Lyon in the 1820s and early 1830s indicate that it was a well-organized social practice that followed a pattern familiar to wealthy and educated Europeans since the late eighteenth century. Newspaper reading was most often done outside the home and away from places of business, in specific public or semipublic locations, and primarily by men. Those who participated in newspaper reading thus had to make a deliberate effort to transport themselves to places where newspapers could be found. Reading the press was a ritual of public life, not an accidental occurrence or one relegated to odd moments of free time during the day. It was part of a larger pattern of public sociability involving regular gatherings in the city's public places. Around the Place des Terreaux, in the neighborhood of the silk-merchants' business houses, 3 P.M. was the customary hour for this interchange.

Les comptoirs sont déserts, les caisses silencieuses, le grand livre fermé. . . . C'est l'instant chéri de la digestion, des rendez-vous, des confidences et des projets du soir. . . . C'est le café du Commerce . . . entrons. . . . Les jeunes gens . . . crient, jouent, jurent et politiquent. . . . [Ils demandent] Quelle est la couleur du *Précurseur* aujourd'hui?[19]

[The offices are deserted, the cash-boxes silent, the order book closed. . . . It is the time set aside for digestion, rendez-vous, confidential conversations and projects for the evening. . . . Enter the *Café du Commerce*. . . . The young men . . . babble, gamble, swear, and talk politics. . . . (They ask) What's the *Précurseur*'s line today?]

Within the cafés and *cabinets de lecture,* newspaper reading had developed into a ritualized practice through which readers defined and affirmed their political identities. Most descriptions of newspaper reading in Lyon from this period describe readers of different political persuasions mixing with each other in the reading rooms, cafés, theater lobbies, and public promenades where newspapers were found. By their dress, their age, and their choice of reading matter, readers signaled to one another their political views. Thus, one account from 1831 portrayed a rich manufacturer catapulted to full citizenship by the previous year's revolution reading the *Précurseur,* while "un jeune homme au front haut, à l'oeil vif" [a young man with a high forehead, a lively eye], who had participated in the street demonstrations of that year called for the more vigorous *Sentinelle nationale.* A third character, "membre de toutes les confréries, trésorier de deux paroisses" [member of every confraternity, treasurer of two parishes], read the Legitimist *Cri du peuple,* while a financially strapped *rentier* made do with the *Journal du commerce.*[20] Humorous sketches of this sort were a journalistic cliché dating back to the revolutionary period, although they undoubtedly reflected a certain reality. Less frequently described but probably more common in actuality were situations in which like-minded individuals gathered to share reading material they approved of. The reading of newspapers was an essential aspect of the sociability at the *cercles* to which Maurice Agulhon has drawn attention in his study of bourgeois social practices in this period.[21] These groups, which frequently maintained reading rooms open only to their members, tended to be more homogeneous in opinions than the gatherings in public places or cafés.

It was in this public space that the city's liberal movement emerged in the late 1820s, and it was literally in the public square in front of the liberal *Précurseur*'s office, which served as a meeting place, that the city's version of the July Revolution began.[22] Ironically, however, the success of this movement, based on a unified "public opinion" whose principal manifestations were the *Précurseur*'s editorials and the crowd that confronted the forces of order in the streets, set the stage for new developments that led to the fractioning of that same public opinion. Lyon provides a textbook example of the process analyzed by social historian Geoff Eley, in his critique of the applicability of Habermas's ideas to nineteenth-century European developments. According to Eley, "the positive values of the liberal public sphere quickly acquired broader democratic resonance, with the resulting emergence of impressive popular movements, each with its own distinctive movement cultures (i.e., form of public sphere)."[23] Just as the liberal *Précurseur* had served to make liberal opinion a force capable of challenging authority, new periodical publications founded after 1830 served as centers around which new "imagined communities," in Benedict Anderson's phrase, could take form and achieve political significance.[24] Thanks to their regular rhythm of appearance and the fact that they always engaged in animated conflicts with their rivals, newspapers were uniquely influential in structuring the conflicts of the class society whose emergence the Revolution of 1830 did so much to promote.

In Lyon, where the press had been of such visible importance in 1830, the creation of new periodicals was an obvious strategy for those who wanted to challenge the hegemony of the new regime and of liberal public opinion. In the years 1831 to 1834, Lyon saw the emergence of the first durable French newspaper to claim to speak directly for the working class, the *Echo de la fabrique,* and of the first French periodicals to use the words *travailleur* and *prolétaire* in their titles.[25] In 1833 and 1834, the city also supported an important feminist periodical, the *Conseiller des femmes* of Eugénie Niboyet.[26] Alongside these two ground-breaking publications, the city also had two major republican periodicals during the early 1830s, the *Précurseur* and the *Glaneuse,* a satirical triweekly. The emergence of these publications, claiming to speak to and for groups and movements that had previously been excluded from the sphere of the periodical press, marked a significant redefinition of the public that deserves to be analyzed in detail.

Of these four publications, only one, the *Précurseur,* was a conventional political newspaper. Founded to represent the city's liberals in the last years of the Restoration, the paper had followed a political line very similar to that of the most outspoken antigovernment paper in Paris, Thiers's *National,* and had played a similar role in galvanizing resistance to the July Ordinances. Like the *National,* too, it had evolved from endorsement of the Orleanist solution in 1830 to overt republicanism by the time of the unsuccessful Paris uprising of June 1832. The *Précurseur*'s transformation demonstrates that even the "bourgeois" daily newspaper in its most classical form did not quietly settle into its presumed role as a pillar of *juste-milieu* society.

The *Précurseur*'s evolution toward democratic republicanism was only one of the ways in which periodicals redefined the public sphere of political discourse in Lyon in the early 1830s. The years following the July Revolution of 1830 saw repeated attempts to institutionalize new forms of journalism that claimed to have either a special relationship to groups of readers previously excluded from the public or a new language for describing politics and society.[27] In place of the unified public opinion posited by the liberal press, whether pro- or anti-regime, these new publications sketched out a vision of a public divided along lines of class and gender, or one fractured by a multiplicity of irreconcilable languages.

The new and unconventional papers that appeared in Lyon from 1831 to 1834 could be seen in some senses as part of a broader movement of opposition to the new order resulting from the Revolution of 1830. From the start, the republican *Glaneuse* and the *Echo de la fabrique* referred to each other with admiration. There was initially some hostility between the *Glaneuse* and the *Précurseur,* but as the latter paper moved into the republican camp and began to share the *Glaneuse*'s difficulties with the authorities, the two papers became friendlier. All three of these papers encouraged Eugénie Niboyet's remarkable feminist periodical, the *Conseiller des femmes,* when it began to publish in 1833. These four papers reprinted articles from each other, and openly expressed sympathy with each other's legal problems. "Nous marchons sous la même bannière" [We are marching under the same banner], the *Echo de la fabrique* asserted in trying to clear up one editorial dispute between itself and the *Précurseur* in 1832.[28] After the April 1834 uprising, when activists associated with the other three papers all found themselves in prison, Niboyet expressed her sympathy for the oppressed by visiting them.[29] A single printer, Léon Boitel, published both the *Précurseur* and the *Conseiller des femmes,* and another printer put out both the *Glaneuse* and the *Echo de la fabrique.*

It would be misleading, however, to construe these periodicals as coordinated manifestations of a single political or social movement designed for different audiences, along the lines of the many special-interest publications sponsored by the Communist Party in the twentieth century. Their common opposition to the Orléanist regime drove these alternative papers together, but each represented a different social or political project and spoke a different language. And each challenged the limits of the liberal conception of political discourse in a different way.

The *Echo de la fabrique* presented itself from the outset as a paper for workers, and particularly for the silkworkers who made up nearly half of Lyon's working-class population. Its subscription bureaus, listed in the initial prospectus, were in very different locations from those of the bourgeois press: the *Echo de la fabrique* hoped to find purchasers in the working-class suburbs of the Croix-Rousse, Vaise, and la Guillotière, and in the poorer areas of Lyon. The paper thus made a bid to establish a new space for political discourse on the margins of the city away from the customary centers of newspaper reading and discussion in the urban center.[30] The paper's initial prospectus explained its purpose and identified its intended audience this way: "Sans défense jusqu'à ce jour contre les menées du commerce, en butte aux brutalités, aux injustices criantes de certains de MM. les négociants . . . les infortunés ouvriers ont choisi, pour arme defensive de leurs droits, la publicité" [Up to now defenseless against the intrigues of commerce, subject to the brutalities and the flagrant injustices committed by certain merchants . . . the poor workers have chosen publicity as a defensive arm to protect their rights.][31] A second prospectus, published in the paper eleven months later, sought to make it clear that its intended audience was not limited to silkworkers. "Nous serons le journal de la CASTE PROLETAIRE, toute entière; à nous donc, artisans de toutes professions, industriels de toutes les classes; ouvriers travailleurs de toute la France" [We will be the paper of the whole PROLETARIAN CASTE; support us, artisans of every trade, productive workers of every class, workers everywhere in France]. This editorial went on to claim to repeat for the benefit of workers the claims for the power of the press familiar from the liberal papers: "la presse est aujourd'hui une puissance supérieure à toutes les forces physiques, nous vous offrons son égide tutélaire. De cette manière, se formera l'association qui leur donnera le pouvoir de résister avec avantage, à l'égoisme, à la cupidité, à la tyrannie des oisifs" [the press is nowadays a power greater than any physical force, and we promise to make it your protecting shield. In this way, a universal association of workers will take shape, which will give them the power to successfully resist the egoism, the selfishness, the tyranny of the idle].[32] Rhetorically, the *Echo de la fabrique* left no doubt of its intention to represent workers as a distinct social group.

Such rhetoric was not unproblematic, however. The researches of historians Fernand Rude, Maurice Moissonnier, and Robert Bezucha leave no doubt that the paper was associated throughout its existence with the organization of the master silk weavers, the Society of Mutual Duty, whose members led the movement for a binding agreement on cloth prices or *tarif* that set off the insurrection of November 1831. The master silk weavers were not, strictly speaking, proletarians. They were small independent pro ducers, firmly subordinated to the wealthy wholesale silk merchants of Lyon, but at the same time heads of family enterprises, owners of their looms, and often small-scale employers in their own right. Although the master weavers were able to mobilize much of the rest of the working population in November 1831, there were clear differences of outlook between this group and others, such as the journeymen silk weavers who worked for the masters and who formed their own association in late 1831. In 1833, when the master silk weavers' Society of Mutual Duty decided to take over direct control of the *Echo de la fabrique,* its former editor, Marius Chastaing, founded a rival paper, the *Echo des travailleurs,* and denounced their narrow conception of working-class interests.[33] It cannot be maintained that the *Echo de la fabrique* directly voiced "the" interests of the Lyon silkworkers, much less those of the entire Lyon working class.

To further complicate matters, the *Echo de la fabrique* employed professional editors of nonproletarian origin throughout most of its existence. The most important of these—indeed, one of the most important early French writers on working-class problems in general—was Marius Chastaing. He devoted twenty years of his life to editing "proletarian" newspapers in Lyon, under such titles as *L'Echo des travailleurs* (fig. 1-2), *Le Tribune prolétaire, L'Union des travailleurs,* and the *Tribune lyonnaise: Revue politique, sociale, industrielle, scientifique et littéraire des prolétaires,* whereas the master silk-weavers' organization gave up its efforts after the passage of the repressive press law of September 1835.[34] Chastaing urged workers to regard him and his associates "comme des frères, qui n'ont pris la plume que pour la consacrer à une classe malheureuse, mais noble par sa conduite et par sa vertu" [as brothers who have taken up the pen only to defend a class unfortunate but noble in its conduct and its virtue], but they spoke to their readers from outside.[35] Their articles reflected a classic dual attitude toward their presumed working-class audience. On the one hand, they denounced its misery and oppression, but on the other they insisted on its need for education and moral improvement. In answer to workers who claimed that they needed their children's income too much to let them attend school, for example, one editorialist, who claimed to have been "né prolétaire" [born a proletarian], insisted on his duty to "parler avec fermeté de l'instruction à la classe qui nous a confié sa défense" [speak firmly to the class that has entrusted us with its defense] and to counter its prejudices.[36] The paper's second prospectus included an appeal for contributions from "tous les littérateurs, aux jurisconsultes, aux médecins, aux artistes. . . . Le peuple a soif d'instruction" [all men of letters, lawyers, doctors, artists. . . . The people is thirsty for knowledge],[37] and the paper regularly printed excerpts from literary classics with the avowed aim

On s'abonne, à Lyon, au bureau du journal, rue de la Fromagerie, n. 7, au 2.ᵉ — Chez M. Baker, libraire, rue St-Dominique. — Goury, au cabinet littéraire, place des Célestins. — Lagras cadet, chef d'atelier, rue Confort, n. 11.

A la Croix-Rousse, au cabinet littéraire, Grande-Rue, n. 40.

A St-Étienne, chez M. Hesse, directeur du Conservatoire des Arts-et-Métiers. — Silvest, place de l'Hôtel-de-Ville, n. 57.

A Paris, à l'Office-Correspondance de MM. Lepellotier et Cᵉ, rue Notre-Dame-des-Victoires, 18.

Et chez tous les Directeurs des postes.

PRIX DE L'ABONNEMENT :

1 f. 25 c. pour 1 mois. — 7 f. pour 6 mois.
3 f. 50 c. pour 3 mois. — 13 fr. pour 1 an.

On ajoutera, pour frais de poste, 2 c. par numéro, pour le département; et 4 c. hors du département.

Ce prix sera augmenté aussitôt que le nombre des 500 souscripteurs sera atteint.

Ce journal paraît les mercredi et samedi soir.
— Les abonnemens se paient d'avance, et doivent partir du 1ᵉʳ ou du 15 de chaque mois.

L'ÉCHO

DES TRAVAILLEURS,

Journal de la Fabrique de Lyon et du Progrès social.

AVIS.

Ce journal s'adresse à toutes les classes de Travailleurs. Il n'est pas le journal spécial d'une industrie, mais celui de toutes.

DE LA

Coalition des Chefs d'atelier de Lyon,

PAR JULES FAVRE, AVOCAT.

M. Jules Favre a compris que ce n'était pas dans l'enceinte étroite d'un tribunal de police correctionnelle que la question de COALITION devait être décidée. Après avoir honorablement succombé sous l'application, que nous croyons avec lui erronée, de l'art. 415 du code pénal, il a eu l'heureuse idée d'élargir son auditoire, et de porter l'appel du procès au tribunal de l'opinion publique. La brochure que cet avocat vient de publier est, dans les circonstances actuelles, un service rendu à la société ; mais le pouvoir saura-t-il l'apprécier ? Par cet éloquent plaidoyer en faveur de la classe ouvrière, M. Jules Favre, connu déjà comme orateur et comme patriote, prend une place distinguée comme écrivain et publiciste. Nous nous bornerons à quelques citations prises au hasard ; mais nous devons auparavant dire quelques mots pour ceux de nos lecteurs étrangers à la fabrique d'étoffes de soie.

Après avoir vainement cherché dans le gouvernement la protection qui leur était due, les ouvriers en soie, provoqués au combat, furent vainqueurs en novembre 1831 ; mais faute d'hommes politiques pour diriger leur victoire, ils se trouvèrent embarrassés, et déposèrent sans contrainte des armes que le hasard leur avait mis à la main. Ils reconnurent en même temps que la force brutale, qui ne donne jamais *le droit*, peut aussi le compromettre lorsqu'il existe, et ils demandèrent à un principe puissant et légal, celui d'association, une force capable de résister pour l'avenir à toutes les exigences. Les compagnons s'associèrent sous le nom de *Ferrandiniers* ; les chefs d'atelier sous celui de *Mutuellistes*. Nous n'avons qu'un reproche à faire à ces sociétés, c'est d'avoir emprunté à d'autres temps des formes que le nôtre repousse, c'est d'avoir cru le secret nécessaire. Partisans sincères des associations, nous aimons qu'elles se montrent au grand jour, et que leurs statuts soient publics et avoués leurs chefs. C'est peut-être le seul moyen de déjouer les trames de la police qui n'a de prise que dans les réunions occultes ; aussi la police se plaît à grossir les ombres du mystère, certaine qu'elle est de trouver quelque part le fil d'Ariane. Nous ne doutons pas que bientôt toutes les sociétés suivront l'exemple de celles *Aide-toi, le ciel t'aidera*, et *des Droits de l'Homme*. La marche constante de l'esprit humain nous donne lieu d'en avoir l'espérance fondée. Revenons à la question. Les sociétés des Mutuellistes et des Ferrandiniers étant organisées, on le sent, l'arbitraire était vaincu. Les ouvriers s'émancipaient de fait ; les négocians devaient donc se résoudre à traiter avec eux sur le pied d'une égalité parfaite, la misère et l'isolement n'étant plus là pour faire pencher la balance en faveur des hommes d'argent. Au mois de juillet dernier, de nombreuses commandes furent faites : la fabrique de Lyon eut par conséquent une grande activité, l'augmentation des salaires devait en être la suite. Il y eut bien quelque augmentation : mais non-seulement elle ne fut pas ce qu'elle aurait dû être, mais elle ne fut pas égale partout, et une anomalie choquante exista dans les mêmes ateliers dont les métiers travaillaient pour divers marchands. La lettre du compagnon Trillat, insérée dans le N. 27 de l'*Echo de la Fabrique*, en fait foi et expose l'inconvénient qui en résulte : « Quel moyen » reste-t-il, disait M. Trillat, aux ouvriers pour ramener » à la raison des hommes placés au dessus d'eux par » leur position sociale et leur fortune, mais qu'aveu- » glent l'égoïsme et la cupidité ? » C'est sans doute à cette lettre seule, qui mit son nom en évidence, que ce compagnon a dû son arrestation et les douceurs qui l'accompagnèrent, le cachot et le secret. Nous avons signalé, dans le temps, ces rigueurs contre un prévenu. Eh bien! ce prévenu était innocent, aucune charge n'a été produite contre lui à l'audience. On n'a pas même admis son avocat à plaider.

Quel moyen reste-t-il, disait Trillat : ce moyen, c'était l'association. Si le travail ne produit pas le salaire, la désertion du travail en est la conséquence immédiate. Les ouvriers quittèrent les ateliers. Ici se présentait une question préjudicielle : le travail pouvait-il être abandonné de suite avant la confection de la pièce acceptée et en fabrication ? M. Anselme Petetin, rédacteur en chef du *Précurseur*, traita cette question avec la haute raison et surtout la bonne foi qui le distinguent. Séduit, nous le pensons, par une idée de justice qui se présenta la première, il décida que non. Nous crûmes pouvoir opposer une opinion contraire (*Voyez l'Echo de la Fabrique N.* 29, p. 236, *et N.* 30, p. 242), et nous entrâmes à ce sujet dans une discussion consciencieuse, mais qui put paraître étrange à quelques-uns. L'*Indicateur Stéphanois* partagea nos principes, et reproduisit notre réponse au *Précurseur*, dans son numéro du 1ᵉʳ août ; M. Petetin ne répliqua pas. Nous devons cependant, pour être exacts, avouer que le nouveau gérant de l'*Echo de la Fabrique* a répudié notre doctrine dans sa profession de foi, et s'est rangé à l'avis des négocians contre les ouvriers, avis adopté, il est vrai, mais non soutenu itérativement par le *Précurseur*.

FIGURE 1-2: Front page, *L'Echo des Travailleurs: Journal de la Fabrique de Lyon et du Progrès social* (6 November 1833). Bibliothèque municipale de Lyon.

of upgrading its readers' intellects. Letters to the editor printed in the paper came from articulate master silk weavers and frequently from silk merchants denouncing the paper's editorial positions, but not from journeymen weavers or from the many women who made up much of the work force.

The extent to which the *Echo de la fabrique* meant to redefine as well as represent its readership was never more clearly demonstrated than when the paper publicized a "Concours ouvert sur l'adoption d'un terme générique, pour désigner la classe des ouvriers en soie d'une manière complète, simple, et euphonique" [Open competition for the adoption of a general term to designate the class of silkworkers in a simple, comprehensive, and euphonious manner]. The aim was to replace the epithet *canut,* which the editorialist claimed had become "une injure, je ne sais pas pourquoi" [an insult, though I do not know why]. The suggested replacements, which included *textoricarien, tissutier,* and *bombitissorien,* suggested that the competitors had a better knowledge of Latin than of working-class argot.[38]

However problematic its relationship to the majority of the actual silkworkers of Lyon, there is no doubt that the *Echo de la fabrique* and the other papers that grew out of it had the effect of reshaping the boundaries of public printed discourse in the city and, indeed, in western Europe as a whole. It is not surprising that members of the Lyon bourgeoisie reacted angrily to the very existence of these enterprises. Several silk merchants tore up copies of the *Echo de la fabrique*'s prospectus in front of one of the public institutions where they normally gathered to read and discuss the press, the Café du commerce.[39] Their gesture was a symbolic effort to deny the working class the access to the public space of debate that the paper was claiming for it. Regardless of its editors' real social standing, the *Echo de la fabrique* established a precedent for the existence of a press claiming to speak for and to an audience defined as distinct from the rest of the population because of its working-class status. The mere existence of such a press was an assertion of the possibility of a proletarian form of publicity, which in turn suggested the impossibility of a unified public opinion, and therefore raised fundamental questions about the entire notion of print journalism as a means of recreating the classical civic assembly.

Much the same could be said of Lyon's pioneering feminist periodical, the *Conseiller des femmes.* It, too, was an initiative undertaken with the explicit justification that the supposedly universal public of the press had excluded a significant social group. The paper's prospectus began,

> Depuis trois ans, . . . la presse périodique fait passer . . . sous nos yeux son prisme aux mille couleurs ou sont réproduits, sans s'altérer, les opin-

ions et les systèmes d'une société qui marche à grands pas dans la voie d'une civilisation plus parfaite. . . . Cependant . . . dans ce grand mouvement de la presse, dans cette active agitation de l'humanité . . . les femmes ont trouvé peu d'organes pour les représenter.

[For the past three years . . . the periodical press has held up to our eyes its prism of a thousand colors, in which are faithfully reproduced the opinions and systems of a society marching rapidly toward a more perfect civilization. . . . However . . . in this great movement of the press, in this energetic agitation of humanity . . . women have found few organs to represent them].

Paris had a women's literary journal and a paper aimed at providing women pleasurable entertainment. These examples showed that "l'élan est donné, l'humanité femme se réveille de sa longue léthargie" [the spark is there, the female portion of humanity is waking from its long lethargy]. But Lyon needed something more: "Nous avons conçu le projet de fonder à Lyon, ville populeuse où les femmes sont en majorité dans les ateliers, dans les fabriques, un journal-pratique ayant pour but d'améliorer leur condition, dans toutes les positions sociales" [We have conceived the project of founding in Lyon, a populous city where most women are in workshops and factories, a practical journal aimed at improving their condition, regardless of their social position].[40]

The *Conseiller des femmes* was not the first Lyonnais periodical to make gender an important part of its self-definition or to address women's issues. Already in the 1820s, the creator of a short-lived periodical devoted to cultural topics had tried to win over a feminine audience.[41] In the wake of the 1830 Revolution, another cultural publication, the *Papillon,* appeared with greater success, lasting—with interruptions—from June 1832 to August 1835. The *Papillon* was subtitled "Journal des dames" and its prospectus argued that art and literature were gendered topics, especially suited to women: "il faut aux femmes des journaux littéraires. Ceux-là sont réellement en rapport avec leurs goûts et leurs habitudes, en harmonie parfaite avec leur âme" [women need literary journals. These really satisfy their tastes and habits (and) are in perfect harmony with their souls].[42] Although this definition of women's proper sphere followed familiar nineteenth-century lines by defining women as especially sensitive to beauty and emotion while implying that they were unfit to deal with issues involving power and money, the *Papillon* did invite Lyonnais women to contribute to its pages and, more important, published a number of strongly written articles, many by future contributors to the *Conseiller des femmes,* demanding major changes in women's social position. The *Echo de la fabrique* and the republican *Glaneuse* also carried occasional articles by women dealing with issues such as the exploitation of female workers.

The *Conseiller des femmes* differed from the other journals published after the 1830 Revolution, however, because its founder, Eugénie Niboyet, intended it to be a journal entirely written by women. Even the *Papillon,* despite its openness to feminist arguments, was edited by a man, and most of its content came from male collaborators. It balanced outspokenly feminist articles with other pieces such as one regular contributor's jocular reflections on the question, "Faut-il battre sa maitresse?" [Should one beat one's mistress?].[43] The project of the *Conseiller des femmes* was to create a press organ in which women contributors were more than guests and their demands for dignity not simply one viewpoint among others. Eugénie Niboyet did not openly polemicize against the *Papillon*—in fact, she wrote a polite letter to its editor, seeking his endorsement of her project, which he duly furnished in the columns of his own journal—but her intention to challenge its definition of women's role and its treatment of women's issues was clear.[44] Like the *Echo de la fabrique,* however, the *Conseiller des femmes* was no simple "voice" of its presumed readership. In one sense, it was closer to women than the *Echo de la fabrique* was to workers: with one exception, every contribution it printed was written by a woman. But the paper's contributors were themselves conscious of the difficulties involved in speaking for all women. Eugénie Niboyet, the journal's remarkable editor, had been influenced by the Saint-Simonian movement,[45] and the journal's collaborators all wanted to improve the lot of the poor woman: "c'est elle, parmi toutes les femmes, qui court le plus de dangers, étant la créature le plus misérablement traitée par nos institutions sociales" [it is she, above all other women, who suffers the greatest dangers, being the creature our social institutions treat the worst].[46] They knew that to achieve this aim, they would have to plead "sa cause auprès des femmes de la classe privilégiée, afin, que voulant bien mettre de côté les distinctions de rang et de fortune, elles aient de l'amour et des soins à donner à cet autre classe intéressante de la société [her cause to women from the privileged class, so that they will put aside distinctions of rank and fortune, and give the love and care needed by this other needy class of society]. Their aim was to promote a sense of unity among all women: "la femme ne sera véritablement forte que lorsqu'elle sera, de bonne foi, l'amie de son sexe" [woman will never really be strong until she is truly the friend of her sex].[47]

The *Conseiller des femmes* had to work, not only to get women to think of themselves as a group with common interests, but to get them to conceive of themselves as oppressed. Precisely because women, as women, had no tradition of collective action, the paper used remarkably forceful language—indeed, despite its respectful references to religion and its contributors' assurances that they aimed to create nothing more than a "coalition pacifique" [a pacific coalition], one might well claim that it was the most incendiary periodical published in Lyon in the early 1830s. The cause of women was "trop juste pour qu'elle ne triomphe pas, dans un prochain avenir" [too just not to triumph in the very near future], one contributor wrote, sure that she would see "les tours féodales de la Bastille tombèrent devant un peuple armé pour la conquête de ses droits" [the feudal towers of the Bastille fall before a people armed for the conquest of its rights].[48] Men were "à l'égard de la femme, ce qu'un monarque absolu est pour le peuple soumis à sa loi; vous avez bâillonné son intelligence, afin qu'elle se soumît sans trop de murmures à votre oppression" [with respect to women, what an absolute monarch is to the people subjected to his law. You have muzzled her intelligence to make her submit to your oppression without too much murmuring].[49] In existing society, woman was in the condition of a helot, but if she protested, man would "croit voir des mains hardies s'élevant pour lui ravir son sceptre" [think he sees bold hands raised to steal his scepter] and react violently.[50]

Despite the force of this rhetoric, the contributors to the *Conseiller des femmes* knew that they faced an uphill struggle to create a social space in which their publication could actually have any impact. The problem was quite simple, as the title of a short story in the paper, "Le mari au café, la femme à la maison" [the husband at the café, the wife at home], suggested.[51] Although bourgeois women, unlike silkworkers, lived in the center of the city, they could not enter most of the spaces where men read their newspapers and discussed their contents, for those spaces—with the exception of such mixed gathering places as the theater and the *promenade de Bellecour*—were part of an exclusively male world. Unlike the male journalist, who was welcomed everywhere, the woman writer was an anomalous figure, rejected by society. Especially in the provinces, contributor Louise Maignaud complained, "on ne saurait parler dans le monde d'une femme auteur sans se la réprésenter prétentieuse et pédante, comme s'il n'était pas aussi simple de confier ses rêves et sa pensée à une innocente feuille de papier que de les dire an mileu d'un salon ou dans une intime causerie" [one cannot speak of a female author without her appearing pretentious and pedantic, as if it was not as simple to put one's dreams and one's thought on an innocent sheet of paper as to speak of them in the middle of a salon or in a private conversation].[52]

The *Conseiller des femmes* sought to challenge women's exclusion from the public sphere with an ambitious plan for an *Athénée des femmes,* an institution that would offer public education for women, taught for the most part by women instructors. Basic courses would teach the uneducated "le langage pur de la bonne compagnie" [the pure language of good company] and prepare them to appreciate the joys of reading, thus fitting them for participation in public discussions, while more advanced lectures would give women who already had some education a grounding in "la science sociale . . . l'économie politique, l'éducation, l'histoire, la littérature et la morale" [social science . . . political economy, education, history, literature, and moral philosophy].[53] Over time, the *Athénée* would have created the public for a serious women's press, but, like the paper itself, it was doomed to a short existence.

Eugénie Niboyet and her associates' bold initiative had much less immediate impact than the *Echo de la fabrique*. Alone among the new forms of press created in Lyon during the early 1830s, their feminist journal failed to achieve the honor of being publicly prosecuted for attacking the regime. Its rhetoric was sometimes revolutionary, but there was no feminist insurrection analogous to the workers' uprising of 1831 to lend dramatic confirmation to its claims for importance. Women journalists were unable to emulate male journalists by holding public banquets and rituals that would underline the importance of their initiatives. In fact, as Niboyet pointed out, the laws that prevented women from being the legal owners of any business enterprises required her to have a male director for her paper and thus deprived her of the ability to use the legal system to defend her paper's rights.[54] In the conditions of the early 1830s, women's patterns of sociability did not lend themselves to representation and restructuring through the periodical press. Despite its limited impact, however, the very attempt to create a women's journal served to challenge the boundaries of the liberal public sphere.

The third major new publication created in Lyon during the period of relative press freedom after 1830 extended the city's political public sphere in a different way than the *Echo de la fabrique* and the *Conseiller des femmes*. Whereas these two periodicals appealed to and claimed to represent social groups that had not previously been represented in the press and that lacked access to the public spaces where newspaper reading was concentrated in the center of the city, the *Glaneuse* sought a general audience and, in effect, a primarily male one. To the extent that the paper's own image of its ideal reader had a social referent, it was the vaguely defined category of "youth." When the paper announced a plan for a demonstration to commemorate the July Days meant to rival the official ceremony, it addressed itself to "jeunes patriotes" [young patriots]. Its editors described themselves as "jeunes hommes" [young men], and, at their political banquet, they made a point of offering a gallant toast "aux dames lyonnaises et aux dames parisiennes" [to the ladies of Lyon and Paris] along with their expressions of political senti-ments. In a sketch of the clientele of a *cabinet de lecture,* the paper imagined itself being read by "un jeune élégant qui, nonchalamment penché sur le comptoir, arrange ses cheveux devant la glace . . . il parle avec le même feu de la guerre des Polonais et de sa maîtresse" [an elegant youth who, leaning casually on the counter, uses the mirror to arrange his hair . . . he speaks with the same enthusiasm about the Polish uprising and about his girl-friend].[55] But these imaginary readers were portrayed as being already at the center of Lyon's public life. Had they not risked their lives during the July Days of 1830?[56] This paper's innovations were thus in its radical political orientation and in its use of an allusive and satirical language not previously seen in the Lyon political press, rather than in a real claim to express the interests of a group hitherto excluded from the realm of public political discourse.

The *Glaneuse* first appeared on 16 June 1831, five months before the insurrection of November 1831. Its ostensible intention was to be entertain-ing rather than political—a tactic for lulling the authorities and for avoiding payment of the caution money required from political journals. The initial issues in fact contained primarily literary sketches, theater reviews, amusing anecdotes, and nothing overtly political, and the paper was distributed at Lyon's two public theaters. From the outset, however, alert readers could have sensed that there was a serious intent woven into the pink-tinted paper that set the *Glaneuse* apart from other local publications. Even the first issue contained a satirical paragraph that asked, "Qu'est-ce que l'aristocratie?" [What is the aristocracy?] and answered, "En 1600, c'était un château-fort; en 89, une place dans une voiture du Roi; en 1800, c'était un sabre; en 1816, un parchemin; en 1831, un billet de 1000 frances" [In 1600, it was a fortress; in 1789, a seat in one of the King's carriages; in 1800, a sabre; in 1816, a parchment title; in 1831, a 1000 franc note].[57]

The *Glaneuse* could not in any sense have been termed a paper for the common people, but the working class soon made an appearance in its columns. One of its favorite humorous devices was the publication of imag-ined dialogues between two invented characters, "Marteau, lockmaker, and Rabot, carpenter." These dialogues, in a mangled French that recalled the *poissarde* tradition of the eighteenth century and the journalistic language of the *Père Duchesne* during the Revolution,[58] were traditional satires in which common people were allowed to voice political truths that should have been obvious to their betters. In the very first of the series, the two tried to understand why they had to pay taxes but were not allowed to vote. One interloctutor told the other, "Je vais t'expliquer ça, moi: Quand il faut se faire tuer, ça nous regarde; alors le peuple c'est nous. Mais quand il faut nommer les deputés, ça nous regarde plus; le peuple c'est les érecteurs [*sic*]" [I'll explain that to you, I will. When it is time to get ourselves killed, that is our affair. Then we are part of the *people*. But when it is time to choose deputies, then it is none of our business. Then the *people* is the erectors].[59]

Unlike the "proletarians" referred to in the columns of the *Echo de la fabrique,* the *Glaneuse*'s articulate artisans were imaginary creations, not even associated with the silk-working industry that gave Lyon its distinctive character. They were typical of the way in which statements made in this paper were never really what they seemed. The young contributors to the paper took a self-conscious pleasure in manipulating the language they used. Even the paper's title was a source of endless play with gendered images. A *glaneuse* was, literally, a gleaner, a poor peasant girl who combed fields looking for the stray grains missed during the harvest. The Lyon paper used pink paper to give itself a feminine look, and it exploited its fictive gender status to make the authorities' assaults on the "fille majeure et légitime de très haute et très puissante Dame *Liberté*" [legitimate adult daughter of the very respectable and very powerful Lady Liberty][60] sound particularly repulsive. "La *Glaneuse* est une fille sage qui n'a jamais vendu ses faveurs, sa robe rose est le seul trésor qu'elle possède, et lorsque cette robe aura été fanée par le contact des mouchards, des gendarmes, des huissiers . . . lorsque vous en aurez arraché le dernier lambeau, la pauvre fille rendra le dernier soupir" [The *Glaneuse* is a well-behaved young lady who has never sold her favors, her pink dress is the only wealth she has, and when that dress has been stained by contact with police spies, gendarmes, court officers, . . . when you have torn off the last remnant, the poor girl will give up the ghost], one editorial announced.[61]

The *Glaneuse*'s constant use of parody, satire, and the presentation of the paper itself as an imaginary female exposed to sexual harassment served a consistent purpose: it allowed the paper to discuss politics in terms that made it, if not impossible, certainly difficult for the authorities to prove that it was doing so. In response to one of the repeated prosecutions brought against the paper, its principal editor, J. A. Granier, openly explained this linguistic strategy. His paper, he insisted, was a literary journal, not a political one. It exemplified

une littérature née de la révolution de juillet, littérature de sarcasme, littérature inspirée par la patriotisme, et qui place dans nos mains le fouet de la satire, en désignant à nos coups les ambitions et les nullités politiques. . . . La littérature que je viens de définir, cette littérature d'allusions, d'épigrammes peut envahir le domaine politique sans contrevenir aux lois sur le cautionnement; car . . . parler politique dans le sens de la loi, c'est discuter les actes du gouvernement.[62]

[a literature born of the July Revolution, a literature of sarcasm, a literature inspired by patriotism and that arms us with the lash of satire, to be applied to political ambitions and nullities. . . . The literature I have defined, this literature of allusions, of epigrams, can invade the political realm without violating the press laws because . . . to speak of politics in the sense of the law is to discuss the government's actions.]

The *Glaneuse* identified its strategy with that of the Paris caricaturists, led by Philipon, for whose benefit it took up a collection in March 1832. "L'ironie est la seule arme qui nous reste" [Irony is the only weapon left to us], it proclaimed.[63] Irony would become, as Richard Terdiman has shown, the principal mode of the pessimistic "counter-discourse" of writers like Baudelaire and Flaubert after 1848. The irony of the republican journalists of the early 1830s, however, was aggressive and optimistic; they made their satirical assaults on the newly installed July Monarchy with the conviction that history was on their side.

The *Glaneuse*'s greatest success in this vein was its publication of a satire entitled "Le Nouveau Petit Poucet, conte traduit de l'arabe" [the new Tom Thumb, a tale translated from the Arabic], which purported to be about "un grand pays bien loin! bien loin! bien loin! qu'on appelait *l'Ile des Dupes*" [a great country far away! far away! far away! called The Isle of Dupes] ruled by "un prince avare, hypocrite et méchant, qui avait les épaules larges, des mains longues, les doigts crochus, et la tête en poire, ornée d'un énorme faux toupet" [an avaracious, hypocritical and evil prince, who had broad shoulders, long hands, crooked fingers, and a pear-shaped head, ornamented with an enormous toupee], and whose chief minister was "un Tiers d'homme qu'on avait surnommé le *petit Poucet du siècle*" [a *tiers* of a man (a third of a man) who had been labeled the Tom Thumb of the century].[64] The references to Louis-Philippe and to the diminutive stature of his minister, Adolphe Thiers, were unmistakable, but the satire set a trap for the prosecutor. He could only call on the jury to convict the *Glaneuse* by admitting that the king did indeed resemble the character in the fable. With the prosecutor as his straight man, the paper's defense lawyer had his course mapped out. "'La tête en poire, ornée d'un énorme faux toupet!' Voyons, y a-t-il ici un buste de Louis-Philippe?" ["a pear-shaped head ornamented with an enormous toupee!" Let's see, is there a bust of Louis-Philippe on hand?] he demanded, inspiring, according to one reporter, "à chaque instant les rires unanimes de l'auditoire" [unanimous and repeated laughter from the audience].[65]

Not everyone, even among the city's republican community, appreciated the *Glaneuse*'s satire. An editorialist in the *Conseiller des femmes* said she had attended a session of the local court to support an "écrivain audacieux" [daring writer]. She had been disappointed when his lawyer managed to treat the incriminated text in such a way that "les expressions . . . decomposées, brisées, détournées de leur sens naturel, amenées à un sens inattendu et forcé, furent ainsi amenées aussi à une innocence compléte. . . . Nous n'avions été frappée que de la flexibilité dangereuse d'une langue faite pour souffler ainsi le chaud et le froid sur toutes les idées" [the expressions . . . decomposed, broken up, twisted from their natural sense, interpreted in a strained and unnatural way, were given a completely innocent meaning. . . . We were struck by the dangerous flexibility of a language used in such a way as to blow hot and cold on every idea].[66]

In reality, satire was only half of the *Glaneuse*'s stock in trade. On many occasions, it made its sympathy for the lower classes and its republican sentiments more than evident. From its earliest issues, the paper had repeatedly proclaimed its sympathy for the poor. Initially confident that the philanthropic instincts of Lyon's wealthy classes would lead them to remedy the workers' misery,[67] the paper had become much more explicit in its treatment of social problems after the workers' insurrection of November 1831. Granier, the paper's editor, had briefly been pushed into a leading role in the evanescent provisional government that took over the Hotel-de-Ville for a few hours during the insurrection. Whether the experience truly radicalized him or merely led him to express his sentiments openly, the paper's treatment of social issues subsequently became much more outspoken. At his trial Granier said he had felt compelled to speak out, "et nos paroles devaient être inspirées par nos sympathies pour cette classe malheureuse dont on s'obstine à méconnaître les droits. Nous avions plaidé la cause des ouvriers; nous avons sondé la profondeur de l'abîme creusé par le désespoir et la faim" [and our words had to be inspired by our sympathies for this unhappy class whose rights have not been recognized. We pleaded the cause of the workers; we measured the depth of the abyss opened by despair and hunger].[68]

The paper soon announced that only a republican regime could improve the common people's lot. Even before the Paris republican insurrection of June 1832, which led many advanced liberals to proclaim their republicanism, the *Glaneuse* had published items such as César Bertholon's poem, "Pourquoi je suis républicain" ["Why I Am a Republican"], which condemned the July Monarchy for putting financial interests ahead of support for freedom in other nations.[69] In April 1833, the paper printed a "Republican Catechism" which represented the program of Lyon's semiclandestine republican movement. While promising that "la république qui s'avance n'est pas celle de 93" [the coming republic is not that of '93] but rather "celle d'une nation éclairée, mûre pour sa liberté" [that of an enlightened nation, ready for its liberty], the paper came out firmly for a long list of civil and social rights, the greatest possible degree of equality, and a spirit of fraternity and mutual aid among all citizens.[70] Nevertheless, the *Glaneuse* never entirely abandoned its original format of light entertainment to become a didactic propaganda organ.

The *Glaneuse*'s unstable mixture of satire, romantic rhetoric, and political indoctrination challenged the primacy of reasoned political discourse exemplified by the *Précurseur* and even by the other antiregime newspapers, the *Echo de la fabrique* and the *Conseiller des femmes*. The *Glaneuse*'s satirical strategy challenged even the basic rationalist assumption that words have intelligible meanings. The reluctance of Lyon juries to convict its editor for his satirical articles showed that the public was a willing accomplice in the paper's subversive language games. To the authorities, this was a warning that the same public might some day endorse the paper's rhetorical violence as well.

The April 1834 insurrections in Lyon and Paris led to increased harassment of the opposition press. In Lyon, the *Glaneuse* was forced out of business. The *Echo de la fabrique*, the *Echo des travailleurs,* and the *Précurseur* had to be restructured, and they appeared under new titles. The *Conseiller des femmes,* whose editors' sympathies for the republican cause were no secret, was not directly targeted by the repression, but in the postinsurrection climate it, too, soon gave up the ghost. A new set of repressive laws in September 1835 gave the government effective tools against subversive journalistic texts, bringing the revolutionary interregnum opened in 1830 to a definitive end.

Although it proved ephemeral, the contestatory press of the early 1830s had lasting historical significance. The periodicals of the postrevolutionary interregnum had shown how the press could claim to be the voice of excluded social groups, such as workers and women, and how it could subvert the liberal bourgeois model of reasoned political discourse. To be sure, the press also served as a buttress for the triumphant liberal regime and as a vehicle for the dissemination of the values of a commercial society. In France's subsequent revolutionary crises, the established press came to be perceived as a part of the system that needed to be overthrown, so that a genuinely democratic system of publicity could be created. But at the same time, journalists and excluded groups never lost their faith in the liberating potential of a properly constituted press, and successive French regimes never forgot the subversive potential inherent in newspapers. The utopian spirit of subversive publications like the *Echo de la fabrique,* the *Conseiller des femmes,* and the *Glaneuse* remained alive, even when those publications had been forgotten. No matter how dull and "bourgeois" the nineteenth-century French press sometimes appeared, it always retained the dangerous potential to transform itself into its revolutionary Other.

Notes

I would like to thank Jack Censer, Sarah Maza, Sandy Petrey, William Sewell, Victoria Thompson, the volume editors, and the audiences at New York University's Institute for French Studies and the University of Kentucky History Department seminar for comments on earlier versions of this essay. Research for this project was supported by fellowships from the John Simon Guggenheim Foundation, the Fulbright Foundation, and the University of Kentucky Research Foundation.

1. Richard Terdiman, *Discourse / Counter-Discourse* (Ithaca, N.Y.: Cornell University Press, 1985), 117, 120.

2. Reddy, *The Invisible Code: Honor and Sentiment in Postrevolutionary France* (Berkeley: University of California Press, 1997), esp. ch. 5, "Condottieri of the Pen: The Political Honor of Journalists." For a contrasting view, in which the weaknesses of the French press are traced to its *unwillingness* to open itself to commercial advertising and its consequent dependence on concealed subsidies, see Marc Martin, *Trois siècles de publicité en France* (Paris: Odile Jacob, 1993).

3. On the revolutionary press of 1789, see Jeremy D. Popkin, *Revolutionary News: the Press in France, 1789–1799* (Durham, N.C.: Duke University Press, 1990).

4. For the idea of "press revolutions," see Jeremy D. Popkin, "Media and Revolutionary Crises," in *Media and Revolution,* Jeremy D. Popkin, ed. (Lexington: University Press of Kentucky, 1995), 12–30.

5. Sandy Petrey, "Pears in History," in *Representations,* no. 35 (1991), 69.

6. "Report to the King," in Percy Sadler, *Paris in July and August 1830* (Paris: Baudry, 1830), 37, 39.

7. For the best-documented narrative of the events of July 1830 in Paris, see David H. Pinkney, *The French Revolution of 1830* (Princeton: Princeton University Press, 1972), 13, 32, 53, 83–6. For a firsthand account of the Paris papers' role, see Charles de Rémusat, *Mémoires de ma vie,* Charles Pouthas, ed., 5 vols. (Paris: Plon, 1959), 2:310–29.

8. Alexandre Saint-Cheron in *Revue encyclopédique,* September 1832, 533, 535, 542.

9. Saint-Cheron, in *Revue encyclopédique,* September 1832, 543, 548, 552.

10. Saint-Cheron, in *Revue encyclopédique,* September 1832, 550.

11. The fundamental works on the Lyon movements are Fernand Rude, *Le mouvement ouvrier à Lyon de 1827 à 1832* (Paris: Domat-Montchrestien, 1944) and *Les révoltes des canuts 1831–1834* (Lyon: Maspero, 1982), Robert J. Bezucha, *The Lyon Uprising of 1834* (Cambridge, Mass.: Harvard University Press, 1974), and Maurice Moissonnier, *Les Canuts,* 4th ed. (Paris: Messidor/Editions Sociales, 1988).

12. Letter of 5 March 1833, in Archives nationales (hereafter AN), CC572.

13. *Précurseur,* 31 October 1832.

14. Gabriel Perreux, *Au temps des sociétés secrètes* (Paris: Rieder, 1931), 103, 58–9.

15. Jürgen Habermas, *The Structural Transformation of the Public Sphere,* Thomas Burger and Frederick Lawrence, trans. (Cambridge, Mass.: MIT Press, 1989).

16. Léon Boitel, "Les tilleuls de Bellecour," in *Lyon vu de Fourvières. Esquisses physiques, morales et historiques* (Lyon: L. Boitel, 1833), 114 (original in *Le Papillon* (Lyon), 21 July 1832).

17. *La Glaneuse,* 28 July 1831.

18. Report of 1 June 1820, in Archives départementales du Rhône, 4M 449.

19. *Glaneuse,* 15 September 1831.

20. *La Glaneuse,* 18 August 1831.

21. Maurice Agulhon, *Le Cercle dans la France bourgeoise 1810–1848* (Paris: Armand Colin, 1977), 18. See also Cathérine Pellissier, *Loisirs et sociabilités des notables lyonnais au XIXe siècle* (Lyon: Editions lyonnaises d'art et d'histoire, 1996), 158–69.

22. On the paper's role in Lyon's version of the Revolution of 1830, see the contemporary accounts in Trolliet, *Lettres historiques sur la Révolution de Lyon, ou Une semaine de 1830* (Lyon: Targe, 1830), 6–10, and J. B. Monfalcon, *Histoire des insurrections de Lyon* (Lyon: Perrin, 1834), 143–5, and the scholarly reconstructions of A. Kleinclausz et al., *Histoire du Lyon,* vol. 3 (Lyon: Pierre Masson, 1952), 73–74, and Pinkney, *Revolution of 1830,* 214–16. Pinkney mentions similar situations in Rouen and Toulouse.

23. Geoff Eley, "Nations, Publics, and Political Cultures: Placing Habermas in the Nineteenth Century," in *Habermas and the Public Sphere,* Craig Calhoun, ed. (Cambridge, Mass.: MIT Press, 1992), 304.

24. Benedict Anderson, *Imagined Communities,* rev. ed. (London: Verso, 1991).

25. A few workers' papers had appeared in Paris in the fall of 1830, but none lasted more than a few issues. William Sewell Jr., *Work and Revolution in France* (Cambridge: Cambridge University Press, 1980), 197–201. For the best treatment of the Lyonnais *Echo de la Fabrique* and of its short-lived rival, the *Echo des travailleurs,* see Bezucha, *Lyon Uprising,* 112–17.

26. On the *Conseiller des femmes,* see Evelyne Sullerot, *Histoire de la presse féminine en France, des origines à 1848* (Paris: Armand Colin, 1966), 186–87; Laura Struminger, "Mythes et réalités de la condition féminine à travers la presse féministe lyonnaise des années 1830," in *Cahiers d'histoire* 21 (1976), 409–24, and Lucette Czyba, "L'oeuvre

lyonnaise d'une ancienne saint-simonienne: *Le Conseiller des femmes* (1833–1834) d'Eugénie Niboyet," in *Regards sur le saint-simonisme et les saint-simoniens,* J. R. Derré, ed. (Lyon: Presses Universitaires de Lyon, 1986).

27. For the way in which the Revolution allowed groups previously excluded from public politics to express themselves, see John Merriman, "The *Demoiselles* of the Ariège, 1829–1831," in John Merriman, ed., *1830 in France* (New York: Franklin Watts, 1975), 87–118, and Peter Sahlins, *Forest Rites: The War of the Demoiselles in Nineteenth-Century France* (Cambridge, Mass.: Harvard University Press, 1994), and Sewell, *Work and Revolution,* esp. ch. 9, "The July Revolution and the Emergence of Class Consciousness."

28. *Echo de la fabrique,* 26 August 1832.

29. Amédée Roussillac, "Description de la prison de Perrache," in *Lyon vu de Fourvières,* 561.

30. On the association between geographic and social marginality in French urban life in this period, see John M. Merriman, *The Margins of City Life: Explorations on the French Urban Frontier, 1815–1851* (New York: Oxford University Press, 1991).

31. *Echo de la fabrique,* Prospectus, n.d. but October 1831. The paper's first issue appeared on 30 October 1831.

32. *Echo de la fabrique,* 9 September 1832.

33. Bezucha, *Lyon Uprising,* 117.

34. The master silkweavers' paper, the *Echo de la fabrique,* ceased publication after the April 1834 uprising, but a continuation, *L'Indicateur,* appeared between September 1834 and July 1835. Marius Chastaing, born in 1800, deserves to be recognized as one of the first great journalists devoted to the cause of workers' rights in France, and indeed in Europe generally. Little is known about his life. According to his own account, he had studied for a legal career and had joined the republican opposition to the Restoration at the age of fifteen. He edited the *Echo de la fabrique* from October 1832 to October 1833, when the master silkweavers who controlled the paper ousted him; he then created the *Echo des travailleurs,* the first of the series of periodicals he produced to publicize his views. Chastaing published several legal tracts and in 1848 he set out his own version of a socialist theory, *Des causes du malaise social et de leur remède, ou Astréologie* (Lyon: Rodanet, 1848). To his dismay, the newly enfranchised voters rejected his bid for a parliamentary seat in the 1848 election. (*Tribune lyonnaise,* 20 April 1848, 10 May 1848.) The date of his death is unknown.

35. *Echo de la fabrique,* 18 December 1831.

36. A. Vidal, in *Echo de la fabrique,* 11 March 1832.

37. *Echo de la fabrique,* 9 September 1832.

38. *Echo de la fabrique,* 28 October 1832.

39. *Echo de la fabrique,* 6 November 1831.

40. *Conseiller des femmes,* prospectus, n.d. but 1833.

41. *Espiègle lyonnais,* 13 June 1824.

42. *Papillon,* 30 June 1832.

43. *Papillon,* 19 March 1833.

44. Bibliothèque municipale de Lyon, Fonds Coste, ms. 1130, letter of Eugénie Niboyet to Eugène de Lamerlière, editor of the *Papillon,* 7 October 1833. The *Papillon* printed a friendly puff piece for the *Conseiller des femmes* on 30 October 1833.

45. Niboyet, the daughter of a doctor, was born around 1800. She had participated in the Saint-Simonian movement in 1831, before leaving Paris for Lyon. After the demise of the *Conseiller des femmes,* she was active in various movements for the disadvantaged. In 1844 she founded France's first pacifist periodical. She resumed her advocacy of women's rights during the Revolution of 1848, editing a Parisian newspaper, *La Voix des femmes,* and serving as president of the *Club des femmes.*

46. Louise Maignaud, in *Conseiller des femmes,* 2 November 1831.

47. *Conseiller des femmes,* 2 November 1833.

48. *Conseiller des femmes,* 2 November 1833.

49. *Conseiller des femmes,* 16 November 1833.

50. *Conseiller des femmes,* 7 December 1833.

51. *Conseiller des femmes,* 5 April 1834.

52. *Conseiller des femmes,* 28 December 1833.

53. *Conseiller des femmes,* 1 February 1834.

54. *Conseiller des femmes,* 14 December 1833.

55. *Glaneuse,* 16 July 1831, 4 August 1831, 18 August 1831.

56. *Glaneuse,* 18 August 1831.

57. *Glaneuse,* 16 June 1831.

58. On the importance of these journalistic traditions for the representation of the lower classes in revolutionary political journalism, see Popkin, *Revolutionary News,* 151–68.

59. *Glaneuse,* 9 July 1831.

60. *Glaneuse,* 31 July 1831.

61. *Glaneuse,* 7 December 1831.

62. *Quatrième Procès de la Glaneuse,* n.d. but March or April 1832. A copy of this pamphlet is tipped in to the Bibliothèque nationale's collection of the paper for 1832.

63. *Glaneuse,* 22 March 1832.

64. *Glaneuse,* 28 October 1832.

65. *Procès de la Glaneuse, contenant les douze articles incriminés* (Lyon: Aux bureaux de la Glaneuse, 1833), 43; *Association républicaine pour la liberté individuelle et la liberté de la presse. Procès de la Glaneuse, journal républicain de Lyon* (Paris: Auffray, 1833), 5, 8.

66. *Conseiller des femmes,* 28 December 1833.

67. *Glaneuse,* 23 October 1831.

68. *Glaneuse,* 22 December 1831.

69. *Glaneuse,* 29 April 1832.

70. *Glaneuse,* 11, 14, 16, 18 April 1833. On the background of the "Catechism," see Bezucha, *Lyon Uprising,* 85–86.

2 The Body Impolitic

Press Censorship and the Caricature of Honoré Daumier

In the face of censorship, the only thing one can possibly do is to keep working.
—Salman Rushdie

Political caricature often thrives at the margins of repressive government.[1] Throughout much of the nineteenth century in France, censorship laws attempted to define strict parameters within which social and political caricature could be published and circulated. Yet the various proscriptions, while largely effective, never completely eradicated political critique in satirical journals. In some instances the laws, the seizures, the prosecutions, and the rhetoric of restriction served only to provoke a more creative response to taboo themes. Some of the most charged political satire of the modern era emerged from the caricaturists who created their art in the face of severe political and economic repression.

While caricature as a form of visual critique has flourished in Western art since the Renaissance, it was only in France in the July Monarchy that its publication in middle-class journals introduced what Baudelaire once termed visual *argot* (or slang) into the concrete social discourse of modern urban society. As Richard Terdiman has observed, the golden age of caricature in the early July Monarchy emerged as a result of several intersecting factors.[2] These include essential technological advances, such as the invention of the lithographic press by Aloys Senefelder in 1798, which made possible the inexpensive production of multiple images in a mass press. Also, the development in the early July Monarchy of journalistic satire of both political and social matters encouraged the sympathetic invention of a visual counterpart.

These illustrated papers delivered the first regular (even serialized) "counter-discourse," to use Terdiman's term, to the hegemonic values of the Parisian bourgeoisie and its chosen form of government, the constitutional monarchy. It is no coincidence that sustained campaigns of press censorship reappeared in the Bourbon Restoration and the early July Monarchy, just as the mass press's audience among the bourgeoisie was becoming larger and more susceptible to the seductive power of images that could reinforce or even generate political and social resistance. In a society where not even all of the middle class was literate, the democratic allure of images was great—particularly in the caricature series in the pages of the press that could entertain as they developed topoi and satiric personages over time. The new satiric press invited a creative intertextual play as images and their captions, essays, and news reports all joined together to construct an unfolding critique of the reader's daily world.

Starting in 1830, caricature developed a momentum of open nose-thumbing and risk-taking that escalated dramatically until 1835, when strict regulations were imposed and the rigid curtain of the September press laws seemed to fall on the stage of satiric political critique. The defiant heroics of the illustrated satiric press in 1830–35 are characteristic of artists working in embattled periods of revolution when ideological opposition is most evident and lines of conflict are clearly drawn. Less obvious, but perhaps more revealing of the dynamics of creativity, are cases of subtle political expression during periods of rigorous surveillance of the arts and the press by political agencies. These are times when the rules and their enforcers appear to reign with uncontested authority; two such periods were the July Monarchy between 1835 and 1848 (when the September Laws regulating political caricature were in effect) and the early years of the Second Empire.

French caricaturists found their most powerful weapon of political resistance in the humor of the body politic. This essay examines the development of Honoré Daumier's use of a particular form of satire in caricature produced between 1831 and 1872. By turning the image of the leader of the French state into a subject for laughter, Daumier and his fellow caricaturists created an unofficial but persuasive political art. I will argue that the mutability of the image of the leader's body—its distortions, exaggerations, and exotic and literary reincarnations—in the hands of the satirists became a visual repudiation of the political authority that attempted to regulate representation. The subject of the leader's body was a loaded one. The image of the king (and, by extension, the image of his self-appointed successor, the emperor) was well protected not only by established codes of aristocratic art, but also by the mythology of absolute monarchy, which held that the king had in fact two bodies—the mere flesh and bones common to all men and the body politic consisting of his policy and government.[3] Prerevolutionary tradition held that while the king's physical body was vulnerable, the God-given powers of his body politic were inviolable. Revolutionary acts of decapitation, regicide, the dissolution of monarchy, and the establishment of a republic had violently dismantled the old system of political symbols. By the end of the Bourbon Restoration in 1830, it was abundantly clear to Monarchists and Republicans alike how vulnerable and replaceable the French head of state was. What followed in the July Monarchy was the birth of a hybrid figure, the Citizen King, at once divine and bourgeois. At this time, the image of the absolute leader became a focus for a compensatory assertion of the old royal authority and power; but it was also a contested focus for Republican opposition to any monarchy, even to a compromised one. Caricaturists asserted new liberties with the crayon that were at one stroke both political and artistic. These freedoms came, of course, at the expense of the decorum and idealized perfection of the royal (and later, the imperial) body politic.

The metaphoric power of the leader's body is made explicit in a caricature by Charles-Joseph Traviès, in which a crowd gathers in front of the lithograph shop of Aubert to view a display of caricatures of King Louis-Philippe (fig. 2-1). The caption "Faut avouer que l'gouvernement [*sic*] a une bien drôle de tête" [Got to admit that the government has a very funny head] makes it clear that the target of the people's laughter is as much the body politic as the body of the king. By claiming the body as sign of political authority through the discourse of satirical humor, caricaturists affirmed that visualized political expression is not some stable commodity that may be harnessed and controlled, but is an adaptive, dynamic process, beyond prediction and often beyond entrapment. There is also a compelling suggestion in the history of caricature that when the dominant ideology seeks to repress its opposition, the less powerful may forge solidarity and identity through humor and satire.[4] To turn the opposition into a good joke in the public forum of the press is to regain the upper hand symbolically. As a consensus-building strategy, laughter is one of the most powerful tools of propaganda, precisely because it may seem so innocuous, spontaneous, and natural (and therefore truthful). Funny as these political caricatures were (and often still are), they were no mere laughing matter in nineteenth-century France.

The most significant political caricaturist to work throughout both the July Monarchy and the Second Empire was Honoré Daumier (1808–79). He published his first political caricature in 1830 at the age of twenty-two, and as an older man his crayon attested to the ravages of Paris in the Franco-Prussian War and in the Commune. His commitment to Republican politics informed his graphic work for more than four decades, and over a third of his lithographic oeuvre of some four thousand prints concerns the political life of Paris. His dramatic career lent itself to legend making. After his death,

Faut avouer que l'gouvernement à une bien drôle de tête

FIGURE 2-1: Charles-Joseph Traviès de Villars, "Faut avouer que l'gouvernement [*sic*] a une bien drôle de tête" [Got to admit that the government has a very funny head], 1831. Lithograph, 24.5 × 28 cm (9⅝ × 11 in.). Courtesy of the Fogg Art Museum. Harvard University Art Museums, Cambridge. Gift of Philip Hofer.

Daumier was claimed as both artistic genius and political martyr by Republicans of the Third Republic.[5] Many of these accounts characterize him as a martyr-hero—praising him for suffering public scandal and personal hardship while displaying moral courage in his early, dramatic encounter with censorship in the July Monarchy.

Almost every biography of the artist mentions that in 1832, at the age of twenty-four, he went to jail because of his art. He served six months in the Ste. Pélagie prison for drawing a satirical lithograph of King Louis-Philippe as the Rabelaisian character Gargantua (fig. 2-2). This episode was the most celebrated of the artist's many encounters with censorship over his long career. In the eyes of fellow caricaturist Étienne Carjat, Daumier was the consummate Republican artist who could inspire subsequent generations to be "toujours fidèles à l'art, à la fraternité et à la République" [always faithful

FIGURE 2-2: Honoré Daumier, "Gargantua," deposited 16 December 1831. Lithograph (2d state), Delteil 34, 24 × 30.5 cm (9½ × 12 in.). [All Delteil numbers are taken from Loys Delteil, *Le Peintre-Graveur Illustré: Honoré Daumier.* 11 vols. Paris: Chez l'Auteur, 1925–30.] Rose Art Museum, Brandeis University, Waltham, Mass. The Benjamin A. and Julia M. Trustman Collection, Brandeis University Libraries, Waltham, Mass.

to art, to fraternity, and to the Republic].[6] (Unless otherwise noted, all translations in this chapter are my own.) After Daumier's death in 1879, obituaries trotted out the familiar tale of his trial and imprisonment, mourning the artist with melodramatic recollections of how his arrest in 1832 was allegedly witnessed by his impoverished, grief-stricken parents.[7] Police archives, which reveal how nervously the Third Republic kept an eye on the remnants of the old left guard, testify that at the 1880 ceremonies of Daumier's reburial in Père-Lachaise cemetery in Paris, Carjat praised Daumier for suffering imprisonment in 1851 at the hands of Louis-Napoléon.[8] In fact, no such second imprisonment had occurred. On the contrary, by this time, Daumier had learned how to negotiate the delicate boundary between the permitted and the proscribed in caricature. Carjat's error draws our attention to the political implications of artistic reputation in the modern era. The Gargantua episode solidified Daumier's association with Republican entrepreneurs who were cultivating a middle-class market for political satire. It was the beginning of a business relationship that lasted thirty years. While we may acknowledge Daumier's political integrity in defending artistic liberty, we should also note that there was some self-interest in his court-ing of notoriety in the name of Art and Freedom. The scandal that sur-rounded Daumier's *Gargantua,* for instance, was not completely uninvited by the idealistic and ambitious artist; a certain amount of grandstanding must be acknowledged. In 1832, artistic freedom was a charged topic in France—the cult of individualism fostered romantic ideals that linked Truth to inde-pendent expression. It was also not a bad career move for a struggling young caricaturist to get involved in the politics of censorship.

At age twenty-two, Daumier's early career would surely not have been so eventful had he not joined the stable of artists employed by artist and entre-preneur Charles Philipon, the "Duc de Lithographie, Marquis de dessin, comte de Bois gravé, Baron de Charge et chevalier des caricatures" [Duke of lithography, marquis of drawing, count of wood engraving, baron of jokes, and knight of caricatures], as he was affectionately addressed by Balzac.[9] As Daumier later recalled, "If Philipon had not been behind me to prod me unceasingly like one does to an ox with a plow, I would never have done anything."[10] Philipon's establishment, La Maison Aubert, dominated the growing caricature business in Paris in the first decade of the July Mon-archy.[11] The Revolution of 1830 had made a recently politicized middle class conscious of its new role in government, and a large audience emerged with a certain self-interest in political satire. Just as this self-interested class now desired a greater role in government and business, they also desired images of themselves and their leaders. For this generation of consumer-connoisseurs, possession and viewing were complementary activities. Car-icature, a quintessential urban art form, offered a new social space where a world of rapidly shifting identities of class and power could be frozen in the comforting, summarizing lines of various urban types.[12]

The new caricature industry also opened a new political space where images of dissent and criticism could be circulated, their seditious content mediated by the screen of laughter. For mere funny papers, caricatures were starting to do serious political work. After the Revolution of 1830, an explo-sion of political caricature sympathetic to Republican philosophy occurred in a climate of disillusionment and broken promises. Louis-Philippe had promised to protect the freedom of the press, a freedom that had been brutally curtailed by his predecessor, Charles X. In the Constitutional Char-ter of 1830, he had promised that censorship would never be reestablished. But even by the end of 1830, new press laws began to introduce new restric-tions. The offenses now punishable under French law fell into three areas: attacks against the person of the king; debate over succession to the throne;

and questioning the legitimate domain of the legislature.[13] The government was, it became clear, nervous not only about demonstrations and strikes, but also about the press's ability to incite unrest. Soon, as had been the case before 1830, papers were required to pay security deposits, a forced prepayment of the government fines they would owe if found guilty of infractions. The press, in short, was now repressed.

In this increasingly embattled atmosphere, Philipon led the satirical charge against both the image of the body and the policy of King Louis-Philippe (fig. 2-3). First in the weekly journal *La Caricature* (founded in 1830) and then in the daily illustrated *Le Charivari* (founded in 1832), he published ardently Republican fare. Between November 1831 and May 1833, Philipon was arrested three times for press offenses, sentenced to a total of thirteen months in prison, and was fined 4,600 francs. His employees and cohorts at La Maison Aubert were often engaged in similar volleys with authority—by July 1832, Philipon boasted that he and his publications had endured twenty seizures by Louis-Philippe's press censors, six arrests, three prison sentences, and fines.[14] Philipon even bragged, with the pride of a bustling entrepreneur, that he had gained subscribers from members of the juries that had heard his cases. He knew that bad press could mean good business.

At stake in the trials was not just Philipon's freedom to do business but the very question of artistic freedom in the political arena—freedom to choose a subject, freedom to render it as one pleased, freedom to put the work on public view in a shop window or in the pages of a journal. Significantly, the satire that first brought the editor-artist to trial was a satiric depiction of the head of state. The specific charge was injury to the person of the king, the form of high treason known as *lèse majesté*, made illegal by the press law of November 1830. Philipon's first trial was in 1831 over the caricature "Boules de savon" [Soap bubbles], in which he depicted Louis Philippe nonchalantly blowing soap bubbles in a Chardinesque parody.[15] Each bubble represents a promise made during the Revolution of 1830 (the "mousse de juillet" [the froth of July]). Prominent among these fragile pledges is "liberté de la presse" [liberty of the press]—demoted from a serious moral right to an ephemeral child's toy of the whimsical monarch.

Although acquitted for "Boules de savon," Philipon was not as fortunate at his trial on 14 November 1831, for a print entitled "Le Replâtrage" [The Replastering] (fig. 2-4) in which the king, dressed as a common mason, whitewashes the past by plastering over his forgotten promises of 1830.[16] Philipon was convicted for publishing this print and received a prison sentence of six months and a heavy fine. He had argued unsuccessfully that the

FIGURE 2-3: Anonymous photographer, "Louis-Philippe I, Roi des Français," 1845. Published in *Dans l'intimité de personnages illustrés 1845–1890* (Paris: Éditions M.D., c. 1900).

caricature only represented the government through the symbolic resemblance of the king, but was not intended as a specific attack on the king's person—a strained defense necessitated by the concept of *lèse majesté*.

While Philipon may have lost the battle at this trial, he nonetheless managed to set out the terms on which he and other caricaturists would ul-

FIGURE 2-4: Charles Philipon, "Le Replâtrage" [The Replastering] in *La Caricature,*
June 30, 1831. Lithograph, 36.8 × 27.6 cm (14½ × 10⅞ in.). Mount Holyoke College Art
Museum, South Hadley, Mass. Gift of Mr. and Mrs. Howard P. Vincent (Mary Wilson
Smith, Class of 1926), 1991.

timately win the war. At his trial, Philipon had pointed out the absurdity of
the court's creating any precedent that would then require every satire in the
future to be tried on the issue of resemblance, that is, on whether it suggested the physiognomy of the king. In a grand gesture that combined wit,
skill, and a flair for visual drama, Philipon drew the famous four-part sketch

LES POIRES,

Faites à la cour d'assises de Paris par le directeur de la CARICATURE.

Vendues pour payer les 6,000 fr. d'amende du journal le *Charivari*.

Sur la demande d'un grand nombre d'abonnés des départemens, nous donnons aujourd'hui dans le *Charivari* les phires qui
servirent à notre défense, dans l'affaire où la *Caricature* fut
condamnée à six mois de prison et 2,000 fr. d'amende.

Si, pour reconnaître le monarque dans une caricature, vous n'attendez pas qu'il soit désigné autrement que par la ressemblance, vous
tomberez dans l'absurde. Voyez ces croquis informes, auxquels j'aurais peut-être dû borner ma défense :

Ce croquis ressemble à Louis-Philippe, vous condamnerez donc ?　　　Alors il faudra condamner celui-ci, qui ressemble au premier.

Puis condamner cet autre, qui ressemble au second.　　　Et enfin, si vous êtes conséquens, vous ne sauriez absoudre cette
poire, qui ressemble aux croquis précédens.

Ainsi, pour une poire, pour une brioche, et pour toutes les têtes grotesques dans lesquelles le hasard ou la malice aura placé cette
triste ressemblance, vous pourrez infliger à l'auteur cinq ans de prison et cinq mille francs d'amende !!
Avouez, Messieurs, que c'est là une singulière liberté de la presse !!

FIGURE 2-5: Charles Philipon, "Les Poires" [The Pears] in *Le Charivari,* 17 January 1832.
Lithograph. Print Collection, Miriam and Ira D. Wallach Division of Art, Prints, and
Photographs; New York Public Library. Astor, Lenox, and Tilden Foundations, New
York.

for the court in which the bulbous face of Louis-Philippe mutates into a common pear (fig. 2-5). The metonymic substitution was not only canny but insulting, as *poire* in French slang had the derogatory connotation of fathead or simpleton. Using the sketch, he argued that law cannot regulate the realm of resemblance, or soon artists would be thrown in jail for merely drawing fruit. He also predicted that the more the courts attempted to impose such restrictions, the more caricaturists would take malicious pleasure in testing their skills and the sacred liberty of the crayon. The gauntlet was down. Ten days after Philipon's conviction, *La Caricature* reproduced his courtroom sketch of the king as pear, and La Maison Aubert began to sell a separate poster of the motif. Authorities stepped in, predictably, and seized the lithograph, but not before the image had made its mark.

Almost immediately artists adapted the new visual code. As Philipon had predicted, the image was beyond the control of the law. If the king's body was off limits to satirists, the fruit was not, even when used metonymically. "Poire-o-mania" exploded among Philipon's satirists.[17] Between the moment of its invention in the courtroom in 1831 and its demise at the hands of the repressive September laws of 1835, *la poire*'s currency was high. As a sign of opposition to the Orléanist regime, it appeared in caricature journals, in print shop windows, in the homes of some bourgeois Republicans, and even on the prison walls of caricaturists jailed for censorship infractions. Years later in 1850, Flaubert noted that the pear had also toured Egypt, where he found the image among the French graffiti on the great pyramid at Giza. The defiant pear thrived as a symbol of resistance in the margins of the law, and in the margins of official culture.

In the early July Monarchy, even the mere outline of the pear carried the message of political resistance and critique. Accounts in *Le Charivari* of the censorious actions of the police were printed in pear-shaped articles.[18] The pear literally gave form to opposition discourse and flaunted its power to defy regulation. Caricaturists exploited its formal potential for obscene and scatological humor. For example, the ponderous jowls of the pear-king invited comparison with his other cheeks—those of his buttocks—in a comic inversion of top and bottom, frontside and backside that was a stock joke of earlier political satire. As fruit, the pear also bore the constant potential of rot and decay, as well as the bispherical shape of a fat human ass, the source of excremental filth. As in the caricature of 1832 by Traviès, "Le Juste Millieu se crotte" [The July Monarchy soils itself], stagnation, decay, and waste are all posited as the realm of *la poire*.[19] In other words, it is the natural state of the pear-king to be dirty and foul.

Daumier's first significant encounter with censorship coincides with the genesis of this provocative, inventive, and insulting imagery of *la poire*. He started work on the print "Gargantua" in November and December 1831, just after Philipon's invention of *la poire* at his trial for "Le Replâtrage." Philipon published both his drawing of "Les Poires" (see fig. 2-5) and his exhortation to the artists of his time: "Oui—nous avons le droit de personnifier le pouvoir. Oui, nous avons le droit de prendre pour cette personification, telle ressemblance qui nous convient! Oui, toutes les ressemblances nous appartiennent!" [Yes, we have the right to personify power. Yes, we have the right to take for this personification whatever resemblance suits our needs! Yes, all resemblances belong to us!][20] Thus Philipon raised the stakes of a battle over images to a veritable crusade for the artistic freedom of the satirist. With "Gargantua," Daumier consciously and somewhat rashly entered the censorship fray. Although he had recently left several provocative prints deliberately unsigned in order to protect himself from prosecution, he now boldly signed his last name at the lower left edge of "Gargantua" so there could be no doubt as to its authorship. He might not have chosen to go to jail, but he was not blind to the advantages of notoriety, or to the benefits of siding with his employer on the issue of freedom of the press. Indeed, he may even have been aware of the celebrated martyrdom of such Republican artists as Pierre Jean de Béranger, the famed author of oppositional songs and poems.[21]

The links between Philipon's *poire* and Daumier's "Gargantua" are incontestable. The pyramidal shape of Gargantua's head, defined by ample whiskers and pointed coiffure, emphatically refigures *la poire*. Even Gargantua's pointed cowlick mirrors the stem of Philipon's pear. The rounded shape of the king's entire body, jammed into its chair, echoes the contours of the ripe fruit. From fat head to fat belly, Daumier's royal figure recalls the newly crowned surrogate, the pear-king.

In "Gargantua," Louis-Philippe sits on a large *chaise percée,* or toilet, and defecates rewards to the tiny ministers of his government gathered beneath the chair. Other ministers collect tribute from the destitute and crippled populace of Paris and then march up a gangplank to feed the baskets of wealth to the ravenous king. The king's body—obese, passive, and immobilized by gluttony—is the agent of his own physical corruption. And it is here that Daumier transgressed the law of 1830 with its proscription of attacking the royal person of the monarch. Daumier's "Gargantua" is the vehicle for insulting both the royal body and the body politic.

Had the image been a mere retelling of the *poire* joke, however, Daumier would probably not have been the target of such rigorous censorship. After all, Philipon was not tried again for creating or printing the pear. But, as I have argued elsewhere, the "Gargantua" image was laden with reference to libelous scatological traditions and to controversial recent events.[22] Its implications clearly made the relatively new and somewhat unstable monarchy nervous. Within days of its appearance in the windows of Aubert's shop, the police confiscated it and ordered Aubert to destroy the original lithographic stone and all remaining proofs; the rarity of impressions of "Gargantua" today suggests they were largely successful.[23]

In February 1832 Daumier was tried for "Gargantua," along with two of his collaborators: Gabriel Aubert (Philipon's brother-in-law and owner of the publishing house and therefore responsible for selling the print to the public) and Hypolite Delaporte (the printer of the lithograph). All were found guilty of arousing hatred and contempt for the king's government and of offending the king's person (the crime of *lèse majesté*). Although all received a sentence of six months in prison and a heavy fine, in the end only Daumier had to serve. *He* was held responsible, as it was his "crayon séditieux a tracé l'image coupable" [seditious crayon (that) had traced the guilty image].[24] The court determined that

> Le but manifeste de l'auteur du dessein [*sic*] était de figurer, sous des traits exagérés et monstreux, la personne du Monarque, qu'il représentait dévorant aux yeux de son peuple famélique, le mets d'un festin dans le goût de ceux que Rabelais prête au personnage dont le nom sert de titre à cette caricature.[25]

> [The goal of the author of the drawing was to figure with exaggerated and monstrous features the person of the king, represented devouring in view of his starving people a feast in the style . . . of Rabelais.]

What was at stake in this judgment was clearly fear: the government feared, and punished, the artist more than his business collaborators. Moreover, pictures were, from the government's point of view, more dangerous than words. This was not only because of widespread illiteracy but also because images were relatively easy to disseminate among various classes and regions. There was also a threat due to the rapidity with which images could convey messages and incite group action. An open fear of caricature surfaced time and again in the debates over censorship in the July Monarchy and later in the Second Empire. One articulation of the threat appeared in a memo from the minister of police in 1852: "Among the means employed to shake and destroy the sentiment of reserve and morality so essential to a well-ordered society, drawings are one of the most dangerous. Drawing offers a sort of personification of thought, it puts it in relief, it communicates it with movement and life, so as to thus present spontaneously, in a translation everyone can understand, the most dangerous of all seductions."[26]

Daumier's conviction did little to alter his commitment to political caricature. In the six months between his trial in February 1832 and his imprisonment later that year, he produced six more satires that were seized by the government (Delteil 35–39). He seems to have teased the government with ever more brazen caricatures to see if they would actually enforce the sentence of his conviction. By the end of summer 1832 he was in Ste. Pélagie prison, which appears in several of his later caricatures as a metaphor for the pervasive climate of Orleanist political repression and control (Delteil 197, 209). He amused himself in jail by drawing variations of Gargantua on the wall, and later in Dr. Pinel's Maison de Santé, where he finished serving his sentence, he joined Philipon in drawing new caricatures to be published by La Maison Aubert. Making caricature was clearly one of the few meaningful acts of political resistance possible while sitting in jail.

After his release in 1833, and for the next two years, Daumier participated fully in Philipon's business of political caricature. One of his key targets continued to be the king. From 1832 until the September laws of 1835 forbade further political caricature, Daumier produced more than two hundred lithographs. Over a third of these depict either Louis-Philippe or his surrogate form, *la poire*.[27] Daumier toys with the issue of resemblance, often coyly covering or turning the king's head away from the viewer to avoid dealing directly with royal facial features. Rather, Louis-Philippe is often identifiable through his attributes: his umbrella and top hat (signs of the so-called Citizen King), his corpulent profile, his muttonchop sideburns and his pointy coiffure. Daumier casts the king in a variety of demeaning roles, figuring him as beggar (Delteil 108), as bloodletting doctor (Delteil 73), as pickpocket (Delteil 95), as villainous butcher (Delteil 97), and as clown (Delteil 86).

In spite of his conviction for "Gargantua," Daumier did not abandon the general theme of the monarch's despotic greed that fueled the Rabelaisian image. He did, however, generally avoid mocking the king with overtly scatological humor, as this particular form of degrading the royal body seems to have been a deciding factor in the government's decision to press charges for "Gargantua."[28] In 1834, Daumier satirized Louis-Philippe's avarice by simultaneously exoticizing and trivializing the king in "Magot de la Chine" (fig. 2-6). Here the king appears as a grimacing Chinese porcelain bibelot, his legs crossed, his eyes slanted, and his earlobes extended in a vulgar parody of imported Buddha figurines. This little statue reflects the middle-class taste for such chinoiserie in the July Monarchy, when the antique *magots*

FIGURE 2-6: Honoré Daumier, "Magot de la Chine" [The Magot of China], in *La Caricature,* 28 August 1834. Lithograph, Delteil 83, 25.5 × 34.8 cm (10¹/₁₆ × 13¹¹/₁₆ in.). Armand Hammer Daumier and Contemporaries Collection, UCLA at the Armand Hammer Museum of Art and Cultural Center, Los Angeles, California.

and *potiches* so popular in prerevolutionary France were once again in fashion.[29] Daumier's satire invokes both senses of the word *magot,* which can mean either a grotesque figurine or a hidden treasure or cache of money. Louis-Philippe clutches a money bag, a sign of greed that resonates with other signs of excess—the swollen belly of the *magot* or the memory of the gluttonous belly of Gargantua. Yet another strain in this heterogeneous satiric discourse is that of the *poire:* from the polished head of the magot sprouts the distinct stem of a pear. Moreover, the rounded pyramidal shape of the figure also echoes the bulbous contours of the infamous fruit. References to greed, stupidity, and excess thus unite in this exoticized body of the ruler. In figuring his monarch as a greedy oriental, Daumier cracks the same joke as George Cruikshank, who two decades earlier had satirized King George IV as a rotund Chinese emperor, enthroned in his new "Chinese Palace" at Brighton.[30] Cruikshank's caricatures of the English king as oriental

FIGURE 2-7: Honoré Daumier, "Récompense honnête décernée 1800 à Louis-Philippe d'Orléans, chirurgien et emigré mais toujours Français, par les sauvages peu délicats de l'Amérique du Nord. (Je vous salue, négresse plein de grâce, le Saigneur [sic] est avec vous. Ave Maria, Namaquois)," [Honest compensation bestowed in 1800 on Louis-Philippe d'Orléans, surgeon and immigrant, but forever French, by the crude North American savages (I hail thee, Negress full of grace, the Savior [and the Surgeon] is with you. Ave Maria, Namaquois)] in *La Caricature,* no. 224, 19 February 1835. Lithograph, Delteil 109, 26.5 × 34.7 cm (10^{7}/16 × 13^{5}/8 in.). Armand Hammer Daumier and Contemporaries Collection, UCLA at the Armand Hammer Museum of Art and Cultural Center, Los Angeles, California.

despot reflected widespread public criticism of the extravagance of the royal pavilion. Daumier successfully adopts a similar trope of orientalism to reembody the French monarch, distancing his subject (and thereby the direct threat of the image) through the strategy of exoticism.

In other satires of Louis-Philippe, Daumier's humor of the body depends not only on the physical dislocation of exoticism, but also on the pointed violation of regal decorum. In "Recompense honnête . . . " (fig. 2-7) he unveils Louis-Philippe in bed with two aboriginal women, "les sauvages peu délicats de l'Amérique du Nord" [crude savages of North America]. The ménage à trois reclines beneath a hanging quiver of arrows, an exotic parody of the amorous symbol of Cupid. The print illustrates a fictional anecdote, recounted in *La Caricature* about Louis-Philippe's youthful adventures in North America, where during his exile of 1796–99 he supposedly saved the life of an ailing Cherokee chief and was given the reward of spending the night with the two eldest noblewomen of the tribe. The satire not only destabilizes the king's authority by removing him physically from Paris and the throne room, placing him *face-à-face* with a cultural "other," but also demeans his power sexually by placing him at the mercy of two partners who are older, aggressive, and conventionally unattractive—typically unsuited to be consorts of a French king. Daumier does not cross over the line of vulgarity here into pornography; he clearly circumvents the risks of a charge of *lèse majesté*. But the baudy circumstances nonetheless humorously compromise the king's royal decorum, as we voyeuristically enter a most private space, that of the king's bed. Had Daumier attempted a similar joke with less exotic partners, the satire would probably not have been tolerated.

Until the September Laws forbade political caricature in 1835, Daumier remained a public defender of freedom of the press. A diminutive figure of Louis-Philippe rants and raves in the margins of "Ne vous y frottez pas" [Don't mess with it] of 1834 (fig. 2-8), in which a young and defiant lithographic printer stands down all interference with freedom of the press. Through his heroic scale and defiant posture, Daumier's worker claims his victory over the impotent efforts of government. But in this final year before the official suppression of political caricature, the government was growing less and less tolerant of oppositional voices. Daumier's sober and poignant "Rue Transnonain" (Delteil 135), an indictment of military repression, was seized as soon as it appeared on public display, and the police destroyed all available prints, as they had in the case of "Gargantua." Freedom of the press was not as unassailable as Daumier's heroic caricature had asserted.

After the demise of *La Caricature* at the hands of the September Laws of 1835, Philipon's major publication was the sister journal *Le Charivari*. (Philipon and Daumier both figure at the center of its masthead, beating the noisy instruments characteristic of the festive rituals of folk charivari. The title of the journal is apt given its mission of social and political critique. As historian Charles Tilly has demonstrated, the "charivari" was a form of popular action, transferred from country to city, that laid the groundwork for political demonstration and revolution in the modern era in France.)[31] *Le Charivari* developed as a less politically aggressive journal than *La Caricature:* its articles and images were largely devoted to the lampooning of bourgeois society. But it was not without its occasional political edge; Philipon used it

FIGURE 2-8: Honoré Daumier, "Ne vous y frottez pas!!" [Don't mess with it!!] in *L'Association mensuelle,* plate 20, March 1834. Lithograph, Delteil 133, 36 × 54.6 cm (14³⁄₁₆ × 21½ in.). Armand Hammer Daumier and Contemporaries Collection, UCLA at the Armand Hammer Museum of Art and Cultural Center, Los Angeles, California.

as a mouthpiece of resistance whenever he thought he could get away with it. After 1835 prior police approval was necessary for the caricatures printed in all illustrated journals. Since text was considered much less a threat than imagery, *it* was not reviewed by censors before publication. Therefore, the journal often resorted to publishing textual descriptions of prints that had been rejected.[32]

In truth, the task of a censor was difficult. In the year 1840 alone, the office of censorship at the Ministry of the Interior had to judge the political content of almost eight thousand images.[33] Archival records suggest that the types of lithographs most frequently censored in the July Monarchy included depictions of the king's guard in undignified actions; views of extreme carnage or crime; particular scenes in the history of the French Revolution; sexually explicit scenes (often located in bathhouses); and political critiques of Louis-Philippe's person and government.[34] Censors had only one shot at these images: once an image had passed, it could not be recalled for second judgment if it was subsequently deemed offensive or unacceptable.

Knowing these rules, the editors of *Le Charivari* often played a clever

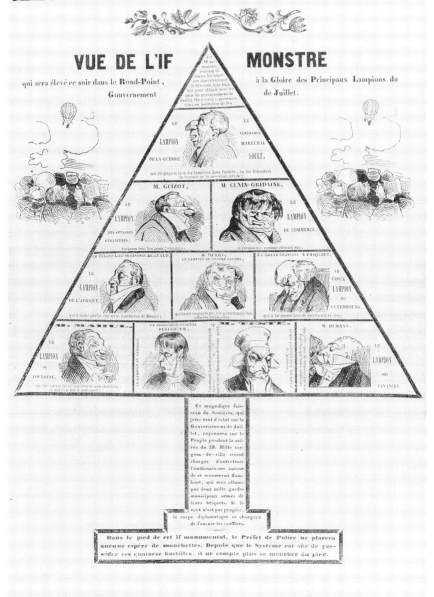

FIGURE 2-9: Honoré Daumier, "Illuminations de Champs-Elysées, Vue de l'if monstre" [Illuminations of the Champs-Elysées, View of the monstrous light-stand] in *Le Charivari,* 29 July 1841. Woodcut, 36.3 × 25.1 cm (14⅓ × 9⅞ in.). The Beinecke Rare Book and Manuscript Library, Yale University Library, New Haven, Connecticut.

game of cat and mouse. One example is the front page of an issue of *Le Charivari* in July 1841 (fig. 2-9). On the date of the anniversary of the July Revolution of 1830, *Le Charivari* published this memorial issue, featuring commemorative songs of the Revolution and small vignettes by Daumier depicting the ministers of the July Monarchy. These caricatures are recycled images, taken from *en-tête* headings printed in the journal in 1833.[35] The heads of the politicians are arranged like *lampions* [fairy lights] hung on a *l'if monstre* [a large light-stand shaped like a pine tree] decorated with the heads of government. The journal envisions the delight with which the French people would attend the light show if these *lampions* were to be lit by two thousand municipal guards.

The insult intended to the ministers was clear—it was literally incendiary—but the individual drawings had been submitted one by one, and not in this particular "ensemble" to the censor. Correspondence between the minister of justice and the minister of the interior about this image reveals their deep frustration in trying to monitor the journal. Even the most vigilant surveillance of individual images as required by the September laws could not prevent editors from giving certain drawings "un caractère répréhensible" [a reprehensible character] by adding oppositional commentary or by creating a certain effect through a suggestive arrangement of the drawings.[36] Not every manipulation of the relationship between images, or of the relationship between images and text, could be foreseen and regulated.

A review of the censorship records of *Le Charivari* between 1835 and 1848 reveals that the number of issues signaled as potentially offensive was far greater than the number that was suppressed; furthermore, the high number of acquittals of press infractions suggests that *Le Charivari* had learned how to negotiate the delicate boundary between the permissible and the proscribed in political satire.[37] The artists, undoubtedly keenly aware of Daumier's history, avoided making that same costly error of *lèse majesté* in caricature. Between 1835 and 1848, the only infraction committed by *Le Charivari* that drew a conviction with a prison sentence resulted from an essay, not an image. In 1839, the journal's manager Beauger was fined heavily for publishing an article "d'offense envers la personne du Roi" [offensive to the person of the king].[38] The article, which plays on a fictional confusion between the king and a common umbrella thief, had represented Louis-Philippe as extremely fat. In 1838, censors were still striving to repress the satirical discourse of royal obesity linked with corruption, as established several years earlier by the Gargantua and pear caricatures. Archival records clearly demonstrate that during the July Monarchy the artists at *Le Charivari* did not avoid political subjects. At least fifty prints submitted by La Maison Aubert to the censor between 1835 and 1848 were rejected; and at least nine of these were by Daumier.[39] As Michael Driskel has demonstrated, Nicolas Charlet published many prints during the July Monarchy that contained subtle Republican protests, in spite of the considerable number of his prints that were censored.[40] Further study of the Republican caricature journals of the period will undoubtedly continue to reveal the pervasiveness of oppositional political discourse, even in this period of surveillance and attempted regulation.

With the Revolution of 1848 and the establishment of the Second Republic, press censorship was once again abolished. Daumier and fellow Republicans could once again openly express political sentiment in caricature as well as in more high-minded forms such as the official competition for the painted representation of *The Republic*.[41] But in the volatile days at the end of the Second Republic, President Louis-Napoléon began to reinstate censorship. Some of Daumier's more brazen colleagues, such as the younger artist Charles Vernier and the journal's *gérant responsable* Léopold Panier, were imprisoned in 1851 for publishing in *Le Charivari* a satire of Louis-Napoléon's acts of favoritism.[42] It is interesting to note here that unlike the earlier case of Daumier, who received a heavier sentence than his business collaborators at the time of his conviction for "Gargantua," the court under Louis-Napoléon now gave a much heavier sentence to the journal's manager than to the artist Vernier.[43] Significantly, the artist was no longer the scapegoat for the business enterprise. In 1832, caricature was still a very new business, and the published image was deemed to be primarily the product of individual artistic intent, or as the court documents regarding "Gargantua" claimed, of the artist whose "crayon séditieux a tracé l'image coupable" [seditious crayon had traced the guilty image].[44] By the Second Republic, Louis-Napoléon had clearly recognized the power of satirical journals as collaborative business enterprises and held the businessman who managed the day-to-day production as the most guilty party.

Rather than quieting the oppositional spirit of *Le Charivari*, Vernier's conviction seemed to heighten the fervor of the journal's attack on Bonapartism. He was little chastised by the prison sentence; one of his caricatures later in 1851 mocks the frequency with which journalists were being sent to prison.[45] Daumier, however, worked more cautiously. In 1850 he lifted a satirical figure from the humorous texts of *Le Charivari* to portray Louis-Napoléon's government—the scurrilous Ratapoil, a fictional, villainous agent of the president's brutal secret police, the "Décembristes" [The Society of the Tenth of December]. Ratapoil became a symbol of all that was corrupt and counterfeit about the Bonapartist Second Republic.[46] In a print

— Belle dame, voulez-vous bien accepter mon bras ?
— Votre passion est trop subite pour que je puisse y croire!

FIGURE 2-10: Honoré Daumier, "Belle dame, voulez-vous bien accepter mon bras?—Votre passion est trop subite pour que je puisse y croire" [Beautiful lady, would you take my arm?—Your passion is too sudden to be believed!] in *Le Charivari,* 25 September 1851. Lithograph, Delteil 2153, 35.88 × 28.58 cm (14 1/8 × 11 1/4 in.). Print Collection, Miriam and Ira D. Wallach Division of Art, Prints, and Photographs, The New York Public Library, Astor, Lenox and Tilden Foundations, New York.

of 1851 (fig. 2-10), the sleazy and untrustworthy Ratapoil—whose moustache, beard, and long roman nose echo the familiar visage of Louis-Napoléon—extends his arm to a noble and virtuous figure of the Republic. Daumier does not always refer to the Second Republic government through the guise of Ratapoil; occasionally President Louis-Napoléon appears as himself, in the company of other identifiable personages of his regime (fig. 2-11). It is the fictional Ratapoil, however, who dominates Daumier's political caricatures in the closing days of the Second Republic; conversely, the more literal-minded Vernier generally represented Louis-Napoléon in direct form.[47] Both satiric personages predictably vanished from the pages of *Le Charivari* with Louis-Napoléon's coup d'etat of 2 December 1851. At that volatile moment, the journal suspended publication for a week and then reappeared featuring a "safe" nonpolitical satire of lawyers by Daumier. The days of openly anti-Bonapartist caricature were, for the moment, over.

Once Louis-Napoléon seized political control in 1851 and subsequently declared himself emperor of France in 1852, rigorous press censorship laws were again established. As in the later July Monarchy, the person of the ruler was off limits to caricaturists. The emperor assembled a massive bureau of censors to police the images of his new regime, and Daumier and colleagues were once again officially ordered to suspend political critique.

The oppositional leadership of *Le Charivari* sought ways to circumvent the new authoritarian restrictions; an obvious ploy was simply to work in exile. A sister journal, *Le Charivari belge,* was published in Brussels during most of the Second Empire.[48] Its articles and images were much the same as those found in the pages of its Parisian version, with one crucial difference: in Brussels, outside the reach of the police censors, oppositional satire could flourish. Anti-Bonapartist caricatures testify to the fires of resistance blazing beneath the surface of the muffled French *Le Charivari*. These images, many by anonymous hands, are keys to the secret agenda of the repressed French journal—marginalized voices that spoke ideas unutterable at the political center. While Daumier did not contribute any political prints to this paper, some of his colleagues, such as the prolific Cham, created political caricatures expressly for the Belgian edition. Daumier and others working for *Le Charivari* in Paris were undoubtedly aware of the agenda of this sister publication in which the anti-Bonapartist satires are direct and unforgiving. In one example, Louis-Napoléon is charged with the murder of Liberty as she lies dead in a coffin marked "Born 1848; died 1851" (fig. 2-12).[49] In this battle of bodies for the soul of France, the emperor stands as victor and executioner. In the background on a pennant hangs the image of Daumier's

M.M. Victor Hugo et Emile Girardin cherchent à élever le prince Louis sur un pavois, ça n'est pas très solide !

FIGURE 2-11: Honoré Daumier, "Victor Hugo et Emile Girardin cherchent à élever le Prince Louis . . . " [Victor Hugo and Emile Girardin trying to lift Prince Louis on the King's shield; it's not very solid!] in *Le Charivari*, 11 December 1848. Lithograph, Delteil 1756, 35.1 × 26.8 cm (13 13/16 × 10 9/16 in.). Armand Hammer Daumier and Contemporaries Collection, UCLA at the Armand Hammer Museum of Art and Cultural Center, Los Angeles, California.

EST-ELLE BIEN MORTE?

FIGURE 2-12: Anonymous, "Est-elle bien morte?" [Is she truly dead?] in *Le Charivari* (Brussels), 18 April 1852. Lithograph, 28.25 × 21.9 cm (11 1/8 × 8 5/8 in.). Copyright Royal Library of Belgium.

Je me suis bigrement sali pour arriver jusqu'ici.

FIGURE 2-13: Anonymous, "Je me suis bigrement sali pour arriver jusqu'ici," [I have dirtied the crap out of myself in order to get this far!] in *Le Charivari Belge,* 14 September 1854. Lithograph, 21.9 × 28.25 cm (8⅝ × 11⅛ in.). Copyright Royal Library of Belgium.

Ratapoil—the symbol of repression—which had just been forced out of the pages of the Parisian journal by the new censorship laws.

In Brussels, a scatological discourse of opposition could flourish. A print of 1854 shows Louis-Napoléon crawling out of the Paris sewers filthy with the muck of his journey and admitting (like Louis-Philippe earlier, in the pages of *La Caricature*) that he has dirtied himself considerably to arrive at the palace of power (fig. 2-13). In Belgian exile, the very subject of censorship and representation could be freely addressed. In a variation of the biblical theme of temptation, a kneeling figure of the Parisian *Charivari* struggles to resist the lure of taboo political subjects (fig. 2-14). A complex game of looking is at work here. The magic lantern of political topics presented to *Charivari* frames the political field of events open to the satirical crayon; *Charivari's* vision in turn is subject to surveillance by the watchful Louis-Napoléon in the background. By implication, it is the Belgian journal in the hands of an actual reader that now keeps Louis-Napoléon under the

VADE RETRO, SATANAS!
PRIERE du CHARIVARI........ Et ne nos inducas in tentationem, sed libera
nos a malo

FIGURE 2-14: Anonymous, "Vado retro, Satanas! Prière du Charivari . . . Et ne nos inducas in tentationem, sed libera nos a malo" [Get thee behind me, Satan! The prayer of Charivari . . . And lead us not into temptation, but deliver us from evil] in *Le Charivari* (Brussels), 5 May 1852. Lithograph, 21.9 × 28.25 cm (8⅝ × 11⅛ in.). Copyright Royal Library of Belgium.

managing surveillance of caricature and the symbolic empowerment of laughter and disrespect.

The Second Empire viewed the Belgian journal as a threat; even into the 1860s, the mere possession within French borders of an issue of *Le Charivari belge* could result in imprisonment.[50] As of 1852 all political satire of the new emperor, Napoléon III, was illegal. He is generally considered to have been thoroughly successful in censoring the opposition press, particularly during the early years of the Second Empire.[51] Napoléon III constructed a public image of himself that drew on the myths of glory associated with his illustrious uncle, Napoléon I. But it is here, with the very image of the ruler, that Daumier took inventive and subtle liberties in order to continue the anti-Bonapartist critique he had begun during the less censorious days of the Second Republic.

This critique begins with the widely understood relationship between Napoléon I and Napoléon III: the latter imitated the former for his own political advancement. During the closing days of the Second Republic, Republicans turned this relationship to their own ends by comparing Louis-Napoléon to another imitator of Napoléon I. Soulouque was the black general who became president of Haiti in 1848 and then proclaimed himself emperor in 1849. A self-declared imitator of Napoléon, he modeled his military and court rituals after the grandeur of the First Empire in France. He was described at length in the French press as an extravagant and authoritarian despot who routinely used violence and intimidation to retain control.

Soulouque emerged in satirical journals of the Second Republic (which did not labor under censorship) as an exotic parallel to President Louis-Napoléon. The caricaturist Cham initiated the satire of Soulouque, making more than sixty caricatures of the black emperor between October 1848 and March 1850. Cham's images emphasize Soulouque's barbaric and despotic behavior. Another caricaturist, known as Nadar, turned to the Soulouque topos in 1850, the year the Haitian leader proclaimed himself Emperor. In 1850 in *Le Journal pour rire,* Nadar directly asserts the parallel between Soulouque and Napoléon by substituting Soulouque for the statue of Napoléon by Émile Seurre that stood atop the Vendôme column in Paris (fig. 2-15). Later in the same journal, Nadar clearly linked Soulouque's Napoleonic makeover to the political ambitions of President Louis-Napoléon.[52] This exotic epithet, coined by the caricaturists of the left, caught on: at the time of Louis-Napoléon's coup d'état in 1851, Republicans ran through the streets denouncing the French president as "Soulouque the Traitor." The international press came to refer to Louis-Napoléon as "The French Soulouque—the Grand Imitator."[53]

Daumier first deployed Soulouque in the censor-free period of July 1850 as a barbaric despot who angrily plunges a terrified journalist into a boiling cauldron (fig. 2-16). Soulouque punishes the European for his articles that criticize the black emperor's regime. The satire does not, as we might expect, concern any current event in Haiti, but speaks in the code of established Republican discourse about the repressive action of Louis-Napoléon, whose government had just seized an issue of the Republican newspaper *Le Siècle* in Paris. The joke here is undeniably racist: long-standing clichés of barbaric behavior among blacks are invoked to underline the despotic nature of the president. The era's Republican ideals of social equality extended only to white males, and their political idealism did not stop caricaturists from exploiting racist stereotypes in their satiric maneuvers. Once strict censorship laws were in effect again during the Second Empire, the use of Soulouque as

Diable de Soulouque! se créer empereur! Le moyen de
doubler un pareil personnage!

FIGURE 2-15: Nadar [Félix Tournachon]. "Diable de Soulouque! Se créer empereur!
Le moyen de doubler un pareil personnage" [That devil Soulouque! Making himself
Emperor! What a way to double the same personage!] in *Le Journal pour rire,* 30 March
1850. Woodcut, private collection.

an exotic surrogate became part of *Le Charivari*'s strategy for continuing
political critique in the face of regulation. The choice of a black surrogate
also coincided with the oppositional discourse of scatology we have seen at
work in caricature of the July Monarchy: casting Louis-Napoléon in black-
face may also be seen as a variation of the ruler "dirtying" or blackening
himself, another form of self-degradation in the argot of the period.

FIGURE 2-16: Honoré Daumier, "L'Empereur Soulouque ayant appris qu'un journaliste européen s'était permis de critiquer quelques uns des actes de son administration, est parvenu à saisir le coupable et le plongé dans une chaudière remplie de goudron brûlant—Tout fait espérer que cela servira de leçon à ce folliculaire et qu'il n'écrira pas un second article contre sa majesté" *(Moniteur officiel d'Haiti)* [The Emperor Soulouque, having learned that a European journalist dared to criticize some of the acts of his administration, has succeeded in seizing the guilty one and plunging him into a cauldron full of boiling tar—in the hopes that this will serve as a lesson to this hack writer and that he will not write a second article against His Majesty (from the newspaper *Moniteur officiel d'Haiti*)] in *Le Charivari,* 15 June 1850. Lithograph, Delteil 2015, 36.8 × 24.3 cm (14½ × 9⁹⁄₁₆ in.). Armand Hammer Daumier and Contemporaries Collection, UCLA at the Armand Hammer Museum of Art and Cultural Center, Los Angeles, California.

Réfléchissant après avoir reçu une roulée des Dominicains, au néant des grandeurs humaines, et

FIGURE 2-17: Honoré Daumier, "Réfléchissant après avoir reçu une roulée des Dominicains, au néant des grandeurs humaines, et commençant à envier le sort des plus simples singes" [After having received a thrashing from the Dominicans, reflecting on the emptiness of human grandeur, and beginning to envy the lot of the simplest monkeys] in *Le Charivari,* 5 March 1856. Lithograph, Delteil 3145, 25.6 × 37.5 cm (10¹/₁₆ × 14¾ in.). Armand Hammer Daumier and Contemporaries Collection, UCLA at the Armand Hammer Museum of Art and Cultural Center, Los Angeles, California.

In defiance of the Second Empire's censorship policy, Daumier and some of his contemporaries at *Le Charivari* continued in the 1850s to parody the regime of Napoléon III through the exotic personage of Soulouque. Daumier used an exaggeratedly simian black body to mock the French emperor as "uncivilized" and "animalistic"—as a coward who hides in the trees while his troops are massacred (a coded reference in 1856 to Louis-Napoléon's absence from the bloody and disease-ridden battlefields of the Crimean War), or as a general lazily sleeping in the jungle, a realm of languor that is suggested as his natural habitat by his physiognomic resemblance to his monkey companions (fig. 2-17). His appearance elsewhere as a brutal despot in a Polichinelle-style puppet show (Delteil 2637) clearly invokes Décembriste violence through the baton, a symbol widely associated through Ratapoil with the repressive acts of President Louis-Napoléon.

In retrospect, it is perhaps hard to imagine how the censors could let such images pass. Yet it was a brilliant ploy for the caricaturists to ground their Bonaparte surrogate in a contemporary context of foreign politics. The multiplicity of meanings in the Soulouque prints—their connections with a diverse field of cultural referents, as had been the case with *La Poire*—made it impossible for censors to discern a single, stable meaning for any image. (One could imagine Philipon arguing that if you arrest one artist for a Soulouque image, you have to arrest any artist who decides to make an image of any emperor.) The actual practice of censorship was a fast-paced business; one-time judgments of images were meted quickly by censors with little knowledge or understanding of the opposition's cultural argot. These official judges were ill equipped to follow the transformations of meaning in a humor generated by a competing ideology. It was hard if not impossible to pin down the subtle sentiments of resistance that survived in a network of coded displacement and surrogacy. The strategy of exoticism in political caricature was successful: there is surprisingly no evidence of any Soulouque prints ever being censored.[54] In fact, the artists at *Le Charivari* during the Second Empire seem to have been generally more adept in escaping censorship than the team that had worked for the journal during the July Monarchy. This is surely due both to the lessons learned from experience and to the savvy strategizing: as Félix Ribeyre observed in 1862, "*Le Charivari* sait se tenir à l'écart du scandale" [*Le Charivari* knows how to swerve to avoid scandal].[55]

And the caricaturists were not alone in devising artistic strategies to stage political critique in the public arena of the Second Empire. A convincing study of Courbet's *The Artist's Studio,* shown in the Universal Exhibition of 1855, identifies the prominent figure of the *braconnier,* or poacher, in the left section of the painting as a coded portrait of Louis-Napoléon, ridiculing him as a common thief who has poached the riches of the Republic of France.[56] Indeed, Linda Nochlin suggests that Courbet intended his massive realist manifesto as "a political cartoon writ large: an allegory of the venality, or at least the futility of present political conduct and hope for a more positive political future."[57] That the ambitious painters of realism shared some of the strategies of the cartoonists for evading the repressive political atmosphere of their time reveals the permeability and cross-fertilization of the so-called spheres of high and low art in this early period of modernism. In spite of Napoléon III's best efforts in the early Second Empire, oppositional political art had its venues and its audiences.

With the liberalization of Napoléon III's government in the 1860s, the reins of press censorship loosened considerably in the late Second Empire. Nonetheless, the Ministry of the Interior continued to watch *Le Charivari*, categorized as a paper of liberal opposition and needing surveillance "plutôt pour ses écarts de plume et de tant que pour son mauvais esprit" [as much for its deviations of the pen as for its bad spirit].[58] With the establishment of the Third Republic, fewer press regulations were enforced, and by 1881 the French government had altogether given up attempting to regulate political caricature.[59] Daumier's final productive period as a caricaturist coincided with the censor-free period of the Commune and the early days of the Third Republic. The persistence of his Republican sentiments emerges forcefully in these latter days. In one of Daumier's last caricatures, the infamous personages from his earlier career—Ratapoil and *la Poire* (inscribed on the sleeve of the baton-carrying Ratapoil at left)—return in "Cette malle n'est a personne" [This chest belongs to no one] (fig. 2-18) as incarnations of the repressive and exploitative past who have returned to urge the new monarchist Republic to loot the abandoned riches of France.

The great power in the humor of satire is to suggest a potentially different world order. During various trials for press offenses, Philipon's defenders often tried to convince the government that these prints need not be taken too seriously, as they were mere safety valves for the release of political tension. Philipon's lawyer appealed to the jury: "Better these sketches than periodic upheavals."[60] But both caricaturists and government knew that political caricature was at some level no laughing matter: its humor and energy nourished the spirit of resistance, critique, and even revolution. Philipon boasted in *La Caricature* of 28 April 1831 that caricature had already become a power, a weapon to strike "the enemies of our liberties." The government of both the July Monarchy and the Second Empire feared the image more than the text, as the image conveyed instantaneously an alternative, a different political and social space where radical dislocations of the status quo existed in the suspended moment of the laugh. Its power was openly acknowledged in 1835: as *Le National* observed, "[the government] made these laws in part to escape from Philipon [and his artists]. . . . They suppressed *La Caricature* because they could not fight with it."[61] These caricatures by Daumier and his contemporaries testify that the censorship laws, however ambitious, could not, in the end, eliminate or effectively police the power of the laugh or the liberty of the crayon.

Political caricature is a provocative and dynamic art form. The satirical press in the days of Louis-Philippe and Louis-Napoléon demanded that the reader/viewer possess both a broad knowledge of the dominant culture of

— Cette malle n'est à personne, donc elle doit être à nous.

FIGURE 2-18: Honoré Daumier, "Cette malle n'est à personne, donc elle doit être à nous" [This chest does not belong to anyone; therefore it ought to be ours!] in *Le Charivari,* 6 May 1872. Lithograph, Delteil 3921, 24.6 × 23.4 cm. (9½ × 9¼ in.). All rights reserved. The Metropolitan Museum of Art, New York, New York. Bequest of Edwin de T. Bechtel, 1957. (57.650.280).

the bourgeoisie, and the humor and independence of mind to share in a pointed critique of that world. Subversive modes of discourse operate with great success when they manage to deploy in new contexts the terms and images already established by the dominant culture. The multivalent image of Soulouque is a good case in point. Daumier and company appropriated to their own oppositional ends the familiar political turf of empire, opportunism, and selfish ambition. Through a farcical recasting of the story of Louis-Napoléon—the Napoléon-imitator—with an exotic outsider, the satirists resisted and reversed the pervasive discourses of political authority. Yet in this textual subversion of the dominant power structures, the artists relied on the deeply embedded codes of racial hierarchy that pervaded French thought of the era. Louis-Napoléon recast as just another white European emperor/despot would not have carried the devastating and malicious humor of the blackfaced Soulouque figure. Contemporary perspectives demand that we recognize the compromised and conflicting sentiments of this decidedly racist campaign devised to swerve the restricting forces of censorship. Yet for the satirists of the mid–nineteenth century, their complicitous means (appealing to racism in an ideology of exploitation) could be justified by the ends of effective political resistance to an imperialist ideology of domination. The new mass audiences for satirical journals needed their humor delivered in easily recognizable forms. Humorous art is seldom as innocent or disinterested as it might at first appear. *Le Charivari* maneuvered brilliantly to escape regulation by censors, but its counter-discourse of political resistance as embodied in the satirical image of the ruler could only wield its power when the audience got the joke.

Notes

1. A nearly identical version of this essay appeared in Elizabeth C. Childs, ed., *Suspended License: Censorship and the Visual Arts* (Seattle: University of Washington Press, 1997), 148–84. Much of the research for this study derives from work supported in 1991 by an ACLS fellowship for recent recipients of the Ph.D. All Delteil numbers in the text are from Loys Delteil, *Le Peintre-Graveur Illustré: Honoré Daumier,* 11 vols. (Paris: Chez l'auteur, 1925–30).

2. Richard Terdiman, *Discourse / Counter-Discourse: The Theory and Practice of Symbolic Resistance in Nineteenth-Century France* (Ithaca, N.Y. and London: Cornell University Press, 1985), chapter 3, esp., 151.

3. See Ernst Kantorowicz, *The King's Two Bodies* (Princeton, N.J.: Princeton University Press, 1953), 7; see also Nicholas Mirzoeff, *Bodyscape: Art, Modernity and the Ideal Figure* (New York: Routledge, 1995), chapter 2.

4. The early history of French caricature supports this idea, as Louis-Philippe's government did not in its own turn use satire to demean those factions it wished to repress. Similarly, the government journals of the Second Empire do not contain satirical derision of competing political ideologies. To grant such attention to the opposition may have seemed unnecessary, or perhaps, may have been seen as an admission not only of the presence but of the power of the opposition.

5. Michel Melot, "Daumier and Art History: Aesthetic Judgement/Political Judgement," *Oxford Art Journal* 11, no. 1 (1988): 3–24.

6. Etienne Carjat quoted in Edmond Bazire, "Les Obsèques de Daumier," *Le Rappel,* 19 February 1879.

7. Anonymous, "Échos de Partout," *La Révolution française,* 13 February 1879.

8. See clippings on the dedication of Daumier's grave, 15 April 1880, Archives de la préfecture de la police, Paris, file E A/42 2 (document 14, page 3).

9. James Cuno, "Charles Philipon, La Maison Aubert, and the Business of Caricature in Paris, 1829–41," *Art Journal* 43, no. 4 (Winter 1983): 347–54.

10. Quoted in Robert Justin Goldstein, *Censorship of Political Caricature in Nineteenth-Century France* (Kent, Ohio: Kent State University Press, 1989), 125.

11. See Cuno, "Charles Philipon, La Maison Aubert, and the Business of Caricature," and James Cuno, "Charles Philipon and La Maison Aubert: The Business, Politics and Public of Caricature in Paris, 1820–1840," Ph.D. diss., Harvard University, 1985.

12. See James Cuno, "Violence, Satire and Social Types in the Graphic Art of the July Monarchy," in Petra Ten-Doesschate Chu and Gabriel P. Weisberg, *The Popularization of Images: Visual Culture Under the July Monarchy* (Princeton, N.J.: Princeton University Press, 1994), 10–36.

13. Goldstein, *Political Caricature,* 122.

14. Cuno, "Charles Philipon, La Maison Aubert, and the Business of Caricature," 351.

15. The caricature, published in February 1831 by Aubert, is reproduced in Goldstein, *Political Caricature,* 135. To a viewer of the July Monarchy, the image of the bubble blower would invariably invoke the genre painting *Soap Bubbles* by Jean Siméon Chardin (1694–1779). Examples are in the collections of the National Gallery of Art and the Metropolitan Museum of Art.

16. The print was published in *La Caricature* on 30 June 1831.

17. See Elise K. Kenney and John M. Merriman, *The Pear: French Graphic Arts in the Golden Age of Caricature* (South Hadley, Mass.: Mount Holyoke College Art Museum, 1991).

18. See *Le Charivari,* 27 February 1834, and 1 May 1835; also *La Caricature,* 17 August 1835.

19. See Gabriel Weisberg, "In Deep Shit: The Coded Images of Traviès in the July Monarchy," *Art Journal* 52, no. 3 (Fall 1993): 36–40.

20. *La Caricature,* 24 November 1832.

21. I am grateful to Robert Herbert for this suggestion.

22. See Elizabeth C. Childs, "Big Trouble" Daumier, *Gargantua,* and the Censorship of Political Caricature," *Art Journal* 51, no. 1 (Spring 1992): 26–37.

23. The only impressions known to me are at the Rose Art Museum at Brandeis University, the Armand Hammer Museum of Art and Cultural Center in Los Angeles, and the Bibliothèque nationale in Paris.

24. Notice presented to M. le Ministre de la justice, le 2 mai, 1832. Archives nationales BB 21 373.

25. Letter from C. Denis to M. le Ministre de la justice, le 19 mars, 1832. Archives nationales BB 21 373.

26. Quoted in Goldstein, *Political Caricature,* 4.

27. For a complete list of the Delteil numbers of these prints, see Louis Provost, *Honoré Daumier: A Thematic Guide to the Oeuvre,* Elizabeth C. Childs, ed. (London and New York: Garland, 1989), 26.

28. Childs, "Big Trouble," 31–33.

29. Hugh Honour, *Chinoiserie: The Vision of Cathay* (New York: Dutton, 1961), 204.

30. See M. Dorothy George, ed., *Catalogue of Political and Personal Satire Preserved in the Department of Prints and Drawings in the British Museum,* microfilm, vol. 9, no. 12749; vol. 10, nos. 13889 and 14400.

31. See Charles Tilly, *The Contentious French: Four Centuries of Popular Struggle* (Cambridge, Mass.: Harvard University Press, 1986), 33. I am grateful to Wayne TeBrake for this reference.

32. Soon after the September Laws went into effect, the journal suffered serious financial setbacks and lower subscription rates, and Philipon sold *Le Charivari.* For a brief history of the administration of the journal, see Childs, "Daumier and the Exotic Vision," 76–84.

33. Michael Paul Driskel, "Singing 'The Marseillaise' in 1840: The Case of Charlet's Censored Prints," *Art Bulletin* vol. 69, no. 4 (December 1987), 621.

34. This summary is based on entries in the ledger at the Archives nationales, F 18* VI 48.

35. For the woodcut *en-tête* designs, see Eugène Bouvy, *Daumier: l'oeuvre gravé du maître* (Paris: Maurice Le Garrec, 1933), nos. 1 and 7.

36. Letter from Minister of Interior to Minister of Justice, 6 August 1841. Archives nationales BB 18 1396 (2289).

37. Archival records of *Le Charivari* for this period include Archives nationales BB 17 A 95 (no. 9); BB 18 1242 (no. 4257); BB 18 1233 (no. 2474); and BB 21 412 (s.9 6465).

38. The article was published in *Le Charivari* on 1 December 1838. Beauger served eight months in prison and paid a very heavy fine of six thousand francs. On his unsuccessful appeal, see Archives nationales BB 24 170–86 (S.2884).

39. For a more detailed history of Daumier's censored prints and the general history of *Le Charivari* and censorship, see Elizabeth Childs, "Honoré Daumier and the Exotic Vision: Studies in French Culture and Caricature, 1830–1870," Ph.D. diss., Columbia University, 1989, chapter 1 and appendices 2 and 3.

40. Driskel, "Singing 'The Marseillaise,'" 604–25.

41. See Marie-Claude Chaudonneret, *La Figure de la République: Le concours de 1848, Notes et documents des musées de France* (Paris: Réunion des musées nationaux, 1987).

42. See *Le Charivari*, 28, 29, 30 May 1851 for reports of the trial. The censored caricature by Vernier is reproduced in Goldstein, *Censorship of Political Caricature,* 177.

43. Léopold Panier, the journal's *gérant responsable,* was given a six-month sentence and a two thousand franc fine; Vernier was given a lighter sentence of two months in prison and a fine of one hundred francs. Results of the trial were reported in *Le Charivari* on 28 May 1851, and responses to the verdict appear on May 29 and 30.

44. Archives nationales BB 21 373 (no. 4172–S8).

45. *Le Charivari,* 10 October 1851.

46. T. J. Clark, *The Absolute Bourgeois: Artists and Politics in France 1848–1851* (Greenwich, Conn.: New York Graphic Society, 1973), 105.

47. Between 1 July and 2 December 1851, seventeen caricatures by Daumier and one by Vernier in *Le Charivari* featured Ratapoil. During the same period, two caricatures by Daumier and eight by Vernier depicted Louis-Napoléon directly.

48. A Belgian edition of the French *Le Charivari* appeared in February 1852. This paper reproduced most of the articles and caricatures in the French edition, but promoted itself as offering readers two uncensored lithographs per week. In 1852 a purely Belgian edition of the paper appeared.

49. The satire is a chilling parody of a well-known history painting, *Cromwell, Examining Charles I's Body,* 1831, by Paul Delaroche (Musée des Beaux-Arts, Nîmes).

50. Archives nationales, BB 24 687–709 (Registre 5.63 no. 3863).

51. See Natalie Isser, *The Second Empire and the Press: A Study of Government-Inspired Brochures in French Foreign Policy in Their Propaganda Milieu* (The Hague: Nijhoff, 1974).

52. See Nadar, "Odyssée du Prince-Président Soulouque accompagné du E. F. Ragotin et Montalenvers," *Le Journal pour rire,* 27 September 1850.

53. For a more complete discussion of the Soulouque series, see Elizabeth Childs, "The Secret Agents of Satire: Daumier, Censorship, and the Image of the Exotic in Political Caricature, 1850–1860," in *Proceedings of the Annual Meeting of the Western Society for French History* 17 (1990): 334–45.

54. We should note that the censorship records for the Second Empire are incomplete. See Childs, "Daumier and the Exotic Vision," 87. Given the longevity of the Soulouque personage in *Le Charivari,* however, it seems reasonable to surmise that the figure was not condemned by censors.

55. Jules Brisson and Félix Ribeyre, *Grands journaux de France* (Paris: Jouast Père, 1862), 411–12.

56. Hélène Toussaint, "The Dossier on *The Studio* by Courbet," in *Courbet,* exh. cat., Arts Council of Great Britain, 1978, 265–66.

57. Linda Nochlin, "Ending with the Ending: The Politics of Place, the Place

of Hope," in Sarah Faunce and Linda Nochlin, *Courbet Reconsidered,* exh. cat., The Brooklyn Museum, 1988, 38–39.

58. Archives nationales, report by A. Langlé, 22 October 1866, A.N. series F 18 294 (193).

59. For a complete history of the breakdown of censorship, see Goldstein, *Political Caricature.*

60. Goldstein, *Political Caricature,* 136.

61. *Le National* as quoted in *Le Charivari,* 9 September 1835.

3 *Réflecs d'un gniaff*

On Emile Pouget and *Le Père Peinard*

Faut faire ton bonheur toi-même!
—*Emile Pouget, 1889*

Sometime at the end of January 1894, Emile Pouget stole quietly away from Paris and made his way, via Antwerp and Brussels, to London. He had good reason to run. Under the aegis of the recently legislated *lois scélérates,* the police had begun a systematic roundup of alleged anarchists on charges of having participated, one way or another, in an *association de malfaiteurs.*[1] The new laws were broad enough in scope to facilitate the incarceration of over four hundred suspects, a number that surely would have included Pouget—whose radical pedigree already consisted of an arrest record, jail time, and a circle of notorious revolutionary associates—had he not sought safe haven. In 1879, at the age of nineteen, he was dismissed from his job as a department store clerk for organizing a union. In 1882 police informants identified him as a member of a group calling itself "La Révolution sociale anarchiste du quartier des écoles."[2] A year later he was detained, along with Louise Michel, when a demonstration of unemployed workers he helped to organize on the esplanade des Invalides ended in violence; the revolver he was carrying at the time of his arrest, as well as the stash of blasting caps and chemicals discovered in the subsequent search of his apartment, earned him eight years behind bars. Upon his early release from the penitentiary at Medun in 1886, Pouget immediately renewed his anarchist ties, and the police their surveillance; he was now a veteran revolutionary. Informants duly noted his participation in groups with ominous-sounding names like "La Sentinelle révolutionnaire" and "L'Aiguille"; and in 1888 they traced him to the editorial board of a short-lived anarchist journal named—again, ominously—*Le Ça Ira.*[3] But it was only when he launched his own newspaper—an inflammatory weekly called *Le Père Peinard*—that the police would learn the full extent of Pouget's talents as a committed activist, a wily conspirator, and a propagandist of considerable imagination.[4]

Le Père Peinard made no bones about its revolutionary objectives, nor about its adherence to a specifically anarchist agenda. Within a few weeks of the inaugural issue in February 1889, the journal had fully disclosed its implacable antiauthoritarianism, anticapitalism, and antimilitarism, as well as its enthusiasm for antiparliamentarianism, theft (when necessary), terrorism (in the form of both *la reprise individuelle* and *la propagande par le fait*), and spontaneous mass insurrection (as a means of overthrowing bourgeois rule and establishing a stateless, classless society). All this, of course, was more than enough to attract the attention of the police, but what distinguished *Le Père Peinard* from over twenty other Parisian anarchist journals published during the late eighties and early nineties were its unique communicative methods. Writing for the most part in working-class vernacular, Pouget (and various anonymous collaborators) assumed the persona of a cobbler *cum* journalist whose informal first-person ruminations—"réflecs d'un gniaff" [a cobbler's reflections], he called them—were designed to address an almost exclusively lower-class readership, *compagnon* to *compagnon*. The narrative fabric of the journal accordingly consisted of both the traditional parlance of the Parisian "bon bougre" (replete with the expletives "foutre!" and "nom de dieu!") and more recent colloquial coinages like "bondieuseries," "politicailleries," and "marchands d'injustices"—in addition to a healthy quotient of scatalogical invective.[5] The militant propagandist Charles Malato gleefully remarked that *Le Père Peinard* horrified "les délicats" and, better still, that it drew into the anarchist movement "des gens de culture primitive, qui, aux jours de lutte, sont les meilleurs" [simple folk who, when push comes to shove, are the best fighters]. (Unless otherwise noted, all translations in this chapter are my own.)[6] In November 1891, just four months before Ravachol's first *attentat* launched the anarchist terror in Paris, the police estimated that Pouget was soon to reach as many as one hundred thousand readers each week.[7] If Malato was right about the journal's audience and the police about their numbers, *Le Père Peinard* enjoyed the potential to function as the quasi-official journal of an *association de malfaiteurs* of enormous proportions.

Hence the Republic's interest in Pouget, and Pouget's hasty retreat to London. Statistics alone confirmed that he was well worth the trouble to prosecute—more so, perhaps, than anarchist *littérateurs* like Jean Grave, Sébastien Faure, Charles Chatel, and Félix Fénéon, who also faced charges during the repressions of 1894. For *Le Père Peinard* seemed to operate at a considerable distance from anarchism's intellectual faction, and it was far less concerned with the nuances of federalism, mutual cooperation, and individual liberty than it was with the pragmatic business of rabble-rousing in the name of *le grand chambardement* (the "great upheaval" that, according to

Bakunin and his followers, would end the reign of capital once and for all).[8] What theory there was in the journal was cleverly woven into the fabric of a homespun narrative devoted principally to news, story-telling, personal reflections, practical advice, and the occasional serial novel, all of which were oriented toward the tastes and predilections of the *classes laborieuses*. Pouget's strategy was to insert the conceptual framework of fin-de-siècle anarchism into a preexistent (if constantly mutating) linguistic system, a lower-class vernacular that, while oppositionally predisposed toward the language of the ruling class, had yet to articulate revolutionary consciousness. The trick, simply stated, was to produce a cultural form that pretended to spring unmediated from *la grande foule* and that served at the same time to acquaint its audience with the desire for revolution they presumably possessed but had yet to recognize.

Such things were easier said than done. Pouget had to master argot, to choose dialects, to distinguish between a wide variety of "speaks" related to *métiers* of which he had no working knowledge. He had to calculate the impact and effects of his pronouncements, and to learn to provoke laughter, skepticism, and rage. He had to construct a convincing set of symbols, myths, and memories, a common language, an approach to the world—in sum, a compelling prototype of a collective working-class identity to be acquired and shared by his readers. His objectives, in other words, were both complex and perilous—especially perilous, since they involved a frontal assault on authority in all its guises and a target audience for whom (under the right circumstances) authority was liable to inspire anything but obedience. This last point is an important one if we are to understand the systems of representations at work in *Le Père Peinard,* for Pouget's commitment to a proletarian readership involved strategies that necessarily ran far afield of those informing event the most oppositional strains of legitimate literature. It is safe to say in this regard that the rhetorical arsenals deployed by the likes of Flaubert or Baudelaire to disrupt the smooth operations of dominant ideological formations—to reveal the most "natural" of beliefs, assumptions, and customs to be contestable structures serving competing interests—were devised to function in discursive conflicts internal to the bourgeoisie. And it is clear too that the nineteenth century's great plans for egalitarianism, for total social reorganization, for Revolution according to Saint-Simon, Fourier, Proudhon, Marx, or Bakunin were conceived largely in terms that spoke *for* the people rather than *to* them. If the oppositional voices of the ruling class were extremely adept at contesting hegemonic structures and proposing alternative social systems, they were markedly less articulate when it came to addressing those who stood to gain the most from the collapse of bourgeois authority.

Parler peuple: the very thought must have evoked notions of linguistic slumming, of a conscious descent into a realm of signification corresponding to disenfranchised social groups whose manner of speaking, whether quaint or boorish, was in either case ill equipped to articulate ideas and negotiate power. But from Pouget's perspective, such misgivings marked the ideological limits of radical bourgeois conceptions of the popular rank and file—the same limits he sought to traverse in *Le Père Peinard.* So it was in the lowly territory of popular parlance that he grappled with tradition, rhetorical convention, stylistic posturing, reception—in short, with the typical concerns of any ambitious writer, but redirected to a readership that most of his *semblables* were unable, or unwilling, to reach. And it was in the pages of his ill-mannered little journal that he formulated a model for ideological warfare that, by the end of the century, would prove to be the most enduring legacy of the ragtag revolutionary movement the Republic saw fit to exterminate in 1894.

1. N'oublie donc pas, mille bombes! que je suis un bouiff.

Pouget was not alone in his search for alternative modes of communication. *Le Ça Ira* had itself been born of a shared concern among militant anarchists that the most visible of the movement's publications, Jean Grave's weekly, *La Révolte,* was too solemn and pedantic in tone to function as anything other than a quasi-academic forum for libertarian proselytizing.[9] The goal, after all, was not simply to proselytize, but also to inspire action— or at least to establish a mode of address through which the written word might contribute, along with the more spontaneous orders of discourse practiced at the *réunion* or the café, to the instigation of revolutionary deeds. As an anonymous writer (perhaps Pouget himself) for *Le Ça Ira* put it ("Ecrire et parler," 24 June 1888: 2):

> Toute médaille a son revers. La parole soulève l'enthousiasme, les applaudissements, mais c'est plutôt de l'emballement qu'autre chose. C'est un feu de paille qui s'éteint comme il s'est allumé.
>
> La pensée écrite a aussi ses inconvénients; qui s'y livre immodérément perd les qualités de l'homme d'action; l'abstraction étant la négation de la vie.
>
> Ce qu'il faut, c'est une pondération des deux, qui allie à la spontanéité

qu'éveille la parole, la réflexion que fait naître la pensée. Grâce à cette union nous gagnerons en force—serons hommes d'action et de résolution—capables de porter des rudes coups au vieux monde et aptes à amener à nos idées les travailleurs inconscients.

[Every coin has its flip side. The spoken word encourages enthusiasm and applause, but it's more a question of packaging than anything else. The flame goes out as soon as it is lit.

Written thought also has its limitations; whoever reads too much of it loses their ability to act—since abstraction is the negation of life itself.

What's needed is a balance between the two, so that the spontaneity evoked by the spoken word is joined with the kind of reflection that induces thought itself. The combination will serve us well; we will become men who—committed both to action and serious thought—will be capable of striking a blow against the old world, while still expressing our ideas to unenlightened workers.]

For *Le Ça Ira,* the role of the revolutionary journal had been to provide a source of reflective thought to complement the provocative tenor of orally transmitted propaganda; for Pouget, who launched *Le Père Peinard* just a few weeks after *Le Ça Ira* ceased publication, the objective was apparently to take the logical next step, and to make a "pondération des deux"—of spontaneity and reflection—the procedural directive of an integrated journalistic enterprise. Which meant, of course, that he required access to a written communicative system that employed oral vernacular forms on the one hand and that was mutable enough to assimilate anarchist ideas on the other. He found it in a long-standing tradition of publications that presumed to speak directly to the people, the progenitor of which was Jacques Hébert's obstreperous *Le Père Duchêne* (1790–93). The trademark revolutionary parlance of Hébert's irascible "marchand de fourneaux" (whose "très grande colère" was typically directed at politicians, the clergy, and "les jean-foutres" in general) had resurfaced in ephemeral publications throughout the nineteenth century and had proven versatile enough to serve a variety of political bents and historical circumstances.[10] Pouget was fully aware of the exploits of his predecessors, and he carefully designed his journal to conform to the basic attributes of the genre: a folksy, commonsensical narrator with an emphatically lower-class lineage and frame of reference; a colloquial narrative voice given to frequent obscene outbursts; and a professed editorial commitment, first and foremost, to *le peuple.*

Le Père Peinard stuck hard and fast by the *Hébertiste* model. The title itself—consisting of the colloquial noun *peinard* [working stiff] affixed to the familiar paternal epitaph *père*—was clever, alliterative, and firmly grounded in folkloric tradition and working-class culture alike.[11] It also provided the appropriate honorific nickname for the journal's narrator, a "vieux gniaff" whose radical identity was implicitly legitimated by the mythic role cobblers (along with tailors and typesetters) had played on the nineteenth-century revolutionary stage.[12] Readers of *Le Père Peinard* could see him hard at work—with pen and paper rather than leather—in the cover illustration (fig. 3-1) Pouget obtained from his friend and collaborator Maximillien Luce. And they could see too that his "intellectual labor" had practical applications, as the phrygian cap appearing to the lower right of Luce's drawing would have suggested. Like a seal of authenticity, this last detail laid claim on behalf of Pouget (and his invented persona) to a mighty revolutionary mythology. Yet his alignment with *Hébertisme* was as shrewd as it was reverential, for *Le Père Peinard* was also devised to usurp the rhetorical power of that tradition in order to establish its own brand of propaganda, replete with a social agenda and a revolutionary solution that would never have occurred to the recalcitrant hero of the *sans-culottes;* when Luce made a new masthead for the journal in May 1890, the phrygian cap was notably absent.

Genealogical maneuvering aside, communicative authority was Pouget's to acquire—and it meant staking out a readership and, by extension, a social territory in which his project stood to gain the most ground.[13] It also meant negotiating the various ways in which *Le Père Peinard* might be consumed by an audience for whom the act of reading was by no means a uniform practice, particularly when that practice encountered oral forms of language in writing.[14] Pouget's *vieux gniaff* accordingly rehearsed his rhetorical strategies in the journal's premier issue (24 February 1889: 3–4):

> Naturellement, en ma qualité de gniaff, je suis pas tenu à écrire comme les niquedouilles de l'Académie. . . .
>
> Les types des ateliers, les gars des usines, tous ceux qui peinent dur et triment fort, me comprendront. C'est la langue du populo que je dégoise. . . .
>
> Etre compris des bons bougres, c'est ce que je veux—pour le reste je m'en fous!

> [Naturally, in my capacity as cobbler, I'm not required to write like the knuckleheads of the Académie. . . .
>
> The guys from the work shops and the factories, everyone who works long and hard, will understand me. I talk the people's language. . . .
>
> All I want is to be understood by regular working stiffs—I don't give a shit about anybody else.]

FIGURE 3-1: Maximilien Luce, Cover illustration for *Le Père Peinard* (6 April 1890).
Photo: A.C.R.P.P., Paris.

On the face of things, the *vieux gniaff*'s aims were simple: to claim a spoken vernacular ("la langue du populo") as his own, to share it with "tous ceux qui peinent dur et triment fort," and to distinguish it from the preferred language of bourgeois society's official intellectual elite. Yet as the impertinent reference to "niquedouilles de l'Académie" suggests, he also wanted to direct its improper linguistic status against institutional authority in terms that effectively impeded recourse to the loci of rationalizations and assumptions upon which authority typically depends to exercise power. The rhetorical damage wrought by calling a priest a "ratichon" [little rat], say, or the state a "putain de République" [whore of a Republic], was hardly to be undone by elegant discourses on theology or universal suffrage. Nor was the *vieux gniaff*'s lambasting of proper French to be reasoned with (24 February 1889: 3): "La grammaire que j'ai eue à l'école ne m'ayant guère servi qu'à me torcher le cul je ne saisis pas en quel honneur je me foutrais à la piocher maintenant" [The only good the grammar I got at school ever did was to give me something to wipe my ass with, so I can't imagine why the fuck I'd slog through it now]. If such turns of phrase smacked of cynicism and malevolence, it is because they bore within them a constellation of lower-class experiences—of subservience, poverty, and humiliation—that begged for retribution, linguistic or otherwise.[15] Hence the countless indignities that formal language suffered in the everyday parlance of colloquial speakers: vulgar suffixes—*ard, o, ote, aille, uche,* etc.—attached to proper words (as in "richard" or "capitalo"); affectatious suffixes—*erie, atif, ité,* etc.—attached to colloquial terms (as in "saloperie"); the pejorative coupling of two words, the second of which metaphorically degrades the first (as in "cléricochon"); the derogatory metaphor—whether animal, alimentary, or fecal (as in "les crocodiles sénatoriaux," "les grosses légumes," or "les lèche-culs de journaleux"). These are just a few of the patterns of linguistic mutilation upon which Pouget drew to position his journal at a critical distance from dominant rhetorical practices. And he clearly relished his work, for *Le Père Peinard*'s colloquial inventiveness was to become one of its trademarks; deputies were called "bouffe-galettes," judges, "salopiots d'enjuponés," the prefecture of police, "la sergocratie."[16] Thus deployed, popular parlance could intimate, through sheer negativity, that language itself was contestable—and innately linked to the material interests at stake in the maintenance and the potential disruption of established social hierarchies.

Pouget, in other words, based his claim to communicative authority on the power of colloquial language to impugn, in the baldest of terms, the rhetorical systems typically employed by the ruling class to represent its own interests as those of subservient social groups. But as a trafficker in linguistic contestation, he inevitably had to compensate for the contestability of his own pronouncements. In October 1889 *Le Père Peinard* reported a well-intentioned reader's observation that the journal's phraseology seemed to him to be "trop grossière." These, for Pouget, were fighting words, if only because the very notion of *la grossièreté* was laden with the kind of disapprobation typically informing upper-class accounts of the culture and practices of the people. The *vieux gniaff* responded by taking his reader, and his readership, to school (20 October 1889: 12):

Si tu avais un peu vécu tu saurais que chaque patelin, chaque société, chaque profession a son argot spécial. Pourquoi le mien qui est celui de la grande foule travailleuse qui ne cherche pas midi à quatorze heures, t'offusque-t-il? . . . N'oublie donc pas, mille bombes! que je suis un bouiff, et un bouiff ne parle pas comme une vieille moule d'académicien.[17]

[If you had a little more experience under your belt, you'd know that each region, each society, each profession has its own special slang. Why are you confused by mine, which is that of the great working masses who don't knock off from noon to four every afternoon? . . . So don't forget, blast it, that I'm a cobbler, and a cobbler doesn't talk like some old twerp from the Académie.]

The correspondence between language and a variegated social landscape; the legitimacy of working-class vernacular; the swipe taken, once again, at the Académie: such refrains are predictable in a journal devoted to the encouragement of working-class solidarity. But the lesson to be learned here is primarily rhetorical, and it takes the form of the exaggerated belligerence with which the narrator insists on his humble social station: "N'oublie donc pas, mille bombes! que je suis un bouiff." The conjuring-up of *Hébertiste* bluster is telling, for if a reader's polite concern about rampant *grossièreté* seemed innocuous enough, it nonetheless implied that the *vieux gniaff*'s linguistic predilections were somehow negotiable or, worse yet, that his narrative identity itself was a fiction dreamt up by a clever journalist looking for a communicative ruse through which to address the people. And nothing stood to undermine Pouget's project more than that.

Nothing, that is, unless the greater part of *Le Père Peinard*'s readership already understood the *vieux gniaff* to be a narrative invention, in which case the relative authority of his utterances was less a matter of perceived authenticity than of proficiency in a game of skill, the objective of which was to seduce readers with daring acts of irreverence or extraordinary verbal dexterity—all the while insisting on the truth of a narrative identity that, in keeping with the rules of the game, was transparently false. The game here is called irony. And the fissure between narrative claims and their resonance *when read* (as true or false, clever or bungling, literal or ironic) is precisely the space in which Pouget and his readership negotiated meaning. For "naive" readers, a literal understanding of the *vieux gniaff*'s alibi ("je suis un bouiff," therefore "c'est la langue du populo que je dégoise") may or may not have justified his bad manners on the grounds of sheer lower-class artlessness; for "sophisticated" readers, however, the recognition of his alibi as an ironic device would have implied that his *grossièreté* was a critical weapon con-

sciously employed to dole out abuse—the legitimacy of which was established by the socially empowered status of his victims ("les ratichons," "les
vieilles moules d'académiciens," et al.) and the attendant possibility of legal
repercussions.[18] Devotion, for a discerning audience, had to be earned, and
it depended on their assessment both of the *vieux gniaff*'s colloquial proficiency and of the relative contemptibility of his preferred targets. Small
wonder, then, that *Le Père Peinard*'s most devoted—and "sophisticated"—
readers were likely to be found among those "gens de culture primitive" for
whom the characteristic patterns of popular parlance were as familiar as the
self-serving pronouncements of their betters, and the oppositional relationship between the two a matter of lived experience.[19]

Through a subversion of normative sociolinguistic hierarchies, in other
words, the experience of subjugation could come to serve as a precondition
of the reader's capacity to contest the journal's narrative function (i.e. the
literal claims of the narrator) in search of alternative meanings, while at the
same time setting a standard against which the credibility of its textual
function (i.e. the impact of narrative as *read text*) might be measured.[20] The
involvement of a proletarian audience in this process of "readerly authorization" was crucial to *Le Père Peinard*'s capacity to seduce its readers—and
crucial too as a means of soliciting their endorsement of the literal imperatives which, as an openly revolutionary form of propaganda, the journal was
bound to make. So Pouget was persistent in his attempts to teach his readers
to read discerningly the (ironic and literal) narratives at work in *Le Père
Peinard*. In response to yet another complaint (16 March 1890: 10–12) about
his penchant for abusive language, the *vieux gniaff* explained with characteristic verve that:

> On m'accuse d'être *mal embouché;* en voilà un crime abominable! Tas de
> gobeurs, qui en ce siècle de fumisteries et loufoquismes ne comprenez pas
> plus qu'on appelle un chat, un chat—un député, un bouffe-galette—un
> patron, un voleur!

> [They accuse me of being *foul-mouthed;* what an abominable crime! In
> this era of swindling and craziness, you'd have to be a real sucker no
> longer to understand that we call a spade, a spade—a deputy, a cake-
> gobbler—a boss, a thief!]

The usual colloquialisms ("gobeurs," "loufoquisme," "bouffe-galette") are
delivered here with the usual implacability, and the reader is once again
solicited with an irony ("en voilà un crime abominable!") that serves to
deflect the subject of the figurative crime from the narrator's truculence to

the "fumisteries" and "loufoquismes" typical, according to the *vieux gniaff,* of contemporary communicative practices. The journal's critics are admonished for their guillibility ("tas de gobeurs"), while concurring readers are rewarded with a sense of belonging to an oppositional collective that knows better. Yet the passage is also constructed to make believers out of antagonists who, once insulted, are invited to participate. Hence the shifting referents of the impersonal pronoun *on,* which serves first to signify the critics as "they" ("on dit que"), and then to propose a collective "we" ("qu'on appelle") to which the critics are welcome to adhere; the shift between "they" and "we," mediated by the curious insertion of the second person plural form of the verb *comprendre* ("qui ne comprenez plus"), suggests that the previously impersonal "they" has become a directly addressed "you" as a prelude to the proposed "we." Partisans and naysayers alike are thus encouraged to learn a language—purged of "fumisteries" and "loufoquismes"—in which one says what one means: "on appelle un chat, un chat." And it goes without saying that the ironic metaphor deployed when calling a *député* a "bouffe-galette" is no less to the point than the literal equation in which a *patron* is a "voleur."

As these last phrases suggest, Pouget attempted simultaneously to secure readerly authorization and to erode the cognitive demarcations upon which such authorization depends—in this case between ironic ("bouffe-galette") and literal ("on apelle un chat, un chat") turns of phrase. Once engaged, the reader was implicitly prompted to register the critique contained within the *vieux gniaff*'s colloquial negations, as well as the literal truth of that critique: a "patron" *is* a "voleur," just as (elsewhere in anarchist thought) "property" *is* "theft." *Le Père Peinard* accordingly functioned as a rhetorical *monde renversé* in which revolutionary directives sprang naturally from the negative assessments implicit in colloquial deformations of legitimate language, and the illegality of revolution was recast as an entirely justifiable response to an illegitimate state of affairs.[21] The *vieux gniaff,* reflecting on distinctions between written and oral forms of communication, put it this way (16 March 1890: 12):

> La langue écrite, qu'on parle dans les livres est une invention idiote, bonne pour embarbouiller les idées et empêcher le populo de comprendre. . . .
>
> Si au contraire les bouquins étaient écrits à la bonne franquette avec des mots connus de tous, tout le monde comprendrait! . . .
>
> Mais la première chose que le populo comprendrait, c'est que les

richards et les gouvernants le volent, et en plus se foutent de lui; alors au lieu d'endurer toute cette racaille, il lui casserait la gueule hardiment.

[The written language spoken in books is an idiotic invention, real good for mucking up ideas and keeping the people from understanding.

If, on the contrary, books were written in a plain and simple language, with words known to all, everybody would understand! . . .

But the first thing the people would understand is that rich folks and politicians steal from them, and don't give a shit about them either; so instead of putting up with those scum, the people would beat the living daylights out of them.]

In the upside-down world of *Le Père Peinard,* these concluding lines made perfect sense; whether they were to be taken literally or figuratively was up to the discretion of the reader.

2. Le Code . . . On chie dessus.

The state, of course, was less interested in the relative discretion of Pouget's readers than it was in the literal letter of the law. In the spring of 1890, *Le Père Peinard* was served with an arrest warrant for having provoked pillage, mutiny, and murder ("non suivie d'effet," the document noted).[22] That the offending article ("La Manifestation du 1er Mai," 6 April 1890: 4) encouraged mass participation in up-coming May Day demonstrations no doubt aggravated government prosecutors, perhaps because such solicitation was legal.[23] That it encouraged civil disobedience and violence, on the other hand, was cause for genuine concern—as well as for aggressive enforcement of the press laws of 29 July 1881. The laws could be stretched when necessary, as they were when the *vieux gniaff*'s observation, "Faut être dans la rue pour traiter des affaires sociales" [you gotta be in the street to deal with social issues], proved inflammatory enough to warrant charges of inciting pillage."[24] But it took considerably less legal stretching to prosecute his musings on an alternative role for the military on May Day:

> Le 1er mai est une occase qui peut tourner à bien. Il suffirait pour cela que nos frangins les troubades lèvent la crosse en l'air, comme en février 48, comme au 18 mars 71, et ça ne serait pas long du coup!
>
> Le gouvernement n'a que cet atout dans sa manche, s'il lui échappe, il est foutu sans remission!
>
> Les soldats, que sont-ils? Nos frères de misère. Pourquoi défendraient-

ils les riches? . . . Qu'ils y songent, nom de dieu, et quand on leur commandera: feu! qu'ils essaient les fusils Lebel sur leurs chefs et qu'ils fassent merveille!

[The May Day demonstrations could take a turn for the better. All it would take is for our brothers, the soldiers, to signal mutiny like they did in February 48 and on March 18th, 1871, and things would happen sooner rather than later.

The army is the only card the government has up its sleeve; if they lose it, they're fucked for sure.

What are soldiers, anyway? They're our brothers in misery. Why do they defend the rich? If they'd just think it over, then the next time they hear the order to fire, they'd try out their Lebel rifles on their officers. It'd work wonders!]

Mutiny, murder, the specter of revolutions past and future: Pouget could hardly have composed a more flagrant violation of a statute designed specifically to discourage the provocation of enlisted men to insubordination and disobedience.[25] Small matter that the text neither provoked, nor directly addressed, potentially discontented soldiers (to whom it referred as "ils" rather than "vous"); when the *vieux gniaff* reported the trial to his readers, he neglected even to mention the prosecutorial sleight of hand.

What he mentioned instead were the objects of his contempt (20 April 1890: 1–4): the law, "dont le Père Peinard se fout comme une merde de chien" [which is nothing but dogshit as far as Père Peinard is concerned]; judges, "une bande de sacripants" [a gang of scoundrels]; and the arrest warrant itself, a "papier torcheculatif" [ass-wiping paper]. Such was the tone of the journal's response to its impending prosecution. Rather than appease his antagonists with tempered rhetoric or halfhearted retractions, the *vieux gniaff* addressed them in the most menacing of terms: "ce n'est que quand le chambardement général vous aura définitivement foutus à cul qu'un peu de raison humaine entrera dans vos caboches obscurcies" [it's only when a mass insurrection has finally stuck it up your asses that a little humane reason will get through your thick skulls]. When the inevitable verdicts (guilty on all counts) and stiff sentences (two years in prison, three thousand francs in fines) came in, he defiantly announced plans to enlarge the format of the journal, to include illustrations, and to redouble his efforts to spread the anarchist message.[26] That he could keep such promises had less to do with commitment and contumacy than it did with the legal provision—at the heart of the press laws of 29 July 1881, and still on the books in 1890—that punitive action against a given periodical was to be directed toward that periodical's *gérant* [publisher] before any members of its editorial staff could be held responsible.[27] Pouget himself was under no obligation to heed the law as long as *Le Père Peinard* could produce the funds necessary to pay fines and the anarchist *compagnons* willing to serve, at the risk of imprisonment or exile, as the journal's *gérant*. "Faites des lois sur la presse," the *vieux gniaff* goaded legislators (20 April 1890: 3), " . . . on ne les lit même pas. On vas droit son chemin sans s'arrêter à des étrons pareils qui fument sur la route" [Go ahead and make your press laws, . . . we don't even read them. We know where we're going, and we're not about to stop for whatever legal turds you drop in our way]. So began a series of skirmishes between the *cour d'assises* and *Le Père Peinard* that would become fodder for the journal's weekly diatribes against authority. Within a year Pouget had lost five *gérants* to press law convictions; with each conviction came another vituperative condemnation of those who presumed to condemn.[28]

An escalation of hostilities was bound to occur, given Pouget's recalcitrance and the judiciary's inability to silence him. In December 1890 *Le Père Peinard* was hit with a barrage of new arrest warrants. The charges had become standard fare (provocation to commit pillage, mutiny, and murder), but the journal now stood trial for ten infractions involving three issues and a total of nine articles. The *vieux gniaff*'s response was predictable (7 December 1890: 1): "Ils veulent serrer la vis au Père Peinard, les charognes. Ça les emmerde que je dégoise des vérités au populo" [They wanna tighten the screws on Père Peinard, the bastards. It pisses them off that I speak the truth to the people]. And it was predictable too that Pouget would turn up the heat by enlisting one of French anarchism's most persuasive orators, Sébastien Faure, to address the court on behalf of the accused. Faure's involvement with *Le Père Peinard* would continue for three years, and it transformed the routine appearances of Pouget's *gérants* before the *cour d'assises* into a series of spectacular public performances. The verdicts were a foregone conclusion, and Faure treated them as such; but a day in court provided the perfect occasion to address authority face-to-face before an overflow audience of anarchist partisans—"une belle chiée de copains" [a shit-load of friends], in Pouget's words.[29] So it was that in trial after trial, *Le Père Peinard*'s defense team systematically ignored the charges filed against the journal's sacrificial *gérant;* what mattered was the opportunity to proselytize against the very foundation of the State's claim to legal authority. In his December 1890 debut, Faure made it clear that the "accused" in the State's proceedings was society itself: "On nous accuse de souffler la haine. Foutre oui! on a raison: le père Peinard excite à la Révolte contre la misère" [They accuse us of spreading hate. Fuck yeah! and we're right: *Le Père Peinard* stirs up rebellion against misery].[30] As his appropriation of the *vieux gniaff*'s phraseology suggests, Faure leaned heavily on the startling effect to be achieved by employing bad language in the most formal of circumstances. But he also delivered a point-by-point critique of the economy, of class hierarchy, of the military, of patriotism, of universal suffrage—of virtually every agent of repression, that is, except for the press laws themselves. Anarchism, Faure explained, recognized the problem and knew the solution:

> Y a que la Force qui domine! Et c'est pourquoi, pour sortir les pauvres bougres de la mistoufle, pour tordre le cou aux patrons et aux gouvernements, nous comptons que sur la Force!
> . . . L'Autorité, qu'elle soit divine ou humaine, n'en faut plus![31]

> [Force alone dominates! That's why we count on Force alone to end the misery of poor folks and to wring the necks of bosses and governments!
> . . . Authority, whether its divine or human, is no longer necessary!]

Authority responded promptly with a guilty verdict. Brought before the bench for sentencing, the *compagnon* Faugoux, interim *gérant* of *Le Père Peinard,* heard judgment passed and, in keeping with convention, concluded the proceedings with the requisite cry of "Vive l'Anarchie!"

The *vieux gniaff* was incensed. Or so it must have seemed to his readers when they saw the front page (14 December 1890: 1) a few days after the trial:

> *Deux ans de sucre, trois mille balles d'amende!!!* C'est le *maximum* . . .
> Ousqu'ils veulent qu'on la prenne, nom de dieu? Faudrait dévaliser quelque juré, pour pêcher trois mille balles. . . .
> Trois mille pains, oui, nom de dieu! Ou s'ils préfèrent, trois mille coup de pieds dans le cul.

> [Two years of hard time and a three thousand franc fine!! That's the maximum!
> Where the hell do they think we'll get it? You'd have to rip off some juror to come up with three thousand francs. . . .
> Yeah right, goddammit, three thousand francs! Or if they prefer, three thousand kicks in the ass.]

The articulation of rage here depends, as typically it did in *Le Père Peinard,* on the aggressive deployment of rote obscenity, on the advocation (figurative or literal) of muggings and ass kickings—on the suspension, that is, of an exchange of ideas between differing parties and its displacement by linguistic paroxysms that would seem to call off discourse altogether. A communicative shut-down made sense, given Pouget's apparent conviction that between oppressors and the oppressed there was simply nothing to discuss. And it made sense too that an annulment of potential dialogue could be figured quite powerfully in visual form; hence the illustration Luce contributed (fig. 3-2) as a graphic complement to Pouget's harangue. Rendered in a suitably objectionable scrawl, the *vieux gniaff* buckles his trousers, having just defecated on an open volume of the *Code pénal;* what he turns to admire is the rude encounter of the literal letter of the law with an *étron* (no less literal) of his own making. The pronominal diction of the accompanying caption, "Le Code? . . . On chie dessus!" [The Code? . . . We shit all over it!] suggests that the defecatory act—and the discursive rupture it promotes—is a collective undertaking; *le peuple* (in the person of the *vieux gniaff*) has figuratively declared war (by shitting) on authority (represented by the *Code pénal*). Pouget's vulgarities openly invited revulsion, incomprehension, and condemnation. "Réunissez tous les jurons possibles," a writer for the *Journal de Saint-Denis* commented in March 1891, "amalgamez avec l'ordinaire langage des pires escarpes et vous ferez un *Père Peinard*" [Assemble every imaginable curse, combine them with the everyday language of the worst kinds of thugs, and you will have made your own *Père Peinard*]; the recipe was crude and unpalatable, especially for readers with whom the journal had no interest in communicating.[32]

Yet one suspects that it communicated quite well with less priggish readers, and that the same vulgarities were a much anticipated feature of each week's issue—if not a welcome source of mirth. After all, Pouget's blasphemous outbursts were delivered for the benefit of an audience for whom propriety counted for very little and the presumed dignity of their masters even less. That his readers might enjoy paroxysms of their own (paroxysms of laughter, of rage) depended on the *vieux gniaff*'s ability to contrive an endless succession of textual and visual incidents in which prevailing social hierarchies were insolently overturned: three thousand *coups de pied dans le cul* for a judge and jury; an unseemly comeuppance for the *Code pénal;* the clever debasement—as in *ratichonneries* or *cléricouillon*—of the clergy and of proper French itself. Assuming a sympathetic reader's delight in such impertinences, Pouget enjoyed access to a nebulous communicative realm defined on the one hand by heightened emotional states (extreme enough to produce physical convulsions) and on the other by the momentary emergence of the unconscious, released (as Freud would have it) along with the suspension of conscious control of the body. Like any effective form of satire, in other words, *Le Père Peinard* intervened in the operation of the most

LE CODE?... ON CHIE DESSUS !

FIGURE 3-2: Maximilien Luce, "Le Code? . . . On chie dessus," *Le Père Peinard* (14 December 1890). Photo: A.C.R.P.P., Paris.

visceral of its readers' cerebral functions—at the expense, presumably, of the determinants ordinarily at work in the process of thought formation.[33] If the resulting effects were difficult for Pouget to anticipate, the rhetorical weapons he employed nonetheless positioned the journal to combat—in emotionally charged terms—the systems of signification through which dominant ideological formations were typically transmitted. Comfortable assumptions about the virtues of patriotism, or the church, or military glory, or jurisprudence were ridiculed with a caustic hostility that potentially served to disrupt, if only fleetingly, the elaborate nexus of influences (material, social, discursive) that constitute the cognitive domain of ideology—if not the very boundaries of conscious thought.[34] In the wake of such disruptions, of course, the problem was to direct readers toward an alternative (anarchist) form of consciousness, while at the same time intimating that its relative validity (as a function of truth, rather than yet another ideological formation) was somehow a matter of intuition; "la réflexion que fait naître la pensée," in other words, had imperceptibly to coexist with "la spontanéité qu'éveille la parole."

Pouget's first concern was to continue to disrupt. Two weeks after the December convictions were handed down, the *vieux gniaff* defiantly announced yet another increase in the format of *Le Père Peinard*. The changes included a larger three-column layout, rubric logos for recurrent "theme" columns, and another new masthead (fig. 3-3) which, in keeping with the belligerence of Pouget's rhetoric, now featured a crude rendition of the narrator—gargantuan in size, leather strap in hand—giving chase to the usual gang of judicial, military, and clerical suspects.[35] Within two years, the journal had transformed itself from a pocket-size pamphlet to a medium-format newspaper fully capable of competing for attention at the corner kiosk, and capable too of expanding its communicative program to include parodies of journalism itself. For if *Le Père Peinard* began to look vaguely like a "respectable" commercial newspaper, it did so with the provision that for every seemingly innocuous "Chroniques," "Variétés," or "Faits divers" served up by the daily press, it could respond with columns of its own, the titles of which—"Au palais d'injustice," "Mort aux proprios," "Saloperies militaires," "Du pain ou du plomb"—signaled the displacement of a familiar configuration of "news" and "features" by a selection of inflammatory articles that was unlikely to grace the pages of *Le Petit Parisien, Le Matin,* or *Le Figaro*.[36] Nor was it likely that the commercial press would have seen fit to print *Le Père Peinard*'s new logo illustrations, especially the one (fig. 3-4) in which the *vieux gniaff* contentedly puffs away at his pipe while squatting, trousers down, on the source of his perpetual difficulties with the law. Next to Luce's

FIGURE 3-3: Anonymous (signed "Pol Cizoc"), Masthead for *Le Père Peinard* (11 January 1891). Photo: A.C.R.P.P., Paris.

ENGUEULADE AUX ENJUPONNÉES

FIGURE 3-4:
Anonymous, Rubric logo for *Le Père Peinard* (11 January 1891). Photo: A.C.R.P.P., Paris.

vitriolic prototype, the image appears more comic in orientation, as if to announce that the adversarial state of affairs aggressively articulated by the original had become a laughably routine consequence of the irreconcilability of working-class interests and the bourgeois judicial system; if the *vieux gniaff* was compelled to live with the *code pénal,* he would at least put it to good use. As always, it was up to Pouget's readers to reject such vulgarities or to enjoy the show as the forces of order, along with their commercial minions, took yet another weekly beating. Now, however, the show was bigger, and in conjunction with Faure's courtroom theatrics and the journal's ongoing (illegal) postering campaigns, the *vieux gniaff* seemed poised to emerge in public consciousness as a working-class media sensation: scabrous, ill-tempered, and potentially dangerous on the one hand; entertaining, and perhaps inspirational on the other.[37]

3. La douce illusion de s'encanailler

The journal's increased notoriety depended to some extent on the willingness of the press to fan the flames. Le Figaro, for one, complied by dedicating an entire issue of its literary supplement to an article called "Le Péril anarchiste" (19 January 1891), a section of which was devoted exclusively to Le Père Peinard and its penchant for "violentes polemiques" [violent polemic] and "furieux coups de boutoir" [furious, hard-hitting attacks]. Pouget could hardly have objected to such observations, especially since they acknowledged his systematic attempts to rehearse a coherent anarchist program amidst all the rhetorical fury. Nor could he have protested the characterization of his narrator's mode of address as "la langue pittoresque de l'habitude de la Boule-Noir et du Moulin de la Galette" [the picturesque language habitually spoken at the Boule-Noir and the Moulin de la Galette]—despite the element of condescension introduced by the adjective "pittoresque."[38] But whether Pouget knew it or not, the invocation of working-class dance halls—and of the lower end of the Parisian entertainment industry in general—pointed to communicative complications that had far less to do with the condescending assessments of the bourgeois press than with the vogue in the eighties and nineties for a wide variety of "popular" entertainments—some of which stood to rival the *vieux gniaff*'s authority as self-ordained representative of the people. Perhaps inevitably, Le Père Peinard was more closely related than Pouget might have liked to the commercial productions that took place nightly at any number of dance halls and bohemian cabarets. For if the journal's preferred rhetorical techniques were effective, they were also public property—and regularly employed in a broad range of cultural practices in which presumably popular systems of signification were recast in the *image* of the people, but in the *interests* of commerce.[39]

There were many forms from which to choose in the early nineties: La Goulue's raucous performances of the *chahut* at the Moulin Rouge, Le Pétomane's renowned farting routine, or the gala ambience of "revolution" peddled at a succession of short-lived *montmartrois* cabarets directed by the former communard Maxime Lisbonne. Or, closer still to Pouget's project, the *chansonnier* Aristide Bruant's renditions of a repertoire of songs and monologues devoted almost exclusively to the culture of the urban underbelly—from the life and times of a *bellevillois* pimp to the last confessions of a convicted murderer awaiting execution at La Roquette.[40] Armed with his own cabaret (Le Mirliton), a newspaper (also called *Le Mirliton*), and a publicity team featuring Toulouse-Lautrec and Théophile Steinlen, Bruant was well equipped to establish a public image which, like *Le Père Peinard*'s, seemed entirely steeped in the most objectionable strata of Parisian society. Every aspect of his production—the abrasive stage routine, the gritty songs about prostitutes, drunks, thieves, and killers, the calculated coarseness of the posters and illustrations he commissioned from Lautrec and Steinlen— contributed to a seemingly authentic representation of life in the Parisian badlands, particularly for consumers whose experience of the Parisian bad-lands was negligible. Singing in the first person and drawing on his acquired knowledge of working-class and criminal argot, Bruant appeared to have the inside track on the so-called *classes dangereuses,* a distinction that won him an enormous following, even among the ranks of *haut*-bourgeois women (for whom he also appeared to be the very embodiment of low-class virility).[41] Edmond de Goncourt, who spent a predictably uncomfortable evening at a Bruant performance in 1892, was appalled by what he heard: "Ce qu'il a chanté, devant les femmes de la société qui étaient là, non, c'est indici-ble! . . . Ç'a été, en ce lyrisme de l'ignoble, des dénominations infâmes, des mots salissants, de l'argot purulent, des vocables de bas bordels et des ma-ladies vénériennes" [What he sang in front of the women of standing who were there—no, it's unspeakable! . . . It was the lyricism of the wretched, composed of dirty words, purulent slang, and the terminology of lowly brothels and venereal diseases].[42] Such indignation boded well for Bruant, since the heady experience of class transgression was precisely the attraction of going to see him perform. One wonders if Pouget would have merited a similarly intemperate response had Goncourt bothered to page through an issue of *Le Père Peinard*.[43]

Or more to the point, one wonders to what extent the resemblance between Bruant's and Pouget's respective communicative strategies—the Rabelaisian vulgarity, the invention of lowly narrative voices, the appropria-tion of *bas langage*—might have obscured the enormous distinctions between their primary objectives: for the former, a hankering for fame and fortune in immoderate doses (his sympathy for *le peuple* notwithstanding); for the latter, nothing less than the total dismantling of bourgeois society. Bruant, for his part, was not insensitive to the marketability of typically bohemian strains of antibourgeois posturing or to the allure, when properly defused and repack-aged, of revolution itself; nostalgic allusions to the Commune, after all, were common fare among the *chansonniers* with whom he worked in Montmartre in the eighties.[44] But looking back on his career thirty years later, he employed distinctly less mnemonically charged terms to describe the effect of his performances on faithful partisans: "Les consommateurs braillaient au refrain, dans la douce illusion de s'encanailler" [the customers howled along with each refrain, under the sweet illusion of rubbing elbows with the riffraff].[45] For Goncourt, the "illusion de s'encanailler" was apparently not "douce" enough; for Bruant, the goal was to scandalize a willing audience while steering clear of materials that might arouse the ire of government censors and prosecutors. The personalities he assumed in his songs were accordingly raunchy, cynical, or fatalistic; but they were almost always content with their lowly social station. Even the narrator of "Belleville-Ménilmontant," a teenage pimp who makes "pas mal de braise" [a pretty penny] by prostituting his friend's younger sister, seems pleased with his lot in life and, in the final stanzas of the song, blithely concludes:

> C'est comm' ça qu'c'est l'vrai moyen
> D'dev'nir un bon citoyen:
> On grandit, sans s'fair' de bile,
>   A Bell'ville,
> On cri': Viv' l'Indépendance!
> On a l'coeur bath et content,
> Et l'on nag', dans l'abondance,
>   A Ménilmontant.[46]

> [That's the real way
> To become a good citizen:
> You grow up with no worries at all,
>   in Belleville.
> You shout: Long live independence!
> You feel just fine and dandy,
> And you're living the good life,
>   in Ménilmontant.]

As Bruant's audiences knew full well, it was hardly likely that "l'on nag' dans l'abondance, à Ménilmontant," at least not by bourgeois standards. So it must have seemed both charming and poignant to hear a small-time pimp declare, confidently and with just a hint of irony, that "On a l'coeur bath et content"—despite the obvious torments of an existence defined by poverty, the sex trade, and the police. The key to Bruant's success was to produce a convincing facsimile of the thoughts and class identity of his characters, while resisting the inclination—typical of bourgeois interlocutors like Zola or the Goncourts—to perform sociological or scientific analyses along the way. The desired effect required a great deal of study, and it hinged on Bruant's capacity to master the vocabulary and speech patterns of the street: slurred elisions ("C'est comm' ça qu'c'est l'vrai moyen"), colloquial turns of phrase ("s'fair' de bile"), and a healthy portion of popular slang ("braise," "bath," etc.). It required disciplined showmanship too, since the credibility of his representations also hinged on the spectator's acceptance of the singer as an authentic *homme du peuple* rather than a clever mimic or, worse yet, an enlightened proselytizer with a social axe to grind.

For the art critic Frantz Jourdain, the relative credibility of Bruant's inventions was apparently never in doubt. Writing for the fashionable literary monthly, *La Plume,* he had this to say about the poster (fig. 3-5) Lautrec made in 1892 to promote Bruant's performances at Les Ambassadeurs:

> [Lautrec] s'est attaché à rendre cet aspect farouche, un peu sauvage mais imposant qu'a ce chantre de la rue. C'est bien là, l'homme à l'amère férocité, au talent âpre et poignant. . . . On lit sur les traits la hardiesse crâne du révolté, la haine de l'audacieux pour les "rupins," la tristesse que lui ont donnée les douleurs humbles.[47]

> [Lautrec has concentrated on rendering the fierceness—impressive, if a little wild—of the street-singer's appearance. There he is, a man of bitter ferocity, of harsh and poignant talent. . . . We read in these lines the gallant boldness of the rebel, the hatred of the iconoclast for "fat cats," the sadness he feels for the suffering of the poor.]

Lautrec could hardly have done a better job of emphasizing—with impudently crude outlines and brazen expanses of unmodeled color—the aura of insolence and vulgarity evoked by Bruant's glowering scowl, by the low-life lurking in the doorway behind him, and by the suggestive position of the singer's staff. Nor could Jourdain have done a better job of promoting Bruant, or of playing the part of "naive reader" in a cleverly orchestrated publicity campaign. Given the configuration of the image, adjectives like "farouche," "sauvage," and "âpre" were fitting, if a bit clichéd; but given the artifice at the heart of the entire Bruant production, Jourdain's choice of words attests rather to his unwitting complicity in the operation of a spectacle designed to obscure the distinctions between the wily implementation of a seemingly popular vocabulary and a "truthful" representation (if such a thing were possible) of an unmediated set of popular practices. It is, after all, patently absurd to consider a term like "révolté" in Bruant's case, or to talk seriously of the hatred he harbored for "les rupins"—especially since the

FIGURE 3-5: Henri de Toulouse-Lautrec, *Ambassadeurs: Aristide Bruant* (1892): San Diego Museum of Art (Gift of the Baldwin M. Baldwin Foundation). Photo: San Diego Museum of Art.

success of his operation depended entirely on bourgeois hankerings for illusory glimpses of the Parisian *bas fonds*. Lautrec promoted such illusions, while circumventing the banal realities of the singer's career: the fact, for instance, that Bruant had experimented with a variety of stage identities (an elegant *boulevardier,* among others) before landing on his definitive public persona—or, more banal still, that he had excelled in Latin at his *lycée* years before undertaking his study of argot.[48] What the poster provides instead are the basic attributes of an elaborate fiction, pictorially pared down to the point that they inspire words like "farouche" and "sauvage" (or for the particularly thinned-skinned spectator, "salissant" and "purulent") while alluding to little else. In the absence of more substantial information, any notions a consumer may have about "marginality" or "virility" or "indecency" are effectively directed toward the fetishized attributes (the scowl, the staff, etc.) of an invented public persona; in the process, the usual anxieties about the underclasses are comfortably focused—with an enticing hint of danger—on the packaged Bruant rather than some unruly collective.

Le Père Peinard, of course, was also a manufactured system of representation, and the *vieux gniaff* no less a contrivance than the fabrications peddled at Bruant's cabaret. The fundamental difference was Pouget's encouragement of class transgression from below rather than consumption from above—a difference that, in practice, would have entailed the mobilization of an unruly collective in ways that involved much more than just a hint of danger. Yet as the similarity of their respective strategies suggests, both Pouget and Bruant operated in a discursive realm in which provocation was habitually exercised for purposes of persuasion. And it suggests too that the promotion of a revolutionary "fête populaire" could be closely related in the eighties and nineties to the routine marketing of popular diversions, closely enough that the distinctions between an enlightened, self-conscious working-class identity and its commercial equivalent could be difficult to recognize.

4. Le moyen: C'est un brin de chambardement.

Pouget's most pressing concern, then, was to devise a means of orchestrating radical thought formation amidst a proliferation of popular forms readily available to fin-de-siècle consumers for a modest sum, with no strings attached.[49] If the possibility for such changes in consciousness was enhanced by *Le Père Peinard*'s deft manipulation of irony and invective, textual solicitation nonetheless had to coexist with substantive forms of critique, so that radical consciousness might seem to the reader to emerge both logically and spontaneously from moments of cognitive destabilization. The *vieux gniaff* described just such an instance in the second issue of the journal (3 March 1889: 16):

> J'étais successivement pour Thiers, pour Barodet, pour Gambetta, pour Rochefort, pour Clémenceau, pour Joffrin, pour Vaillant.
>
> J'étais pour me foutre à la queue du cheval du Boulanger, quand j'ai réfléchi et je me suis dit:
>
> Et, merde, on se fout de toi mon vieux Peinard!
>
> T'as trimé toute la vie; t'as défendu ta patrie en 70; t'as fait tout ce que tu devais faire, et t'es toujours dans la mélasse.
>
> Tous les jean-foutres en qui tu au eu confiance t'ont foutu dedans— faut pas continuer à faire le daim! . . .
>
> Je me suis vu, braillant à pleine gueule, sans raison, après n'importe quoi!
>
> Puis, après des réflecs à perdre haleine, j'ai repris mes sens, . . . et j'ai conclu: "Faut faire ton bonheur toi-même!"
>
> Le moyen, c'est un brin de chambardement qui vienne mettre les choses en l'état où elles devraient être.

> [One after the other, I was for Thiers, for Barodet, for Gambetta, for Rochefort, for Clémenceau, for Joffrin, for Vaillant.
>
> I was even ready to jump on Boulanger's bandwagon when I stopped to think it over and said to myself:
>
> "What the hell! They don't give a shit about you, old Peinard.
>
> You've busted your hump all your life; you fought for your country in 1870. You've done everything you're supposed to and you're still up to your neck in muck
>
> It's all those fucking good-for-nothings you believed in who put you there—you gotta stop playing the fool! . . .
>
> I caught myself screaming at the top of my lungs like a lunatic howling at the moon!
>
> Then, after some serious soul-searching, I regained my senses, . . . and I realized: "If you wanna be happy, you gotta rely on yourself!"
>
> A little dose of insurrection: that's all it'll take to make things the way they ought to be.]

Pouget's remedy for states of agitation extreme enough to leave one "braillant à pleine gueule" was reflection. And it was for the sake of reflection that, along with the weekly quotient of inflammatory provocation, the pages of *Le Père Peinard* were filled with articles that provided readers with a system of thought to be drawn upon at precisely those moments when (inflammatory provocation having done its work) the smooth operation of dominant ideological formations was most vulnerable to disruption. While the journal's partisans undoubtedly enjoyed a good laugh at the expense of their oppressors, they also stood to learn a great deal about anarchism's critique of liberal capitalism, about working-class history, about possible courses of action (given a state of affairs in which "Faut faire ton bonheur toi-même")—and, in a more general sense, about utopian dreams that surely went unmentioned as the audience at Bruant's cabaret "braillaient au refrain" of a song they already knew by heart. An anarchist education once in hand, Pouget's readers would presumably conclude—like the *vieux gniaff* before them—that "un brin de chambardement" was the ultimate social panacea.

That conclusion, of course, involved a leap in faith that was unlikely to be inspired by conscientious explications of "ideology" or "false consciousness," even though the journal's principal raison d'être—revolution notwithstanding—was ideological contestation. *Le Père Peinard*'s educational program accordingly relied less on conceptual analysis per se than it did on an incessant vilification of those institutions and individuals responsible for the administration of power—as well as on Pouget's ingenious knack for identifying, in its most objectionable forms, the full range of their transgressions. In one remarkable instance, a critique of authority was mounted in a brief article (12 January 1890: 9) about regulations limiting the access of workers to factory toilets in a steel mill in Saint-Chamond. According to the *vieux gniaff*'s on-the-scene source:

> Quand on a envie d'écrire au pape, il faut pour entrer aux chiottes, passer devant un pipelet et prendre un jeton. Les gardes-chiourmes constatent le temps qu'il vous faut pour vider vos tripes.
>
> Si par malheur vous vous trouvez obligés d'aller deux fois dans la même journée faire la même commission, voilà le cerbère qui vous apostrophe:
> "—Si vous êtes malades, allez voir le médecin."

> [Whenever you wanna to write the Pope, you have to get a token from an attendant to get into the shitter. The prison guards check on how much time it takes you to empty your bowels.
>
> If you're unlucky enough to have to go twice in the same day on the same errand, the watchdog's right there to bark at you:
> "—If you're sick, go see a doctor."]

Given his subject, Pouget could hardly have resisted the ironic headline, "La liberté de chier," nor the occasion to provide his readers with a case study of the ways in which authority regulates the body. Nor, for that matter, could the *vieux gniaff* have resisted the opportunity to offer helpful advice to the steel mill's administrators: "Eh bandits! Foutez leur un bouchon au derrière à vos ouvriers; de cette façon, vous pourrez les régler à votre fantaisie" [You crooks! Why don't you stick corks up the butts of your workers? That way, you can really keep them in line]. These are harsh words, particularly since they address in concrete terms a state of totalizing subservience in which even the most personal of bodily functions are surveyed and controlled. Yet they are funny too, assuming that the reader would have laughed at the narrator's outrageous proposal, at the absurd coincidence of a conceptual ideal ("la liberté") with a defacatory obscenity ("chier")—at the ironic twist, that is, with which the text turns a lamentable state of affairs into a jocular assault on the sheer efficiency of exploitative labor practices. The transmission of meaning here depends on the reader's participation in that maneuver and, as we have seen, on the momentary release of the unconscious generated by the successful solicitation of laughter. So it is predictable that the *vieux gniaff*, in order for his readers to experience the disruption of ideological determinants in textual proximity to revolutionary directives, would conclude his (ironic) counseling of factory administrators with a (literal) threat: "Un jour viendra où ils [vos ouvriers] vous boucheront autre chose" [A day will come when your workers will use more than corks on you].[50] Pouget's critique of power was almost always linked to a revolutionary solution. Its potential for communicative effectiveness, however, was also a function of its capacity to direct critical conceptualization to the everyday experience of domination—and to establish seemingly instinctual connections between conscious analysis and spontaneous response.

So it was even in those instances when *Le Père Peinard* indulged in critique of a more conventional variety. When, for example, Pouget provided his readers with a brief essay on property (6 April 1890: 8–10), he made do with a bare minimum of social and economic theory:

> On vient sur la terre, nus commes les asticots du fromage. . . .
> Dès que nos quinquets s'ouvrent à la lumière du soleil et des camou-
> fles, nous avons un tas de sales exemples qui nous introdufibilisent des
> mauvaises pensées dans la caboche encore vide.
> Autour de nous y a les prêtres, les maîtres d'écoles, y a toute la séquelle
> des administrations et du gouvernement qui nous rengaînent sur tous les

tons le respect de la propriété des riches: c'est-à-dire le respect de ce que ces bandits-là ont volé au populo.

[We land on earth naked, like a snail without a shell. . . .

As soon as our eyes can distinguish sunlight from shadows, we're exposed to a bunch of bad examples that put corrupt ideas in our empty noggins.

All around us there are priests, school teachers, and all the agencies of governments and administrations that employ every possible means to maintain our respect for the property of the rich: respect, in other words, for the very thing those thieves have stolen from the people.]

The *vieux gniaff* says nothing here about the power of property to consume without producing, nor about its capacity to appropriate the results of labor (in the form of rent or interest) without in turn rendering an equivalent value; what little is left of Proudhon has been whittled down to the point that property is characterized, quite literally, as what the rich steal from the poor. Similarly literal, and—for a journal promoting the collapse of bourgeois society—similarly pertinent, is the pointing of fingers at those representatives of authority, from priests and school teachers to administrations and governments, under whose direction a critique of property was unlikely to be encouraged in the first place.[51] Having (again) challenged the presumably rational foundations of bourgeois rule, the *vieux gniaff* concludes by proposing (again in textual proximity to that challenge) that: "Sans le distinguo du tien et du mien, les frères vivraient en frangins, heureux d'être ensemble et ne pensant qu'à être utiles les uns aux autres" [If we got rid of the distinction between "yours" and "mine," brothers would live fraternally, happy to be together and thinking only about how they can help each other out]. If such utopian musings were transparently speculative, they could nonetheless serve both as idealistic visions of a better world and as conceptual alternatives to the underlying assumptions that lent power—in a less tolerable, yet more familiar world—the appearance of legitimacy.

This less tolerable world was at the heart of the *vieux gniaff*'s most thoroughgoing attempt to educate his readers—a project for which Pouget enlisted the assistance of a team of artists, Luce and Lucien Pissarro principal among them, to launch an appropriately pedagogical visual program for the journal.[52] With their help, he began to publish a series of illustrated lessons in anarchist thought adapted from the dossier of drawings that Lucien's father made for two of his nieces at the end of 1889. *Turpitudes sociales*, as Camille called his project, was designed as an exposé of capitalist exploitation, the drawings (and explanatory captions) serving to identify in their most typical forms the malevolent effects of economic and cultural domination; a wide range of all-too-familiar urban phenomena—a beggar at a fashionable restaurant, a late-night mugging, a pair of working-class drunks tossed from a wine shop—are treated as symptoms of a diseased society, and their unpleasant familiarity as evidence of the advanced stage of the malignancy rather than the particular failings of dysfunctional individuals.[53] Beginning in May 1890, a closely related version of the same image/text prototype (the explanatory captions now substantially longer and colloquially rephrased) began to appear regularly in *Le Père Peinard*. In keeping with Pissarro *père*'s model, it consisted largely of a visual typology of commonplace victims whose destitute circumstances could be traced, one way or another, to the characteristic inequities of bourgeois society: *L'Affamé*, a starving vagabond in need of sustenance but unable to find work; *La Misère en chapeau noir,* a low-level clerk who moonlights as a musician in a *musette* to make ends meet. Or *Fille-Mère* (fig. 3-6), a provincial servant girl who, the *vieux gniaff* explains (20 July 1890: 8–10), is left pregnant by her master's son, fired by his father, hounded by shame and disparagement—and whose destiny is inexorably linked to the brothel, the street corner, the orphanage, and the hospital. The villainous treatment she receives on her way to disaster—at the hands of her seducer (authority once removed) and her master (authority personified), or owing to social taboo (authority's ideological offspring)— establishes a behavioral pattern of domination from which others like her will suffer "jusqu'au jour où foutu à cran par toutes ces horreurs le populo se rebiffera carrément" [until the day when the people, having had their fill of such horrors, strike back in no uncertain terms].[54] If *Le Père Peinard*'s revolutionary corrective was predictable, then so too were the chronic abuses Pouget rehearsed in case studies week after week. The point, of course, was to underscore the frequency with which abuse occurred, and to ensure that everyday casualties were not to be characterized as aberrations from an otherwise healthy state of affairs—despite the Republic's apparently high-minded investment in public assistance and solidarism. The sheer ubiquity of quotidian misfortune, in other words, was made to serve an alternative form of ideological transmission that depended (like the dominant forms it opposed) on the power of ordinary assumptions about ordinary events to determine seemingly intuitive assessments of lived experience.

What was ordinary for sympathetic readers of *Le Père Peinard* was the assumption that where capitalism was concerned, exploitation was a given. So it was also a given that the two peasant children whose fates are the subject of *Le Sort des petiots* (fig. 3-7) were doomed to tragic lives—the daughter as a domestic-turned-prostitute for whom disease and suicide are a mat-

FILLE-MÈRE

FIGURE 3-6: Lucien Pissaro, "Fille-Mère," *Le Père Peinard* (20 July 1890).
Photo: A.C.R.P.P., Paris.

LE SORT DES PETIOTS

FIGURE 3-7: Anonymous (signed "DAB"), "Le Sort des petiots," *Le Père Peinard* (22 June 1890). Photo: A.C.R.P.P., Paris.

ter of course, and the son as a conscript destined to catch a bullet in yet another of the military skirmishes periodically initiated by his superiors.[55] If the *vieux gniaff*'s prophecies were mawkish and overdetermined, they nonetheless conformed to a simple paradigm of demonstrable causality and cyclical inevitability. "Les mères faites des gosses, . . . " he concludes tersely (22 June 1890: 8–10): "Les riches en feront des soldats ou des putains" [Mothers, go ahead and have your kids . . . The rich will turn them into soldiers or whores]. The remedy was also simple, and it involved the pragmatic business of insurrection; a drawing wishfully entitled *Ça arrivera! Nom de Dieu!* (fig. 3-8) makes perfectly clear the kind of work required to interrupt the cycle of exploitation once and for all.[56] Revolution, for the *vieux gniaff*, was as straightforward as the labor performed by a miner for the benefit of his oppressor; routine common sense, he seemed to imply, was all it would take for his readers to conclude along with him that the same miner might put his pick to better use as a weapon.

Common sense dictated too that *Le Père Peinard*'s illustrators would stick closely by the *vieux gniaff*'s narratives, or closely enough at least that their images would serve to complement Pouget's texts regardless of any liberties taken in terms of formal handling. The liberties taken were considerable: the

ÇA ARRIVERA! NOM DE DIEU!

FIGURE 3-8: Anonymous (signed "Pol Cizoc"), "Ça arrivera! Nom de Dieu!" *Le Père Peinard* (26 October 1890). Photo: A.C.R.P.P., Paris.

Le Capital et la Charité

FIGURE 3-9: Lucien Pissarro, "Le Capital et la Charité," *Le Père Peinard* (8 March 1891). Photo: A.C.R.P.P., Paris.

crude, abbreviated lines employed (somewhat in the manner of William Morris) in *Fille-Mère* to produce an effect reminiscent of popular *imagerie;* or the combination of bold outlines and subtle tonalities which, for aficionados of the Parisian avant-garde, might have suggested connections between *Le Sort des petiots* and the similarly primitivizing work of the Pont-Aven group; or, finally, the sheer clumsiness of *Ça arrivera! Nom de Dieu!* which, in formal terms, laid claims to an artlessness that must have seemed downright proletarian. While the stylistic posturing of these images is arguably well suited for their respective subjects, it is unlikely that aesthetic issues were of particular importance to the journal's rough-and-tumble readers. Pouget was concerned enough about their ignorance of artistic matters to publish the occasional art review (in which Félix Fénéon posed as the *vieux gniaff*). But he was more concerned with the overall communicative effectiveness of *Le Père Peinard,* and he tended to keep a vigilant eye on the contributions of his illustrators—and to balk when he thought they strayed too far into avant-garde territory.[57]

The limits of that territory were formally defined when he complained about the symbolic program at work in the allegory, *Le Capital et la Charité* (fig. 3-9), Lucien submitted in the winter of 1891: "[Pouget] préfère le fait,"

Pissarro *fils* explained to his father, "car il prétend que la synthèse est faite pour les cerveaux déjà très développés et que le *P. Peinard* s'adresse juste-ment aux simples." [Pouget prefers facts, because he thinks that synthesis is for highly sophisticated minds and that the *P. Peinard* addresses simple folk instead].[58] Lucien was only half right, for while Pouget targeted an aesthet-ically unsophisticated audience, he was nonetheless concerned with "la synthèse"—one in which anarchist critique intersected, in the minds of his readers, with observable social inequities in order to produce revolutionary consciousness. The problem with *Le Capital et la Charité* was that the opera-tive terms of the allegory (the monster, the waif, the mask, the rising sun) were *too* allegorical—that is, too abstract to assist in the recognition of the characteristic forms that "capital" and "charity" assumed in the world of lived experience. The solution involved finding the middle ground between the conceptual and the concrete, or rather to *conceptualize the concrete*—as Luce did a few months later in a drawing called *Capital et Travail* (fig. 3-10): en-trapped in the "earthly" sphere of the composition, working people bear the burden of the surplus capital produced by their own labor, as well as the accumulated wealth and elevated social position of the idle rich; but in order to avoid a wholly symbolic program, Luce transformed the allegorical cap-italist into a portrait of Baron Rothschild, one of the Left's preferred whip-ping boys in the eighties and nineties, and an entirely suitable figure with which to remind his readers of the faces capital was likely to wear in the world outside the image.[59] "On appelle un chat, un chat—un député, un bouffe-galette—un patron, un voleur!"; in keeping with his linguistic pro-gram, Pouget's visual strategies were designed to encourage the literalization of conceptual critique (right down to physiognomy, in this case) and to help his readers negotiate the distance between critical abstractions and their concrete manifestations.

The success of such negotiations, of course, was the necessary precondi-tion for the implementation of Pouget's most urgent objective: the literaliza-tion of revolution itself. So in issue after issue, the *vieux gniaff*'s complete arsenal of narrative and visual techniques was focused on what Lucien called "le fait"—on the familiar abuses of authority as well as an unfolding history of anarchist deeds. The uprising at Décazeville in 1886; the massacre at Fourmies in 1891; Ravachol's *attentats* in 1892, and Vaillant's and Henry's in 1893–94: these were momentous events, and well suited to establish the topical foundation of a militant collective consciousness. But when it came to revolution itself, nothing stood to serve Pouget better than the Paris Commune.[60] The *dix-huit mars* and the *semaine sanglante* were constant points of reference for the *vieux gniaff*, and an endless source of material from

CAPITAL ET TRAVAIL

FIGURE 3-10: Maximilien Luce, "Capital et Travail," *Le Père Peinard* (16 August 1891). Photo: A.C.R.P.P., Paris.

which he fabricated emotionally charged reflections on both the factual (if ephemeral) existence, and the conceptual possibility, of a society purged of the iniquitous effects of bourgeois domination. By way of insisting on the facts, Pouget devoted an entire issue of *Le Père Peinard* (25 May 1890) to a selection of citations drawn from press accounts—foreign as well as

French—of the brutal repression of the Commune by the *versaillais* in the spring of 1871; the reports of random executions, of squadrons that took no prisoners, of officers who bragged of having thrown wounded insurgents in the Seine, were enough to provoke the ire of the *vieux gniaff* (and, presumably, his readers as well):

> Foutre non, la Sociale n'est pas morte! Elle est vivante, nom de dieu, plus vivante que jamais. Les tueurs de 71 avaient pourtant bien crû l'enterrer pour toujours,—là haut, dans un coin du Père Lachaise.
> Thiers, Gallifet et l'affreuse clique, se sont foutu le doigt dans l'oeil. Dans les champs fumés avec du sang, le blé pousse mieux: kif-kif pour les idées! Les mitraillades de 71 n'ont réussi qu'a foutre de la haine au coeur des pauvres bougres.[61]

> [Hell no, the social revolution's not dead. It's alive, goddammit, more alive than ever. The murderers of 1871 thought they'd buried it for good—up in a corner of Père Lachaise.
> Thiers, Gallifet, and their disgusting cohorts pulled the wool over their own eyes. Wheat grows better in blood-soaked fields: the same goes for ideas. The massacres of 1871 did nothing but plant hatred in the hearts of poor folks.]

As for retribution, *Le Père Peinard* proposed the resurrected figure of "La Sociale" who, in the lithograph (fig. 3-11) Luce made to go along with Pouget's text, leads the people out of their graves and back into the fray, passing along the way from darkness to light—both visually and allegorically.

The almost hallucinatory program of the image had been anticipated two months earlier when, in an article devoted to the *dix-huit mars*, the *vieux gniaff* had waxed poetic about the first hours of liberty (25 May 1890: 1):

> Il n'y en a pas épais de jours comme celui-là, nom de dieu, dans l'existence d'un homme!
> Quelle joie, quand je vis à Montmartre les troubades que Thiers avait envoyé pour chaparder les canons, lever la crosse en l'air et foutre leur képi à la pointe de leurs baïonnettes!
> Il me semble que le ciel changeait de couleur, devenait brillant, brillant! . . . et bienfaisant pour tous. Je nous voyais libres, tous égaux! Finis les emmerdements! Evaporée la misère, telle qu'un mauvais rêve!

> [There sure aren't enough days like that in a man's life, goddammit.
> What joy I felt, when up in Montmartre I saw the troops that Thiers had sent to rip off the canons signal mutiny by raising their rifle butts in the air, and impaling their caps on the points of their baïonnettes!

Elle n'est pas morte, foutre!!!

FIGURE 3-11: Maximilien Luce, "Elle n'est pas morte, Foutre!!!" *Le Père Peinard* (25 May 1890). Photo: A.C.R.P.P., Paris.

It seemed like the sky changed color and became brighter and brighter! . . . Our spirits soared. We were all free and equal! The bullshit was over! Misery evaporated like a bad dream!]

The *facts* of an historical event could thus serve as catalyst for the *figurative* sensation of revolution Pouget wanted to etch in the minds of his readers: the elation brought on by the sudden collapse of the state apparatus; the exhilaration generated by the spontaneous passage of utopian dreams into the realm of the possible; the euphoria that accompanied the sudden realization by Parisian proletarians of their new role as makers of history.[62] The *vieux gniaff* accordingly suspended all forms of satire (if not the provocative deployment of vulgarity) in favor of a passionately unpolished lyricism—"le ciel changeait de couleur, devenait brillant, brillant"—designed to elicit yet another form of readerly authorization. For if Pouget's readers knew to negotiate the distance between the narrative and textual functions of *Le Père Peinhard,* they might also have suspected that any representation of the "revolutionary moment" was necessarily figurative, precisely because it presumed to describe an emotional state that was literally unknowable before the fact. Pouget's revolutionary come-on, after all, was no less an invention than his assumed identity, and no less obvious as such to the knowing reader; but the same reader would perhaps have found the fiction of revolution compelling enough to follow the journal into the uncharted territory of insurrection, if only to get a glimpse of what lay just on the other side of the epiphanic shift in consciousness the *vieux gniaff* claimed to have experienced back in 1871.

5. On fait mieux: on agit.

Or perhaps not. In spite of Pouget's efforts to establish alternative forms of ideological transmission, the relative effect of *Le Père Peinard*'s communicative program on its readers remains indeterminable. Circulation was reportedly up to forty thousand by the end of 1893, but the incessant charges filed by the *cour d'assises* were always followed by the disclaimer, undoubtedly annoying to Pouget, that the journal's habitual violations were "non suivi d'effet."[63] While rumor had it that Ravachol himself had been an avid reader, there were also apologies made on *Le Père Peinard*'s behalf by a bourgeois press that saw its own liberties threatened as conservative legislators looked for ways to stamp out the anarchist menace.[64] One thing is sure; *le grand chambardement* never occurred, and it seems too as if the *vieux gniaff*'s vaunted commitment to insurrection ("nous comptons que sur la Force!," as

Faure had put it) accomplished little more than to exacerbate the climate of heated rhetoric and scattered terrorist activity that seized Paris from 1892 to 1894. It was the Republic, finally, that resorted to force—and Pouget who found himself holed up in London to wait out the repressions.[65] By the time the dragnet sanctioned under the *lois scélérates* had culminated in the much publicized *procés des trente*, French anarchism's sensational revolutionary program was yesterday's news and the *vieux gniaff*, a memory. It hardly mattered that all but three of the participants in the notorious *association de malfaiteurs* were acquitted; the state had managed to silence radical talk, while dispatching those whose offenses involved more than talk to prison, or to the guillotine.[66] That such strong measures were deemed necessary, of course, attests to the success of *Le Père Peinard*—at least as far as the judicial system was concerned. Its greatest liability, despite the ingeniousness of Pouget's rhetorical strategies and educational program, was its penchant to fight force with force—or rather, to propose spontaneous insurgency as the only viable response to force. The journal's unyielding stance against all forms of authority—bourgeois and proletarian alike—effectively precluded its endorsement of nonrevolutionary opposition, particularly of the parliamentary variety (Guesde's Marxist Parti ouvrier and Brousse's and Malon's Fédération des travailleurs français were the focus of especially venomous commentary).[67] In the absence of a workable middle ground between complicity and active resistance, even its most devoted partisans were likely to balk when the *vieux gniaff,* having won their support with irony, or invective, or tantalizing images of revolutionary euphoria, urged them to take to the streets. Oppositional thinking was one thing, self-annihilation quite another. And *Le Père Peinard* was hard pressed to supply its readers with a cure for the frustrations generated by the nagging irreconcilability of theory and practice—if, in fact, they had experienced such frustrations at all.

Pouget surely had, but as a veteran propagandist and a staunch advocate of the revolutionary solution, the standards of success to which he held his journal probably ran far afield of the thoughts and impressions that hundreds of thousands of readers had taken from its pages over the years. The *vieux gniaff*'s revolutionary fervor aside, *Le Père Peinard* was well suited to lend itself to nonrevolutionary, yet deeply felt oppositional reflexes: of rage, at the typical fate of yet another working-class casualty; of hilarity, as proper French was subjected to unimaginably inventive vulgarizations; of vindictive delight, when arrest warrants were put to use as *papier torcheculatif;* of retribution, as conscripts turned on their officers; of satisfaction, when heartless magistrates received well-deserved thrashings. The textual effect produced by the sympathetic reader's interaction with the narrative configuration of *Le Père Peinard* was already a form of oppositional entertainment, and entirely capable of producing the intellectual preconditions for a critique of dominant ideological formations. Yet it also ran the risk of encouraging cynicism and complacency, if only because of the sheer improbability—materially, socially, conceptually—of revolution itself. As the discursive nucleus of an alternative ideological formation, "revolution" was perhaps more easily identifiable as an enticing invention than those (*la patrie, la démocratie,* etc.) it presumed to contest. And it was no less conceptually linked to a myth-inscribed vocabulary (*le peuple, La Commune,* etc.) than the preferred rhetoric of church and state alike.

Pouget, however, was never to relinquish his faith in revolution, nor his conviction that revolutionary activism constituted the only tenable working-class challenge to the Republic's monopoly on power. Soon after his return to Paris in February 1895, he launched a weekly called *La Sociale,* the insurrectional tenor of which was as overt as its name implied; by the end of October 1896, he had suspended publication of the journal in order to make way for a new series of *Le Père Peinard,* with the *vieux gniaff* back at the narrative helm and revolution once again on the horizon. While his promotion of the *grand chambardement* would proceed unabated, Pouget's thinking had changed during his year in exile, not only because of his increasing involvement with revolutionary syndicalism, but also because he had begun to study British tactics of resistance—sabotage, boycotting, labeling—which, while falling short of revolution itself, had nonetheless proved effective in exerting control (with varying degrees of success) over the exploitative environment of the workplace. In the 26 July 1896 issue of *La Sociale,* he made his case for sabotage (the typical forms of which involved intentionally poor workmanship and the temporary disabling of machinery) as a pragmatic means by which laborers could force negotiations on an unwilling management. The article was reprinted in *Le Père Peinard* (19 September 1897: 2–3), and its basic tenet—"à mauvaise paye, mauvais travail" [bad work for bad pay]—officially adopted at the congress of the Confédération générale du travail in Toulouse a month later.[68] Beyond its importance in determining the direction of the nascent CGT, the conceptual basis of sabotage provided the ideal solution to the difficulties implicit in a propagandistic program that promoted a revolution it could never deliver. Readers of *Le Père Peinard* could now resort to a relatively risk-free course of action that promised immediate material gains. And Pouget could rest assured that, in practice, an act of sabotage represented the literal transfiguration of concepts into deeds, while helping the perpetrator to take the first steps toward a state of enlightenment in which (the boundaries of legality having already been transgressed) revolution might appear as a practical solution rather than a distant abstraction. Sabotage, in other words, was a hands-on educational tool, a radical lesson in "self-help," a rehearsal for participation in bigger and better things—things like *la grève générale* which, in a motion passed at the Congrès de Toulouse, had acquired official CGT status as a "synonyme de révolution."[69] Sabotage, strikes, revolution: here, at last, was a realizable pattern of resistance that had the distinct advantage of encouraging changes in working-class consciousness while simultaneously redirecting ideological contestation—through substantive action—to the material world itself.

L'Action directe: that, for Pouget and the CGT, was the logical solution to the theory/practice dilemma, as well as to the cynical resignation potentially elicited by a form of propaganda which, regardless of its revolutionary program, functioned primarily on a rhetorical level. *Le Père Peinard* ceased publication for good in 1900, when Pouget became editor in chief of the CGT's weekly newspaper, *La Voix du peuple,* and one of the organization's most active pamphleteers; the *vieux gniaff*'s penchant for irony and invective disappeared too, and along with it a circulation that had far exceeded the reach (six thousand copies per week in 1904) of the new journal. If *La Voix du peuple*'s readership was narrower, it was more committed, and with the leadership and the considerable manpower of the *syndicats* behind him, Pouget was free to speak as a professional propagandist without drawing on the assistance of a working-class narrative middleman. He was also free, in the somewhat highbrow pages of Hubert Lagardelle's *Le Mouvement socialiste,* openly to discuss the relationship between dedicated militants and his former target audience:

> La minorité n'est pas disposée à abdiquer ses revendications et ses aspirations devant l'inertie d'une masse que l'esprit de révolte n'a pas animée et vivifiée encore. Par conséquent, il y a pour la minorité consciente obligation d'agir, sans tenir compte de la masse réfractaire.[70]

> [The minority is unwilling to give up its demands and its aspirations in the face of the inertia of the masses who have yet to become animated and invigorated by the spirit of revolution. Consequently, the conscious minority is obliged to act, without paying heed to the unthinking masses.]

Pouget, then, was apparently no longer in the business of manufacturing revolutionary consciousness; that transformation would result from the inspirational example set by an enlightened minority whose goal was active self-determination. And since *l'action directe* was by definition "une manifestation spontanée ou réfléchie, mais sans intervention d'agent extérieur, de la conscience et de la volonté ouvrière" [a demonstration of working-class consciousness and willpower that, whether spontaneous or reflective, is realized without outside intervention], ideological combat of the *Hébertiste* variety had presumably become irrelevant.[71] For a journalist who had published a weekly "intervention d'agent extérieur" for over a decade, it was probably difficult to put all one's eggs in a basket fashioned "de la conscience et de la volonté ouvrière"; but for an anarchist who had seen revolutionary rhetoric muffled by the repressions of 1894, it must have seemed logical to question the communicative efficacy of inflammatory propaganda—and to envision a form of oppositional transubstantiation in which ideological conflict was brought to bear directly on the material world. Pouget's pithy slogan for the CGT said it all: "Dans les syndicats, on philosophe peu. On fait mieux: on agit" [In the unions, we rarely philosophize. We do better than that: we act].[72]

The new formula, of course, was as rhetorically clever as the clever rhetorical mechanisms it displaced—and no less a function of an axiom designed to provide eager militants with theoretical legitimations for syndicalist interventions of a more material order. It helped, no doubt, to inspire the strikes waged, often with considerable success, during the formative years of the CGT.[73] But it could also inspire the imagination of a figure like Georges Sorel, whose propitious advocation of both the heroism of proletarian violence and the utility of revolutionary myth might have seemed, with the publication of *Réflexions sur la violence* in 1908, like an erudite synopsis of the weekly dispatches Pouget dutifully sent off from the trenches.[74] For obvious reasons, the rank and file of the CGT had no use for Sorel, nor for his Bergsonian vision of an autonomous and indivisible socialist unity generated by faith in the potential power of the general strike. Nor apparently did Pouget, for whom the very notion of the general strike *as myth* probably represented a negation of years of grind-it-out propaganda in which revolution figured *as imminent*.[75] The difference was more than a matter of conceptual niggling, for despite his prowess as a manipulator of symbolic language, Pouget was driven by a sincere conviction that revolution constituted the sole means by which the working class might free itself of economic enslavement. If, over the years, his rhetorical strategies had been reconfigured to operate primarily on a level of material relations, there was no denying that in Pouget's universe substantive social change had always been contingent upon a thoroughgoing transformation of those same material relations—heady ruminations about the heroism of proletarian violence and the utility of revolutionary myth notwithstanding.

Conclusion. Quand ej'pète, ej'dis: j'ai pété.

Not that Sorel was wrong. In fact, his assessment of the unique integration in syndicalist thought of ideological and economic contestation—and of the decisive role played by militant activists in establishing its working parameters—could hardly have been more accurate.[76] Pouget, however, was less interested in assessments than he was in action. Hence his pointed reminder to readers of *Le Mouvement socialiste:* "il est logique qu'on 'prépare' la grève générale et très prétentieux de prétendre l' 'organiser' " [it is logical that we make "preparations" for the general strike, and very pretentious to think that we can simply "organize" it].[77] *Le Père Peinard* was all about such preparations, and the *vieux gniaff*'s cantankerousness thoroughly informed by the workaday business of maintaining productive relations with a "masse réfractaire" that was unlikely to greet flat-footed overtures to working-class unity with any more enthusiasm than they reserved for the most predictable of unkept official promises.

Their profound indifference to the efforts of would-be liberators was Pouget's albatross, and Bruant's bread and butter. And it was Bruant, needless to say, who found the words with which to cloak indifference in a blanket of sorry hilarity, and the narrative voice with which to make of destitution the stuff of comedy. The voice belongs to a drunken *clochard* whose ruminations are the subject of a monologue called "Philosophe," and whose system of thought is entirely foreign to Sorel's remote idealizations of noble proletarian sentiments—foreign, that is, to the extent that Bruant's narrative focuses on the act of farting, and on farting as an ennobling act of civil disobedience:

> D'abord ej'comprends pas qu'on s'gène,
> Ej'suis ami d'la liberté,
> J'fais pas ma Sophi', mon Ugène,
> Quand ej'pète, ej'dis: j'ai pété.
> Et pis nous somm' en République,
> On n'est pus su' l'pavé du roi;
> Va, va, mon vieux, va, pouss'ta chique,
> T'es dans la ru', va, t'es chez toi.[78]

> [First of all, I don't understand what all the fuss is about,
> I'm all for liberty,
> And I'm not about to put on lofty airs,
> So when I fart, I say: I farted.

Now that we have a Republic,
We're no longer in the King's streets;
Go ahead, old friend, go ahead and squeeze your cheeks.
You're in the street, go ahead, you're at home.]

Here, then, is another form of *action directe,* another order of oppositional transubstantiation, and (assuming a relative degree accuracy in Bruant's simulations of proletarian consciousness) another model of class identity in the making. That it warrants comparison with the rhetorical timbre of *Le Père Peinard* is telling, not only because of the coincidence of off-color humor with political irreverence, but also because of the marked absence in the *philosophe*'s operative frame of reference of alternatives to a world in which wind-passing amounts to a form—be it comic or pathetic—of social self-expression. Similar forms of self-expression were well known to the *vieux gniaff,* and regularly deployed to recall similarly cynical states of mind; yet it was Pouget's singular talent to make of them the cognitive materials out of which revolutionary consciousness might little-by-little be wrought. If the task required a thorough understanding of the shifting terrain of proletarian discourse, it required persistence too—the persistence of a propagandist who conceived of his work as an ongoing practice, as a job-never-done, as a form of labor, in other words, that took as its product the transformation of the very circumstances that made labor a template of oppression. And it was his persistence, finally, that created a discursive situation in which Pouget, as *l'éminence grise* of the fledgling CGT, could lay the *vieux gniaff* to rest and propose an integration of ideological and material contestation with any hope of support from the *pauvres bougres* on whose behalf he had worked for years.

Notes

ABBREVIATIONS

A.N., Archives nationales, Paris.

A.P.P., Archives de la préfecture de police, Paris.

I.F.H.S., L'Institut français de l'histoire sociale, Paris.

Many thanks to Erika Naginski, Tim Clark, Armand and Marie-Jacques Hoog, Carrie Weber, and Leslie Dunton-Downer for their suggestions, and to Sarah Kennel for her timely assistance.

1. The so-called "lois scélérates" [villainous laws] were legislated within a few days of Auguste Vaillant's bombing of the Chambre des députés during the session of 9 December 1893. The first of the new laws was aimed at the anarchist press and

extended the reach of the laws of 29 July 1881 against the direct incitement of subversive activity to include published apologies for such activities. The second prohibited any association of individuals maintained for subversive purposes, thereby defining as illegal the participation in an "association de malfaiteurs" [conspiracy of wrongdoers] for which all thirty defendants (nineteen "intellectuals" and eleven "thieves") were prosecuted during the *procès des trente* in September 1894. See Jean Maitron, *Le Mouvement anarchiste en France,* (Paris: Editions François Maspero, 1975), 1: 251–61. See also Henri de Varennes, *De Ravachol à Caserio* (Paris: Garnier frères, 1910), 78–79.

2. A.P.P., B a/152, report signed "Valère," 22 July 1882.

3. A.P.P., B a/75, "Organisation des forces socialistes révolutionaires à Paris," December 1887; B a/76, report signed "Jean," "Au sujet des anarchistes," 16 November 1889. *Le Ça Ira* ran for less than a year, before succumbing to fines levied against it for press law violations; ten issues appeared (irregularly) between 27 May 1888 and 13 January 1889.

4. On Pouget, see Emile Pouget, *Le Père Peinard,* Roger Langlais, ed. (Paris: Editions Galilée, 1976); Christian de Goustine, *Pouget: Les matins noir du syndicalisme* (Paris: Editions de la tête de feuilles, 1972); Edward Peter Fitzgerald, *Emile Pouget, the Anarchist Movement, and the Origins of Revolutionary Trade-Unionism in France* (Ph.D. diss., Yale University, 1973). Pouget also figures in Max Nettlau's magisterial *Geschichte der Anarchie,* 4 and 5 (Vaduz: Topas Verlag, 1981, 1984).

5. Needless to say, late nineteenth-century French vernacular is difficult to translate, since English equivalents tend to follow dissimilar patterns of linguistic mutilation—and since correspondences in colloquial vocabulary from one language to the other are especially imprecise. For "bon bougre" one might suggest "good old boy" (but without the "redneck" associations) or "regular guy" (but without implying conformity); the expletive "nom de dieu!" translates equally well to "goddammit!" "by God!" or "in the name of God!"; "foutre!" can translate to "shit!" "fuck!" "hell!" and so on. It is even more problematic to find English colloquial equivalents for expressions like "bondieuseries" [religious hocus-pocus], "politicailleries," [sleazy political machinations], and "marchands d'injustice" [magistrates]. In order that the general flavor of my translations not seem overly quaint or retrograde, I have employed contemporary (as opposed to late nineteenth-century) American equivalents for Pouget's phraseology; in the absence of appropriate late twentieth-century colloquialisms, I have resorted to proper—if somewhat awkward—English rather than distort the primary meaning of a given text. It should be noted that grammar, syntax, and orthography are irregular in *Le Père Peinard.*

6. Charles Malato, *De la Commune à l'anarchie* (Paris: V. Stock, 1894), 267. See also A. N., F[7] 12506; *Le Père Peinard*'s subscription list, seized by the police in 1894, reveals little about its readership, although the conspicuous absence of "intellectual" readers

(Huysmans, France, Mallarmé, Aljabert, and Lecomte, among others, subscribed to Grave's *La Révolte*) is itself noteworthy.

7. A.P.P., B/a 77, "Bulletin de quinzaine," 5 November 1891. The police estimated that circulation was soon to reach twenty thousand and that each copy was likely to be passed around to as many as five readers. For discussions of the anarchist press in general, see Maitron, *Le Mouvement anarchist,* 1: 111–50; Richard D. Sonn, *Anarchism and Cultural Politics in Fin-de-Siècle France* (Lincoln, Ne., and London: University of Nebraska Press, 1989), 16–28, 78–87, 97–101. See also René Bianco, *Un siècle de presse anarchiste d'expression française,* 7 vols., Doctorat d'Etat, Université de Provence, 1988.

8. For Pouget, the *grand chambardement,* a massive, spontaneous working-class assault on the existing social order, was distinct—at least prior to his participation in the CGT's *congrès* of 1897—from hotly debated socialist notions of the "general strike" (i.e. a large-scale, simultaneous shutdown of crucial industries). He did, however, allow for the latter's potential to lead to the former (12 January 1890: 11): "La Grève générale proclamée à un moment donné, il peut n'y avoir que 1000 ouvriers qui marchent. Seulement, ces 1000 ouvriers se disent: 'la Grève générale, c'est la cessation complète du travail, faut donc nous arranger comme si tous les copains étaient en grève . . .' Quand le populo verra les zigues d'attaque aller de l'avant, il se dira: 'ils ont raison les bougres! . . . faut les suivre.' Et de fil en aiguille, la Grève générale deviendra vraiment la Grève générale!"

9. *Le Révolté* was founded by Kropotkin in 1879 and published in Geneva until its offices moved to Paris in 1885. Its name changed to *La Révolte* in 1887 (in order to avoid payment of outstanding fines levied against it in accordance with the press laws of 29 July 1881). Grave edited the journal from 1883 until publication ceased during the repressions of 1894; in 1895 he resumed publication under the title *Les Temps nouveaux.* According to Malato ("La Presse," *L'Attaque,* 10–17 August 1890: 2), Grave's was one of only three anarchist journals in print around 1890 that warranted respect: "Parmi les journaux que le manque de fonds—içi, plus que jamais, pauvreté n'est pas vice—force de paraître plus rarement, j'en connais trois, pas plus, dont la rédaction n'est ni vendue ni à vendre: *La Révolte, Le Père Peinard,* et *L'Attaque.*"

10. For "jean-foutres" read "good-for-nothings," the wordplay consisting of the phonetic similarity of "jean" to "gens" [people] in combination with the obvious negative implications of the explicative "foutre!" For nineteenth-century assessments of Hébert's journal, see Charles Brunet, *Le Père Duchêne d'Hébert* (Paris: Librarie de France, 1859); G. Tridon, *Les Hébertistes: Plainte contre une colomnie de l'histoire* (Paris: G. Tridon, 1864). For a standard account, see Walter Gérard, *Hébert et le Père Dushesne* (Paris: J. B. Janin, 1946). Hébert's journal spawned a family tree that, between 1790 and 1934, would include as many as thirty journals and pamphlets of the same name, or that of a close relation like *La Mère Duchêne* (1791, 1797, 1848, 1869–70, 1871) or *Le*

Fils du Père Duchêne (1871). Eugene Vermesch's pro-Commune *Le Père Duchêne* (1871) saw its circulation skyrocket to fifty thousand after only three issues. On Vermesch's journal, see Maxime Vuillaume, *Mes cahiers rouges au temps de la Commune* (Paris: A. Michel, 1971), 145–59.

11. See Maurice Tournier, "*Le Père Peinard* et le burlesque populaire" and "Subversion des valeurs sociales et subversion des valeurs de langue. L'Exemple du *Père Peinard,*" *Des mots sur la grève: Propos d'étymologie sociale* (Paris: Klincksieck, 1992), 1: 237–52, 253–64.

12. See Jacques Rancière, "The Myth of the Artisan: Critical Reflections on a Category of Social History" in *Work in France,* David H. Lake and Cynthia J. Koepp, eds., (Ithaca, N.Y., and London: Cornell University Press, 1986), 317–35.

13. I.F.H.S., AS 14 158, "*Le Père Peinard, Le Temps nouveau*" (unpublished manuscript by the anarchist militant Paul Delasalle). According to Delasalle, *Le Père Peinard* was particularly well-received by joiners, cabinet-makers, and cobblers.

14. On *Le Père Peinard* and "oral culture," see Sonn, *Anarchism and Cultural Politics,* 115–40.

15. Consider this, from Victor Hugo's exhaustive study of argot in *Les Misérables* (Paris: Pagnerre, 1867), 7:382. "L'argot véritable . . . n'est autre chose . . . que la langue laide, inquiète, sournoise, traître, venimeuse, cruelle, louche, vile, profonde, fatale, de la misère. Il y a, à l'extrémité de tous les abaissements et de toutes les infortunes, une dernière misère qui se révolte et qui se décide à entrer en lutte contre l'ensemble des faits heureux et des droits régnants; lutte affreuse où, tantôt violente, à la fois malsaine et féroce, elle attaque l'ordre social à coups d'épingle par le vice et à coups de massue par le crime. Pour les besoins de cette lutte, la misère a inventé une langue de combat qui est l'argot." By "l'argot véritable," Hugo meant to distinguish the speak of the so-called *classes dangereuses* from the specialized parlances of countless *métiers;* by the end of the nineteenth century, however, such distinctions had become difficult to maintain (due in part to the general effects of urbanization), and a wide variety of argots (criminal as well as professional) had begun to coalesce into a larger linguistic phenomenon that Lazare Sainéan would call "le bas langage parisien." See Lazare Sainéan, *Le Langage parisien au XIXe siècle* (Paris: E. de Bocard, 1920), 482–83; see also Marcel Schwob and Georges Guieysse, "Etude sur l'argot français," *Mémoires de la société de linguistique de Paris* (Paris: Emile Bouillon, 1892), 7:33. On Pouget and argot, see Sonn, *Anarchism and Cultural Politics,* 95–114.

16. For a nuanced account of Pouget's linguistic strategies, see Tournier, *Des mots sur la grève,* 237–264; see also Sainéan, *Le Langage,* 56–7. For a study of the linguistic practices of organized workers in late nineteenth-century France, see Michelle Perrot, *Workers on Strike: France, 1871–1890,* Chris Turner, trans., (New Haven, Conn., and London: Yale University Press, 1987), 188–242.

17. Pouget's phraseology here, "chaque patelin, chaque société, chaque profession

a son argot spécial," is likely derived from Hugo's *Les Misérables,* 7:379: "[O]n peut nous dire que tous les métiers, toutes les professions, on pourrait presque dire que tous les accidents de la hiérchie sociale et toutes les formes de l'intelligence, ont leur argot."

18. For a "naive" reading of *Le Père Peinard,* see Félix Dubois, "Le Péril anarchiste," *Le Figaro* (19 January 1891): 3. Dubois rightly distinguishes Pouget's linguistic preferences from the more sober tone of Grave's *La Révolté;* but apparently taking the *vieux gniaff* at his word, he "naively" describes the editor of *Le Père Peinard* as a "former cobbler." Anarchist partisans, at least those who attended meetings where Pouget regularly spoke, would presumably have been under no such illusions. Nor, for that matter, would the lower-class Parisians who poured over the pages of *Le Père Duchêne* in the early 1790s (or in the Spring of 1871) have been likely to read the classic *Hébertiste* refrain—"Je suis le véritable Père Duchêne, foutre!"—in literal terms.

19. I.F.H.S., AS 158, "*Le Père Peinard, Les Temps nouveaux.*" Delasalle described the journal as one of: "le plus lu, le plus discuté, je crois bien le plus goûté dans les milieux ouvriers. J'ajoute, et cela n'est pas le symptomatique, que des centres ouvriers très actif jusque là sont devenu quasi indifférents une fois le PP a disparu [*sic*]."

20. The terminology ("narrative function," "textual function") is adapted from Ross Chambers, *Room for Maneuver: Reading the Oppositional in Narrative* (Chicago: University of Chicago Press, 1991), esp. 35–39. By "a subversion of normative sociolinguistic hierarchies," I mean to suggest: 1) that, by definition, the "sophisticated" reader of *Le Père Peinard* possesses an experiential knowledge of subjugation; 2) that he/she is capable of employing that knowledge as a means of assessing the claims (and the acquired *bas langage*) of Pouget's narrator; and 3) that any resulting concurrences (whether ironically or literally negotiated) between reader and narrator involve both the former's assessments of the journal's mode of address and the relative effectiveness of the latter's powers of seduction. So by "readerly authorization" I want, again following Chambers, to suggest that the successful transmission of meaning (i.e., the "textual function" of *Le Père Peinard*) involves both the reader (in the act of reading) and the narrator (whose ability to seduce hinges in any case on his relative understanding of his readers' predilections). *Room for Maneuver,* of course, focuses on the workings of "oppositional" narratives, a category of texts to which *Le Père Peinard,* as an openly revolutionary, or "resistant" journal, only partially corresponds (assuming we take "oppositional" and "resistant" here to conform to the famous distinctions between "tactics" and "strategies" rehearsed—as Chambers notes—in Michel de Certeau's *Arts de faire*). Chambers also notes that there exists "a very large gray area straddling the categories of resistance and opposition" (12); Pouget's journal, I think, is "gray"—and its simultaneous deployment of irony and literal revolutionary imperatives a model for the potential transmutation of ideological antagonism into material contestation.

21. On popular parlance and subversion, see Tournier, *Des mots sur la grève,* 238–39.

Tournier approaches Pouget's project (and the *Hébertiste* tradition in general) via Bakhtin; accordingly, the subversive engagement in the journal of "popular" vulgarities is taken to contribute, on linguistic and social levels alike, to what Tournier calls a " 'Révolution' burlesque."

22. I.F.H.S., AS 14 16, "Papiers d'Emile Pouget." This carton contains many of the legal documents pertaining to *Le Père Peinard*'s interminable difficulties with the *cour d'assises*.

23. No provisions were made in the press laws of 29 July 1881 to prohibit periodicals from assisting in the organization or promotion of *peaceful* demonstrations. For legislative transcripts, see J. Duvergier, *Collection complète des lois, décrets, ordonnances, règlements et avis du conseil d'état* (Paris: L. Larose et Forcel and Ch. Noblet, 1881), 290–325.

24. Duvergier, *Collection complète des lois,* 300–01. *Le Père Peinard* frequently ran afoul of Article 24 of the law of 29 July 1881: "Ceux qui . . . auront directement provoqué à commettre les crimes de meurtre, de pillage et d'incendie, ou l'un des crimes contre la sûreté de l'Etat . . . seront punis, dans le cas où cette provocation n'aurait pas été suivie d'effet, de trois mois à deux ans d'emprisonnement et de 100 fr. à 3,000 fr. d'amende."

25. Duvergier, *Collection complète des lois,* 301. The violation here has to do with Article 25: "Toute provocation . . . adressée à des militaires des armées de terre ou de mer, dans le but de les détourner de leurs devoirs militaires et de l'obéissance qu'ils doivent à leurs chefs dans tout ce qu'ils leur commandent pour l'exécution des lois et règlements militaires, sera punie d'un emprisonnement d'un à six mois et d'une amende de 16 fr. à 100 francs."

26. "Chouette Nouvelle!" *Le Père Peinard* (21 December 1890): 3.

27. Duvergier, *Collection complète des lois,* 292, 305–06. Article 42 was crucial to Pouget's legal strategies: "Seront passibles, comme auteurs principaux, des peines qui consituent la répression des crimes et délits commis par la voie de la presse, dans l'ordre ci-après, savoir: 1) les gérants ou éditeurs, quelles que soient leurs professions ou leurs dénominations; 2) à leur défaut, les auteurs . . . " (305–06). As Article 6 made perfectly clear, a *gérant* could be just about anybody: "Tout journal ou écrit périodique aura un gérant. Le gérant devra être Français, majeur, avoir la jouissance de ses droits civils, et n'être privé de ses droits civiques par aucune condamnation judiciaire" (292).

28. See *Le Père Peinard* (13 December 1892). By December 1892, Pouget had seen seven of his nine interim *gérants* receive maximum sentences; his statistics were cited, with considerable venom, directly from *Le Journal officiel*.

29. Pouget urged his readership to attend Faure's performances; upcoming trial dates and times (the location, of course, was "au palais d'injustice") were published as a matter of course. See, 'for example, "Aux camaros," *Le Père Peinard* (7 December 1890): 3.

30. "Aux palais d'injustice," *Le Père Peinard* (14 December 1890): 5. Pouget routinely published blow-by-blow accounts of Faure's courtroom presentations.

31. "Aux palais d'injustice," 6.

32. Edgar Jégut, "Le Père Peinard," *Journal de Saint-Denis,* 12 March 1891: 1.

33. See Mary Douglas, *Implicit Meanings: Essays in Anthropology* (London: Routledge and Kegan Paul, 1975): 90–114 and Sigmund Freud, *Jokes and Their Relation to the Unconscious,* James Stachey, trans. (New York: W. W. Norton, 1960). I am drawing here on Douglas's reading of Freud and jokes: "The joke is an image of the relaxation of conscious control in favor of the subconscious. . . . The joke merely affords opportunity for realizing that an accepted pattern has no necessity. Its excitement lies in the suggestion that any particular ordering of experience may be arbitrary and subjective" (96). Freud himself, in his discussion of "hostile" (as opposed to "innocent") jokes, remarked: "A joke will allow us to exploit something ridiculous in our enemy which we could not, on account of obstacles in our way, bring forward openly or consciously; once again, then, the joke *will evade restrictions and open sources of pleasure that have become inaccessible*" (103). One of the primary functions of *Le Père Peinard,* I think, was to engage "hostile" forms of joking (irony as well as rote invective) and the "sources of pleasure" they elicit (via the unconscious) in close textual proximity to a literal critique of bourgeois authority and, as often as not, to an open call for revolution; a substantive challenge to the smooth operation of dominant ideological formations (something akin, I want to suggest, to "the obstacles in our way") may be close at hand when the reader *consciously* understands the implications of the unconscious realization "that an accepted pattern has no necessity." Michel Pêcheux has observed that "the common feature of the two structures called respectively *ideology* and the *unconscious* is the fact that they conceal their own existence within their operation by producing a web of "*'subjective' evident truths*"; but he has also underscored the "yawning absence of a worked-out conceptual articulation of *ideology* and the *unconscious.*" See "The Mechanism of Ideological (Mis)recognition," in *Mapping Ideology,* Slavoj Žižek, ed. (London: Verso, 1994), 147. While such conceptual articulations have been undertaken— notably in Žižek's *The Sublime Object of Ideology* (London: Verso, 1989)—my objectives here are more modest and, I hope, clearly focused on the historically specific case of *Le Père Peinard.*

34. The effect on Pouget's readership of continuous textual assaults on the conceptual foundations of bourgeois rule (universal suffrage, nationalism, egalitarianism, justice for all, etc.) is virtually impossible to determine. One might speculate, however, that the sheer persistence with which such notions were challenged in *Le Père Peinard* may have contributed: 1) to a weakening of their claims to inevitability or "rightness"; 2) to a concomitant questioning of the institutions and interests they served; and 3) to a reader's willingness—and this, for Pouget, would have been the ideal scenario—to defy conceptual foundations and institutions alike. The cognitive chain reaction I am

describing here would have amounted to a systematic dismantling of what Laclau and Mouffe (expanding on Lacan and Derrida) have called the "nodal points" of discursive domination—that is, the privileged signifiers that serve to fix meaning in a discursive chain while interrupting the operation of potentially oppositional meanings (*différence*, in their preferred terminology). See Ernesto Laclau and Chantal Mouffe, *Hegemony and Socialist Strategy* (London: Verso, 1985).

35. The drawing, as well as the new rubric logos, were contributed by an illustrator who employed the pseudonym "Pol Cizoc." Camille Pissarro, for one, strongly disliked his work and complained to Lucien (13 January 1891) that: "Le *Père Peinard* paraît toujours, il a changé de format, il est bien plus grand, comme *l'Art des deux mondes*. Mais le premier numéro est tellement mauvais, tellement idiot que je n'ai pas cru devoir te l'envoyer. Je ne comprends pas Pouget qui a sous la main des artistes, se laisse forcer la main par cet amateur. Ce n'est pas son affaire à cet homme, il fait un grand tort à son journal." See Janine Bailly-Herzberg, ed., *Correspondance de Camille Pissarro* (Paris: Editions du Valhermeil, 1988), 3: 19. Pissarro's objections notwithstanding, Pol Cizoc's masthead is reminiscent of certain varieties of *imagerie populaire* widely disseminated in France during the eighteenth and nineteenth centuries. In terms of subject matter (an enormous cobbler enacting an inversion of normative social hierarchies) and formal handling alike, the drawing warrants comparison with an image like *Le Grand Saint-Lundi* (serially published beginning in 1834 by the Maison Pellerin in Epinal), in which a similarly gargantuan cobbler presides over a *Saint-Lundi* celebration. See Musée de Québec, *Images d'Epinal*, (Paris: Editions de la réunion des musées nationaux, 1995), 116–17. When, in October 1891, Luce made yet another new masthead for *Le Père Peinard*, he closely followed Pol Cizoc's thematic and compositional example; Luce's would prove to be the definitive version, running unchanged until the journal ceased publication in 1900.

36. On the development of the commercial press in Paris and its claims to "objectivity," see Richard Terdiman, *Discourse / Counter Discourse: The Theory and Practice of Symbolic Resistance in Nineteenth-Century France* (Ithaca, N.Y., and London: Cornell University Press, 1985): 117–46.

37. Pouget distributed posters (bearing the headline, "Le Père Peinard au populo") throughout the journal's eleven-year run—sometimes as a "supplement" folded into the journal itself. An edition of as many as 130,000 posters was distributed in August 1893, although typical publication figures range from 8,000 to 50,000 copies.

38. Dubois, "Le Péril anarchiste," 2.

39. On the various interests at stake in the production and consumption of "popular culture," see Stuart Hall, "Notes on Deconstructing 'The Popular,'" *People's History and Socialist Theory,* Raphael Samuel, ed. (London: Routledge and Kegan Paul, 1981), 229–39.

40. The literature devoted to fin-de-siècle Parisian entertainment, as well as to

individual performers, is enormous. For general accounts, see Anne de Bercy and Armand Ziwès, *A Montmartre . . . le soir: Cabarets et chansonniers d'hier* (Paris: B. Grasset, 1951); Charles Rearick, *Pleasures of the Belle Epoque: Entertainment and Festivity in Turn-of-the-Century France* (New Haven, Conn., and London: Yale University Press, 1985).

41. On Bruant, see Henri Marc, *Aristide Bruant: Le maître de la rue* (Paris: Editions France-Empire, 1989); Jerrold Seigel, *Bohemian Paris: Culture, Politics and the Boundaries of Bourgeois Life* (New York: Viking Penguin, 1986), 235–41; Sonn, *Anarchism and Cultural Politics*, esp. chapter 5. Bruant, whose status as marginal "sex symbol" was apparently well known, makes an appearance (as a fictional *chansonnier* called Legras) in Zola's *Paris* (Paris: Bibliothèque Charpentier, 1898), 281–82: "Et, quand [Legras] eut fini, ce fut du délire, les belles bourgeoises ne s'essuyaient même pas de tant d'affronts, elles applaudissaient frénétiquement, la salle trépignait, s'enrouait, se vautrait éperdue dans son ignominie."

42. Edmond de Goncourt, *Journal: Mémoires d'une vie littéraire, 1891–1896* (Paris: Robert Lafont, 1956), 4: 677.

43. In the absence of such distinguished readers, Pouget would settle for a less violent, but equally dismissive description of his journal: "Une sorte de feuille ordurière n'ayant droit à aucune prétention littéraire, rédigée en un style dont la bassesse n'a même pas la drôlerie pour excuse: c'est le *Père Peinard*." See Jégut, "Le Père Peinard," 1. Disparaging readers were equally subject to ridicule; hence a socialist defense of the journal's *bas langage*: "Les miniaturistes du beau style, les gourmets de bon ton, les laveurs de vaisselle aimant à se ganter, sans doute, sont décontenancés, la plupart, à la lecture de cette langue crue, de ces phrases plus que vertes, de ce salé vocabulaire." See "Jean qui passe," "Deuxième lettre aux exploités: *Le Père Peinard*," *La Voix du peuple de Marseille* (13 October 1891): 2. Since Freud assumes a close relationship between "hostile" and "lustful" joking (*Jokes and Their Relation to the Unconscious*, 101), it is worth noting that Pouget's narrative voice, while vulgar, masculinist, and highly scatological, was entirely devoid of what Freud took to be "smut." Sexual references are virtually nonexistent in the *vieux gniaff*'s parlance, with the exception of his penchant for terms like "putain" or "garce" to refer to the "infidelity" of the Republic.

44. Camille de Sainte-Croix's classic *montmartrois* refrain is typical in this regard: "A nous Gloire et Fortune! / Massacrons les bidards / Et faisons la Commune / Des Lettres et des Arts!" Cited in Michel Herbert, *La Chanson à Montmartre* (Paris: Editions de la table ronde, 1967), 134.

45. Aristide Bruant, *Fleurs de Montmartre* (Paris: J. Tallandier, 1929), 12.

46. Aristide Bruant, "Belleville-Ménilmontant," *Dans la rue: Chansons et monologues* (Paris: Flammarion, 1896), 1:87–90.

47. Frantz Jourdain, "L'Affiche moderne et Henri de Toulouse-Lautrec," *La Plume* (15 November 1893): 490.

48. Bruant's interest in colloquial parlance culminated in the publication of his *L'Argot au XXe siècle: Dictionnaire Français-Argot* (Paris: Aristide Bruant, 1901).

49. Pouget was well aware of the popular appeal of *chansonniers* like Bruant, and he regularly published songs—"La Ravachole" is one such example—that served to inject a powerful communicative tradition with anarchist medicine. The 6 August 1893 issue of *Le Père Peinard* featured Victor Barrucand's "Je suis contre le gouvernement," an anarchist parody of Bruant's more sanguine monologue, "Je suis de l'avis du gouvernement."

50. For further discussions on the subject of toilets, see "Impots sur les chiottes," *Le Père Peinard* (11 December 1892): 5.

51. For related anarchist reflections on the nature of property, see Alain Gouzien, "La Propriété," *Le Ça Ira* (19 September 1888): 3.

52. Over the years, Pouget's stable of illustrators would also include H.-G. Ibels, Adolphe Willette, Charles Maurin, Georges Pissarro, and many others. Given the journal's precarious legal circumstances, most of the illustrations are unsigned (or signed with pseudonyms); Luce, who contributed over one hundred (unsigned) drawings, was arrested and incarcerated at Mazas prison during the repressions of 1894.

53. Pissarro's *Turpitudes sociales* (Collection Skira, Geneva) is reproduced in facsimile as Camille Pissarro, *Turpitudes sociales* (Geneva: Editions d'art d'Albert Skira, 1972), with an introductory essay, "Pissaro et l'anarchie," by André Fermigier. On *Turpitudes sociales,* see Richard Thomson, "Camille Pissarro, *Turpitudes sociales,* and the Universal Exhibition of 1889," *Arts Magazine* 56, no. 4 (April 1982): 82–88; John G. Hutton, *Neo-Impressionism and the Search for Solid Ground: Art, Science, and Anarchism in Fin-de-Siècle France* (Baton Rouge and London: Louisiana State University Press, 1994), 181–91. For articles that similarly describe society's down-and-outers as victims of exploitation, see *L'Attaque* ("Il est saoûl," 18–25 January 1890: 3, and "Les Trimadeurs," 1–8 March 1890: 3).

54. As for prostitution itself, the *vieux gniaff* was quick to advise his readers that the "oiseaux de la nuit" were not to be further victimized by taboo of the proletarian variety (14 December 1890: 10):

> Chaque fois que je vois un type crachant une saloperie au visage de ces malheureuses, ça me fait quelque chose, nom de dieu.
>
> On les méprise,—pourquoi? C'est pas pour raison: c'est encore les jean-foutres de la haute qui en sont cause.
>
> Car enfin, quand on rumine un tantinet, on est obligé de s'avouer que le métier qu'elles font n'est pas plus dégueulasse que de turbiner au profit d'un singe.

As usual, les "jean-foutres de la haute" were to blame, just as they were for the exploitative economic circumstances under which prostitutes and wage laborers both worked. But the *vieux gniaff* challenges conventional morality here by arguing that the prostitute (who effectively separates the bourgeois from his money) helps to compensate for the ineptitude of the wage laborer (whose work generates bourgeois wealth in the first place). "Ne leurs foutons pas la pierre, nom de dieu!" he continues, "En turbinant nous faisons de l'inégalité, en faisant la noce elles font de l'égalité."

55. The illustration is apparently signed "DAB" (or perhaps "DBM"); I have been unable, in any case, to assign authorship. *Fille-Mère* and *Ça arrivera! Nom de dieu!* are signed respectively by Lucien Pissarro and Pol Cizoc.

56. See "Insurrection," *Turpitudes sociales,* no. 28.

57. Fénéon's articles appeared in the 9 April, 30 April, and 14 May 1893 issues of *Le Père Peinard.*

58. Anne Thorold, ed., *The Letters of Lucien to Camille Pissarro* (Cambridge: Cambridge University Press, 1993), 195.

59. Rothschild, according to the socialist bimonthly *L'Aurore sociale* (16–30 Avril 1889: 1), was the wealthiest man in France, commanding as much as one billion francs in capital from which he drew an annual income of fifty million francs. For an example of Pouget's ongoing interest in Rothschild, see *Le Père Peinard* (30 March 1890): 1–4.

60. Because of the constant threat of legal reprisal, *Le Père Peinard*'s commentary on Ravachol, Vaillant, and Henry was muted (and often involved direct citations— delivered with considerable irony—of the bourgeois press). Pouget's journal, of course, was not the only leftist periodical to eulogize the Commune. For a related examples, see *L'Aurore Sociale* (16–30 March 1889: 1) and *Le Chambard socialiste* (24 March 1894: 1, and 31 March 1894: 1).

61. "La grande mitraillade racontée par les bourgeois," *Le Père Peinard* (25 May 1890). Pouget is drawing here on remarks by a reporter for *L'Indépendance belge* (24 April 1871) who: "n'entend que des gens parlant de fusiller par ci, de déporter par là: de tel ou tel corps de l'armée qui ne font pas de prisonniers; je ne les nommerai pas, . . . pas plus que je ne voudrais nommer des officiers qui se vantaient hier, d'avoir fait jeter dans la Seine des insurgés blessés." Pouget's article was originally published in *Le Ça Ira* (27 May 1888: 2–3).

62. See Guy Debord, Attila Kotányi, and Raoul Vaneigem "Thesis on the Paris Commune" (1962) reprinted in *Situationist International Anthology,* Ken Knabb, trans. (Berkeley: Bureau of Public Safety, 1989), 314. On "spontaneity" and the "realm of the possible" see Henri Lefebvre, "La Commune: dernière fête populaire," in *Images de la Commune,* James Leith, ed. (Montreal: McGill-Queen's University Press, 1978), 33–45; Lefebvre's text, while considerably reworked and expanded, is closely related to his article of 1962, "La Signification de la Commune" in *Arguments,* nos. 27–28 (1962): 11–19, as well as to the original Situationist International essay.

63. See Théo Praxis, "La disparition du *Père Peinard,*" *Le Libre parole* (1 February 1894): 1. When, at the end of January 1894, Pouget was finally driven into exile by the enforcement of the *lois scélérates,* Praxis reported that: "le journal révolutionnaire,

soutenu par un tirage considérable de 40,000 exemplaires, continuait à paraître et le directeur présumé, Emile Pouget, se dérobait aux plus active recherches de la police."

64. "Mon ami," Ravachol is said to have told a police informant (*Le Petit Journal*, 31 March 1892), "vous devriez lire le *Père Peinard*, c'est le journal de ceux qui souffrent, de ceux que le capital exploite." *Le Figaro* (26 April 1892) told a different story: "Prenons Ravachol, par exemple, croyez-vous vraiment qu'il ait attendu la lecture du *Père Peinard*, on du *Révolté*, ou des autres papiers anarchistes, pour devenir l'enragé que nous voyons? . . . La loi, à en juger par les condamnations qui frappent de temps en temps les anarchistes militants, est suffisamment armée contre cette fâcheuse littérature; il n'y a aucune raison d'aller plus loin et de sacrificier à une panique même légitime et justifiée la seule liberté qui nous ait été vraiment donnée par la République."

65. During his year in exile, Pouget (still under constant police surveillance) produced a London series of *Le Père Peinard*, as well as short manuscripts on "Impressionism" and "Positivism" (see I.F.H.S., 14 AS 16). He was also accused by fellow *compagnons* of having written five articles about French anarchists for the *Evening News* in December 1895 (see A.P.P., B/a 1509, "Une Infamie"). *L'Almanach du Père Peinard* (1894) was apparently produced prior to Pouget's exile; upon his return, it appeared annually between 1896 and 1899.

66. Despite the fanfare, the only convictions obtained during the *procès des trente* were for burglaries committed by three working-class anarchist thieves. The terrorists Ravachol, Vaillant, and Henry, whose *attentats* had to some extent provoked the legislation of the *lois scélérates*, had already been executed at La Roquette. See Maitron, *Le Mouvement anarchiste*, 1: 251–61. For transcripts of the trial itself, see *La Gazette des tribunaux* (7–13 August 1894).

67. From a Marxist perspective, of course, anarchism was roundly critiqued (as early as 1872, with the publication of Marx's and Engel's *Fictitious Splits in the International*) for both its petit bourgeois individualism and its abstentionism.

68. Pouget's increased involvement after 1895 with Fernand Pelloutier, Victor Griffuelhes, and other leaders of the CGT is similarly emblematic of his developing interest in pragmatic tactics of resistance. For a general account, see F. F. Ridley, *Revolutionary Syndicalism in France* (Cambridge: Cambridge University Press, 1970), 256–61. See also Jeremy Jennings, *Syndicalism in France: A Study of Ideas* (London: Macmillan in association with St Antony's College, Oxford, 1990), 11–55.

69. Emile Pouget, "Confédération générale du travail," in *La Grève générale et le socialisme: Enquête internationale* (Paris: *Le Mouvement socialiste,* 1904), 177.

70. Emile Pouget, *La Confédération générale du travail* (Paris: Marcel Rivière, 1908), 34–35.

71. Pouget, *La Confédération,* 36.

72. Emile Pouget, "Les Débats et les résolutions du congrès syndical de Bourges,"

Le Mouvement socialist, no. 142 (1 November 1904): 42. As Pouget's slogan suggests, the CGT took the enactment of opposition in the work place (sabotage, strikes, etc.) to be a matter of revolutionary consciousness rather than a habitually practiced (and therefore less self-consciously revolutionary) method of "making do" with an objectionable set of circumstances. It is here, of course, that we might imagine a "gray area" between what Michel de Certeau describes as "strategies" and "tactics" (see above, note 20); *Le Père Peinard* was already a form of journalism in which "opposition" and "resistance" (taking textual form, respectively, as irony and literal revolutionary imperatives) coexisted; it was the goal of Pouget and the CGT, I think, to propose a coalescence of the two in which oppositional tactics might—in practice—be refigured as self-conscious acts of resistance.

73. Judging by the CGT's own statistics (see Pouget, *La Confédération,* 51–52), strikes were waged in France with increasing success between 1890 and 1905: "Grèves terminées favorablement: De 1890 à 1900, 56%; de 1901 à 1904, 62%; en 1905, 65.67%." For assessments of the influence of anarcho-syndicalism on the nascent CGT, see Patrick de Laubier, *La Grève générale en 1905* (Paris: Editions Anthropos, 1979), 85–119; Maitron, *Le Mouvement anarchiste,* 1: 440–81.

74. See Georges Sorel, *Réflexions sur la violence* (Paris: Marcel Rivière, 1946). According to Sorel, "La violence prolétarienne, exercée comme une manifestation pure et simple de lutte de classe, apparait ainsi comme une chose très belle et très héroïque" (130). On the utility of the "myth" of the general strike, Sorel famously concludes that: "Il faut juger les mythes comme des moyens d'agir sur le présent: toute discussion sur la manière de les appliquer matériellement sur le cours de l'histoire est dépourvue de sens. *C'est l'ensemble du mythe qui importe seul;* ses parties n'offrent d'intérêt que par le relief qu'ils donnent à l'idée contenue dans la construction" (180).

75. Imminent to the extent that in 1909 Pouget, along with Emile Pataud, published a fictionalized primer on the mechanics of revolution, *Comment nous ferons la révolution* (Paris: J. Tallandier, 1909); see Jeremy Jennings, "Syndicalism and the French Revolution," *Journal of Contemporary History,* vol. 26, no. 1 (January 1991): 77–78.

76. Sorel's assessment of the role played by militant propagandists in the workers' movement is both condescending and laudatory (*Réflexions,* 181): "Ces hommes peuvent se tromper sur une infinité de questions de politique, d'économie ou de morale; mais leur témoinage est décisif, souverain et irréformable quand il s'agit de savoir quelles sont les représentations qui agissent sur eux et sur leurs camarades de la manière la plus efficace."

77. Pouget, *La Grève générale,* 276.

78. Aristide Bruant, "Philosophe," *Dans la rue,* 1: 13.

Readers and Consumers

4 Utopia Commodified

Utilitarianism, Aestheticism, and the *presse à bon marché*

1848: Critical wisdom views this year as a watershed of cultural history, particularly in France, the moment of an irremediable rupture between the intellectual avant-garde and the triumphant bourgeoisie.[1] Surely the contagion of revolution across Europe in that year, the publication of Marx and Engels's *Communist Manifesto,* and a significant retreat (or, in the case of Victor Hugo, exile) from active political *engagement* among artists, writers, and intellectuals, from Baudelaire to Delacroix soon thereafter, have all contributed to this perception of 1848. It is a commonplace that, as we look back to the middle years of the nineteenth century, the most blessed of writers and embraced of artists are the *poètes maudits* and *peintres refusés.* Indeed, with Sainte-Beuve's and Baudelaire's reviews of Flaubert's *Madame Bovary* (1857), the innovations of Manet and the impressionists, and especially the advent of the formalisms and attendant critical discourses of high modernism and postmodernism,[2] Western literary and cultural critics, still in thrall to romanticism's cult of originality, have privileged the aesthetic over the utilitarian.[3] One might even maintain that much of recent materialist literary and cultural history is a very *personal* attempt to rescue and co-opt the now canonical, intentionally (but not necessarily successfully) ahistorical, solipsistic, or decadent qualities of an aesthetic tradition that privileges form over content and that consciously, at times vociferously, eschews the very social critique that its inscription in the larger social text of the nineteenth century would seem to demand.[4] The social question in 1848—the division of labor and the distribution of wealth and property—is driven underground or into exile (or, in the case of the Hugo of *Les Misérables,* both), where irony becomes "the linguistic repository of difference. In itself, it represents something like a minimalist subversion, a zero-degree counter-discourse."[5] With 1848, according to this version of events, the utopian, progressive impulse within romanticism is abandoned once and for all for an obsessive aestheticism—Gautier and the Parnassians, Baudelaire, Flaubert, and later Huysmans—an aestheticism eventually salvaged from charges of political irrelevance by a largely Marxist critique that privileges irony as subversive counter-discourse, almost *faute de mieux*. My intention in the pages that follow is to demonstrate the considerably more complex relationships in the 1830s of both aestheticism and utilitarianism to the development of an inexpensive mass press. I will contend that *l'art pour l'art,* despite—or indeed, as we shall see, because of—its uselessness, models itself on the utopian, if not utilitarian, ideal of productivity. As a superfluous commodity produced for consumption, the literary text invites comparison to the useless, mass-produced products of industry and culture that were circulating with increasing ubiquity in the July Monarchy, and of which the newspaper stands as both the emblem and conduit. For, in the daily paper were (con)fused the ostensibly conflicting discourses of utopian socialism, capitalism, utilitarianism, and aestheticism.

Flaubert's aversion to journalism is well known (although his earliest surviving literary attempt was a schoolboy newspaper of his own creation—with the utopian title *Art et progrès*); as for Baudelaire, he writes, "Je ne comprends pas qu'une main pure puisse toucher un journal sans une convulsion de dégoût" [I cannot fathom how an unsoiled hand could touch a newspaper without recoiling in disgust].[6] (All translations from the French are my own unless otherwise indicated.) But perhaps the most famous of all antijournalistic diatribes is Théophile Gautier's satirical preface to *Mademoiselle de Maupin* (1835), which spares no one. Despite their clear contempt for the periodical press, however, Baudelaire, Flaubert, and especially Gautier all depended on journalism at one time or another for income. Like Balzac before and Zola after them, they were thus *collaborateurs,* in both senses of the word, with the dominant public discourse shaped by the mass press. Of course the very notion of a monolithic, dominant bourgeois discourse finding expression through the mass press begs the question: to what extent can we speak in black-and-white terms of discursive hegemony, when in fact the press permitted, even throve upon the clash of opinion generated by a vast array of partisan publications of every conceivable political shade? Emile de Girardin, usually considered one of the three or four "creators of the modern press,"[7] would be the first to conceive of a *colorless* information-based daily, which simultaneously and paradoxically seeks to make itself invisible *and* foreground its own materiality *as commodity*. His conscious reordering of the press's priorities marks a fundamental shift that in turn allows us to examine the actual formation of the dominant discourse we still know today as the mass press.

What, then, can be the relation between the ephemeral, disposable newspaper and the creation of enduring works of literature? While the extent of writers' journalistic activity, from Flaubert's slight involvement with serialized publication to Gautier's twenty-year relationship with Girardin's *La Presse,* is well known, it is seldom discussed beyond the realms of biography or bibliography. It could be that too close an association with the press contaminates the aesthetic (and, by extension, ironic counter-discursive) credentials of these writers, implicating them as it does in the production of the "littérature industrielle" denounced in Sainte-Beuve's article of the same title.[8] Indeed, the use of the press as a vehicle of naked ambition—at the expense of feeling, morality, or artistic integrity—becomes a recurrent topos in the nineteenth-century novel itself, from Balzac's *Illusions perdues* (1839) to Maupassant's *Bel Ami* (1885). Perhaps the first, and certainly the most dramatic, example of designed obsolescence, the newspaper is so ephemeral that it depends for its very existence upon the "freshness" of today's news and its "staleness" tomorrow.

The belief in the eternal qualities of great art and literature is at least as old as Homer, of course, but it was to become a master trope of romanticism. In the face of the sweeping changes brought first in the wake of the Revolution, then by massive industrialization and urbanization, writers and artists doubtless clung to the originality of their works as anchors in an uncontrollable and largely incomprehensible storm. Gautier, that "poète impeccable" to whom Baudelaire would dedicate his *Fleurs du mal* (1857), provides the model for the aloof, apolitical aesthete who chooses to shut out the storm of current events and focus on the creation of objets d'art in the preface to *Emaux et Camées* (1852): "Sans prendre garde à l'ouragan / Qui fouettait mes vitres fermées, / Moi, j'ai fait *Emaux et Camées*" [Paying no heed to the storm lashing my closed windows, I fashioned *Emaux et Camées*].[9] Yet Gautier was hardly Proust in his cork-lined room, or even Flaubert hibernating at Croisset, for he was named editor of the "feuilleton littéraire" of *La Presse* in February 1848, and between 1836 and 1855 he contributed some 1,200 *feuilletons* to Girardin's paper.[10] This apparent contradiction, between the eternal qualities of art and the ephemera of journalism, tempts one to draw a clear distinction between Gautier the journalist and Gautier the poet. After all, first in his own "L'Art" (the concluding poem of *Emaux et Camées*) and later in the *Parnasse contemporain* he inspired, the *durability* of art is made palpable, it becomes sculpted metal or stone and is thus rescued from the disintegration to which the quotidian is subject:

Tout passe.—L'art robuste
Seul a l'éternité.
Le buste
Survit à la cité.

Et la médaille austère
Que trouve un laboureur
Sous terre
Révèle un empereur.

Les dieux eux-mêmes meurent,
Mois les vers souverains
Demeurent
Plus forts que les airains.

Sculpte, lime, cisèle;
Que ton rêve flottant
Se scelle
Dans le bloc résistant![11]

[Everything passes.—
Only robust art is eternal.
The bust outlives the city.

And the simple coin
Unearthed by a peasant
Reveals the image of an emperor.

Even the gods die,
But triumphant verse lives on,
Stronger than bronze.

Sculpt, file and chisel;
Let your insubstantial dream
Be sealed in enduring stone!]

Yet Gautier, like most of his contemporaries, published much of his work first in periodicals, and this multiple inscription of poetic texts—prose and verse alike—blurs the line between ostensibly separate discursive realms[12] and suggests the need for a refinement of any assertion that "[i]n the nineteenth century, much of 'literature' defines its condition of existence as counter-discursive."[13] I would argue that not only does most literature not define its condition as opposition, but also that many of the texts we view as subversive or counter-discursive also, and often *first,* collaborate with and legitimate the dominant discourse of journalism. If it is true that various competing cultural and ideological discursive strands under consideration here are nevertheless interwoven, some more tightly than others, then to untangle them—utopianism, consumer capitalism, aestheticism, and utilitarianism—would prove a particularly instructive exercise. To do so is to move from the end of the July Monarchy to its beginning.

1830: In Stendhal's *Le Rouge et le noir,* whose alternate title is "Chronique de 1830," the narrator steps out of the narrative frame and, in a scene whose metafictionality is reminiscent of Diderot, confides that:

(Ici l'auteur eût voulu placer une page de points. Cela aura mauvaise grâce, dit l'éditeur, et pour un écrit aussi frivole, manquer de grâce, c'est mourir.

—La politique, reprend l'auteur, est une pierre attachée au cou de la littérature, et qui, en moins de six mois, la submerge. La politique au milieu des intérêts d'imagination, c'est un coup de pistolet au milieu d'un concert. Ce bruit est déchirant sans être énergique. Il ne s'accorde avec le son d'aucun instrument. Cette politique va offenser mortellement une moitié des lecteurs, et ennuyer l'autre qui l'a trouvée bien autrement spéciale et énergique dans le journal du matin. . . .

—Si vos personnages ne parlent pas politique, reprend l'éditeur, ce ne sont plus des Français de 1830, et votre livre n'est plus un miroir, comme vous en avez la prétention.)[14]

[At this point the author would have preferred a page of ellipses. "That will be ungainly," said the editor, "and in a text this frivolous, if you lack grace you're dead."

"Politics," the author responded, "is a stone hung round the neck of literature, which will sink it in less than six months' time. Politics amid the interests of imagination is like a pistol shot in the middle of a concert. It's all sound and fury, and clashes with the sound of every instrument. These political questions will end up mortally offending half of the readers, and boring the other half—who nevertheless found them quite engaging in that morning's paper. . . . "

"If your characters don't talk politics," replied the editor, "then these are no longer Frenchmen of 1830, and your book is no longer the mirror you claim it to be."

The press is explicitly invoked as the appropriate vehicle for the ephemeral political details of the moment, which threaten to doom his work with oblivion.

Stendhal's ambivalent attitude toward social and political phenomena suggests an aesthetic that somehow simultaneously conveys the particularity of the real as it aspires to the universal and yet, like Gautier's chiseled verse, escapes the ravages of time. His editor prevails, however, and this is fitting enough, for the events of the "*trois glorieuses*" of 1830 came about as a direct result of the Restoration government's proscription of the press as "un instrument de désordre et de sédition" [instrument of disorder and sedition].[15] Indeed, in this year the novelist was also a contributor to Adolphe Thiers's *National,* the paper primarily responsible for setting off the chain of events that would lead to the installation of Louis-Philippe as Citizen King.[16] Moreover, it can be argued that the July Revolution created the two conditions most necessary for the development of the first truly mass medium, the inexpensive daily newspaper: a hitherto unknown degree of freedom of the press, and educational reform culminating in the Guizot Law of 1833, which guaranteed French males access to elementary education, ultimately raising literacy rates considerably. These combined with innovations in printing and marketing techniques to allow the capabilities of production and consumption that would in turn enable the introduction in 1836 of the first mass dailies.[17]

In the meantime, 1830 also witnessed the definitive triumph of romanticism in literature with the premiere of Victor Hugo's *Hernani* in February. Already in 1829 Hugo had argued for the autonomy of art, which meant not only independence from classical models, but from any connection whatsoever with contemporary social and political affairs. This is the passing heresy of the preface to *Les Orientales,* which even goes so far as to abandon a familiar cultural frame of reference:

> Si donc aujourd'hui quelqu'un lui demande à quoi bon ces *Orientales?* qui a pu lui inspirer de s'aller promener en Orient pendant tout un volume? que signifie *ce livre inutile de pure poésie,* jeté au milieu des préoccupations graves du public et au seuil d'une session? où en est l'opportunité? à quoi rime l'Orient? . . . Il répondra qu'il n'en sait rien, que c'est une idée qui lui a pris; et qui lui a pris d'une façon assez ridicule, l'été passé, en allant voir coucher le soleil.[18]

> [And if today the author is asked what the point is of these *Orientales?* Who or what could have inspired him to go traveling through the Orient for an entire volume? What's the meaning of *this useless book of pure poetry,*

tossed in the midst of the public's serious concerns and as a new session of parlement is about to begin? Is this timely or appropriate? What does the Orient have to do with anything? . . . He will answer that he hasn't the slightest idea, that it is an idea that simply came to him, and that came to him in a rather ridiculous way, last summer, as he was going to watch a sunset.]

This Hugo has not supplanted the committed author of *Le Dernier Jour d'un condamné,* which dates from the same year, but he has set the tone and outlined the program—or absence of one—of a characteristically modern, paradoxically militant aestheticism, if such an oxymoron may be permitted. The "useless book of pure poetry," momentary lapse that it is, nevertheless announces Gautier's 1834 preface to *Mademoiselle de Maupin* (novel published 1835–36), as well as Flaubert's dream of a "livre sur rien," an art of modernity whose signifying power is freed from the shackles of accepted aesthetic, social, religious, and political referents—in short, usefulness of any kind— and whose duty is to its aesthetic integrity alone. Yet the autonomous work of art has an internalized, specialized utility, which paradoxically mimes in its operations the specialization of labor under the increasingly industrialized society that was anathema to so many of aestheticism's proponents.

What, one might reasonably ask, does the aesthetic innovation suggested by these frequently cited literary passages—we might even call them "touchstones of modernity"—have to do with the price of newspapers? Everything, I would suggest, for the creation of a new *presse à bon marché* is intimately tied to the so-called social question as it was raised by various utopian socialists under the Restoration and July Monarchy. While aestheticism, most brashly represented by Gautier's *l'art pour l'art,* is by all appearances antithetical to both the social meliorism of the utopians and the pragmatic mercantilism of the daily press, its emphasis on the *production* of the superfluous at the expense of the useful will ultimately become a defining gesture of a modernity at once divorced from and inscribed in society. At its center is what Roland Barthes has called "une sorte de fétiche de la forme *travaillée,* située sans doute hors du pragmatisme de l'activité bourgeoise, et pourtant insérée dans un ordre de travaux familier, contrôlé par une société qui reconnaît en elle, non ses rêves, mais ses méthodes" [a kind of obsession with *well-crafted* form, most likely situated outside the pragmatism of bourgeois activity, and yet inscribed in a familiar pattern of work and controlled by a society that sees in that very form, perhaps not its dreams, but certainly its methods].[19]

Indeed a few pages later in *Le Degré zéro de l'écriture,* Barthes compares this new self-referential mode of writing to "une écriture de journaliste, si précisément le journalisme ne développait en général des formes optatives ou impératives (c'est-à-dire pathétiques)" [journalistic writing, if in fact journalism did not generally develop optative or imperative (which is to say pathetic) forms].[20] I would argue that it was just this imperative, pathetic, or subjective brand of journalism that Emile de Girardin sought to replace with a new objective, *dispassionate,* nonpartisan daily newspaper, *La Presse.*

The facts of the "revolution in the periodical press" are well known and often cited: Girardin and his erstwhile collaborator Armand Dutacq introduced, respectively, *La Presse* and *Le Siècle* in July of 1836 for an annual subscription of forty francs, half the amount then charged by the established papers. Profits were to come from advertising revenues rather than subscription, and as Terdiman points out, "the effect of commercializing information was to reduce the influence of *other* social and ideological determinants upon the formation of newspaper discourse . . . then, like money, it began to seem colorless."[21] This shift from political to commercial frames of reference and editorial goals, however, was no nebulous, impersonal sea change; it was the direct result of an intential effort by Girardin to transform the role of the newspaper in social, intellectual, and economic life.

Until 1836, daily newspapers were typically the organs of opposing political parties; each paper had its "color," which was in fact the word in use at the time. The metaphor is particularly apt, for it allows us to see the objectivity Girardin claimed for his paper, which was to be an undistorted, utilitarian instrument, a mirror of the world whose clarity would depend upon an *absence* of ideological shading. Positioning *La Presse* as a philanthropic enterprise whose sole aim was to disseminate information for the good of the public,[22] Girardin addressed his paper's colorlessness with pride in an editorial published 13 August 1836. Quoting *Le Journal du commerce,* in which it was written that "le journal *la Presse* n'est entré dans aucune classification" [the newspaper *la Presse* is impossible to classify], he responds: "Non, certes, nous n'avons aucune des couleurs qui forment l'arc-en-ciel de la politique actuelle, et Dieu nous en garde! . . . Ainsi, et ceci sera déclaré une fois pour toutes, nous sommes bien aises que les vieux journaux nous disent que nous sommes *sans couleur*" [No, certainly, we don't have a single one of the colors that make up the rainbow of contemporary politics, and heaven forbid! . . . And so—let us declare it once and for all—how delighted we are to have the newspapers of the old school call us *colorless*].[23]

And yet Girardin claims to belong to a party of sorts: "Ce parti, dont nous sommes, a entrepris d'organiser la nouvelle France que la révolution sociale de 1789 a créée, et d'agir pendant que les autres parlent" [Our party is the one that has undertaken the organization of the new France made possible by the social revolution of 1789, acting while others only talk].[24] The new, free France will be based on the full exploitation of its natural and human resources; if the editor's language is reminiscent of Saint Simon, Fourier, and their disciples, it is not by chance. It could be argued that Girardin, almost single-handedly, adopted and popularized the broadest of the utopian socialists' common concerns and, in the context of growing literacy and rapid industrialization, ultimately transformed them into a marketing tool.

After all, Girardin's credentials as a *vulgarisateur* were unrivaled; in 1828 he had cofounded *Le Voleur [The Thief]*, his first great success; it was one of those weekly digests described by the anonymous *Physiologie de la presse* (1841) as "des feuilles reproductrices qui ont une paire de ciseaux pour redacteur en chef" [digest rags whose editor in chief was a pair of scissors].[25] As early as 1831 Girardin seems to have grasped just which elements of utopian socialism could be adapted to the development of the mass press, particularly its desire to find unity of purpose and to create a new *organisation sociale* that would benefit the greatest number of people. He seizes the pragmatic and rejects the visionary or mystical; if we compare his 1831 statement of purpose in *Le Journal des connaissances utiles* to early socialist formulations, the similarities are striking: in *L'Organisateur* of 1819 Saint Simon writes that "la question de l'organisation sociale n'aura été ni assez promptement, ni assez complètement éclairée, car les hommes ne se battent jamais que faute de s'entendre" [the question of social organization cannot be too promptly or completely illuminated, for men only quarrel through a lack of mutual understanding].[26] In the "prospectus" for *Le Producteur* of 1825, we learn from his disciples that the journal "aura pour but le plus grand developpement possible de la production, prise dans son acceptation la plus étendue" [will have as its goal the greatest possible development of production in its broadest sense].[27] For *Le Producteur,* journalism is "ce nouveau moyen de rapports, créé par les sociétés modernes, [qui] n'a jamais été plus nécessaire qu'aujourd'hui, et jamais ceux qui se chargent de faire agir ce puissant ressort n'ont eu à remplir une mission plus belle et plus importante" [that new means of communication created by modern societies, [which] has never been more necessary than it is today, and never have those whose task it is to wield this powerful tool had a more noble mission to accomplish].[28] Before it has even come into existence, the mass press is assigned a social task—one for the masses—to be *useful* by spreading understanding, disseminating knowledge in its multiplicity of forms, and enabling and promoting production in every sense of the word.

Perhaps no one was better placed to take up this civilizing mission than Girardin, whose *Journal des connaissances utiles* [Journal of Useful Information] was in fact ostensibly published by a Société nationale pour l'emancipation intellectuelle that received considerable praise from various individuals and newspapers, all of which was duly reprinted in the *Journal* itself and recycled for the further edification of its readership: "La Société . . . publie un journal, dont le bas prix doit résoudre le problème de l'éducation morale, politique, agricole et industrielle du peuple des villes et des campagnes" [The Society . . . publishes a newspaper, whose low price should solve the problem of the moral, political, agricultural, and industrial education of the masses in both city and country].[29] Indeed, the Society would have its members join in the crusade, asking that "les dignes citoyens qui accepteront le titre de correspondan de n'épargner aucun effort pour réunir au moins cinq abonnemens" [the noble citizens who would accept the title of "correspondant" do their best to sell at least five subscriptions].[30] And if one's social conscience were not sufficient motivation, "UNE MEDAILLE EN ARGENT est décerné aux membres correspondans qui se chargent dans leur localité du placement de vingt-cinq abonnemens" [A SILVER MEDAL is to be awarded to those "correspondent members" who can obtain twenty-five subscriptions in their area].[31]

Thus, with the liberalization of the press ushered in by the July Revolution and educational reform underway, the *Journal des connaissances utiles* solemnly assigns itself the following goals:

> Concourir au maintien et à l'amélioration de l'ordre social, en enseignant simultanément à chaque classe: SES DROITS, SES DEVOIRS, SES INTERETS. Ranimer l'industrie nationale en donnant aux découvertes des arts et des sciences, aux inventions nouvelles, aux procédés économiques, enfin à tous les objects UTILES, une publicité si grande qu'elle les rendra USUELS.[32]

> [Take the lead in the maintenance and improvement of the social order, teach each class at once: ITS RIGHTS, ITS DUTIES, ITS INTERESTS. Reinvigorate national industry by giving new discoveries in the arts and sciences, new inventions, and new economic techniques—in short all USEFUL objects—a publicity so great that it will bring forth their prompt implementation].

The paper is to serve as an educational economic mediator between producer and consumer; like today's *Consumer Reports,* the *Journal des connaissances utiles* both encouraged consumption and sought to educate the consumer. For Girardin this incipient consumerism is inseparable from the social ques-

tion: [Q]ue le peuple, étant le plus grand des consommateurs, toute l'économie politique, toutes les questions de bien être social pourraient se résumer
dans ces mots de comptoir: VENDRE BON MARCHE pour VENDRE BEAU-
COUP;—VENDRE BEAUCOUP pour VENDRE BON MARCHE" [Since the masses
are the greatest [potential] consumers, all political economy, all questions of
social well-being could well be summed up by these shopkeeper's words:
SELL CHEAP, SELL A LOT;—SELL A LOT, SELL CHEAP].[33]

This slogan, the very soul of mass marketing, will remain Girardin's
throughout his long career, and it is under its aegis that *La Presse* will be
founded four years later. Social well-being is tied to production, production depends upon consumption, and consumption can spread among the
masses only if their own productivity rises and the cost of the products they
wish to consume falls. In Girardin's epigrammatic remarks is inscribed the
circular logic (some would call it the myopia) of the utopian socialists' emphasis on *production,* on "trickle-down" economics *avant la lettre.* Internal,
political strife and partisan bickering has stifled the industrial revolution in
France, and only the harmonization of competing ideologies will foster a
productive society.

The success of the *Journal des connaissances utiles* is due to the application of
these "economic doctrines," as Girardin calls them.[34] Already he is laying the
groundwork for *La Presse; publicité* will replace *polémique,* and the newspaper
of the future will seek to transcend party differences (or *couleurs*). In his first
article for *La Presse* he will make plain how closely linked his paper is—
indeed how it depends upon—the suppression of ideological differences:

> [L]es plus éminentes intelligences bâtissaient sur un fond d'idées presque
> identiques. En creusant, nous avons trouvé les mêmes couches, comme
> nous le ferons voir plus tard, sous l'edifice de leurs discours et de leurs
> écrits.
>
> Il n'y a guère, socialement, qu'une idée mère dans les esprits. Le prob-
> lème à résoudre est toujours celui-ci: *Le plus de bonheur pour le plus grand
> nombre possible.*

> [Most of the eminent minds of our time have built upon a foundation of
> almost identical ideas. By probing, we have uncovered the same layers—
> as we will later reveal—under the edifices of their speeches and writings.
>
> Socially there is little more than a single idea in men's minds: *The most
> happiness for the greatest number possible.*]

Of course at this time *publicité* meant not just advertising but publicity,
making information public. Terdiman and others have underscored the ten-

dency to blur such distinctions, yet Girardin leaves little room for doubt about what he intended. Later in life, and with a characteristic lack of modesty, the great journalist—perhaps hoping to rival Pascal and La Rochefoucauld in one fell swoop—allowed his *Pensées et maximes* to be excerpted from his journalistic writings. Under the rubric "Publicité" he bluntly states: "Sans la publicité marchande, point de progrès véritable, point de concurrence sérieuse, point de progrès utile aux masses" [Without commercial advertising, there can be no true progress, no serious competition, no progress of use to the masses], and "Où ne règne pas la publicité ne règne pas la liberté" [Where there is no publicity, there is no freedom].[36] Only then can we understand what Girardin meant when, under the July Monarchy, he referred to himself by the apparently oxymoronic label "conservateur progressiste."

It is also only in this larger discursive context that one can truly appreciate Théophile Gautier's brilliant, ironic, raving manifesto for the autonomy of art in his preface to *Mademoiselle de Maupin*. In it he attacks virtually everything sworn sacred by Girardin, above all *l'utilité;* indeed, the journalist's popularization of utopian ideas seems quite consciously invoked:

> A côté des journalistes moraux, sous cette pluie d'homélies comme sous une pluie d'été dans quelque parc, il a surgi, entre les planches du tréteau saint-simonien, une théorie de petits champignons d'une nouvelle espèce assez curieuse.
>
> Ce sont les critiques utilitaires.[37]

> [Next to the moralistic journalists, in this rain of sermons as in a summer rain in some park, there has sprung forth, between the planks of the Saint-Simonian platform, a theory of little mushrooms of a new, rather curious species.
>
> These are the utilitarian critics.]

Where Girardin argues "Mais surtout soyez utile" [Be useful above all] Gautier retorts: "Il n'y a de vraiment beau que ce qui ne peut servir à rien" [The only true beauty is that which is useless] and "L'endroit le plus utile d'une maison, ce sont les latrines" [The most useful place in a home is the toilet].[38] In short, Gautier's preface excoriates the holy trinity of the nineteenth-century bourgeoisie: usefulness, progress, and commerce, particularly as they coalesced in the press of the July Monarchy. His "journalistes progressifs"[39] naturally remind one of Girardin, and any doubt is removed by an ironic reference to the *Journal des connaissances utiles.*[40]

Tongue firmly in cheek, Gautier promises to write a poem in honor of Louis-Philippe, if only the latter, "une bonne fois pour toutes, supprimait tous les journaux littéraires et politiques" [once and for all, were to suppress all of the literary and political papers].[41] Of course the author remained a journalist himself, and only a year after the publication of *Mademoiselle de Maupin,* Gautier found himself working at none other than Girardin's revolutionary experiment, *La Presse.* As strange as it may initially appear, this turn of events was in the end altogether fitting. After all, in the first paragraph of his celebrated preface, Gautier asserts that every last newspaper has turned moral or didactic, "tous les journaux, de quelque couleur qu'ils soient, rouges, verts ou tricolores" [all the papers, regardless of their color, red, green, or tricolor].[42] How appropriate, then, that he should land a regular position with the *journal sans couleur*—the new information-based daily—for despite his scorn for the utilitarianism that had "mushroomed" from utopian sermonizing, Gautier's aesthetic privileges an art that serves no didactic or political purpose and whose impassive, unemotional devotion to form and craftsmanship (Barthes's "fétiche de la forme travaillée") is the aesthetic Other of Girardin's professed vision of a colorless newspaper serving no master but the "objective truth" in the service of social progress. Indeed, Girardin's self-effacing, colorless newspaper undergoes a curious transformation in its effort to avoid becoming—as were the traditional papers—an extension or representation of something beyond itself, and the text of the paper is, perhaps unexpectedly, splendidly autonomous. Its purely referential project—presenting the news—is ultimately self-referential, for in doing away with a known political "color" that would filter or mediate information in order to promote a political agenda, it is presented *for its own sake,* as a commodity to be consumed along with the other "articles"[43] listed in the advertising section on the paper's final page or pages.

Today it is perhaps all too easy to forget that in Girardin's view (and those of many early socialists) there existed no fundamental contradiction between increased industrialization and productivity on the one hand and social harmony and even equality on the other. Indeed, it was widely held that the first would of necessity entail the second; the genius of Girardin is revealed in his relentlessly practical application of socialist "rhetoric" to the business of selling newspapers. While he doubtless was not alone, his master coup of popularization was to take the potentially subversive utopian discourse of Saint-Simon, Fourier, and others and commodify it, by harnessing it at the most opportune moment to advertising, industry, and a growing desire for information (all of which, of course, were then further promoted in Girardin's papers). The social question and the cult of objectivity—as much the legacy of the Enlightenment as it was of the utopian socialists who followed—fuse in Girardin's project to create the first instance of the mass press, a press for the masses that will at once respond to public opinion and help to create (by enlightening) it. As Terdiman has pointed out, Girardin (and later, Moïse Millaud) "turned the daily into a commodity in terms of both its means of circulation and its content. . . . [T]he newspaper was adapted to the implicit needs of commerce. It *became* the institutional incarnation of the dominant discourse . . . for which . . . it could be taken—and indeed was taken—as a characteristic figure."[44]

What seems most compelling here, however, is the extent to which an implicitly subversive political discourse has been domesticated and *made to serve* the interests of a stratified bourgeois capitalism devoid of—if not openly hostile to—any efforts to resolve the "social question." Like Gautier's art for art's sake, *La Presse* owed allegiance to no one but *La Presse;* how splendidly appropriate, then, was its name. Unlike other papers, it referred not to a political tendency or abstract quality, but to itself, to its own *reproduction.* The paper that would represent the world of reality suggests by its very title a self-enclosed, self-referential text whose objectification (in both senses of the word) will recommend it as an alternative to the highly contextualized, subjective discourse of the traditional political press. And it is in the ambiguity of the "objective" that we can, in conclusion, trace the parallels—and divergences—between the *presse à bon marché* and the aestheticism that developed alongside it.

Two coins: one—Gautier's "médaille austère"—upturned by a plowman after centuries of subterranean oblivion, the other—Girardin's "médaille en argent"—minted for and awarded to his faithful "correspondents" for their subscription sales. The first is valued by Gautier precisely because it has been dislodged from its historical context, outliving its currency as it were, its referentiality, its usefulness. In short, it is pure form or object, and its opacity occludes any referential function whatsoever; it has neither the symbolic (monetary) nor the ideological (political) meaning it was originally intended to carry. The second "médaille" is a symbolic reward, a mass-produced token of appreciation that functions as an incentive to those who would participate in the philanthropic enterprise of the *Journal des connaissance utiles.* While, like Gautier's "médaille austère" Girardin's is useless in that it cannot function as currency, it does carry the ideological weight of an agenda of social and industrial progress. It represents the incentive to *all* literate Frenchmen to participate in the new France envisioned by the utopians through increased production, consumption, and the dissemination of information. It is also the perfect emblem for the vapidity of Girardin's rhetoric of progress.

There is a third coin here, the real currency of which Gautier's is consciously the antithesis and Girardin's is a counterfeit. Financial wealth, of course, was recognized under the July Monarchy as increasingly synonymous with social and political power. The third coin—cold, hard cash—brings Gautier and Girardin together in *La Presse*. Literature's uneasy inscription within journalism allows it to flourish,[45] but also generates a rift—at times more rhetorical than substantive—between pure (autonomous and thus unprofitable) and prostituted (profitable, because in the service of an implicit or explicit ideological agenda) writing.

In the end, the autonomy to which both aestheticism and the *presse à bon marché* aspire is *formally* identical. Girardin's *La Presse* and art for art's sake position themselves above or beyond the partisan conflicts of the day, and both attempt to create an objective distance and a structural independence that removes them from the *couleurs* of political and ethical discourse. Both develop a cult of the object (or product), a cult of objectivity (impassivity; critical, "impartial" distance). But the aesthetic object is designed to endure, while the newspaper's survival is predicated upon its own obsolescence. Gautier's medallion has value because it can no *longer* function as currency, while the newspaper relies on its decontextualized presentation of *l'actualité* to create profits, one kind of currency generating another.[46]

Modernity encompasses multiple counter-discursive strands (all of which owe their origins to romantic or utopian ideological networks) that most clearly begin to unwind under the aegis of *progress*. But modernity is also the dominant cultural hegemony, largely shaped by the development of the "objective" decontextualized mass press with which—even *through* which—we continue to live in the late twentieth century. Art for art's sake, too, partakes of a *double vie:* it is both a continuation of the classical view of art and a new aesthetic framed by the cult of scientific objectivity and unconsciously modeled on the utopian socialists' goals of industrial productivity. The financial project of the *presse à bon marché,* and particularly Girardin's *La Presse,* drew its ideological breath from the totalizing views of the Enlightenment and early utopian socialists and yet participated in the elaboration of the cult of objectivity. I have argued that objectivity subtends discourses as disparate as the Parnassian school of poetry—lasting, sculptured verse largely inspired by Gautier—and the development of the *presse d'information,* the beginnings of a true mass press that paradoxically is at its most powerful when it is at its most ephemeral, promoting consumption, including especially its own. It may be that this final word—"consumption"—embraces the only truly significant distinction between two uniquely modern cultural phenomena, born under the July Monarchy but destined to dominate, as polar opposites, the cultural field of the later nineteenth and early twentieth centuries: the mass press and the artistic and literary avant-garde. And because of this polarization, promoted tirelessly by the proponents of decadence and high modernism—Gautier's epigones—we too often lose sight of the seminal interrelations and common origins of modernity in all its multifariousness, a complexity without which our understanding of the role of the mass press in the formation of modern life is significantly impoverished.

Notes

1. See the "Introduction" to Richard Terdiman's *Discourse / Counter-Discourse: The Theory and Practice of Symbolic Resistence in Nineteenth-Century France* (Ithaca, N.Y.: Cornell University Press, 1985), particularly pages 71–75. In a general but pervasive way, 1848 also functions as an *année charnière* in Fredric Jameson's *The Political Unconscious Narrative as a Socially Symbolic Act* (Ithaca, N.Y.: Cornell University Press, 1981) and Roland Barthes's *Writing Degree Zero* (New York: Hill and Wang, 1973). See also art historian T. J. Clark's influential interdisciplinary studies, *The Absolute Bourgeois: Artists and Politics in France, 1848–1851* and *Image of the People: Gustave Courbet and the Second French Republic, 1848–1851* (both, London: Thames and Hudson, 1973).

2. Gene H. Bell-Villada has recently examined this as "the outcome of the aestheticist and modernist legacy in an age of criticism" (*Art for Art's Sake and Literary Life* [Lincoln: University of Nebraska Press, 1996], 277).

3. By utilitarian I do not mean to suggest the contemporaneous philosophical concepts of a Bentham or a J. S. Mill, but rather a more banal opposition to the aestheticism of art for art's sake, *utile* versus *dulci*. A perusal of the journalism of the July Monarchy makes it clear that *utilitaire* denotes instrumental usefulness, and that it is an outgrowth of the progressive, productive ideology that the early socialists inherited from the Enlightenment. For a further discussion, see my "Going Nowhere Fast: Utopia, Progress, and Narrative in Nineteenth-Century France," *Esprit Createur* 34, 4 (1994): 65–76.

4. Terdiman's *Discourse / Counter-Discourse* is an excellent example of a cultural study that seeks to attribute qualities of symbolic resistance to texts—especially Flaubert's and Baudelaire's—that are themselves devoid of a systematic social vision. Such texts, as Terdiman points out, function negatively through irony (and, I would add, fragmentation). See Terdiman, 76.

5. Terdiman, *Discourse / Counter-Discourse,* 76–77.

6. In "Mon coeur mis à nu," quoted in Terdiman, *Discourse / Counter-Discourse,* 117.

7. See Jean Morienval, *Les Créateurs de la grande presse en France: Emile de Girardin, H. de Villemessant, Moïse Millaud* (Paris: Editions Spes, 1934); Pierre Pellissier, *Emile de Girardin: Prince de la presse* (Paris: Denoël, 1985); Maurice Reclus, *Emile de Girardin: Le*

Créateur de la presse moderne (Paris: Hachette, 1934); Jacques Wolgensinger, *La Grande Aventure de la presse* (Paris: Gallimard [Découvertes], 1989), esp. 67–85 and 130–33. For Girardin's early years in the press, see Roland Chollet's *Balzac journaliste: Le Tournant de 1830*.

8. "De la littérature industrielle" (1839).

9. Théophile Gautier, *Emaux et Camées* (Paris: Gallimard, 1981), 25.

10. See the appendix to vol. 1 of Gautier's *Correspondance générale,* Claudine Lacoste-Veysseyre, ed. (Genève-Paris: Droz, 1985), 399. The alphabetic index of correspondents gives helpful biographical and anecdotal sketches of Gautier's relationships with Girardin and his wife, Delphine (Gay) de Girardin.

11. Gautier, *Emaux et Camées,* 149–50.

12. Terdiman draws the common distinction between the literary of the "high cultural realm" and the press, which occupies a space "drearily down to earth," *Discourse/ Counter-Discourse,* 76.

13. Terdiman, *Discourse/Counter-Discourse,* 117.

14. Stendhal, *Le Rouge et le noir* (Paris: Garnier-Flammarion, 1964), 419.

15. Jean Tulard, *Les Révolutions, de 1789 à 1851* (Paris: Fayard, 1985), 362.

16. For a brief discussion, see Tulard, *Les Révolutions* 361–70. See also Philippe Vigier, *La Monarchie de Juillet* (Paris: PUF, 1962).

17. See Claude Bellanger et al., *Histoire générale de la presse française* (Paris: PUF, 1969). Of particular interest in this context is Tome *2: De 1815 à 1871,* 11–26 (on the evolution of printing techniques) and 114–24 (on the *presse à bon marché*).

18. Victor Hugo, *Oeuvres poétiques* (Paris: Gallimard [Pléiade], 1964), 1: 578. Italics are mine.

19. Roland Barthes, *Le Degré zéro de l'écriture* (Paris: Seuil, 1972), 48.

20. Barthes, *Le Degré,* 56.

21. Terdiman, *Discourse/Counter-Discourse,* 126.

22. In his *Balzac journaliste,* Chollet notes that the elaborate administrative and philanthropic apparatus surrounding Girardin's publications—including the "Société nationale pour l'emancipation intellectuelle" discussed here in connection with *Le Journal des connaissances utiles*—was "en partie imaginaire sans doute" [in all probability partly imaginary], 79, n.29. They were, in fact, largely fictive.

23. *La Presse,* 13 August 1836: 1.

24. *La Presse,* 13 August 1836: 2.

25. Anonymous, *Physiologie de la presse* (Paris: n.p., 1841): 81.

26. *L'Organisateur,* vol. 1 (1819): 1.

27. *Le Producteur,* vol. 1 (1825): 3–4.

28. *Le Producteur,* vol. 1 (1825): 5.

29. *Le Journal des connaissances utiles,* September 1832: 241.

30. *Le Journal des connaissances utiles,* September 1832: 241.

31. *Le Journal des connaissances utiles,* September 1832: 241.

32. *Le Journal des connaissances utiles,* September 1832: 241.

33. *Le Journal des connaissances utiles,* September 1832: 241.

34. By the end of its first year of existence, the monthly *Journal des connaissances utiles* had 132,000 subscribers and Girardin was making a fortune, even though he claimed to be publishing it only "in the interests of the country." See Reclus, *Emile de Girardin,* 68–78.

35. *La Presse,* 1 July 1836: 1. Emphasis is mine.

36. *Pensées et maximes extraites des oeuvres de M. Emile de Girardin,* par Albert Hetrel (Paris: Michel Lévy Frères, 1867), 612. The volume is arranged alphabetically by topic, and bears a suggestive resemblance to Flaubert's ironic *Dictionnaire des idées reçues.*

37. Théophile Gautier, "Préface," *Mademoiselle de Maupin* (1834; Paris: Garnier-Flammarion, 1966), 19.

38. Gautier, *Mademoiselle,* 23.

39. Gautier, *Mademoiselle,* 30.

40. Gautier, *Mademoiselle,* 25.

41. Gautier, *Mademoiselle,* 38.

42. Gautier, *Mademoiselle,* 1.

43. Terdiman's entire chapter on "Newspaper Culture: Institutions of Discourse, Discourse of Institutions" in *Discourse/Counter-Discourse* (117–46) may be said to turn on this revealing pun.

44. Terdiman, *Discourse/Counter-Discourse,* 129.

45. The *roman-feuilleton* dates from 1836, and was first published in Girardin's *La Presse* and Dutacque's *Le Siècle,* the founding newspapers of the *presse à bon marché,* although there existed already a long tradition of literature in and of the press, as well as a distinctly literary press. On the *roman-feuilleton* see Maria Adamowicz-Hariasz's contribution to this volume.

46. Maxime du Camp reports that Girardin felt Gautier incapable of managing his career. In *Théophile Gautier,* du Camp quotes Girardin's comments from a meeting that took place between them in 1862 or 1863: "Gautier est un imbécile, qui ne comprend rien au journalisme; je lui ai mis une fortune entre les mains; son feuilleton aurait dû lui rapporter 3000 ou 4000 f par an; il n'a jamais su lui faire produire un sou. Il n'y a pas un directeur de théâtre qui ne lui eût fait des rentes, à condition de l'avoir pour porte-voix. Actuellement et depuis qu'il a quitté *La Presse,* il est au *Moniteur Universel,* c'est-à-dire au journal officiel de l'Elysee; il n'en tire aucun parti; je vous le répète, c'est un imbécile qui n'a jamais profité d'une bonne occasion" [Gautier is an imbecile who understands nothing about journalism. . . . I handed him a fortune. . . . His column should have brought him 3,000 or 4,000 francs per year, but he's never been able to make a penny from it. There's not a single theater director who wouldn't have paid him a yearly salary

to have him as spokesman. Now, since he's left *La Presse,* he's at the *Moniteur Universel,* in other words at the official organ of the Elysée, and he's making nothing from it. . . . I'll say it again, he's an imbecile who has never taken advantage of a good opportunity]. Quoted in Théophile Gautier, *Correspondence générale,* Claudine Lacote-Veysseyre, ed. (Genève-Paris: Droz, 1985), 399.

5 From Opinion to Information

The *Roman-Feuilleton* and the Transformation

of the Nineteenth-Century French Press.

During the course of the nineteenth century, as its readership multiplied, the French press went through a period of great expansion and profound alteration. Two facts are often cited as examples of the transformation that, by making the press more profit oriented and accessible to a wider public, changed its predominantly political character: Emile de Girardin's introduction in 1836 of an inexpensive newspaper and the 1863 launching of the even less expensive *Le Petit Journal,* the "true" beginning of the mass press.

The radical lowering of the price of newspapers was only part of the story, however. The popularity of the *roman-feuilleton,* the serial novel, also contributed to the success of the new press. Its influence was far-reaching, transforming both the press and its readers, for it helped to create a new type of newspaper based more on transmitting information and providing entertainment than on shaping or discussing political opinions. Although the older type of journalism was not entirely eliminated, the political press became increasingly marginalized. Moreover, the previously small, homogenous group of privileged consumers of the dailies became diversified and expanded as the new journalism began attracting lower-middle-class and working-class readers. The *rez-de-chaussée,* the bottom of the newspaper page, began the cultural democratization of French society—from the bottom up.

The *roman-feuilleton* came to life as a result of complex sociopolitical and economic forces, and it in turn became a source for profound changes in the social and cultural history of France. I will examine these forces and transformations through an analysis of the history of one newspaper—*Le Constitutionnel*—and the serial novel it published from 1844 to 1845, Eugène Sue's *Le Juif errant,* the most frequently cited example of the *littérature facile* or *littérature industrielle* capable of transforming the most respected political newspaper into a commercial venture. Indeed, the history of *Le Constitutionnel* provides a clear illustration of this, as *Le Juif errant* saved the newspaper from bankruptcy—but not, however, without radically changing its character. Extremely popular and enthusiastically received—especially by lower-class readers—*Le Juif errant* also provided the impetus, according to many critics, for an attempt at altering the entire social and political order during the 1848 Revolution; as Irene Collins laconically but correctly avers, "the serial stories were not without political consequences."[1]

The history of the nineteenth-century French press corresponds closely to the chronicle of social and political upheavals of that period. The revolutionary changes of regimes invariably brought about an abolition of censorship followed by a proliferation of newspapers and, subsequently, a return to law and order, which often meant the disappearance of many of the new, ephemeral *feuilles*. Such was the case in 1815 during the *Cent Jours*, in 1830 after *les Trois Glorieuses*, and again in 1848 and 1870. Nevertheless, the number of newspapers and readers steadily grew: according to Albert Joseph George, "in 1824, only 13 papers appeared in Paris, 7 pro-government, 6 opposed, and all together they could claim only 55,600 subscribers."[2] In 1836 there were already 70,000 subscribers to the Parisian press, and this number grew in 1846 to 200,000.[3] During the Second Empire, the launching of *Le Petit Journal* and of the other dailies that tried to follow in its footsteps increased circulation figures even more dramatically. But the press underwent its greatest expansion and diversification during the Third Republic: from 1870 to 1914 the number of Parisian dailies went up from fifty to seventy, and their circulation from 1.5 million to 5.5 million.[4]

There were three principal reasons for this unprecedented growth. The first is related to the industrial progress of the period, wherein technological advances directly contributed to the development of the printing industry. By 1830, new speedier presses with rollers instead of tampons had been installed, new inks concocted, and new methods for manufacturing larger sheets of paper invented.[5] Later, a new invention, the rotary press, first installed in England in 1848, and in France in 1867 (at *Le Petit Journal*), allowed for an even greater increase in printing capabilities and, consequently, in circulation. Additionally, technical advancements created new industrial centers and attracted rural populations to the cities. New kinds of work required skilled, literate workers, a need that in turn gave impetus to widespread educational efforts. The new environment created a new urban working class, dissolving old cultural forms and replacing them with new ones.[6]

The second reason for growth was the steady rise in the level of literacy, especially since the introduction of the Guizot Law in 1833 guaranteeing male pupils the right and access to elementary education. As a result, a spectacular increase in the number of school children occurred: it rose from 987,667 in 1817–20 to 3,228,250 in 1841–50.[7] This is exactly the group from which new readers of the press, and the *roman-feuilleton,* were recruited. Although Allen rightly points out that "the history of literacy is simply not identical with the history of reading,"[8] the numbers clearly show a steadily growing demand for the written word among the newly literate. For example, *cabinets de lecture,* or reading rooms, mushroomed throughout the country, and especially in the cities. Claude Pichois notes their rapid multiplication in Paris: only 23 in 1819, but already 207 in 1843, 215 in 1844, 198 in 1845, and 209 in 1850.[9] Cuvillier-Fleury, in an article published in the *Journal des débats* in June 1842, just days before the paper was to begin its publication of the first installment of Sue's *Les Mystères de Paris,* talks about the public's new and ferocious appetite for reading: "[L]a consommation de romans, bons ou mauvais, qui se fait à Paris et en province est prodigieuse; et comment y suffire, je le répète, comment assouvir cet immense appétit qui attend la bouche ouverte sa pitance littéraire de chaque jour . . . " [The consumption of novels, good or bad, occurring in Paris and in the provinces, is phenomenal; and how to meet the need, I repeat, how to satisfy this immense appetite that awaits—mouth open—its daily literary sustenance . . .].[10] (Unless otherwise noted, all translations in this chapter are my own.)

The third reason for the general growth in press readership and for the development of a taste for fictional works was the political climate of the period. The voting system—based on a poll tax that allowed only a small fraction of society to participate in political life—alienated many active social groups from politics. In addition, the law of September 1835, introduced after Fieschi's attempted assassination of Louis-Philippe, considerably limited the liberty of the press. In order to avoid violating the law, editorials and political commentaries had to be toned down and as a result their previously vigorous and direct critique of the regime gave way to masked allusions. This situation further contributed to the loss of interest in political journalism, as only a small portion of readers were capable of reading between the lines.[11] Moreover, the growth of an increasingly educated public gave birth to a new class of readers who lacked experience with, and were initially indifferent to, politics. It was to accommodate and attract these readers that, during the July Monarchy, the existing papers sought to evolve from associations of individuals linked by common political views into more commercial enterprises.

Many scholars agree that the transformation of the press began in 1836 as the result of a single phenomenon: the inauguration of the *presse à bon marché* or "penny paper." Emile de Girardin's *La Presse* appeared alongside *Le Siècle,* launched by his former collaborator—and now rival—Armand Dutacq. Both newspapers were founded upon the same principle, the lowering of the subscription price from eighty to forty francs. Increased circulation and paid advertisements were supposed to make up for the loss of subscription revenues. Yet Girardin knew that price alone, even if capable of attracting more subscriptions, would not keep new readers interested for an extended period of time. Hence, the second innovation Girardin introduced: the *roman-feuilleton.* Balzac's *La Vieille Fille* (23 October 1836) is considered "the first French novel in France to be published originally in installments in a daily."[12] The publication of a novel in parts was not entirely new in that monthlies and literary reviews had published novels before. Now, however, a long fictional work would occupy the lower front page of a daily. Previously, this part of the page—the *feuilleton*—had been reserved for literary, theatrical, musical, or Salon reviews, society gossip, or the latest session of the Académie des sciences. The introduction of a novel in a daily that had been until 1836 essentially an organ of a political orientation or party changed the newspaper drastically and forever. Girardin and Dutacq's gamble had paid off and their newspapers became over time two of the most read during and subsequent to the July Monarchy.[13] New readers were certainly attracted by the lower price but above all they were attracted by the serial novel:

> The rapidly mounting subscription to the *Presse,* the *Siècle* and the *Constitutionnel* were due not to their cheapness but to the serial story. The *Constitutionnel* provided the clearest evidence of this fact. In 1830 it had 22,000 subscribers, but the numbers had dwindled rapidly until they were only 5,000 in 1841. In 1844 the newspaper was acquired by a shrewd business man, Dr. Véron, who followed the example of Girardin and Dutacq and changed the character of the newspaper. On 16 January 1845 Véron published the first installment of Eugène Sue's *Juif errant,* and on the same day he was able to announce that the subscription list had risen to 24,000.[14]

Irene Collins is mistaken when she claims that the number of subscriptions to *Le Constitutionnel* grew magically overnight; from the lowest 3,428 in March 1843, it increased to 16,120 in August 1844[15] and to the highest 25,000 in January 1845,[16] a change that coincided with the run of *Le Juif errant* from 25 June 1844 to 26 August 1845. But she is definitely right in stressing the importance of the *roman-feuilleton,* citing as proof the *Journal des débats,* which did not lower the price of subscription yet retained its readership. According to Ledré, the newspaper's circulation was 10,008 in 1836; 10,583 in 1840; and

9,844 in 1845.[17] Those newspapers that resisted the serial novel saw a substantial decrease in their circulation. For instance, *La Gazette de France* boasted 5,500 subscriptions in 1837, but only 2,950 in 1846.[18]

Le Journal des débats introduced its first fictional work in 1837 with the publication of *L'Histoire de Madame F. D.* by Frédéric Soulié and soon followed this with a partial publication of his enormously successful *Mémoires du diable*. However, it was only in 1842 that the newspaper started to publish Eugène Sue's *Les Mystères de Paris* which became a true bestseller in France as well as in Europe.[19] The success of *Les Mystères de Paris* not only made Eugène Sue a dominant figure in the literary market, but also created a *roman-feuilleton* frenzy, as other newspapers and authors tried to profit from his success. According to René Guise, in the years 1842–47 the very existence of many papers depended on the success of the serial novels they published, as readers no longer based their decisions to subscribe on papers' political affiliations, but on the kind of fictional works offered.[20]

The influence of the *roman-feuilleton* was not limited to transforming the character of the papers, now depoliticized and focused on *divertissement*. By imposing certain constraints, publication in installments also changed the novelistic genre. It influenced, for instance, the rhythm of writing, as novels—more often than not—had to be hastily produced, often during the few days preceding publication. Not only did it dictate the size of the installments and of the entire work, but often it also influenced the content of the story. A reader subscribing to a newspaper, a consumer paying for a material commodity had a right to voice objections if the content of the product did not suit his or her morals or fancy. This was especially true in a work of fiction whose progress could be monitored every morning. The very first *roman-feuilleton*, Balzac's *La Vieille Fille,* provoked numerous complaints from the readers of *La Presse,* forcing the author to take notice of them.[21] In November of the same year, 1836, Balzac received a letter from Girardin urging him to change the subject of his next novel (*La Torpille*) to be published in the newspaper, the editor having received too many complaints.[22] Likewise, many other writers, forced by the book market to prepublish their novels in installments, had to endure the tyranny of the public and of the newspaper owners.

By signing the contract with Balzac, Girardin hoped to gain publicity for the newspaper, since the author's excellent reputation at that moment was a great asset. The audience, however, did not like to read Balzac in installments, complaining not only about moral issues but also about such things as the narrative containing overly long descriptions and too many details. Later, in 1844, concerned by a significant drop in subscriptions and by the readers' discontent, *La Presse* interrupted its publication of Balzac's *Les Paysans,* and replaced it with Dumas's *La Reine Margot.* Indeed, Dumas along with Soulié and Sue, but not Balzac or Sand, were the masters of the new mode of publication, and there may be evidence that the *roman-feuilleton* can be considered a distinct novelistic genre. There is no doubt that—because it forced the *hommes de lettres* to write as fast as journalists and because the product of their work had to attract and sustain the interest of as many consumers as possible—serialization had a great impact on narrative discourse and on the structure of the novel. A successful *roman-feuilleton* made frequent use of clichés, it privileged dialogue over description, and it delighted readers through swift action and rapidly and unexpectedly changing events. The chapters of a serial novel, written for immediate consumption, tended to be entities in and of themselves, resembling often sensational short stories. Open-ended and somewhat independent in relation to the text as a whole, they allowed (when necessary) for new developments of secondary plots and multiplication of characters. The fragmentary style of the *roman-feuilleton* reflected the novelty-oriented content and the look of the new press and further strengthened their symbiotic connection.[23]

The cutting technique—wherein each chapter is constructed so as to create powerful suspense at its end, thereby delaying the development of the story even as it seduces the reader into coming back for more—is likely the most important aspect of the serial novel. The manner in which some writers, for instance Balzac and Sue, worked is indeed very telling. According to René Guise, Balzac wrote the first drafts of his novels without any cuts, only afterward dividing them into chapters and giving them titles.[24] Sue, on the contrary, though he usually had a general outline of the story beforehand, wrote by creating single chapters, sometimes not even knowing exactly what would happen next. Manifestly, there is a huge difference between a novel conceived as a novel and a novel conceived as a *roman-feuilleton* and produced as such (by chapters), in that the latter aims at providing immediate satisfaction to the readers of dailies.

The ambiguity of the term *roman-feuilleton* thus requires further clarification. It is sometimes considered a distinct genre, defined by its content and aesthetic quality. It is also often wrongly identified with the nineteenth-century *roman populaire,* an even more polysemous term as it eludes any univocal definition. Is it created by representatives of the people as a socioeconomic class or is it to be read by the people? And who are the people? Rural population and/or working class? Is the *roman populaire* destined for, or consumed by, a large reading public comprising various social classes?

Considered as a mode of publication the term "roman-feuilleton" is no less confusing. If we adhere to its strict interpretation, then even the first novel published in installment, Balzac's *La Vieille Fille,* cannot be called a *roman-feuilleton* because it was not published at the bottom of the first page of the daily, the usual place for a *feuilleton.*

To use the term "roman-feuilleton" requires great caution precisely because of its strong association with those lengthy novels of the mid—nineteenth century whose ultimate purpose was to help sell the paper, while at the same time providing a source of income for the authors (for Sue, money made from his novels was indeed a lifesaver, the young dandy having spent all his inheritance). Because of a perceived strong incompatibility between the laws of the free market and art, between uniformity and originality, repetition and creativity, immediate consumption and preservation of universal aesthetic values, these novels tend to be associated with the very bottom part of a severely hierarchized structure called literature.

The recently proposed theory of paraliterature by Daniel Couégnas[25] enumerates several criteria that can be used to distinguish between high and popular literature. Couégnas's analysis seems to offer the most coherent model for studying noncanonical literature, which in France truly became mass literature only at the end of the nineteenth century. According to Couégnas, paraliterary text refers to phatic, cognitive, and referential functions of the language rather than poetic ones, to use Jakobson's terms. Some characteristics that decide whether a literary work adheres to the paraliterary model are the following: material and textual signs identifying the work as a paraliterary model for a potential reader (cover illustration, title); a tendency toward repetition of settings, situations, simplified and quasi-allegorical characters, with no hint of irony or parody by the narrator that would invite readers to critical reflection; a maximum of textual elements producing *illusion référentielle* (dialogues, clichés); a system of redundancy that excludes dialogism. Couégnas's theory also stresses the indissoluble link between text and reader, suggesting the possibility that the same work can be read from a paraliterary or literary perspective.

Toward the end of the publication of *Les Mystères de Paris* (its epilogue appeared in the *Journal des débats* on 15 October 1843), Louis Désiré Véron, one of the shareholders of *Le Constitutionnel,* approached Sue and offered him 100,000 francs for his next novel, *Le Juif errant.* It was an enormous amount of money, one never before offered for a fictional work, and all the more surprising since, as some claimed, not even the first line had been written. Sue happily accepted the offer but the validity of the agreement was almost immediately challenged in the courts on the grounds that Sue had made some vague promises to deliver his future works to two other major newspapers, *La Presse* and *Le Journal des débats*. The court sided with Véron and the trial itself—understandably—contributed enormously to making *Le juif errant* even more popular than *Les Mystères de Paris*.[26]

When Véron acquired the novel, he was determined to turn it into a literary and financial success. The former proved elusive, however, as professional journalists and critics greeted the novel coldly, in part due to its publisher's bad reputation and manipulative character. A shopkeeper's son, Louis Désiré Véron had reportedly been a brilliant student of medicine, yet his professional medical career went nowhere, and he turned to journalism as his second passion. For some time at the beginning of his journalistic career he wrote a weekly political column for *La Quotidienne;* later he reviewed theater for *Le Messager des chambres*. In 1829 he founded *La Revue de Paris,* which by publishing well-known writers as well as still obscure talents, enjoyed considerable success. After two years Véron quit *La Revue* to take charge of the Paris Opera, which he was able to restore to its former splendor, at the same time securing a substantial income for himself. His personal gain did not go unnoticed and in 1835 Véron was relieved of his duties. Afterward he threw himself back into political journalism by becoming first a shareholder and later a managing editor and director of *Le Constitutionnel*. He was very well known in various social milieus, and as one observer rather sarcastically put it, "tint pendant la première moitié du dix-neuvième siècle, autant de place dans la chronique parisienne que Napoléon Ier dans l'Histoire de France" [in the first half of the nineteenth century [Véron] took up as much place in the Parisian chronicle as did Napoléon I in the history of France].[27]

Véron's idea was to use *Le Juif errant* to resuscitate *Le Constitutionnel,* which he had bought when it was on the brink of extinction. Save it he did, but his action created a major scandal, and numerous critics condemned his enterprise. What inspired the critics' indignation? Could the printing of a novel really change a well-respected newspaper?

Le Constitutionnel was one of the most influential and widely read dailies between 1815 and 1830, when it battled the Restoration regime. As such, it played a major role in the July 1830 Revolution.

> Autour de lui s'étaient groupés tous les éléments sains de cette révolution. Un moment, dans les premières semaines qui suivirent le succès des trois journés, le bureau du *Constitutionnel* fut le vrai centre de la direction politique, le siège réel du gouvernement. Il eut alors un grand pouvoir.[28]

> [All the sound elements of this revolution rallied round it. At one point, during the first weeks that followed the success of the Three Days, the

office of *Le Constitutionnel* was the true center of the political leadership, the actual headquarters of the government. In those days it had a great amount of power.]

It was founded as the *Indépendant* in May 1815, during the short period of *Cent Jours* when Napoleon lifted censorship, and later frequently changed its title, especially during its first few years of existence: it became the *Courier,* then *Le Constitutionnel,* later the *Journal du commerce,* finally returning to *Le Constitutionnel.* All this was done in order to escape the laws designed to suppress opposition journals. The legal maneuvers of the paper's proprietors, who were also its editors and journalists, did not alter its political orientation: from the beginning, and even after the July Revolution, when the paper was no longer an organ of the opposition, *Le Constitutionnel* positioned itself at center-left of the French political spectrum.

Moderate royalists, liberal and anticlerical, the readers of *Le Constitutionnel* represented above all the *petite* and *moyenne bourgeoisie:* industrialists, military men, white-collar professionals, and merchants. The data concerning working-class access to the newspaper is vague and does not permit precise conclusions to be drawn. However, given that *Le Constitutionnel* was one of the dailies most read in the *cabinets de lecture* and cafés, particularly in the towns of the northern, most industrialized, regions of France, the newspaper's penetration of the working-class environment seems very likely.

The number of subscriptions to *Le Constitutionnel,* which rose steadily during the Restoration (4,200 in 1817 to 22,000 in 1830), went downhill after the July Revolution. As Mouchot writes: the year 1832 "marque pour *Le Constitutionnel* une charnière entre son époque de prospérité et celle de sa décadence" [marks for *Le Constitutionnel* a turning point between its era of prosperity and its decline].[29]

Three principal reasons can be cited for this fall. First, the general political situation: the constitutional monarchy for which *Le Constitutionnel* had tirelessly fought was a fait accompli and the paper was no longer in opposition to the governing regime. For this reason, it was much less interesting, and it alienated many of its readers. According to Hatin, "souscrire au *Constitutionnel,* ce fut désormais . . . prendre une patente d'*épicier*" [to subscribe to *Le Constitutionnel* was from now on . . . to take a license of *épicier.*[30] Second, the situation of the press changed dramatically after 1836, the year of Emile de Girardin's introduction of the "penny press." Other papers did not have room to maneuver: in order not to disappear completely from the market, they had to follow the example of *La Presse* and introduce the *roman-feuilleton* into their pages. Third, the internal situation of *Le Constitutionnel,* according to Véron, became unbearable, mostly because financial difficulties created personal and power conflicts among its editors and shareholders.

In his capacity as shareholder, Véron decided to buy out *Le Constitutionnel* in order to make it a newly profitable enterprise. However, he encountered strong resistance from those shareholders who were also founders of the paper: MM. Jay, Roussel, and Etienne, among others, rejected Véron's conditions and refused to sell him *Le Constitutionnel*. The conflict was resolved only by the arbitration of the courts which on 17 January 1844 pronounced a dissolution of the joint stock company. Five days later, on 22 March 1844, a new company, which was to finance the new *Constitutionnel*, was officially founded.

Véron wanted total control of *Le Constitutionnel*, not so much to save it from bankruptcy—although he did have an initial investment in the paper— but rather to enrich himself with the help of a popular fiction writer whose name, so Véron thought, would attract tens of thousands of new subscribers. In his letter to Sue from 21 February 1844 he wrote:

> Mon cher Sue,
>
> Aujourd'hui que la dissolution de la société du journal *Le Constitutionnel* est prononcée et publiée, je suis prêt à vous acheter, moyennant la somme de 100,000 francs, que je vous ai offerte, votre nouveau roman, ayant pour titre: *Le Juif errant*, qui dans ce cas, aurait au moins dix volumes.
>
> Voici seulement deux conditions nouvelles auxquelles je suis forcé de tenir:
> 1. Pour tous les ouvrages nouveaux que vous publierez après *Le Juif errant*, j'aurai de droit à prix égal la préférence sur tout autre acquéreur;
> 2. J'aurai le droit de publier *Le Juif errant*, soit dans *Le Constitutionnel*, si je m'en rends acquéreur, soit dans un journal nouveau que je fonderais si le prix du *Constitutionnel* était trop élevé au feu des enchères.
> Mes amitiés,
> Véron[31]

> [My dear Sue,
>
> Now that the dissolution of *Le Constitutionnel*'s company has become public, I am ready to buy from you, in return for the sum of 100,000 francs, which I have offered you, your new novel entitled: *Le Juif errant*, which, in this case, will have at least ten volumes.
>
> Here are the only two new conditions on which I am forced to insist:
> 1. For any new works that you will publish after *Le Juif errant*, you will grant me preference over any other equal bidder.
> 2. I will have the right to publish *Le Juif errant* either in *Le Constitutionnel* if

I purchase it, or in a new paper that I would found if the price of *Le Constitutionnel* became too high in the heat of the auction.
Best regards,
Véron.]

This letter makes it clear that Véron did not want to buy the novel in order to rescue *Le Constitutionnel:* true, he needed a still-respected paper in which to publish *Le Juif errant,* but with that constraint he was ready to publish it in some other, or even any other, newspaper.

It is telling that none of the founding "fathers" of *Le Constitutionnel*—those who created it in 1815—joined Véron's enterprise, so incompatible was its new character with their principles. If they preferred to break off their contact with Véron and "his" *Constitutionnel,* it was not because of a difference in their political opinions: Thiers, who was now protecting Véron, had been a protégé of M. Etienne, former managing editor of the paper. Neither was it because of a sudden change in the readership sought: the new *Constitutionnel* still wanted to represent the *petite* and *moyenne bourgeoisie.* The problem was, so it seems, the publication of a novel in installments. The regular publication of a fictional work over a long period of time relegated politics to a position of secondary importance, and for many new readers the presence of a *roman-feuilleton* was a primary reason for subscribing to the paper. Such commercialization of a paper, which had until recently been highly praised and esteemed for its political content, can explain the hostility of its former readers toward the first long serial novel published in *Le Constitutionnel.* For them *Le Juif errant* became the symbol of the paper's reorientation and concomitant moral failure. The old type of newspaper, based on people and ideas rather than capital, had ceased to exist. From a more general perspective this represented the death of a certain type of journalism:

Le cas du *Constitutionnel* . . . est un exemple très significatif du passage de "l'ancien journalisme" au "nouveau." La nouvelle presse, dépouillée de son intérêt politique, n'était plus la petite entreprise artisanale qu'elle avait été: elle n'était plus poussée par l'idéal politique de quelques hommes: un journal fut désormais une affaire financière dans laquelle on vit surtout un placement lucratif.[32]

[The case of *Le Constitutionnel* is a very significant example of the transformation from an old type of journalism to a new one. The new press, stripped of its political interest, was no longer the small craft enterprise that it had been; it was no longer driven by the political ideals of a few men: from then on, the newspaper became a financial deal and above all a lucrative investment.]

Véron's *Constitutionnel,* launched to assure profits, was the result of capitalist speculation. Published every morning, even on Sundays, it contained four pages of three columns each, the fourth page reserved for advertisements. Véron kept all the principal sections of the former *Constitutionnel:* an editorial that commented on the current political and social situation; Parisian, national, and international news; reports from the *Assemblée nationale;* the stock exchange list; court reports. One big change was the expansion of the advertising section. Before Véron, this occupied one third of the fourth page, but on 23 March 1844, in the very first issue of the new *Constitutionnel,* whose price had been lowered by half, advertisements occupied the entire fourth page.[33] The biggest and most striking change, however, was the *roman-feuilleton.* Before Véron, *Le Constitutionnel,* like most papers, had reserved a limited space at the bottom of the first page, called the *feuilleton,* for theater reviews, travel letters, fragments of old chronicles, and the like. During Véron's reign, a serial novel occupied the bottom of the second and even third pages.

However, Véron's plan was not to transform the newspaper entirely and exclusively into a commercial venture. In an attempt to reassure its old readers, the new editorial staff declared a continuation of the old *Constitutionnel*'s line, as well as a cultivation of its traditions. For this purpose the editorial staff sought and received the cooperation of eminent representatives of the *Assemblée nationale* and *Sénat,* such as Thiers, Rémusat, and Cousin.

It was the *roman-feuilleton,* however, and not its political articles that made Véron's new enterprise a success. The profits obtained from the publication of *Le Juif errant* allowed him to introduce changes that would push *Le Constitutionnel* even farther along the path of commercialization. On 1 June 1845, the newspaper was issued in a new and larger format of four folio pages of five columns each (an increase from twelve to twenty columns)—and all for the former price. It had more space for news and articles on science, agriculture, industry, and commerce, but its truly major innovation was the creation of the *Bibliothèque choisie* (pages to be cut, folded, and stapled), which effectively increased the nonpolitical content of the paper.[34] Also noticeable was the change in the size of advertisements; smaller and thus more numerous, they brought in even more revenues.

A lower subscription price and the name of a famous author were probably the significant features attracting new readers to *Le Constitutionnel.* But also important in enlarging the newspaper's subscription base was the modern use of publicity and marketing, and the manipulation of readers' interests. A shrewd capitalist and skillful businessman, Véron had experience in pharmaceutical advertising. He was behind the campaign that made throat expectorant a universally appreciated product.[35] Later as a director of the Paris Opera (1831–35), he handsomely profited from this experience by attracting the public through the use of posters and ads placed in newspapers. Even an ordinary performance was presented, on his orders, as a unique event: "Demain, dernière représentation de . . . qui, désormais, ne jouera plus qu'à de rares intervalles. Demain, trentième représentation de . . . La troisième scène du second acte sera jouée comme le premier soir" [Tomorrow, the last performance of . . . which, in the future, will play only at rare intervals. Tomorrow, thirtieth performance of . . . The third scene of the second act will be put on as it was the first evening].[36]

Véron used the same methods to promote *Le Constitutionnel*. Indeed, his promotional efforts were so apparent that some of his contemporaries attributed the success of *Le Juif errant* exclusively to the relentless ad campaign:

> Vous entrez [aux bureaux du *Constitutionnel*] et vous demandez un abonnement:—"C'est sans doute pour *Le Juif* que monsieur s'abonne. Vous recevrez *Le Juif* tout entier. . . . " Telles sont les paroles qui se succèdent. Il ne s'agit plus au *Constitutionnel* que du *Juif*, *Le Constitutionnel* c'est *Le Juif*, il n'y a plus d'autre question pour *Le Constitutionnel* que celle du *Juif* et, pour peu que cela dure, il faudra débaptiser le journal et l'appeler *Le Juif*. . . . Ainsi l'a voulu le nouveau propriétaire du journal, homme habile s'il en fut, grand politique sans doute, mais qui a étudié la politique à l'Opéra.[37]

> [You enter [the offices of *Le Constitutionnel*] and ask for a subscription, and these are the words that follow:—"It's no doubt because of *Le Juif* that you subscribe. You will receive absolutely all of the *Juif*. . . . " At *Le Constitutionnel* it is no longer a matter of anything but *Le Juif*, *Le Constitutionnel* is *Le Juif*, there is no other question for *Le Constitutionnel* than *Le Juif* and if this will last a little longer, one would have to rename the paper and call it *Le Juif*. This is how the new owner of the paper wanted it, a skillful man, a big politician no doubt, but who studied politics at the Opera.]

The analysis of Véron's advertising campaign shows that, if rather moderate at the beginning, the promotion of *Le Juif errant* became excessive over time. The newspaper advertised the novel while it was being published as well as during interruptions; it announced book editions of each volume by Paulin (these announcements appeared just after the newspaper completed its publication of their contents); it printed letters from enthusiastic readers, as well as other accounts of the novel's popularity. It even cited parodies and critical articles from other papers. Véron cleverly manipulated the novel's publication schedule, interrupting it for a few weeks at the height of a dramatic event in the narrative, an interruption that would, of course, coincide with the time for subscription renewal. This system obviously worked, as demonstrated by the example of one seven-week interruption between volumes 4 and 5 (18 November 1844 through 17 January 1845), when the number of subscriptions rose by almost 4,500. The *roman-feuilleton* became, like the newspaper itself, a commodity, susceptible to modifications, cuts, and other intrusions, all in order to please the public and sell more copies.

Sue first thought about writing *Le Juif errant* as early as 1843 and by the time of the contract with Véron had probably written at least two or three volumes. My research indicates that during the course of the novel's publication, he was probably asked to change certain aspects of his story in order to accommodate Véron's agenda. Having discovered his socialist mission, in large part thanks to an enthusiastic reception by the readers of *Les Mystères de Paris,* Sue wanted to continue in this direction and conceived *Le Juif errant* as an effort to popularize the socialist ideas of Saint-Simon and Fourier, thus contributing to the improvement of the working-class situation. Véron, however, the principal owner of *Le Constitutionnel* (whose title was still associated and almost synonymous with an extremely anticlerical and, during the Restoration, even quasi-militant ideology) wanted Sue to capitalize on the sociopolitical conflict that, since 1840, had been dividing French society into liberals and Catholics. The "Jesuit question"[38] thus became equally important in the novel, and some critics even accused the author of writing not a fictional work, but an anti-Jesuit pamphlet.

Le Juif errant is an ideological novel criticizing the existing socioeconomic order and proposing necessary reforms to emancipate those who suffer the most, namely, women and the masses. The principal plot opposes forces of good (the seven descendants of Marius Rennepont) against forces of evil (the Jesuits). The latter try to eliminate the members of the family in order to get hold of an immense heritage and the written will left by Marius 150 years earlier. In the will Marius reveals some of the terrible machinations of which the Jesuits are capable and orders his family to form an association that, by putting into action Christ's words, "Love each other," would work against Jesuits and for the improved life and happiness not only of women and the poor, but of all humanity. The narrative recounts a series of events in which

Jesuits try to prevent the Renneponts, who have come from as far as India and Siberia, to gather in Paris, by detaining them in prisons and asylums, or through acts of treason, kidnapping, bribing, and the like. Later they will eliminate them one by one through elaborate lies leading the protagonists to suicide, duels, death by overdrinking, and by cholera raging in Paris. The Jesuits will perish as well, or otherwise go mad; the money will burn, but Marius's idealist vision will one day become reality—so says the Wandering Jew at the close of the narrative, beholding the rising sun of emancipation.

The combination of anti-Jesuit agenda and socialist ideas presented in a fast-paced narrative full of suspense and sudden reversals made *Le Juif errant* extremely popular and widely read. The numbers show that it was one of the most, maybe *the* most, widely read novel of the July Monarchy, one that attracted elite as well as lower-class readers. At the peak of its popularity, *Le Constitutionnel*'s circulation was about 25,000 copies. There were also numerous book editions of the novel both at the time of its newspaper publication and later.[39] Additionally, a good number of the newspaper copies and book editions of the novel were read by multiple readers, either in the *cabinets de lecture* or cafés or through a shared subscription. Thus the actual number of readers of *Le Juif errant* would have been between 425,000 and (as high as) 850,000.[40]

Another measure of the popularity of the novel and its widespread influence is revealed in the reactions of professional critics and journalists whose writings demonstrate how deeply *Le Juif errant* penetrated the consciousness of the lower classes. On 13 November 1844, in an article published in *L'Univers,* Veuillot mentions copies of the novel glued to store windows, and talks about *la canaille* and *la populace* that reads everywhere: "pas une échoppe, pas un cabaret où quelque mauvais drôle ne se pénètre d'une haine bestiale en savourant l'épopée bâtarde dont il a le temps d'apprendre par coeur toutes les feuilles" [not one workshop, not one tavern where some poor scamp does not become permeated with bestial hate while savoring the bastard epic whose pages he has the time to learn by heart].[41] Sainte-Beuve also indicated that Sue had dethroned Balzac and was read by high and low audiences, "dans le salon comme dans l'échoppe" [in the salons as in the workshops].[42] In his book, *Des Jésuites et de quelques engouements littéraires à propos du "Juif errant,"* Victor Joly signaled with indignation that the novel was devoured by *badauds* and *commis-voyageurs,* an especially easy crowd to seduce.[43]

Critics attributed this popular attention to the ascent of a new public with no refined tradition or good taste, and they pointed to the cultural dangers it implied. The unsophisticated readers' demand for the *roman-feuilleton* effectively silenced "real" writers and critics since the latter traditionally occupied the bottom part of the paper before the advent of the serial novel. Now, however, they had to take refuge in literary reviews, sometimes even abroad (as Saint-Beuve in *La Revue Suisse*) or in a few remaining conservative papers that refused to bow to the serial novel folly, as *La Gazette de France,* whence Nettement would, for almost two years, launch his attacks against the *roman-feuilleton.* According to these professional readers, the serial novel, this "sewer of literature," which did not require any serious intellectual effort and which sought the immediate satisfaction of popular demand, led to a lowering of the standards of literary discourse and made the novel a commodity like the newspaper itself.

However, a closer reading of the critics' articles and books reveals that for them the essential problem was not just the cultural danger but above all the moral and political danger inherent in the fact that this *littérature facile* was being consumed by a public that had only recently become a factor in the literary market. The lack of general education and literary tradition made these readers easy prey, incapable of defending themselves from the influence of immoral ideas or views that questioned the existing order and led to social and political anarchy. A commentary by Charles Nisard, director of the *Commission d'examen des livres du colportage* (created in 1852 in order to censure and to control what the people read), explicitly distinguishes between high- and low-culture reception:

> J'estimai . . . que si, dans l'intérêt des personnes faciles à séduire, comme le sont les ouvriers et les habitants des campagnes, la Commission ne devait pas manquer d'interdire le colportage aux trois quarts de ces livres, cette prohibition ne regardait pas les gens à l'épreuve des mauvaises lectures, c'est-à-dire, les érudits, les bibliophiles, les collectionneurs et même simples curieux de littérature excentrique.[44]

> [I have deemed . . . that if, in the interest of easily seducible people like workers and the rural population, the Commission could not help but ban the peddling of three quarters of these books, the prohibition did not concern those impervious to bad books, that is, scholars, bibliophiles, collectors, and even ordinary people interested in eccentric literature.]

As soon as the first pages of *Le Juif errant* were published, the critics signaled the dangers of corrupting the lower classes. Nettement warned that the hatred and disorder provoked by the novel would lead to the destruction of social order.[45] Babou indicated that the seeds of discontent sown among the masses could be disastrous.[46] It is in the reception of these and other professional critics that one can examine the degree to which the *roman-feuilleton* was indeed a lower-class phenomenon, since, during the July Monarchy, these "simple" readers, barely literate and with very little free time, left very few, if any, written traces of their literary or cultural habits. Another powerful and violent indication of the lower classes' wide readership of the *roman-feuilleton,* until 1850 greatly inspired by social romanticism and socialist ideas, was their subsequent realization of the inequalities and divisions along class lines, which manifested itself in the social upheaval of 1848. Without the serial novel—which, often in order to become accessible to the unsophisticated reader, popularized socialist ideas under sensationalist or sentimental plots—the intellectual and political emancipation of the people would not have occurred so soon.[47] According to many critics, Sue was among the most responsible, having shown the masses the legality of insurrection and having encouraged workers to revolt:

> Ainsi, frappant d'abord la société dans sa triple base: la religion, . . . la morale, . . . la famille, . . . M. Eugène Sue achevait son oeuvre en excitant les classes ouvrières à la plus terrible de toutes les guerres, la guerre sociale. . . . Pendant vingt ans, sous toutes les formes, dans tous ses romans, M. Eugène Sue a par degrès inoculé au peuple ces idées, ces calomnies, ces excitations, ces appels à la révolte et à la guerre. Lorsque, le 24 juin 1848, la société eut à se défendre contre la plus formidable des insurrections, que disaient ces malheureux qui l'attaquaient avec un courage inhumain? Ils disaient et pensaient ce qu'avait pensé M. Eugène Sue. Ils mettaient en action ses romans.[48]

> [Thus, striking society at its triple base—religion, morality, and the family—M. Eugène Sue completed his work by inciting the working classes to the most terrible of all wars, social war. For twenty years, bit by bit, in many ways, in all his novels, M. Eugène Sue has inoculated the people with these ideas, these calumnies, these exhortations, these calls to revolt and to war.
>
> When on 24 June 1848, society had to defend itself against the most formidable of all uprisings, what were those poor souls saying who were attacking it with inhuman courage? They were saying and thinking what M. Eugène Sue had been thinking. They were acting out his novels.]

Sue was indeed widely known and respected by the lower classes as was demonstrated by his election in 1850—decided mostly by working-class and bouregois neighborhoods of Paris—to the National Assembly.[49] Twenty years later, during the Paris Commune, yet another generation of workers found inspiration and guidance in Sue's writings, once again published in installments.[50]

Another measure of the far-reaching influence and popularity of the *roman-feuilleton* is revealed in an attempt by the government to silence the newspapers that were publishing the serial novel. The law passed in 1850 to curtail the freedom of the press contained a special amendment, introduced by Representative Riancey, imposing a one-centime stamp on each issue of a newspaper publishing a serial novel. Riancey's goal was to combat the "immoral" literature being spread by the newspapers and to prevent its "subtle poison" from penetrating and demoralizing society and its structures. For some time his measures worked and only well-established newspapers that could afford to pay the price of Riancey's stamp continued to publish the *roman-feuilleton.* Those who could not or did not want to pay it either disappeared from the market (such was the case with many of the cheap *feuilles* that specialized in reprinting serial novels from other newspapers) or resigned themselves to publishing travel journals, old chronicles, and so on.

On the cultural plane, reaction manifested itself in the form of literary awards bestowed by various institutions on works that were highly critical of the literary production of previous years. Also, the disgruntled critics could now regain their place in the newspapers. For instance, in 1849 Sainte-Beuve became a literary critic at *Le Constitutionnel.* His appearance in the newspaper, which not so long ago had been attracting thousands of subscriptions thanks to Sue's *Le Juif errant,* was indeed symbolic. It was in fact the end of the first *âge d'or* of the serial novel. The articles of Sainte-Beuve and others are clearly a revenge for the last years of the July Monarchy when easy literature dominated the readers' market.

However, the effect of the draconian press laws imposed between 1848 and 1852 was that the newspapers had to turn, much more than originally intended, to *frivolité:* society chronicle, gossip, *faits divers* and again the serial novel, which after Riancey's amendment was repealed in 1852, was often the only appealing part of the newspaper.

These circumstances effectively opened the door to the development of the popular press launched on 1 February 1863. Polydore Millaud's *Le Petit Journal,* a five-centime small-format daily, the first modern mass-circulation newspaper, created another revolution in the history of the French press. Its success should be attributed most of all to the existence of the wide reading public that had been formed by the newspaper *romans-feuilletons* published during the July Monarchy. It also benefited from new methods of printing, such as the rotary presses, capable of printing 18,000 copies an hour, which enabled the production of newspapers on a mass scale and at minimal cost.

A fundamental change occurred in the distribution of these large quantities of newspapers: they were now sold not through subscriptions but by individual copy. With this change, the process that began in 1836 seems to have come to a conclusion. The introduction of the "penny press" by Girardin and Dutacq triggered the transformation of the previously political and opinion-shaping press into a material commodity. The paper, however, was still being sold through subscriptions and created or maintained some sense of ownership, of mutual engagement, of belonging to a distinct group of consumers. It was not uncommon for readers to collect copies of the newspaper, or at least to cut out certain parts (like the serial novel) for further use. Now, however, the newspaper would be sold on a daily basis at a very low price. The decision to buy it or not, to read it or not, would be made every morning according to the proposed content of the newspaper, and, once read, the paper would be immediately discarded. A commercial product of limited use, the newspaper had to find new ways and means to make profits.

The distribution network created by Millaud, taking advantage of the significant development of the railroad, enhanced the newspaper's circulation. By the end of the century, in big cities and small villages, there were 18,000 depositories of *Le Petit Journal*[51] from which the newspaper's criers, all 1,200 of them,[52] would take to the streets in search of prospective readers. *Le Petit Journal*'s circulation figures were indeed astounding: in July 1863 it sold "only" 38,000 copies and in 1865 already 259,000.[53] Its example was quickly followed and other *petits journaux,* such as *La Petite Presse* and *Le Petit Moniteur du soir,* appeared on the market, creating a whole new class of readers.

As a nonpolitical daily, *Le Petit Journal* promised in its prospectus a wide range of information for its readers, randomly juxtaposing stock summaries and accounts of court proceedings, news from abroad and theater reviews. Richard Terdiman, in his analysis of *Le Petit Journal*'s prospectus, signals its striking "absence of organic logic."[54] However, he notes that the accumulation of disparate information corresponded to the new manner of distribution by individual copy: "By offering numerous categories of information, however disparate, the chances that one or another of them might correspond to a particular consumer's desire tended to increase. . . . So *Le Petit Journal* was a daily not only by its frequency of publication, but also, for the first time, in its conception of the content by which it sought each day to present itself as uniquely desirable."[55]

The prospectus also proclaimed that because of a general disgust with the *roman-feuilleton,* the newspaper would rather publish short stories. However, noting in 1866 the increase in circulation that occurred after the publication of *La Résurrection de Rocambole* (223 feuilletons), *Le Petit Journal* decided to publish additional original serial novels alongside the *faits divers,* which were, so it seems, more appealing to the new public. Indeed, detailed crime descriptions, which sometimes filled many pages of the paper, could make circulation figures soar. According to Crubellier, *Le Petit Journal's* dramatic retelling of one criminal's murderous activities increased the number of copies by close to 50,000, and these numbers grew proportionally as new corpses were discovered.[56]

The *roman-feuilleton* remained, however, a permanent and necessary feature in most of the new journals. According to Queffélec, *Le Matin,* created in 1884 to compete with the almighty *Petit Journal,* announced initially that it would publish only the *faits divers.* A couple of months later, however, the readers' demands forced it to start a regular publication of the serial novel.[57]

In 1857 Eugène Poitou, a member of the council at the Cour impériale of Angers, in his *Du roman et du théâtre et de leur influence sur les moeurs,* which was given the first prize by the Académie des sciences morales et politiques, offered a dismal appraisal of literary production and its influence on social life:

> Nous avions applaudi pendant quinze ans à l'orgie littéraire; nous avons failli avoir à la suite l'orgie sociale. . . . Notre société a été réveillée en sursaut par une révolution, . . . elle a entrevu l'abîme. . . . Aujourd'hui, nous avons à peu près repris notre sang-froid. De cet accès de fièvre . . . il ne nous reste plus que la honte de nos aberrations, et les remords du mal que nous avons fait ou laissé faire.[58]

> [For fifteen years we had commended a literary orgy; we very nearly had a social orgy as a result. Our society was awakened with a start by a revolution, it saw an abyss. . . . Today, we have almost regained our sangfroid. From this bout of fever, we are left only with the shame of our aberrations and the remorse over the evil that we committed or allowed.

Poitou claimed that a certain part of society, either because of the satiety provoked by the excesses associated with the *roman-feuilleton,* or because revolutionary events made it realize the perils of such literature, stopped reading the serial novel.[59] He acknowledged however that other groups in society still needed and read the serial novel: "Les miettes de ce honteux festin où nous n'avons pas rougi de nous asseoir, elles sont tombées à terre: d'autres aujourd'hui les ramassent et s'en rassasient à leur tour, et n'en seront peut-être pas dégoûtés de si tôt" [The crumbs of this shameful feast at which we sat without blushing have fallen on the ground: today others take their turn picking them up and satisfying their hunger, and maybe they will not tire of this so soon].[60]

Cultural division was an important part of the social polarization that followed the 1848 Revolution. The reception by the public of *Le Juif errant* had demonstrated the existence of strong differences in perception between classes. The "proof" of the political and social danger represented by the *roman-feuilleton* as confirmed by the events of 1848 gave new strength to the accusations against this mode of publication and distribution and further solidified cultural differences. Later, in 1863, the creation of the *petite presse,* a popular press for the masses, contributed even more to the separation of high and low publics. Critics and authors became aware of the differences in writing for the elite as opposed to the lower classes, and between publishing in the popular press as opposed to the *grands journaux*. Such a neat distinction was impossible during the July Monarchy, for the mass press did not yet exist and popular readership was still being formed. Even if *Le Siècle, La Presse* or *Le Constitutionnel* were commercialized, they nevertheless kept a certain balance between *roman-feuilleton, faits divers,* and political or social issues, and they were still oriented primarily toward middle-class readers. However, after 1863, the creation of the mass press (mass produced for the broad mass of unsophisticated readers) separated the popular press from the *grands journaux,* along with their respective publics and the kinds of novels they read. Anne-Marie Thiesse cites a telling anecdote about Jules Mary (1851–1922), one of the most widely read and wealthiest authors of the Third Republic:

> Piqué au vif par une remarque blessante sur sa production littéraire, l'écrivain se serait exclamé: On peut avoir un feuilleton au *Petit Parisien* et un autre au *Temps* ou au *Figaro!*" Déclassant dans le premier cas, parce qu'il est publié par un journal populaire, le roman-feuilleton est valorisant lorsqu'il est accepté par un journal intellectuel ou bourgeois.[61]

> [Hurt to the quick by a cutting comment about his literary production, the writer allegedly exclaimed: "One can have a *feuilleton* in *Le Petit Parisien* and another one in *Le Temps* or *Le Figaro.*" Demeaning in the first case, because published in a popular newspaper, a *roman-feuilleton* can be status-enhancing when it is accepted by an intellectual or bourgeois paper.]

Indeed, the serial novel became increasingly associated with low culture and the popular press, especially during the Third Republic when the press was the most diversified: the *petits journaux* on one end of the spectrum and the literary journals or reviews on the other aimed at highly distinct groups of the reading public.

The *roman-feuilleton* directly changed the press during the July Monarchy first by taking a firm hold of the *rez-de-chaussée* and then by spreading its influence over the entire paper, which in order to satisfy new customers, gradually had to diversify its content and include more eclectic information—to the detriment of the political discussions and commentaries, its unique *raison d'être* before commercialization. Between 1836 and 1863, as a magnet that attracted readers to the newspaper, and after the creation of popular press in 1863, as an attraction that sustained their interest, the *roman-feuilleton* initiated and subsequently accustomed members of lower social classes to a new cultural practice: the daily consumption of information provided by a mass-circulation press.

Notes

1. Irene Collins, "The Government and the Press in France during the Reign of Louis-Philippe," *English Historical Review* 271 (April 1954): 263.

2. Albert Joseph George, *The Development of French Romanticism: The Impact of the Industrial Revolution on Literature* (Syracuse: Syracuse University Press, 1955), 61.

3. See Eugène Hatin, *Histoire politique et littéraire de la presse en France* (Paris: Poulet-Malassis, 1861), 8:570.

4. See Lise Queffélec, *Le roman-feuilleton français au XIXe siècle,* Que sais-je? no. 2466 (Paris: Presses Universitaires de France, 1989), 76.

5. George, *The Development of French Romanticism,* 59.

6. For a detailed presentation of those cultural changes see Maurice Crubellier, *L'Histoire culturelle de la France* (Paris: Armand Colin, 1974).

7. See James Smith Allen, *In the Public Eye: A History of Reading in Modern France, 1800–1940* (Princeton: Princeton University Press, 1991), Appendix, table A5.

8. Ibid. 56.

9. See Claude Pichois, "Les cabinets de lecture à Paris durant la première moitié du XIXe siècle," *Annales* 3 (1959): 521–34.

10. Article quoted by Harry Alis in "Le Roman-feuilleton," *Le Livre du centenaire du Journal des Débats, 1789–1889* (Paris: Plon, 1889), 519.

11. "Et l'on peut légitimement se demander si la partie proprement de polémique politique des grands quotidiens parisiens n'intéressa pas, dans cette période 1840–1848, que des lecteurs capables de porter attention à des textes souvent atténués." J.-P. Aguet, "Le tirage des quotidiens de Paris sous la Monarchie de Juillet," *Revue Suisse d'Histoire* 10 (1960): 216–86.

12. Lucienne Frappier-Mazur, "Publishing Novels," *A New History of French Litera-*

ture, Denis Hollier, ed. (Cambridge, Mass., and London: Harvard University Press, 1989), 693–98; quotation on 696.

13. In 1836 *Le Siècle* had about 11,000 subscribers; 33,666 in 1840; and 34,966 in 1845. During the same time period, *La Presse*'s subscribers numbered 10,000, 10,106, and 22,409 respectively. See Charles Ledré, *La presse à l'assaut de la monarchie. 1815–1848* (Paris: Armand Colin, 1960), 244.

14. Collins, "The Government and the Press in France during the Reign of Louis-Philippe," 267.

15. See *Le Constitutionnel,* 9 August 1844.

16. See *Le Constitutionnel,* 19 January 1845.

17. Ledré, *La presse à l'assaut de la monarchie, 1815–1848,* 245.

18. See Claude Bellanger, Jacques Godechot, Pierre Guiral, and Fernand Terrou, *Histoire générale de la presse française,* vol. 2, *De 1815 à 1871* (Paris: Presses Universitaires de France, 1969), 127.

19. For an account of the novel's enthusiastic reception see, for example, Jean-Louis Bory, *Eugène Sue: Le roi du roman populaire* (Paris: Hachette, 1962), 269–97.

20. See René Guise, "Le Roman-feuilleton et la vulgarisation des idées politiques et sociales sous la Monarchie de Juillet, *Romantisme et politique 1815–1851. Colloque de l'Ecole Normale Supérieure de Saint-Cloud (1966)* (Paris: Armand Colin, 1969), 316–28, especially 319.

21. "On se plaint aussi généralement qu'il y ait des détails trop libres pour un journal qui doit être lu par tout le monde et traîner partout." René Guise, "Balzac et le roman feuilleton," *L'année balzacienne* (1964): 283–338, quotation from 292.

22. "Il nous vient de si nombreuses réclamations contre le choix du sujet et la liberté de certaines descriptions que le gérant de *La Presse* demande à l'auteur de la *Vieille Fille* de choisir un autre sujet que celui de *La Torpille.*" Ibid. 292.

23. I am indebted to Jeannene Przyblyski for pointing out this relation to me.

24. See Guise, "Balzac," 300.

25. Daniel Couégnas, *Introduction à la paralittérature* (Paris: Seuil, 1992).

26. *La Gazette des Tribunaux* of 29 February 1844 gives a detailed report of the trial.

27. *Un Anglais à Paris. Notes et souvenirs,* J. Hercé, trans., 3d ed. (Paris: Plon, 1893), 81.

28. Hatin, *Histoire politique et littéraire de la presse en France,* 8:587.

29. Marion Mouchot, "*Le Constitutionnel:* Contribution à l'histoire de la presse sous la Restauration," Ph.D. diss., Ecole Nationale des Chartes, 1968, 19.

30. Hatin, *Histoire,* 588.

31. *Gazette des Tribunaux,* 29 February 1844.

32. Mouchot, "*Le Constitutionnel,*" 241.

33. The newspaper's revenues from advertisements grew considerably: from 172,505 francs in 1848, to 205,200 in 1844–45, and to 300,000 in 1846–47. See Bellanger et al., *Histoire générale de la presse française,* 2:122.

34. The *Bibliothèque choisie* was to be printed on pages 3 and 4, in addition to pages 1 and 2 on which the paper would print a *feuilleton,* be it a novel, literary review, chronicle of Paris, etc.

35. "Mais surtout, et partout, cette *Pâte pectorale de Regnauld aîné* qui, jusqu'à la fin du siècle, multipliera sa publicité dans les journaux les plus divers." Marcel Galliot, *La publicité à travers les âges* (Paris: Editions hommes et techniques, 1955), 95.

36. *Un Anglais à Paris,* 86.

37. Alfred Nettement, *Etudes critiques sur le feuilleton-roman* (Paris: Lagny Frères, 1845), 1:60–61.

38. See, for example, Jules Michelet and Edgar Quinet, *Des Jésuites* (Utrecht: J. J. Pauvert. Libertés 35, 1966) or Alain Guillermou, *Saint-Ignace de Loyola et la Compagnie de Jésus* (Paris: Presses Universitaires de France, 1960).

39. The Catalogue des imprimés of the Bibliothèque Nationale cites twelve known editions of *Le Juif errant* from 1844 to 1852. It does not, however, include cheap editions or *contrefaçons belges.*

40. For a further explanation of these numbers see Maria Adamowicz-Hariasz, "*Le Juif errant* d'Eugène Sue. Poétique et politique d'un roman populaire," Ph.D. diss., University of Pennsylvania, 1994, or Pierre Orecchioni, "Eugène Sue: Mesure d'un succès," *Europe* 643–44 (1982): 157–66.

41. See *L'Univers,* 13 November 1844. See also Edgar Knecht, *Le mythe du Juif errant: Essai de mythologie littéraire et de sociologie religieuse* (Grenoble: Presses Universitaires, 1977), 245. Knecht quotes another fragment of the same article.

42. Charles Auguste Saint-Beuve, "M. Eugène Sue," *Portraits contemporains* (Paris: Didier, 1847) 2:69–92.

43. Vincent dit Victor Joly, *Des Jésuites et de quelques engouements littéraires à propos du Juif errant* (Bruxelles: E. Landoy, 1846).

44. Charles Nisard, *Histoire des livres populaires ou de la littérature du colportage depuis le XVe siècle jusqu'à l'établissement de la Commission d'examen des livres du colportage (30 novembre 1852)* (Paris: Librairie d'Amyot, 1854), 1:iv.

45. Nettement, *Etudes critiques sur le feuilleton-roman,* 2:53.

46. *La Revue de Paris,* 17 September 1844.

47. "Le roman-feuilleton a permis, en contribuant à l'instruction du peuple, en vulgarisant les idées politiques et sociales, cette prise de conscience fondamentale . . . qui n'est pas sans effet pratique. La Révolution de février 1848 est là pour l'attester." Guise, "Le Roman-feuilleton et la vulgarisation des idées politiques et sociales sous la Monarchie de Juillet," 327.

48. Charles Menche de Loisne, *Influence de la littérature de 1830 à 1850 sur l'esprit public et les moeurs* (Paris: Garnier Frères, 1852), 318–19.

49. See Bory, *Eugène Sue,* chapter 6 for the dramatic account of the election.

50. During and immediately after the revolutionary events, the *rez-de-chaussée* of the

dailies was suspended in favor of information and political discussions. However, "une exception vis-à-vis de l'attitude hostile aux publications littéraires se trouve dans le *Journal Officiel de la République Française,* c'est-à-dire l'organe officiel de la Commune dans son édition à bon marché. . . . C'est ici que paraît en mars et avril 1871 un texte d'Eugène Sue, inédit en France: *Jeanne et Louise ou Histoire d'une famille de transportés,* dans lequel le romancier dénonce la persécution des républicains après le coup d'état du 2 décembre 1851. Cette publication démontre le prestige extraordinaire de Sue considéré comme le feuilletonniste de gauche le plus important." Klaus-Peter Walter, "Le Roman-feuilleton et la révolution de 1848 et 1871," *Richesses du roman populaire. Actes du colloque international de Pont-à-Mousson, Octobre 1983,* René Guise and Hans-Jorg Neuschäfer, eds. (Nancy: Centre de recherches sur le roman populaire, 1986), 57.

51. See Queffélec, *Le Roman-feuilleton français au XIXe siècle,* 58.

52. See Theodore Zeldin, *France 1848–1945: Intellect, Taste and Anxiety* (Oxford: Clarendon Press, 1977), 526.

53. See Ballanger et al., *Histoire générale de la presse française,* 2:327.

54. Richard Terdiman, *Discourse / Counter-Discourse. The Theory and Practice of Symbolic Resistance in Nineteenth-Century France* (Ithaca and London: Cornell University Press, 1985), 133.

55. Ibid. 133–34.

56. Crubellier, *L'Histoire culturelle de la France,* 177.

57. See Queffélec, *Le Roman-feuilleton français au XIXe siècle,* 78.

58. Eugène Poitou, *Du roman et du théâtre contemporains et de leurs influence sur les moeurs* (Paris: Auguste Durand, 1857), 314.

59. "[L]a portion éclairée du public ne lit plus ces grands romans en dix ou vingt volumes." Ibid. 315.

60. Ibid. 316–17.

61. Anne-Marie Thiesse, *Le Roman du quotidien. Lecteurs et lectures populaires à la Belle Epoque* (Paris: Le Chemin vert, 1984), 85.

6 Linking Producers to Consumers

Balzac's "Grande Affaire" and the Dynamics of Literary Diffusion

Habent sua fata libelli [Books have their own destiny].
— *Terentianus Maurus*

In the economy of the psyche, the mass article appears as an obsessive idea.
— *Walter Benjamin,* Gesammelte Schriften

W hat is the fate of the text? What factors permit, control, or disrupt the production and dissemination of texts, particularly literary ones? In the early nineteenth century, these questions became particularly relevant and urgent because the printed word, especially the book, "était devenu production industrielle avant d'avoir conquis un marché de masse" [had become an industrial product before having conquered a mass market] (Parent-Lardeur, 1981, 98). (Unless otherwise noted, all translations in this chapter are my own.) This contradiction between the mode of production and the mode of distribution found an uneasy dialectical resolution when Emile de Girardin founded *La Presse* in 1836 and inaugurated the serial novel or *roman-feuilleton*. Yet this contradiction was also experienced, if not lived, by Honoré de Balzac, who—despite the fact that his *La Vieille Fille* (1836) was the first French serialized novel published in France—remained convinced that the ultimate "value" or glorious "destiny" of his literary writings required a system of production and distribution superior to the one dominant in his time. This essay describes how Balzac cobbled together his own resolutions to the crisis in the book trade, concentrating on the strategies he employed—including his Société d'abonnement général, a prototype of the Book-of-the-Month Club—to reconceptualize and restructure the reading (consuming) practices and habits of those he called "la masse lisante."[1] Following Walter Benjamin's observation, we shall read Balzac's "obsession" with the "mass article" through his polemical, reformist, and literary texts, focusing primarily (but not exclusively) on those written in the early 1830s.[2]

The contradictions inherent in the developing industrialization of the book market were obvious to Balzac, who nostalgically recalled the situation of writers in the *ancien régime*, when the benevolence of a secular paternalistic presence guaranteed both their livelihood and their readership. After the Revolution, the situation of the writer changed dramatically; as Balzac puts it in an 1841 address to a government commission on literary property:

> Tout grand prince, dans les époques antérieures aussi bien que de nos jours, a regardé comme une des obligations de la couronne de protéger et les écrivains et les lettres. Je suis fâché de dire que cette protection active, sérieuse, matérielle manque aux classes lettrées, et qu'elles souffrent beaucoup de leur alliance nécessaire avec la Presse périodique. (Balzac 1956c, 723–24)[3]

> [Every great prince, from earlier times to the present day, considered the protection of writers and literature one of the obligations of the crown. I am sorry to say that this active, committed financial support is no longer available to the literary classes, and that they are suffering greatly from their imposed alliance with the periodic press.]

In order to improve what he calls "la propagation" (ibid. 724) of the published work, which previously was ensured by the "glory" of the sponsor, Balzac devoted much time and energy to defining and defending the notion of intellectual property, and he attempted to implement innovative reforms in the inefficient and unfair bookseller's trade, in order to improve both the lot of the writer and the "fate" of the literary text within the market system. The problem, as Balzac lamented, resided in the failure to resolve the contradictions inherent in the industrial market: "il n'y a aucune analogie entre la production et la consommation [de la littérature]" [there is no analogy whatsoever between the production and the consumption (of literature)].[4] The complex organization of the book trade did not solve, but perpetuated, this basic contradiction at all levels of exchange, such that there was "aucune correspondance entre l'offre et les besoins, entre les besoins et la demande, entre les prix et le pouvoir d'achat, entre le tirage et la vente, entre la vente et le nombre réel de lecteurs" [no relation whatsoever between supply and demand, between need and demand, between prices and buying power, between print-run and sales, between sales and the actual number of readers] (Chollet 1975, 154).

The difficulty of comprehending the anarchic and contradictory nature of emergent capitalist exchange is characteristic of the nineteenth century, and Friedrich Engels was no stranger to this phenomenon. As he writes in his

Origin of the Family, Private Property, and the State: "The more a social activity, a series of social processes, becomes too powerful for conscious human control, grows beyond human reach, the more it seems to have been left to pure chance, the more do its peculiar and innate laws assert themselves in this chance, as if by natural necessity. Such laws also control the fortuities of the production and exchange of commodities; these laws confront the individual producer and exchanger as strange and, in the beginning, even as unknown powers" (Engels [1884] 1972, 163). The mode of production, exchange, and distribution characteristic of capitalism forsakes or overrides the paternalistic presence of a guarantor, be it God, the muse, the prince, or even the reader and author, and the text becomes a thing, a commodity whose "fate" depends upon "economic fortuities." In short, literary texts acquired a dynamic whose "innate laws" appeared "strange" to Balzac. Indeed, the incorporative structure of *La Comédie humaine* can be understood as an attempt to reclaim and control the fortuitous economic peregrinations of his individual works, which had become "alienated" in their original appearance in the periodic press.

In order to counter this alienation in the meantime, Balzac needed a notion of literary production that would ground this process in nonmarket or metamarket terms. In 1834 he boasted that literary works are "propriété sacrée" whose value is "indépendant et du sol et des transactions sociales" [beyond soil and social transactions] (Balzac 1956b, 224). In 1841, his defense of the "rights of genius" borrowed its metaphors from classical mythology, in particular the voyage to the underworld: "Entre concevoir et produire, il est un abîme, et le génie seul a des ailes pour y descendre et en sortir, tenant à la main des fleurs immortelles" [There is an abyss between conception and production, and only the author's genius has the winged ability to descend into it and to emerge clutching immortal flowers] (Balzac 1956c). Despite its Orphic undertones, Balzac's mythology of the creative act is Promethean, since these "fleurs immortelles" are to be offered to mankind as a sacred gift bestowed on present and future generations. This conception of the "rights of genius" goes hand in hand with Balzac's lifelong attempts to find and increase the size of the readership, that is, the market, for his works. Balzac's conviction that a literary work is an "offrande écrite" [written offering] (1956b, 232) whose destiny is immortality permitted him to critique the system of production and distribution dominant in his time from a coherent, albeit grandiose, vantage point.

As he was all too aware, the literary marketplace in the early nineteenth century was based on a system of distribution largely unsuited to the full diffusion of the products of the author's labor, primarily on account of its reliance on meddlesome intermediaries. These intermediaries, as we will see, were the "libraires-commissionnaires," who bought books in quantity from the publishers and sold them to bookstores and the popular "cabinets de lecture" or reading rooms where books and magazines could be "rented." The periodic press, despite its greater efficiency at the level of distribution, fragmented the author's work at the level of production and dispensed these fragments piece by piece into the realm of alienated consumption and thus can be considered another intermediary. To this situation, Balzac opposed his belief in the private and privileged nature of literary communication, which underlies his fetishism for the book and ultimately the synthesizing strategy of the *Comédie humaine* itself. His entry into the world of the periodic press involved more than desperate financial need: he hoped to further diffuse his writings and augment his readership in ways the book trade could not or would not provide. Roland Chollet captures the motives behind this decision, what he calls "le grand tournant de 1830," when he says that from this point on, "Balzac . . . n'accordera plus jamais à la librairie, qui s'est montrée si inférieure à sa mission, le privilège exclusif de diffuser ses oeuvres" [Balzac . . . will never again grant the booksellers, who proved incapable of accomplishing their mission, the exclusive privilege of distributing his works] (Chollet 1971, 60).[5]

Balzac always remained very attached to the format of the printed book; and it was the book trade, more than the nature or practices of the periodic press, that especially aroused his ire. Convinced that the economic relations between novelist, publisher, and reader should be as direct as possible, Balzac, in a series of texts written from 1830 to 1841, pointed the finger at three disruptive practices: "l'exhérédation" ("disinheritance," the practice of not extending publication rights to the author's family), the "libraires-commissionnaires," and the "cabinet de lecture." Perhaps because Balzac would never come to believe that the periodic press was in a position to offer a solution to these problems, his "grand tournant" was accompanied by attempts to reform the book trade by applying to it practices already in use in the *feuilleton* industry as well as in the "cabinets de lecture." For this reason, Balzac's proposed solutions to the anarchy of the book trade, and in particular his Société d'abonnement général must be situated in the context of reading practices prevalent in his time. These practices had everything to do with money and its Other, credit.

One of the biggest differences between the book industry and the periodic press, Balzac realized, was starkly pecuniary: novelists were "paid" in notes that could not be cashed for months, if not years, whereas journalists were paid immediately in cash. After meeting Emile de Girardin in 1829,

Balzac began publishing, in four journals (*Le Voleur, La Mode, Feuilleton des journaux politiques, La Silhouette*),[6] what would amount to about sixty articles by July 1830. Among these were many of his short stories, which would later be incorporated into *La Comédie humaine*. These *contes et nouvelles* served as a buffer between the two realms of the novel and the periodical, and eventually allowed him, beginning in 1831, to double his pay by prepublishing them in the feuilletons then releasing them in book format. Among these articles is the first of many he devoted to the crisis in the book publishing industry, and possible solutions to it.

In "De L'État actuel de la librairie," Balzac describes how the publishing industry of the early 1830s was actually composed of a complex series of intermediary structures that combined to inflate the eventual price of the book to a level unacceptable to the general public:

> Les libraires sont divisés en trois classes: (1) les libraires-éditeurs qui achètent les manuscrits, ou réimpriment les anciens auteurs, et les confectionnent en livres; (2) les libraires-commissionnaires et de détail, auxquels les premiers livrent des parties considérables d'éditions; (3) les libraires de province qui se mettent en communication avec l'acheteur. Nous ne parlons pas des bouquinistes ou étalagistes, qui paient des livres comptant, et vendent de meme. Cette absurde hierarchie, qui a pour but de faire payer trois impôts à un livre, avant qu'il ne parvienne au public, est la cause de tous les malheurs de ce déplorable commerce. (*Feuilleton des journaux politiques,* 3 and 10 March 1830; reprinted in *L'Universel,* 22 and 23 March 1830, and in 1956d, 547)

> [The booksellers are divided into three groups: 1) the publishers who buy the manuscripts or reissue the works of dead authors and print them; 2) the salesmen working on commission, to whom the first party delivers most of the books; 3) the provincial booksellers who are in direct contact with the buyer. We will not mention the secondhand booksellers or stall-keepers who buy and sell books for cash. This absurd hierarchy, whose goal is to have all three pay taxes on one book before it reaches the public, is the cause of all the misfortunes of this deplorable trade.]

A shortage of cash, combined with high interest rates on borrowing, often led the "libraires-éditeurs" to sell most of their stock to the "libraires-commissionnaires" at a sizable discount, sometimes for cash but often on deferred payment; like authors, printers, too, were often "paid" in long-term "billets d'échéance." It was the "libraire-commissionnaire" who actually distributed the books to provincial markets, often with the help of the "colpor-

teur," the traveling salesman of the literary market, who sold books (generally to "gens de province") and received a percentage of each sale. It was, of
course, the consumer who ultimately paid for this percentage. Like his
counterpart the "libraire-commissionnaire," the "colporteur" disrupted the
triangular relationship linking author, editor, and public and rendered the
book unaffordable for many. Balzac's solution was to do away with such
middlemen, and when it was his turn to edit four issues of the *Feuilleton,* he
offered a 25 percent rebate to readers willing to buy a book directly from a
"libraire-éditeur," the only middleman being himself. Although this strategy
failed to catch on, and the *Feuilleton des journaux politiques* folded a few months
later, Balzac was already attempting to bring the dynamics of the periodic
press to the rescue of the book industry.

Whereas others argued that the problem with the book trade resulted
from overproduction and they sought to rein in the number of "libraires-
éditeurs," Balzac repeatedly affirmed that there existed even (and, he would
add, especially) in rural areas a strong demand for reading material at the
right price. His "Préface de la première partie [des *Illusions perdues*]" of 1837,
concludes by apologizing for the slowness of his composition, and contrasts
his patience and perseverence as a writer with the impatience of a public
indifferent to the "grande mais difficile tâche" of the author: "[le public] veut
ses livres, sans s'inquieter de la manière dont ils se produisent" [(the public)
wants its books and does not care how they are produced] (Balzac 1976,
5:112). Confronted with a surplus of books priced too high to sell, many
printers and publishing houses blamed the trade deregulations inaugurated
in the aftermath of the Revolution, and called for restrictive trade laws (such
as limiting the number of "brevets de libraire" awarded) and production
caps (Chollet 1971, 66–67). Instead of blaming overproduction, however,
Balzac ascribed the book industry's difficulties to underconsumption and
argued that the reading public's demand for books was actually insatiable,
though poorly understood and addressed. As he stated in the opening para-
graphs of his "Acte préliminaire de la Société d'abonnement général (1830)":

> La publication des romans nouveaux, des ouvrages historiques et des
> voyages constitue, dans le commerce de la librairie, une exploitation spé-
> ciale. Le goût et les besoins du public rendent toujours nécessaires ces
> sortes de productions. Leurs [*sic*] bénéfices commerciaux qu'ils sont sus-
> ceptibles de donner procèdent d'une source intarissable. . . . Or, si l'on
> compare la cherté des livres à la rapidité de la lecture et à la nécessité de
> renouveller souvent les plaisirs qu'elle procure, et qui ont créé un besoin
> nouveau par suite de la propagation des lumières, et du nombre de lec-

teurs qui augmente annuellement, il est facile de découvrir un vice capital dans le monde actuel de l'exploitation de cette branche du commerce de la librairie; car il n'y a plus aucune analogie entre la production et la consommation. (Chollet 1971, 88–89)

[The publication of new novels, of historical works, and of travel narratives is of particular importance to the book trade. The taste and the needs of the public always make such productions necessary. Their [*sic*] profits they could yield arise from an inextinguishable source. . . . However, if one compares the high price of books to the rapidity of reading and the frequent need to renew the pleasures that reading procures, and which have created a new demand resulting from the spread of literacy and from the increasing number of readers annually, it is easy to discover a capital vice in the present state of the bookselling trade: for there is no longer any analogy between production and consumption.]

Balzac's proposed solution to this dilemma was to attempt to organize what he and his collaborators called the Société d'abonnement général, which Chollet and Parent-Lardeur consider the first "Book-of-the-Month Club." The goal of this Société was to place at the disposal of the public low-cost editions mailed directly from the publisher, available on a subscription basis, and free from the additional expenses tacked on by intermediaries. With equal prescience, Balzac also proposed that the author receive a percentage based on the number of books sold and not, as was the practice then, on the number of books printed. The trick, of course, was to enroll a significant number of subscribers; Balzac thought the plan would require that at least one thousand readers agree to receive four volumes every other week, for a yearly total of ninety-six, for a fee equivalent to a year's subscription to a single periodical. This project, which he referred to only as his "grande affaire" in his correspondence, was never realized, but is described in detail in two texts unearthed by Roland Chollet: the "Acte préliminaire de la Société d'abonnement général" (1830) and the "Acte de société de 1833."

Balzac was well aware that most readers of his time obtained, or rather rented, books from "cabinets littéraires." According to his estimation, there existed in all of France about fifteen hundred of these nineteenth-century versions of today's video-rental stores (Chollet 1971, 94); in his "Lettre aux écrivains français" (1834), he pities the "pauvre libraire français [qui] vend à grand peine un de vos livres à un millier de misérables cabinets littéraires, qui tuent notre littérature" [the poor French bookseller (who) sells with great difficulty one of your books to a thousand contemptible reading rooms that are killing our literature] (228). These "cabinets littéraires" or "cabinets de lecture" were often poorly stocked, especially outside of Paris: on the one hand, their managers (licensed by the state) were often unwilling to invest in a book they did not think would prove popular; and on the other, a book that proved popular would rarely be available on the shelves. This same dilemma confronted the periodic press, since the "cabinets" had to subscribe (invest) in new periodicals of unknown popularity in order to receive them, whereas books, at least, could be obtained on credit. The words of the well-read Mme de Cosmelly to the deflated poet Samuel Cramer, the antihero of Baudelaire's *La Fanfarlo*, would surely sound familiar to earlier authors: "Le maître de mon cabinet de lecture dit qu'il ne vous connaît pas" ["The proprietor of my reading room says that he does not know you"] (Baudelaire 1975, 1:558). What is more important, Balzac objected to the whole notion of "renting" books, and to the effects of this business on the literary marketplace: fewer books sold to individuals, hence smaller print runs averaging about a thousand; the expressed preference on the part of "cabinet" owners for sturdy, expensive, oversized multivolume formats that could withstand frequent use;[7] and needless to say, the fact that not even a fraction of the rental fees, which were charged by the volume and even by the hour, were set aside for the publisher or the author.

In a tirade worth quoting at length, Balzac bitterly adumbrates the disruptions such a mode of distribution created for the reading public:

En France, messieurs, dans ce beau pays où les femmes sont élégantes et gracieuses comme elles ne sont nulle part, la plus jolie femme attend patiemment, pour lire Eugène Sue, Nodier, Gozlan, Janin, V. Hugo, G. Sand, Mérimée, que la modiste ait lu le volume en compagnie, le soir, dans son lit; que la femme d'un charcutier ait achevé le dénouement et l'ait graissé, que l'étudiant y ait laissé son parfum de pipe, y ait cloués ses observations lascives ou bouffonnes. En France, un livre, le livre où l'auteur a mis une offrande écrite, se promène dans les alentours d'une famille. Oui, c'est à qui se soustraira même à l'impôt des deux sous du cabinet littéraire. "Prêtez-moi Notre-Dame, envoyez-moi Jacques!" sont dits par des gens riches dont la voiture passerait au besoin sur le corps d'un mendiant qui veut deux sous pour une roquille, sa littérature à lui. . . . [I]l n'est pas encore admis qu'on envoie douze francs à un libraire pour lire à son aise, dans un livre propre et vierge, l'œuvre nouvelle la plus intéressante qui donne quelques journées de lecture ou quelques heures de méditation. . . . Aristocratie, vous êtes morte: l'égalité triomphe; la duchesse attend que sa couturière ait lu *La Salamandre* avant de la lire. . . . Il est des villes où la *Revue de Paris* de janvier est lue en décembre. Des femmes élégantes éternuent au milieu des *Feuilles d'automne,* par le fait d'un bourgeois qui a laissé couler du tabac en tournant un feuillet. Qui de nous n'a pas entendu dire à des millionnaires: "Je ne puis avoir tel livre, il est toujours en lecture!" (Balzac 1956b, 232–33)

[In France, my dear sirs, in this lovely country where the women are gracious and elegant beyond compare, the prettiest among them who wishes to read Eugène Sue, Nodier, Gozlan, Janin, V. Hugo, G. Sand, or Mérimée, must wait until the milliner has read the volume with a friend, at night, in her bed; until the pork butcher's wife has reached the end and smeared grease on it; until the student has left the smell of his pipe in it, after inserting his lascivious or clownish observations. In France, a book, the book where the author has placed his written offering, is haphazardly passed from one family member to another. Yes, it has even come to the point where people try to avoid paying the two bits charged by the reading rooms. "Lend me Notre-Dame, send me Jacques!" utter rich people whose carriage would drive over the body of a beggar if need be, a beggar who wants two bits for a cup of wine, his only literature. . . . (I)t is not yet recognized that one could send twelve francs to a bookseller in order to read at one's leisure, in a clean and virginal book, the most interesting new work providing several days of reading or a few hours of meditation. . . . Aristocracy, you are dead: egalitarianism triumphs; the duchess waits until her seamstress has finished *La Salamandre* before reading it herself. . . . There are some towns where January's *Revue de Paris* is read in December. Elegant women sneeze in the middle of the *Feuilles d'automne* because a bourgeois spilled some tobacco while turning the page. Who among us has not heard millionaires exclaim: "I can never obtain this book, it is always signed out!"]

The egalitarian[8] reading practices forced upon patrons of the "cabinet de lecture" are unworthy of the sacred nature of the author's "written offering," which is intended to be personally presented to and treasured by the individual, not consumed en masse by other readers—or even family members. Since the whole point of Balzac's "grande affaire" is, as he states in "L'Acte de société de 1833," to find "un moyen quelconque de faire arriver l'ouvrage produit entre les mains des consommateurs" [some way to bring the written product into the hands of consumers] (in Chollet 1975, 164) as directly and as quickly as possible after publication, he is clearly opposed to middlemen such as the "libraires-commissionnaires" and, presumably, the "cabinets de lecture." However, he carefully insists that the alternative, his Société d'abonnement général will in no way detract from the business of existing "cabinets" because his readership will consist of those who do not frequent them to begin with: "des personnes ou trop riches pour se soumettre à l'insuffisance des livres loués par les cabinets littéraires, . . . ou des personnes trop éloignées des chefs-lieux où se trouvent des cabinets" [people who are either too rich to put up with the paucity of books available for rent in the reading rooms, . . . or those too far removed from the larger towns where these reading rooms are located] ("Acte préliminaire," in Chollet 1971, 94). If it is objected that since these people are not reading now, there is no reason for them to begin, the author of *Scènes de la vie de province* continues:

> L'observation la plus superficielle des mœurs provinciales révèle qu'il existe une masse considérable de propriétaires habitant la campagne même pendant l'hiver, auxquels il manque entièrement des sujets d'amusement et de distraction. Ainsi la compagnie qui se formerait créerait plutot des débouchés nouveaux et réveillerait plutôt des besoins non satisfaits qu'elle ne s'addresserait aux consommateurs actuels. (Ibid. 94)

> [The most superficial observation of provincial customs reveals that there exists a considerable number of landowners dwelling in the country even during the winter who are entirely lacking in activities providing fun and distraction. Instead of addressing the needs of current customers, the proposed company will create new outlets and will awaken unsatisfied needs.]

His plan, then, involves more than a reconfiguration of the marketing and distribution of books; it also seeks to redefine the way people read them, treat them, and feel about them. To be sure, the "cabinet," along with the periodic press, played an important role in sensitizing the reader by encouraging him or her to read regularly, if not daily. What Balzac sought to tap (or create) was a personal, private, and fetishistic relationship linking the individual reader to the literary artifact. When he invites us (actually, fellow and potential investors, since this text was not intended for publication) to consider, as favoring his enterprise, "le nombre des lecteurs, qui, même dans les villes populeuses, préférera, pour un prix presqu'égal à l'abonnement des cabinets de lecture, recevoir des livres directement et les conserver" [the number of readers who, even in big cities, would prefer to receive books directly and keep them for a price almost equal to the subscription price of a reading room] ("Acte préliminaire," in Chollet 1971, 95); or when he praises the "livre propre et vierge," to be read "à son aise" (Balzac 1956b, 233) without worrying about due dates and fines, he is affirming the reader's equivalent to the author's right to his "propriété littéraire."

Beginning with his "Lettre aux écrivains francais" (1834), Balzac attacked legislation dating from 1791 and 1793 (and still in effect in his time) that disallowed authors to pass on the rights to their literary works to their inheritors ("l'exhérédation") and that defined literary property as public property. It stands to reason that if members of the reading public are accustomed to books that reach them indirectly, bearing the traces and even the smells of previous readers, it will be difficult to convince this same public that these books emanate not from the public domain but directly from an author who conveys them to his or her readers: for if a reader can't own ("conserver") a book, how can an author? The fetishized "livre propre et vierge" is Balzac's solution to the contradiction between the sacred, personal offering of the book and the transient, soiled, and "used" mass article.

Balzac's Société d'abonnement général is perhaps best understood as an attempt to reconcile the subscription-based mode of distribution characteristic of the periodic press with the sense of permanence arising from the long-term physical possession of a fetishized object. This sense of permanence is essential to Balzac's argument against "l'exhéreditation," since books don't acquire their true "value" for years:

> La propriété littéraire ne devient fructueuse que dans un temps déterminé. Tout livre, dans sa première édition, est à l'état de semailles. Le soleil du succès ne fait pas toujours mûrir la moisson du vivant de l'auteur, malgré la vigueur des moyens créés par la publicité moderne. (Balzac 1956c, 726)

> [Literary property does not become profitable until a certain amount of time has passed. Any book, at its first printing, is still in a germinative stage. The sunlight of success does not always cause the harvest to ripen during the author's lifetime, despite the vigorous means employed by modern advertising.]

The literary periodic press was in no position to guarantee that such an accretion of value would take place. Pursuing the same agricultural metaphor, during the very time he was trying to establish his Société, Balzac, in what Chollet considers the harshest words he ever directed at literary journalism, compares the latter to a bottomless pit into which writers

> jettent en holocauste au fantôme de la civilisation, sous prétexte d'éclairer les masses, de leur nature peu perméables à la lumière, et des ouvrages en germe, fruits précoces, et des pages remarquables, fruits mûrs, oubliés tous, et qui tous eussent donné plus que de la gloire en viager à leurs auteurs. (*La Quotidienne*, 22 August 1833, in Chollet 1975, 157)

[sacrifice to the ghost of civilization (under the pretext of enlightening the masses, who are rather impermeable to light) both immature works (precocious fruits) and remarkable pages (ripened fruit), all of them forgotten, despite the fact that they all would have granted more than a lifetime of glory to their authors.]

The purpose of this agricultural metaphor was to emphasize the disparity between the temporality particular to the success of the novel and the temporality characteristic of the periodic press. First, the content (if not the very existence) of the feuilletons was necessarily transitory and ephemeral because writers and publishers were subject to shifting political and financial allegiances (see *Illusions perdues*); this is why Balzac explicitly prohibits the publication, by the Société, of "aucun ouvrage ayant une tendance politique" [any work tending toward the political] ("Acte de société de 1833," in Chollet 1975, 169). Second, because the periodic format is dependent on rapid production and consumption, individual issues become outdated quickly: no one, as we have seen him suggest, wants to read January's *Revue de Paris* in December. For this reason, Balzac planned to publish low-cost yet durable editions belonging to three traditional genres: "des romans nouveaux [i.e., in the private domain], des mémoires historiques, des relations de voyages" (ibid. 163). Specifically, there is little doubt that Balzac planned to use the Société to publish and distribute his own works, since he alone would be in charge of the "choix des manuscrits et de la confection des ouvrages" [the choice of manuscripts and the production of books] (ibid. 169), and furthermore because, as Chollet points out, Article 16 would have allowed Balzac "Directeur" to use the society's funds to purchase manuscripts from Balzac "auteur" (ibid. 161). This circular and internal economy prefigures the narrative structure of *La Comédie humaine,* where a totalizing metanarrator collects, organizes, and subsumes the productions of particular novelistic narrators.

Balzac's attempt to unite the book trade with the periodic press thus required him to adopt for himself the role of the "maître littéraire" of the "cabinet de lecture," and to an extent his planned Société was a privatized version thereof. Yet the key to Balzac's plan was the subscription format, which bypassed the "libraires-commissionnaires" in addition to supplying immediate cash. He saw that the solution to the crisis in the book trade lay not in an association of sellers and distributors—which was clearly the problem in the first place—but rather in an association of readers, a sort of "buyer's collective" along the lines of a modern co-op. Such associations of readers' or subscribers' collectives had already been formed during the *Res-*

tauration: groups of readers—often members of a *salon littéraire*—would pool their money to obtain one subscription to a periodical (particularly the *Constitutionnel*) and would share each issue.[9]

Balzac proposed adapting and applying the dynamics of the periodic press to the distribution of the novel; Girardin, for his part, favored adapting the format of the novel to suit the dynamics of the periodic press. Although Girardin's position won in the short term, Balzac's plans would become realized much later, although no one gives him credit for it. Two studies (Lee 1958; Rubin 1992) devoted to the history of the American Book-of-the-Month Club, for instance, trace the association's origins to German book societies in the aftermath of World War I. Yet in his lifetime, Balzac fashioned his own solution to the economic crisis of the book trade by pre-publishing stories and chapters from novels in the periodic press, by signing book contracts well before he had actually written the work in question (for works he more often than not never completed), and finally by creating the overarching structure of the *Comédie humaine,* which allowed him to re-release previously published novels in an expanded format. In this way he could profit three times from the same work: thus the feuilleton is to the book what the book is to the *Comédie humaine.*

Although readers of the *Comédie humaine* will find no direct allusions to his Société d'abonnement général (indeed, even in his correspondence Balzac only referred to it obliquely as his "grande affaire"), many of the issues that led Balzac to perceive a need for "private" reading arise in it. Whereas *Illusions perdues* describes but does not attempt to resolve the anarchic state of the book trade, many of Balzac's stories and novels emphasize the private, leisurely consumption of the written word, contrasting it with rapid public consumption. The reader of *Le Père Goriot* (1834) is addressed directly in the following terms: "vous qui tenez ce livre d'une main blanche, vous qui vous enfoncez dans un moelleux fauteuil en vous disant: peut-être ceci va-t-il m'amuser" [you who are holding this book in a white hand, you who are ensconced in an armchair saying to yourself: "Perhaps this will amuse me] (Balzac 1976, 3:50). The whiteness of the reader's hands, in addition to connoting purity if not naïveté, suggests that these hands have not been soiled by the kind of worn, stained books available at the "cabinet de lecture" and perpetuates the "sale/propre" metaphor invoked by Balzac to justify private ownership of the literary artifact.

The narrator of the short story "Le Message" (prepublished in the *Revue des deux mondes* in 1832, and included in the second volume of the *Scènes de la vie de province* the next year) invokes a version of the "sacred" social function of the author, while implying a dream of total narrative diffusion, when he proclaims "Il faut tout dire" [Everything must be told] (Balzac 1976, 2:400). He witnesses the accidental death of his traveling companion, who begs him to inform his mistress personally of his demise so as to spare her "la peine qu'[elle] ressentirait si elle apprenait brusquement sa mort par un journal" [the pain she would feel if she suddenly learned of his death from a newspaper] (ibid. 397). The dynamics of a personalized narrative, accompanied by the direct transmission of objects belonging to the deceased other (a pendant, a lock of hair), are coded here as preferable to an alienating public text. Similarly, "Etude de femme" (prepublished in *La Mode* in 1830, published in the third volume of the *Romans et contes philosophiques* in 1831, and eventually included in the first volume of *La Comédie humaine* in 1842) shows the marquise de Listomère confronting Eugène de Rastignac over a love letter intended for his mistress, which he "accidentally" sent to her. While the marquise points out that love letters—the epitome of the privatized utterance—can hardly be addressed accidentally, her husband sits by the window reading *La Gazette de France* "pour acquérir," the narrator tells us, "le journaliste aidant, une opinion à lui sur l'état de la France" [in order to obtain, with the help of a journalist, his own opinion on the state of France] (Balzac 1976, 2:177). When, echoing *Le Message,* the marquis finds a death notice in the *Gazette* ("Ah! Mme de Mortsauf est morte" [178]), the opposition between direct interpersonal exchange and indirect public consumption becomes clear. These few examples[10] suggest that what might have pleased Balzac the most would have been an opportunity to personally deliver his "message" directly to the reader, which to some extent was the purpose of his "grand affaire."

It is Balzac's short story "L'Illustre Gaudissart," however, that best illustrates the problems involved in recruiting provincial readers; in fact, this story can be interpreted as explaining why the author's "grande affaire" never got off the ground. Written in one night, as Balzac boasted to Mme Hanska, in November 1833, so as to fill out the second volume of his *Scènes de la vie de province,* this story literally reflects what one commentator calls the "horreur du vide" or the "désir de complétude" (Dällenbach 1979, 431) characteristic of the incorporative strategy of the *Comédie humaine.* The protagonist is Gaudissart himself, the "commis voyageur" par excellence, whose job is to link Paris to the provinces:

> Le commis voyageur n'est-il pas aux idées ce que nos diligences sont aux choses et aux hommes? il les voiture, les met en mouvement, les fait se choquer les unes aux autres; il prend, dans le centre lumineux, sa charge

de rayons et les sème à travers les populations endormies. (Balzac 1976 4:561)

[Is not the traveling salesman, with respect to ideas, the equivalent of what stagecoaches are to things and men? he transports them, he puts them into motion, makes them rub up one against the others; he takes from the radiant center his quiver of rays and plants them throughout the sleeping population.]

These "populations endormies" living far from the "centre lumineux" constitute the same group of provincial readers targeted as subscribers to Balzac's "grande affaire." Indeed, "commis voyageurs" like Gaudissart might presumably have been instrumental in selling subscriptions to the Société d'abonnement général, since they were already busy selling subscriptions to periodicals. Gaudissart can sell anything to anyone because he possesses "le pouvoir de la langue" (ibid. 563); he is therefore assigned the difficult task of selling door-to-door, as it were, subscriptions to politically oriented newspapers, a *Journal des enfants,* and more important (since more profitable), policies for an *assurance de capitaux* to the recalcitrant Tourangeaux. Upon discovering the nature of his mission, the "boute-en-train du bourg" [the town's most energetic character] (ibid. 577), of Vouvray, a Monsieur Vernier, who holds all Parisian "spéculateurs" in contempt, directs Gaudissart to "un homme à peu près fou, nommé Margaritis" [a practically crazy man, named Margaratis] (ibid. 579) and claims that the latter is an "ancien banquier" and a respected figure in the community. The remainder of the story describes the misunderstandings that nonetheless lead to an eventual (though ultimately illusory) agreement between the two men.

Gaudissart can be considered an exemplary "libraire-commissionnaire," not only since he sells magazine subscriptions on commission, but more metaphorically because he is (as many townfolk gleefully remind him) selling nothing, the invisible, the "useless." Surely Balzac realized that as an author himself dependent upon the "pouvoirs de la langue," he had much in common with this "colporteur," all the more because his planned Société would require reaching out to the provincial markets. Surely Balzac also realized that the inhabitants of the provinces would greet Parisian salesmen selling subscriptions with great suspicion, especially if their reading habits were underdeveloped. Although, as we saw, Balzac had attempted to dispense with the intermediary figure of the "libraire-commissionnaire," "L'Illustre Gaudissart" demonstrates a more evenhanded appreciation for his social function: for these traveling salesmen, significantly called "représentants," serve as localized stand-ins for the author to his reading public:

Personne en France ne se doute de l'incroyable puissance incessamment déployée par les voyageurs, ces intrépides affronteurs de négociations qui, dans la dernière bourgade, *représentent* le génie de la civilisation et les inventions parisiennes aux prises avec le bons sens, l'ignorance ou la routine des provinces. (Ibid. 563)

[No one in France is unaware of the incredible power incessantly deployed by traveling salesmen, these intrepid warriors of negotiation who, in the most remote town, represent the genius of civilization and Parisian inventions grappling with the common sense, the ignorance, or the routine of the provinces.]

Margaritis, along the same lines, can be considered a "model" for this reading public. The madman, we are told, does enjoy reading very much, and at minimal expense: "Au logis, il demandait à tout moment le journal; pour le contenter, sa femme ou sa servante lui donnait un vieux journal d'Indre-et-Loire; et depuis sept ans, il ne s'était point encore aperçu qu'il lisait toujours le même numéro" [At home, he was always asking for the newspaper; in order to satisfy him, his wife or his servant would give him an old newspaper from Indre-et-Loire; and for seven years, he still hasn't noticed that he's been reading the same issue] (ibid. 579). Obviously, his reading habits would prevent him from responding by mail to advertisements for new subscriptions printed in such newspapers, which necessitates the physical presence of a "commis voyageur" at his door. He is not, however, a "passive" consumer once confronted with the powerful, seductive discourse of the salesman: instead, he comes to imitate precisely such a discourse. Margaritis is, as we are told, obsessed with selling two illusory casks of wine and therefore proceeds in turn to negotiate their sale with Gaudissart, who eventually agrees to buy them if Margaritis agrees to buy a subscription to the *Journal des Enfants*. Since they are speaking the same language, an agreement is reached:

—Revenons à notre affaire, dit Gaudissart.
　　—Nous y sommes, monsieur, reprit le fou. Mon vin est capiteux, capiteux s'accorde avec capital en étymologie; or, vous parlez capitaux . . . hein? *caput,* tête, tête de Vouvray, tout cela se tient. (Ibid. 587)

[—Let us get back to business, said Gaudissart.
　　—We're already there, replied the madman. My wine is heady, and "head" is etymologically linked to capital; and in fact, you're talking about capital . . . right? *caput,* head, barrelheads of Vouvray wine, it all holds together.]

Indeed, that which holds everything together is the language of capitalism, the "irrésistible éloquence" of "cette folie de notre époque" (ibid 567), which weaves its way through the extensive word play, puns, and double entendres of the text.

Paradoxically, the end result of the discourse of capitalism is that nothing is sold. Gaudissart is undone, as he can offer nothing concrete to the madman but words; as Shoshana Felman notes, "la défaite de Gaudissart comme sa victoire dépendent du langage" [the defeat of Gaudissart, as with his victory, depends on language] (1978, 128). It is the salesman's position as intermediary that forces him to rely on language; and because the referent "behind" his language is absent, his words are all the more subject to displacement, ambiguity, and even any other seductive discourse. The discourse that motivates the dynamics of marketing ultimately relies on the same absence of the real as does literary discourse and is thus condemned to its own version of "uselessness" and failure.

In "L'Illustre Gaudissart," the real power of language resides not on the side of the salesman but on the side of the discourse that represents the failure of his discourse: that is, with the narrative discourse of the *Comédie humaine*. "Literary" language can recuperate the failure of a capitalistic exchange by inserting this failure into a larger narrative structure within which everything must become narratable, hence marketable:[11] Gaudissart's failure to sell becomes a story that can be sold and included in the *Comédie humaine*. This story can be considered both as Balzac's revenge upon an industry that he thought denied his books an audience, and as the proclamation, within the *Comédie humaine* itself, of the power of literary discourse to account even for the conditions limiting its full diffusion in the marketplace. Constantly rebuffed in his paradoxical attempts to increase the "propagation" of his literary writings while retaining personal control over them, Balzac is able to incorporate even the story of his failure to do so into the narrative dynamics of his fictional world. When Margaratis and Gaudissart agree to a deal (the former pays seven francs to subscribe to the *Journal des enfants* and the latter agrees to purchase two casks of wine), we know that there is no wine and that the madman is hardly the target reader of a magazine for children: there is still an abyss separating the mass product from the consumer. Yet it is the madman's quite sane resistance to and subversion of the language of capitalism that ultimately reveals how it, and not he, embodies "cette folie de notre époque" [this madness of our time]. Indeed, Margaratis as a consumer displays the same kind of resistance to and distrust of the realm of distribution that Balzac displayed as a producer.

Notes

1. Chollet (1975, 154, n. 5) discusses the appearance of this striking expression in Balzac's writings of the early 1830s.

2. The polemical texts include "De l'état actuel de la librairie" (1830), "Lettre aux écrivains français" (1834), and "Notes remises à Messieurs les Députés composant la commission de la loi sur la propriété littéraire" (1841). The reformist texts are the "Acte préliminaire de la Société d'abonnement général" (1830) and the "Acte de société de 1833," in Chollet 1971 and 1975, respectively. Literary texts include *Le Message* (1832), *Etude de femme* (1830), and *L'Illustre Gaudissant* (1930). Since these texts all have a common goal, the "Balzac" in question is not the biological subject, the reformer, the author, etc., but a writing machine in search of disseminatory plenitude.

3. Although this text was signed by the "Comité de la Société des gens de lettres," it is usually ascribed to Balzac.

4. "Acte préliminaire de la Société d'abonnement général" (ms. A 257 of the Bibliothèque Louvenjoul), in Chollet 1971, 89.

5. Those interested in this period should consult Chollet 1983, where the term "grand tournant" is coined. For a summary of this period informed by Chollet, see Pierrot 1994, 167–76.

6. Balzac's entry into journalism placed him immediately in a position of "bad faith": *Le Voleur,* as the name indicates, published articles that had appeared in other periodicals without compensating these periodicals or the original author. The extent of Balzac's collaborative writings at this time also problematizes his stand on originality as justifying literary property. *Hypocrite auteur?* Perhaps; yet this shows to what extent Balzac was living the contradictions of the marketplace, all the while trying to resist and reform it.

7. See Chollet 1971, 69. The expansion (or packaging) of printed matter into multiple volumes "in-12" obviously benefited the "cabinets" who rented by the volume.

8. Balzac's monarchism, as we have seen, is a form of nostalgic resistance to the "fortuities" of the marketplace, which here take the form of "egalitarianism." Balzac's political beliefs, as expressed in November 1830, seem primarily intended to protect literary property: Balzac favors a hereditary constitutional monarchy, a powerful Chambre des pairs "qui représente la propriété, avec toutes les garanties possibles d'hérédité" [that represents property owners, with all possible hereditary guarantees], and laws whose purpose is "*d'éclairer le plus possible le peuple*" [to enlighten the people as much as possible], so they can reach an "état d'aisance" [state of ease] (in Pierrot 1994, 173–74) presumably conducive to reading—and owning—literary texts.

9. See Chollet 1975, 165, n. 1. Balzac had no objections to groups splitting the subscription rates for his Société.

10. There are many other examples, too numerous to explore here, such as the daily offering of personalized "bouquets" in *Le Lys de la vallée*.

11. Fredric Jameson suggests that Balzac's narrative project imitates the economic stage of "primitive accumulation of capital" dominant in his time by "stockpiling" stories (1971, 10). The question is, where is this stockpile to be located, how is it to be distributed, and what is its "fate"? The transformation of the "raw" into the "market-able" is a process that turns back upon itself when there is no market, a process demonstrated by "L'Illustre Gaudissart."

Works Cited

Balzac, Honoré de. 1956a. "De l'état actuel de la librairie." First published in *Feuilleton des journaux politiques,* 3 and 10 March 1830. Reprinted in Balzac 1956d, 547–50.

———. 1956b. "Lettre aux écrivains français." First published in *Revue de Paris,* 2 November 1834. Reprinted in Balzac 1956d, 223–38.

———. 1956c. "Notes remises à Messieurs les Députés composant la commission de la loi sur la propriété littéraire." Paris: Hetzel, 1841. Reprinted in Balzac 1956d, 717–35.

———. 1956d. *Oeuvres diverses.* Vol. 23 of *Oeuvres complètes.* 24 vols. Edition established by the Société des études balzaciennes. Paris: Club de l'Honnête Homme.

———. 1956e. "Sur les questions de la propriété littéraire et de la contrefaçon." First published in *Chronique de Paris,* 30 October 1836. Reprinted in Balzac 1956d, 298–306.

———. 1960–. *Correspondance.* 5 vols. Paris: Garnier Frères.

———. 1976–81. *La Comédie humaine.* Edited by P-G Castex. 12 vols. Paris: Gallimard.

Baudelaire, Charles. 1975. *Oeuvres complètes.* Pléiade ed. 2 vols. Paris: Gallimard.

Chollet, Roland. 1971. "Un Episode inconnu de l'histoire de la librairie: La Société d'abonnement général avec le texte inédit de Balzac." *Revue des sciences humaines* 36, no. 141 (January–March 1971): 55–109.

———. 1975. "Balzac et sa 'Grande Affaire' de librairie: L'Acte de société de 1833." *L'Annee balzacienne,* 145–75.

———. 1983. *Balzac journaliste, le tournant de 1830.* Paris: Klincksieck.

Dällenbach, Lucien. 1979. "Du fragment au cosmos." *Poétique* 40 (November): 420–31.

Engels, Friedrich. [1884] 1972. *The Origin of the Family, Private Property, and the State.* Reprint, New York: Pathfinder.

Felman, Shoshana. 1978. *La Folie et la chose littéraire.* Paris: Seuil.

Jameson, Fredric. 1971. *Marxism and Form: Twentieth-Century Dialectical Theories of Literature.* Princeton, N.J.: Princeton University Press.

Lee, Charles. 1958. *The Hidden Public: The Story of the Book-of-the-Month Club.* New York: Doubleday.

Parent-Lardeur, Françoise. 1981. *Lire à Paris au temps de Balzac: Les Cabinets de lecture à Paris, 1815–1830.* Paris: Editions des Hautes Etudes en Sciences Sociales.

Pierrot, Roger. 1994. *Honoré de Balzac.* Paris: Fayard.

Rubin, Joan Shelley. 1992. *The Making of Middlebrow Culture.* Chapel Hill: University of North Carolina Press.

Engendering
the News

7 Unfashionable Feminism?

Designing Women Writers in the *Journal des Femmes*

(1832–1836)

Je suis donc content qu'elles fassent leurs romans et leurs chiffons. Le temps viendra
peut-être bientôt où l'homme qui fera un roman sera aussi ridicule que ceux qu'on
voit aujourd'hui faire des robes et des bonnets. [*I am then happy to let them*
(women) make their novels and their clothes. The time will come perhaps when the
man who makes a novel will be as ridiculous as the ones who today make dresses
and bonnets.]
—*Auger, 1827*

Le goût du siècle, la toute-puissance des hommes, a dépossédé les femmes d'un
genre de littérature qui, après plus d'un siècle, leur semblait dévolu, car ce sont les
hommes aujourd'hui qui font les romans. [*The style of the century, the omnipotence*
of men, has dispossessed women of a literary genre that, after more than a century,
seemed granted them, for it is men today who make novels.]
—*Choiseul-Meuse,* Journal des femmes, *1833*

"Oh, women's magazines," the journalist said with contempt. "Everybody knows
they're catalogs—but who cares? They have nothing to do with journalism."
—*Anonymous male journalist quoted by Gloria Steinem, 1990*

I really miss the old Ms., *the one more interested in what women say and do than*
what they wear!
—*Linda M. Steele, letter to* Ms., *1990*

Toward the end of the Bourbon Restoration (1815–30), the French academician Auger told men that it made good sense to leave the novel to women since it was "almost exclusively for their use." Around the same time, however, Félicité de Choiseul-Meuse, author of licentious novels and didactic literature for girls, offered an alternative but equally gendered view of novel production in which male

*Unless otherwise noted, all translations from French to English are my own.

authors had wrested the novel from female writers.[1] Subsequent developments contradicted Auger when both the novel and the fashion industry
became big business for men. However shortsighted Auger's prediction
about the future of the novel, his rhetorical pinning of novels by women to
the trifling stuff of fashion ("chiffons") nonetheless anticipated a major
strategy for devaluing modern print forms "contaminated" by the feminine
and fashion. More than 150 years later and on another continent, Gloria
Steinem's interlocutor performed a similar deprecating flourish. Invoking
"women's magazines," *Ms.* magazine included, the anonymous male journalist reduced them to unadulterated advertising copy. If Auger's remarks belie
anxiety about the feminizing effects of novel writing, "women's magazines"
seem to pose no such risk; since they are not "real" journalism, they are
simply beside the point.

My chronological and geocultural leap from the *roman de femme* (woman's
novel)[2] to "women's magazines" is prompted by a persistent tendency of
critics to deploy what I call a rhetoric of the *chiffon* that maps women's writing
onto a vast, unexplored no man's land. In the context of nineteenth-century
France, a long ribbon cordoned off the *roman de femme* and then the *press
féminine* from the larger print culture. Tied into a fashion knot, this ribbon
strained to check the frivolous and nefarious effects of commodification by
fashion taken in its least playful sense. Such marginalization has resulted in
the exclusion of the *presse féminine* from scholarship on nineteenth-century
French print culture in general, and more particularly, on the status of
French female authorship in that culture. This essay centers on one such
under-read periodical, the *Journal des femmes,*[3] to make the case for factoring
the *presse féminine* into the context of the "vertiginous changes" in July Monarchy print culture.[4] The *JDF* is an important example of writing women's
entanglements with the rhetoric of the *chiffon* and it is of value to feminist
cultural work on the writing of French women.

It can be argued that the July Monarchy press offered women—whether
exiting the literary salons of the Restoration or just coming to writing—new
venues for varied textual production and publication experiences. Their
excursions into journalism represent a key moment of female authorship in
nineteenth-century France that has yet to be adequately historicized. Literary criticism still treats the *presse féminine* as paraliterary, and while women in
the press are not absent from histories of journalism or of French feminisms, those identified with either fashion or bourgeois feminism do not
generate intense scholarly interest. The *JDF* is a case in point for more
careful examination of the ways in which various issues—fashion, literary,
and feminist—intersected and clashed within a given periodical. Following

Nancy K. Miller's contention that "the story of the woman who writes is *always* another story," this essay argues that the *JDF,* despite its service to fashion and the political status quo, was feminist in its attempt to stake new territory for writing women.[5]

The *JDF*'s hybrid status serves as an important reminder that our inherited, rigid categories of women-centered print forms—feminine, feminist, and fashion—are unstable and subject to change. Like the feminist *Ms.* magazine and its successive phases, the *JDF* had a vexed publication history. This so-called women's magazine underwent several facelifts before being taken over in 1836 by men and advertising. Moreover, its initial, uneasy presentation of an alliance between fashion and pedagogy was undermined from within by an unexpected and multivoiced literary feminism on the part of certain regular collaborators. Their resistance to both *chiffons* and prevailing discourses on the *femme auteur* had much "to do with" the paper's final makeover into a more straightforward and male controlled fashion magazine.

The *JDF* appeared at a critical moment in the history of French print culture when the July Monarchy press became a major actor in producing and organizing culture for a more broadly conceived public. Dependence upon and service to capital marked the beginnings of mass communication and prompted a change in critical focus from the woman's novel to the women's press. This shift was by no means simple, bound up in concerns with the changing status of literature in a period identified with modernity, understood here as the particular conditions and responses to urban culture in an increasingly industrialized Paris. Around 1830, Auger's gendered boundaries of genre were neither fixed nor respected by the expanding and diversifying press and novel. Critics of various stripes blamed the press, seen both to have lost its political rigor by opening itself to new discourses and to have corrupted literary purity. Even before the arrival in 1836 of the serialized novel in the new, cheaper daily newspapers, the critic Désiré Nisard attacked "facile literature," and Philarète Chasles spoke of an epidemic in novel writing encouraged by the press. According to Chasles in 1834, "everyone had to be a man of letters."[6] The new commodification of print materials eventually coincided with their feminization to produce hyperbolic images of the July Monarchy journalist as a prostituted writer. Whether a sell-out or an intrepid survivor, the male author was "seduced" by the new press.

Critics from Walter Benjamin to Richard Terdiman have articulated the role of the July Monarchy press in configuring modern authorship, whereby the *homme de lettres* taking to the streets in search of copy is best personified by the *flâneur,* a double of the journalist as prostitute.[7] But there has been little analogous analysis of the writings, place, and transformation of the *femme de lettres* in this urban print culture. Although writing women were subject to eroticized representation (exhibitionism, lack of modesty), other images entrapped them in a semantic vestiary network, or rhetoric of the *chiffon.* Like the pre-1830 *roman de femme* synonymous with *chiffons,* the developing *presse féminine* of the July Monarchy became a new target for critics who ridiculed both the desexed, down at the heels *bas-bleu* (bluestocking) and her alter ego, the hyperfeminine, well-heeled muse.

Are there connections between these pronouncedly clothed caricatural figures of literary women and the "invisible," silent *flâneuse?* Must we turn to the *grands magasins,* which according to Anne Friedberg, mobilized the gaze and gait of the Parisian *flâneuse?*[8] Is the *bas-bleu* just another truant from the domestic sphere, sited and surveyed by the discursive networks of what Roddy Reid calls "familialism"?[9] Or might the underside of the risible *bas-bleu* and the sublime muse reveal women writing themselves—ambivalently, reluctantly, and even optimistically—into journalistic spaces permeated with the fashion concerns of modernizing Paris? Before 1836, the year the poet Delphine Gay de Girardin metamorphosed into a weekly columnist for the *Presse* and proclaimed the centrality of *chiffons* in urban Paris,[10] she and other less well-placed women writers had spent the early 1830s coming to terms with writing in the nascent *presse féminine.* Distinct from the radical, working-class Saint-Simonian women of *La Femme libre* (1832–34), these middle- and upper-class women in pursuit of professional authorial status crossed boundaries and negotiated the contradictions and ironies of feminism and fashion.

Richomme et Cie: Founding Le Journal des femmes: Gymnase littéraire

Created in March 1831, the Paris-based *Journal des femmes* attracted over seventy female collaborators of whom thirty contributed regularly from May 1832 to January 1836. Managing director Fanny Richomme represented the silent partners of "Fanny Richomme et Cie" and received one hundred francs an issue for bookkeeping, organizing the contents, and remunerating her writers. Advertisement-free, the *JDF* was expensive at fifteen francs a trimester. Announced as a biweekly, but appearing weekly, the *JDF* boasted circulation in sixty-nine bookstores throughout the provinces and in twelve foreign cities, including New York and New Orleans. Each in-quarto issue of approximately twenty-four pages included a plate or color lithography of instructional or, less frequently, fashion interest.[11] Richomme modified the layout over time but maintained major divisions between literature, arts, and the sciences on the one hand, and miscellaneous pieces of domestic advice, brief fashion blurbs, theater reviews, and visual material on the other (see fig. 7-1). Any given issue included a section of book reviews, poems, stories, and articles covering the natural sciences, the fine arts, history, travel sketches, public lectures, theories of education, women's rights and condition in the nineteenth century, and their artistic and intellectual achievements. Still others examined the death penalty, suicide, and even animal rights. With the early exception of a small number of articles by men on science or the law and many brief fashion pieces by Herbinot de Mauchamps, women (signing their full names, maiden or married) were the authors.[12]

A hybrid, the *JDF* drew upon eighteenth-century journals that had sought to educate women, while structurally it resembled fashion magazines financed by companies of shareholders.[13] The title sounded a modern note; the substitution of *femmes* for *dames* immediately distanced the *JDF* from both the *Journal des dames* (1759–78) and the well-established contemporary fashion magazine the *Journal des dames et des modes* (1797–1839). The subtitle *Gymnase littéraire* built upon the familiar formula from Horace to "instruct and amuse" adopted by previous literary periodicals. The few periodicals addressing women in the eighteenth century, such as the *Journal des dames,* also used this formula to make "light literature" serve what Nina Gelbart calls "necessary camouflage" for the "serious" matters of their educational agenda.[14] Again though, the *JDF* distinguished itself by proposing two primary goals. According to Richomme, it sought both to create "la femme telle que le siècle la veut" [woman such as befits the century] (1: 18) and to circulate publicly "la parole des femmes" [women's word] (3: 249) and "leur manière de voir les choses" [their manner of seeing things] (4: 246).

The format and layout of the *JDF* reinforced tensions between these two objectives. The magazine structure, which replaced the centralized editorial authority of essay periodicals, offered a variety of texts by numerous authors, consequently diffusing editorial authority along multiple lines. The imagined readers, from the class with "money and time" (4: 247), were divided among the learned, the literate, and those who only cared about the visual material (1: 314). However, the *JDF* frequently addressed readers as potential writers. Thus, published reader responses and contributors combined to unsettle Richomme's dominant ideological framework. An insistent and multifaceted emphasis on women's writing paradoxically undermined the stated instructional agenda designed not to challenge the status quo, thereby exposing the slender thread connecting "women's word" to the familiar

Supplément.

TABLE DU CINQUIÈME VOLUME

Du Journal des Femmes.

PREMIÈRE PARTIE.

MORALE, SCIENCES ET ARTS.

Sciences naturelles. 1re série. 1er article. Migration des oiseaux. Mme A. *Dupin*. 3
2e article. 28
3e article. 47
4e article. Oiseaux sylvains ou fringilles. 70
5e article. 88
6e article. 107
Des Femmes sous le rapport des arts, de l'industrie, et sous celui de l'exposition de 1833. Mme Alex. *Aragon*. 7
Société française de Statistique universelle. F. de *M*. 24
Notice sur Provins. Mlle Lina *Jaunès*. 25
Quelques conseils (préambule). Mme Aline de *M*. 45
1er article. Vanité. 65
2e article. Vanité. 149
Rêverie. Végéter c'est vivre. Mlle S. U. *Dudrezène*. 47
Société pour l'enseignement élémentaire. Séance du 19 mai 1833. La *Directrice*. 63
De la Politesse. Mme Alex *Aragon*. 67
Maison de refuge. La *Vieille Femme*. 85
Sur l'origine des vêtemens et des modes, 3e article. M. *Coubard d'Aulnay*. 101
4e article. 165
Les Mendians à Paris. Mlle Clémence *Robert*. 105
Société d'horticulture. Exposition de 1833. Mme Alex. *Aragon*. 124
Cours normal gratuit. Mme Laure *Bernard*. 129
Monumens du moyen-âge (Arques). Mme Alex. *Aragon*. 132
Id. (Cathédrale de Milan.) La même. 232
Sciences naturelles (Botanique). 1re série. 1er article. M. *P. Ollion*. 151
2e article. Des Feuilles. 171
3e article. 192
Chronique musicale. Mme Alex. *Aragon*. 153
Françoise de Rimini. 168
Le Duel. Mme Angélique *Arnaud*. 169
Rêverie. Mlle S. U. *Dudrezène*. 170
Les Cours publics à Paris. Mlle Clémence *Robert*. 190
Des Etablissemens de charité en France et en Bavière. Mme Laure *Bernard*. 209
Rêverie. Du Sens moral. Mlle S. U. *Dudrezène*. 212
De quelques superstitions et de leur origine. Mlle Clémence *Robert*. 229
De la Tendresse, de l'Exaltation, du Dévouement. Mlle Félicie *d'Ayzac*. 253
Toujours la Gloire ! Boutade. Mlle V. *de Sénancour*. 254

DEUXIÈME PARTIE.

LITTÉRATURE.

Le Castel de Verneuil. Mœurs des dixième et onzième siècles. 1024. 1er article. Mme *Piet*. 11
2e article. Ermance la brune. 50
3e article. Le Serf et l'Archevêque. 111
4e article. La Potence. 234
L'Hirondelle. Mme Julia *Limno*. 16
La nouvelle littérature, ou les puissances d'argent. Mme Alex. *Aragon*. 31
La première composition d'une femme. Mme Elisa *Souty*. 34
Lucy. Mme Emma *Ferrand*. 54
Légende groenlandaise. Mlle Emilie *Marcel*. 55
Les Jardinières. 64
Le Kidouschim. Scène de mœurs hébraïques. Mme Eugénie *Foa*. 78
Les Polémiques du jour. 1re soirée à l'île Saint-Louis. 91
2e soirée. 137
3e soirée. 176
4e soirée. 217
5e soirée. 263
Les Journaux. Mlle Clémence *Robert*. 94
Croquis de plusieurs célébrités modernes. Madame Desborde-Valmore. M. *Bouilly*. 96
Les deux Frères (fragment) Mme Laure *Bernard*. 116
La Matinée. Congrès féminin. Mme *de Saint-Surin*. 125
Qu'a-t-il donc fait? Mme *Mahault*. 134
L'Enfant aux cheveux blonds. Mme Coraly *Thiéry*. 142
Traduction de Manzoni. Mlle Pauline *Roland*. 143
Elle fut sage. Mme Adèle *Janvier*. 154
La Vieille Femme. Mme Elisa *Souty*. 160
Un Ange de marbre, ou ne vous y fiez pas. Mlle Pauline *de Stolz*. 173
Prétentions. Mlle Virginie *de Sénancour*. 181
Miroir du monde. 1er article. Mme de *Senithes*. 195
Pouzoles. Mme Hortense *Allard*. 198
La Paulina et les Journaux. La *Vieille Femme*. 199
Correspondance, à Mme la Directrice du *Journal des Femmes*. Mme A. *Dupin*. 201
Histoire d'une Bague, conte imité de l'anglais. Mme Alex. *Aragon*. 213
De l'Influence que les femmes pourraient avoir sur la littérature actuelle. Mme Mélanie *Waldor*. 222
Les Laides de Paris. Mme *Souty*. 238
Les Pyramides et Fontainebleau. Mme Victorine *Maugirard*. 240
Une Grimace. Mme Anaïs *Ségalas*. 255
A quoi servent les Femmes. M. *Blanqui* aîné. 267

BULLETINS LITTÉRAIRES.

Correspondance d'Orient, de 1830 à 1831, par Michaud, de l'Académie française, et M. Poujoulat, 1er vol., 18. — Les Ombrages, contes spiritualistes, par M. Gustave Drouineau, 37 — Le Livre des Conteurs; un Jour de coquetterie, par M. Ancelot, 38. — Une Grossesse, par M. Jules Lacroix, *ibid.* — Chroniques du Café de Paris; le Jeune Homme, tome 1er, la Province, 40. — Histoire des anciennes villes de France. 1re série, Haute-Normandie, Dieppe, per M. Vitet, 56 — A l'Ouest, roman américain de Poulding, traduit par Mlle Sobry, 79. — Dalilah, par M. Jules de Saint-Félix, *ibid.* — Un Enfant, par M. Ernest Desprez, 80. — Une Méchante Femme, par M. Hippolyte Bonnelier, 98. — Saconthala à Paris, par M. Eusèbe de Salle, 99. — Souvenirs d'un Sexagénaire, par M. Arnault, de l'Académie française, *ibid.* — Une Fantaisie de Louis XIV, par M. Bignan, 122. — Les Contes de

FIGURE 7-1: "Table du cinquième volume," *Journal des femmes* (1833). Bibliothèque nationale de France, Paris.

FIN DU TOME CINQUIÈME.

feminine curriculum and the minimal fashion content. Within the cautious program to rehabilitate women's social position through education, the discourse on writing women articulated a surprising resistance to feminine norms and a hostile literary marketplace. Once a source of private amusement, writing became a necessary tool for the personal and cultural transformation of the *femme de lettres* turned journalist.

In the following sections I examine three major areas of the *JDF* in which the "women's word" on women's writing slants the pedagogical will to create "woman as befits the century" toward advocacy of public female authorship. In the first section I examine the tone and mission of the periodical in Richomme's Prospectus. I then turn to articles by collaborators to show how their preoccupation with the *femme auteur* revised Richomme's original curriculum and produced a blurred vision of the domestic and public spheres. Following this I return to Richomme's editorial comments to track the evolution in her own discourse on women's writing. In these sections, I am primarily concerned with efforts of writing women to speak and encourage other women to speak within a periodical dismissed as either a "fashion magazine" or a "women's magazine." In my conclusion I place such endeavors within the context of the periodical's vexed publication history to measure the extent to which the appropriation of "feminine" press space by writing women was ultimately deemed unfashionably feminist.

Fanny Richomme: *"Ce que femme veut, Dieu le veut"*

Opening the Prospectus, the literary sketch "What woman wants, God wants" (1: 9–16) stages a taking of the private and public pulse to both soften and ironize the drama of women entering the press. Mme Reynaud defines the journal while her adviser (an old professor who owns a gazette) uses his know-how to secure the necessary capital. Allaying her husband's fear of financial ruin, Mme Reynaud reassures him that her idea is "in the air"; unlike those journals that alarm him, hers is "a matter of literature and education." While wanting to challenge ideas about her "sex," she shrewdly characterizes the journal as a "speculation," thus winning spousal approval. Mme Reynaud sets off with her adviser in search of their primary resources: "celebrated literary women" and "capitalists." At a ball, both men and women are confounded by the idea of a journal for "women" and not "ladies." The clichés activated by the guests who are themselves stereotypes—the young republican for whom a woman's paper can only mean "compotes and jams"; the hen-pecked marquis fearful of insurrectionary women; and society women for whom woman author is synonymous with "ugliness"—serve Richomme's humorous response to received ideas about women in the press and her lesson that men and women need educating about literary women. As a first contact with readers, Richomme's sketch performs as amusing "camouflage" for her will to change public opinion.

Adopting the editorial "we" in the subsequent prospectus proper, Richomme places the *JDF* in the existing field of discourses on women but ventures no further than to present "emancipation" as training for companionate marriage and responsible mothering of future citizens. However, her wish that woman may "faire entendre sa voix" [in turn make her voice heard] is bolder: "Nous ferons appel aux femmes elles-mêmes; elles seront les organes de leurs voeux et de leur besoins" [We shall call upon women themselves; they shall be the organ of their wishes and their needs] (1: 17).[15] Richomme's pains to define the emancipated, modern woman whose desires do not bring down the house signal a central tension in her mission between resistance and submission to dominant notions of womanhood. Richomme's stance is progressive but equivocal. She only asserts through negative repetition what the woman of the century is not. She is neither the "free woman" of the Saint-Simonians, nor the "austere Christian," nor the affected *"précieuse,"* and even less the depraved woman of the Regency. She shall materialize only when she rejects the "prejudice" that "la condamne à la frivolité dans ses études et qui en exige des vertus surhumaines" [condemns her to frivolous studies and demands superhuman virtues] (1: 18).

The new woman does not exist because she has yet to be formed. Such namelessness participates in the strategy by which a periodical invents a need for its readers that it proposes to satisfy. This is in keeping with Richomme's moderate view that women's emancipation was to come about gradually in a vague future. The linguistic void also suggests cautious avoidance of the stereotype of the *femme-auteur*. Ultimately, the Prospectus offers only the sketchy figure of a potentially creative but silent woman, "douée d'une imagination vive et fertile" [possessed of a lively, fertile imagination], whose "regard pénétrant a découvert un horizon plus étendu" [penetrating gaze has discovered a broader horizon] (1: 19).

Et Cie: Writing for One's Life

Contributors filled in the contours of this figure by repeatedly invoking the name Richomme's sketch dared not say, the *femme-auteur*. Their articles depict her activity as a means of connection to the literary world and to a private space of her own. In its personal context, writing rehabilitates, enhances, or even replaces domestic space. At the same time, though, it enables women to make contact with other women, earn income, and lay claim to professional status in the public sphere. Figures of the writing woman emerge as both anomalous and heavily stereotyped in pieces where the authors attempt to question the equation of significant womanhood with marriage and maternity. Although decidedly bourgeois in these representations, the writing woman is not a monolithic figure; she is young, mature, or aging; single, married, or widowed; well-to-do, comfortable, or struggling. Challenging the stereotype of the unseemly *bas-bleu,* contributors sought to set different terms for writing women in print culture.

Their quest for new identities and locations raised primary questions of space and voice that determined the *femme-auteur* as a figure in the making, neither at home in so-called safe, domestic space nor welcome in the literary marketplace. Ambiguously situated in relation to their privileged social position and desire for a recognized *droit de cité* as authors, the contributors viewed the act of writing as a means of self-determination and self-representation available nowhere else.

The domestic sphere came under frequent scrutiny from within reflexive, appeasing arguments that household management and mothering were perfectly compatible with writing. However necessary such rationalizations were in contesting women's use of leisure time, the collaborators challenged modern bourgeois constructs of the domestic as the only place where the female spouse could exert a civilizing influence. "Home" was simply not enough. Mme Aragon used a spatial metaphor for women's uncertain relationship to knowledge in "On the Judgment of Some Men Regarding Women's Writing." Pointedly addressing a masculine interlocutor, Aragon claimed that intellectually emancipated women who "dare . . . observe, judge, and write" find "another life in life" (2: 45). The life of the mind helps women endure the life that "vous nous avez gâtée et rendue si pesante, si perilleuse" [you have spoiled for us and made so burdensome, so perilous!]. The "domaine de la pensée" [domain of thought] is women's "vraie terre de liberté" [true land of liberty], beyond reach of the "pouvoir d'homme" [power of man] (2: 48). Here, although Aragon, like some others, does not dynamite the foundations of domestic life, she builds into it a utopian space of retreat.

In "On Women Authors," Emilie Marcel's response to clichéd ideas about writing women eliminated the spouse altogether from the domestic scene to focus primarily on motherhood. Pointing out that the mother who favored her literary work over her children would just as likely neglect them for her other "pleasures and . . . passions," Marcel argued that the majority of writing women no longer or never did exercise a maternal function.

Stressing that life continues beyond motherhood or without children, Marcel opens a space in which writing itself replaces family ties. Intellectual activity, and not the husband's presence, keeps women company; without its "sweet pleasures" life would be nothing but a state of "vegetation" (3: 75).

Adding to such arguments, Clémence Robert (a frequent contributor of essays, stories, and poems) declared in "On the Future of Women" that "knowledge" was a means of possessing "l'espace et le temps, c'est agrandir notre étroit horizon de tout l'espace de l'univers" [space and time, of extending our narrow horizon to all the space of the universe]. Women's enforced state of ignorance is tantamount to "homicide." Thus, she proclaimed, "savoir c'est vivre" [knowledge is life] (6: 225).[16]

In another piece, "On Girls," Robert asserted that while writing was inherently pleasurable for women and kept them good company, it was also their lifeline. Decrying the material inequality between a few women with everything and those with nothing, Robert nonetheless concentrates on women from "la classe moyenne" [the middle class] with both the time and means to become "artists" and "women of letters." She condemns the excessive importance of fashion and feminine activities in the life of the bourgeoise who not only takes three months to choose a "winter dress" but also stakes "her entire future on the perfection of her scarves, sewing, and jellies." Having neatly dispensed with the majority, Robert makes her main point: growing numbers of women from this class find study and writing an antidote to their most "banal" of existences (3: 167).

Like Marcel, Robert reasons that women with "an interior to care for" write because they simply choose to spend their free time this way. In a typical, deflective move Robert describes this minority group of bourgeois literary women as isolated, unmarried, or no longer married. With no "domestic duty" to fulfill, they devote themselves to literary work "pour attacher leur vie à quelque chose" [in order to attach their life to something] (3: 168). Robert's shift in emphasis from the writing wife to the woman alone conveniently steers critical scrutiny away from the former but it also importantly invests the full span of women's lives with meaning. The tactical maneuver underscores the problems of invisible women from "the middle class" for whom lived reality does not conform to the bourgeois feminine norm. Such emphasis transforms the important "interior to care for" into the space of bourgeois female subjectivities.

"On Girls" proceeds to take on the old "prejudices" against women writers through ironic rebuttal, before concluding with an oblique reproof of male-female personal relations. Women writers, claims Robert, do not step out in public to perform "a few tricks of the mind in search of praise, alms-bowl in hand! Why not recognize the most simple cause? They write because in them are thoughts that need to pour out." Robert ends her article by figuring women's vital need for self-expression and connection to the world through a metaphor of women as dryads, or wood nymphs. While this figure preserves the idea of women as naturally dependent, Robert makes it clear that not just any tree will do. Most women, she explains, attach their lives to the man of their choice; sometimes he is "the kindly oak" with protective branches; more often though he is the "poison upas whose shade is fatal." Once again, the fundamental bourgeois social unit, the heterosexual couple, is found wanting. And again, Robert immediately introduces the right of "other" women to choose without impunity the "immense tree of knowledge" whose "sap" alone can calm their "suffering souls" (3: 168).

Eugénie Foa—who published countless volumes of stories for both children and adults—reiterated but personalized the theme of female alienation in her article "How I Became an Author." Presenting a younger self at odds with the times, Foa reviews a number of unsatisfying pastimes that failed to ease her melancholy. She had spurned the quintessentially feminine ones: "Courir les marchands?—J'achetais mal. . . . Causer chiffons?—Un quart d'heure après je baillais à me démonter la machoire" [Shopping?—I was bad at it. . . . Fashion talk?—After fifteen minutes, I'd be yawning my head off]. The disaffected child who told herself bedtime stories later found writing both amusing and a relief from her *chagrins*. The narrator compares her earlier writing self to a slave who "drinks opium, falls asleep, and forgets; as for me, I wrote" (7: 171). Not Lamartinian ennui, or even a "male malady,"[17] Foa's ailment was rooted in the prevailing feminine culture; its remedy was the dream work of writing stories.

In these articles, the authors frequently justified clearing their calendars and a space to work in the household. However, their questioning and redefinition of the domestic as a "protected locus"[18] for the woman who wrote went hand in hand with critical responses to the larger publishing world. When collaborators turned their gaze to the public sphere they anticipated hostile male response and responded vigorously. Writing acquired power as an instrument by which the *JDF* consciously shaped a community of women writers determined to make inroads into the print culture. Critical interventions took several forms: they ranged from refutations of "detractors" of women's writing to celebrations of women's publications and of the *JDF*'s role as both a forum and a haven for women writers.

The male critic, high priest of the most pernicious commonplace thinking about the *femme-auteur*, received his share of censure from the *JDF*. Wondering what could be "more malicious, intolerant, sullen, demanding, quarrelsome than the humor of a man" when judging women's writing, Mme Aragon advised readers to publish but warned them to prepare for "a real war of petty quarrels" (2:45). Since women had shown themselves capable of more than "light literature," Emilie Marcel demanded their right to "publish their thoughts" without having their "private life" slandered or the "title of author" used against them. Such behavior, according to Marcel, belonged as much to the past as that "commonplace" of conversation, that "banal formula" that women lose the "charm of their sex" when they cultivate the faculties of the mind (3: 75). Robert's more caustic responses to such "prejudices" were tinged with a desire to find an unproblematic term for writing women. Critics, she stated dryly in "On Girls," reason that women writers are denatured because in taking up the pen "elles ont passé dans je ne sais quelle nature de force, d'audace, d'indépendance, où elles sont devenues des . . . êtres sans nom" [They have passed into I know not what force of nature, of audacity, of independence, where they have become . . . nameless beings] (3: 168).

Robert also took issue with the critic Désiré Nisard's double reproach of women writers for being "women and having the time to write" and for producing "easy, useless, and harmful literature." Hearing no other "woman's voice," Robert broke the silence to argue that more women had turned to writing because of fundamental changes in their lives. Girls hid to write novels rather than read them and dreamt of editors instead of suitors. The convent, where women could once build "a world far from the world," no longer offered a refuge. Robert found it inconceivable that these women, the "hermits of our time," accept "the silence of the mind" and the "stagnant life" of English and German women: "amuse oneself the year long tending a scrawny carnation on the windowsill? No thank you!" (8: 46).

The step from figuring writing and thought as women's latest "world far from the world" to celebrating the *JDF* as their new sanctuary was logical even if the press was hardly a sheltered space. In "*Le Journal des femmes*" (7: 133–34) Robert rejoiced that the periodical had brought together so many women "in the same category, equal here in rank and privilege . . . diversely placed in the world!" From the most well-to-do wife to the humblest woman of letters, "il faut qu'elle écrive" [she must write]. Her "jouissances intellectuelles" [intellectual pleasures] draw her to her desk like the "vine to its support."

Other writers concurred with Aurore Dupin's description of the *JDF* as an "organ for her complaint" about publishing problems and condescending reviews of her work. To write in the *JDF* meant she was no longer "a voice crying in the wilderness" (5: 203). Elise Voiärt urged women to submit work to the magazine despite their fear of the label "woman author" or lack of support for their "literary vocation." They might never be a Sévigné or a Staël, but they could discuss their "true interests" in a "special publication" (1: 58–59).

In "On the Influence Women Could Have on Contemporary Literature," Mélanie Waldor took the published works of contributors as concrete signs of the "new era" for writing women. United en masse, they were "smoothing the way" to a century "rich" in "women-authors" and proving to men that the literary profession was no longer shameful or perilous for women. Writing, Waldor insisted, had opened as a "career" (5: 224). In "A Quick Look at Light Literature," Alida de Savignac identified the *JDF* as the champion of writing women. She noted that as demand for their talent was growing, women no longer needed to hide behind a masculine name whereas men "do us the honor of disguising themselves as women" (4: 260). Even Pauline Roland, one-time Saint-Simonian turned freelance journalist, sent New Year's greetings in 1834 to "women, my sisters" and congratulated the *JDF* for opening its columns to so many talented young women writers (7: 174).

Cumulatively, these articles point to what was at once an energizing and intimidating endeavor: to free up "women's word" and invent relations among women writers. Laying claim to a textual space that extended beyond "light literature" and fashion reviews, the collaborators employed ambiguous coping strategies to get around the gendered boundaries of literary and journalistic practices. By their own textual examples and conscious appraisal of their anomalous place in culture, these women revised Richomme's cautious curriculum and resisted the dictates of fashion and domesticity to take authorial position. Transmitted clearly is their perception that the very act of writing reconfigured their position in the world. Suffering from what Carolyn Heilbrun has called "problems with no names," they labored to rewrite the heavily stereotyped *femme-auteur* and to clear their troubled vision of the public and private spheres.[19] Hence the double insight that neither space made room for them; they remained, in effect, "nameless beings."

Designing Woman Writers

Richomme's coming to terms with the anomaly of the "nameless being" was especially fraught with hedging due to her dual agenda to create "the woman as befits the century" and to let women speak for themselves. Women's writing initially occupied a subordinate position in her program to train readers to discuss subjects traditionally belonging to men. Moreover

Richomme did not initially view the literary section of the *JDF* as key to its "durable success" (1: 513). Instead, in her earliest letters to subscribers (addressed as *abonnés* and not *abonnées*), she spent much time responding to readers' comments and debates she had called for. Serving her educational mission, these responses allowed Richomme to define her editorial position regarding divorce, women's legal rights, and Saint-Simonianism. However, Richomme shuttled back and forth between two vantage points striving to occupy what she called a "juste-milieu" position between radical and conservative opinions about women's legal rights (1: 265).[20] When Richomme responded to two Saint-Simonian letters about the *JDF* published in *La Femme libre*,[21] she offered her own "profession de foi" [profession of faith]: "Nous ne voulons et nous ne prétendons pas amener avec notre innocent receuil une révolution . . . Amélioration graduée et arrière les révolutions" [We neither wish nor claim to bring about a revolution with our innocent publication. . . . Gradual improvement and down with revolutions] (2: 246). Ultimately though, what Richomme denied at the level of the sociopolitical, she sanctioned in the world of letters: a "revolution."

When Richomme first addressed the issue of women's writing, she established a hierarchy of types to which women should aspire. Her lessons in writing privileged the useful over the pleasing. As writers in the making, her readers were to progress gradually from "the gauzy veils of a light tale" to texts with more overt persuasive designs in which they would "expose an injustice, criticize an institution, even give advice" (4: 245). Thus, at the end of the first trimester, Richomme apologized for the overabundance of frivolous writing in the *JDF* and begged reader indulgence for those writers who had not dared "tackle delicate questions head on; they have in war terms, turned position" (1: 313).

While Richomme herself "turned" away from certain "delicate questions" raised in the debates, she applied herself earnestly to the task of distancing her periodical from the light fare associated with fashion magazines. Women needed to produce writing that demonstrated their talent for "reflection" as well as "style." Instead of producing "historiettes" [little stories] (1: 314), "reasonable women" should aspire to writing capable of effecting serious change (3: 250).

Unwilling to declare a social "revolution," Richomme called for writing as an instrument of persuasion which eventually led her to resistance of another order, a literary one. Although she regularly "turned" to the subject of women's writing when hemmed in by her *juste-milieu* position concerning nonliterary issues, Richomme's "profession of faith" turned out to be a faith in the profession she wanted open to women. Upon closing her discussion of the two Saint-Simonian letters, Richomme ended her piece with an encomium to the *JDF*, the first periodical to receive articles by women "under their names." The *JDF* had so shamed other periodicals that they now take pride "in a feminine name," even composing entire publications with works by women.[22] Unconcerned with the motivation for this change, Richomme claimed that the result was the same she pursued: "ouvrir aux femmes de nouvelles carriéres, en faisant connaître leurs talens" [to open new careers to women by making their talents known] (2: 247).

Richomme devoted her entire final letter of the first year to assessing the *JDF*. Thanks to its "original idea," the *JDF* had inspired "semirival publications." Originally the object of public derision, the periodical was now "une mode" [a fashion]:

> Les vendeurs de pensées, avides d'offrir au public une marchandise nouvelle, exploitent maintenant les femmes de mille manières, en leur demandant des contes de toutes les couleurs et sous tous les titres. Les détracteurs des écrits de femmes frondent en renvoyant les auteurs à leur ménage et à leur quenouille. . . . La révolution n'en est pas moins faite et avec le temps, on en recueillira les fruits. (4: 245)

> [The vendors of thought, eager to offer new merchandise to the public, now exploit women a thousand ways by asking them for stories of all colors and under all titles. The detractors of women's writings scoff by sending the authors back to their household and their distaff. . . . The revolution is no less complete and with time, we shall gather its fruits.]

Wishful thinking and marketing hyperbole aside, Richomme's perception of women's writing as a hot commodity was canny even if the irony of the term "révolution" here may have been lost upon her. But whether or not Richomme exaggerated the impact of the *JDF*, she unquestionably situated it in a specific moment of flux for writing women. For all the increased marketability and vogue of something identified as "women's writing," Richomme underlined the paradox that its authors were still perceived as escapees from the domestic sphere and trespassers in the press.

From Textual Designs to Fashion Statement

Beginning in late 1834, the inexorable possession of the *JDF* by fashion interests proceeded in stages. On October 1 Richomme informed readers that the *JDF* had been sold at public auction; henceforth she was sole owner and manager. Promising not to change its format, Richomme announced, however, a few modifications destined to extend readership from elegant society "à toutes les classes instruites" [to all the educated classes]. She returned the job of literary reviews to women, halved subscription rates, increased page length to include more visual material, and added an "article magasin" [shopping rubric] (8: 85). Despite Richomme's optimistic tone, some of these changes suggest financial difficulty and, indeed, they portend more drastic alterations of the periodical that had become "a fashion."

Just a year later, on 16 October 1835 the *JDF* fused with *Le Protée,* to become *La Revue fashionable.* The new codirectors, J. de Gaston, director of *Le Protée,* and Fanny Richomme, told readers that the periodical would no longer be exclusively written by and for them even though its columns remained open to their talents (12: 169). Louis Janet[23] became manager and one out of two visual pieces was a fashion plate. In late 1835 Delphine Gay de Girardin's poem "La Jeune Fille enterrée aux Invalides" (12: 89) and George Sand's "Cri d'une âme souffrante" (12: 153) appeared in *La Revue fashionable*'s pages. The publication of texts by better-known women writers coincided with Richomme's gradual disappearance; from October to December 1835, she contributed only brief theater and fashion articles and the odd piece for the Miscellany section.

By 1 January 1836, Richomme had vanished, but new director-owner, Paul Simon, resurrected the original title. Sounding a markedly different note, the new management promised to banish politics from "notre coquet journal" [our coquettish journal] unless "elle ne devienne joyeuse et gaie, coureuse de bals et de modes . . . à moins qu'elle ne quitte ses moustaches et sa longue barbe pour une couronne de roses et sa redingote brune pour une robe de crêpe. . . . En changeant de propriétaire, le *Journal des femmes* veut conserver sa même ligne" [it becomes joyful and gay, a follower of balls and fashion . . . unless it abandons its moustache and long beard for a crown of roses and its brown fitted coat for a crepe dress. . . . In changing owners, the *Journal des femmes* wants to keep its figure] (2d ser. 1: 1). In contrast to Richomme's "broad horizon," the new angle focuses on a restricted field of fashion and society to which politics can only gain entry by appearing in chic drag. The male administration savvily employed a rhetoric of *chiffons* in which the *JDF* is represented as a fashionable, body-conscious woman.

No more than the editorial voice, the feminine "figure" of the new *JDF* was not that of the original. Text occupied one column per page instead of two, full-blown advertising appeared for the first time, and the number of articles decreased, often signed only with initials. In July 1836, a full page advertisement for Emile de Girardin's forthcoming daily *La Presse* appeared, announcing the principal male collaborators. These adjustments signal converging and diverse interests in the *JDF*. Had the periodical (and which version?) successfully mobilized an audience Emile de Girardin sought for his new cheaper daily or did the latest administration of the *JDF* seek Girardin's intended public?

The last phase of this fashion makeover occurred in August 1836, when the *JDF* merged with the *Gazette des salons* (1835–37) and the *Miroir des dames* (1835–37). With Emile de Champeaux, the "Napoleon of the fashion press,"[24] as director, the ghost of "la mode" that had haunted Richomme's periodical took up permanent residence to redomesticate the unruly *JDF*. First among Champeaux's proposed "amélioration utiles" [useful improvements] (2d ser. 2: 210) was to make "La MODE" one of the periodical's "principal specialties" (2d ser. 2: 114): "[S]ince everything attached to private life is henceforth subject to [fashion's] whim," the new *JDF* promised to report not only on attire and hairstyles but also on furnishings, the latest manners, carriages, and amusements in vogue (2d ser. 2: 210–11). Thus did the domestic interior emerge and merge with the social sphere of appearances as center of reader attention.

Other notable "improvements" specifically put women's writing (back) in its place. All the while playing off the first *JDF*, "veritable monument raised in honor of women's literature" (2d ser. 2: 209), Champeaux stipulated that curricular revision was in order. The 19 August notice informing readers that "efforts by an as yet unknown muse . . . will be considered with serious attention" marked such "efforts" as amateur and subject to editorial refusal. The *JDF* gallantly offered this as a new service: rejected articles would be returned to their authors with "annotations that could serve to enlighten them" (2d ser. 2: 152). Finally, struck by the "gravity" of the title, Champeaux diminished its force by referring, unlike Richomme, to readers as "lectrices" [female readers] and to women writers as "ladies who want to write." He conceded that their work rightfully belonged in the public eye, but only because men had abandoned literature for "politics and its "passions." To women went the honor "of occupying our Parnassus too often deserted for the Forum" (2d ser. 2: 210).

Champeaux's takeover redesigned Richomme's *JDF* into a "ladies" magazine, a feminized Parnassus where women writing for women were to engage in "une sorte de confidence intime, de causerie sans prétention" [a sort of intimate confidence, an unpretentious chat] (2d ser. 2: 210). Champeaux shushed Richomme's "women's word" into polite drawing room conversation. His soft touch expunged the most compelling features of Richomme's *JDF* and erected hard boundaries between public and private spheres, between politics on the one hand, and fashion, literature, and consumer society on the other. Shored up, the new walls tightened the bonds between fashion and letters by enclosing them under the sign of a tamed femininity where women were to speak only in hushed tones.

Afterlife

The last trace of Richomme's journal, its title, disappeared in February 1837 when the periodical was absorbed by the *Journal des dames et des modes,* the successful and longest-running fashion periodical of the early nineteenth century, which itself merged with the *Gazette des salons* by the end of the year. However inescapable the makeover of the *JDF* by "the vendors of thought," its short history suggests more than either a simple failure in publication terms or capitulation to predatory fashion concerns. The subject of women's writing and the collaborators' conscious pursuit of professional authorial status created sufficient friction within the developing *presse féminine* for the *JDF* to appear unfashionable because feminist. Richomme's efforts to keep the *JDF* alive anticipated in surprising ways the negotiations of *Ms.* magazine's editors with rich advertisers who sought to shape its content and readership. That the latest reincarnation of this well-known American feminist magazine was possible only by doing without advertising revenues is a reminder that independence from networks of commercial interests comes at a high cost to readers. Unlike *Ms.* magazine, though, the *JDF* had no third life as an advertisement-free publication. However, its spirit and community of women writers did not disappear so much as migrate.

In January 1836, coincident with Richomme's total eclipse from the *JDF,* Alfred de Montferrand launched *Les Femmes: Journal du siècle.* Most of the twenty-eight listed collaborators of this monthly, which vowed to publish only women's writing, had contributed to Richomme's *JDF.* In its first and only issue, *Les Femmes* modeled itself on, but did not name outright, the journal "founded four years ago . . . for them and by them." *Les Femmes* promised to recover that specialty "abandoned in part" by its founders: giving women a voice in the press (1: 1).

The very same year, Montferrand also created the *Biographie des femmes auteurs contemporaines françaises* to be published in monthly installments at eight francs each.[25] Every ten-page issue would offer portraits of the authors featured in bio-bibliographical articles. Women wishing to appear in the *Biographie* were invited to send the necessary information to Montferrand. Of the thirty-six women profiled in the *Biographie,* fourteen had collaborated on Richomme's *JDF;* of those writing the entries, some of which were written by men, eight were former *JDF* contributors (see fig. 7-2).

ARMAND-AUBRÉE, ÉDITEUR-LIBRAIRE, RUE TARANNE, 14.

Biographie

DES

FEMMES AUTEURS

CONTEMPORAINES FRANÇAISES,

avec portraits

DESSINÉS PAR M. JULES BOILLY,

ET SOUS LA DIRECTION

DE M. ALFRED DE MONTFERRAND.

—————

Collaborateurs :

Mesdames la duchesse D'ABRANTÈS, la comtesse DE BRADI, la baronne DE BAWR, Camille BODIN, la baronne Aloïse DE CARLOWITZ, DUPIN, la comtesse D'HAUTPOUL, la comtesse Eugène D'HAUTEFEUILLE, Marie DE L'ÉPINAY, Joséphine LEBASSU, MENESSIER-NODIER, Sophie MAZURE, Émilie MARCEL, Clémence ROBERT, RICHOME, la princesse DE SALM, Anaïs SEGALAS, George SAND, la duchesse DE SAINT-LEU, Alida DE SAVIGNAC, Amable TASTU, ULLIAC-TRÉMADEURE, DE TERCY, Marceline DESBORDES-VALMORE, Mélanie WALDOR, Elise VOÏART, Céleste VIEN, etc., etc.

MM. AIMÉ-MARTIN, AZAÏS, ANCELOT, ALLETZ, AUDIFFRET, BALLANCHE, BIGNAN, BOUILLY, BERTHEVIN, le vicomte DE CHATEAUBRIAND, CHATELAIN, Philarète CHASLES, DANIELO, Emile DESCHAMPS, DES ESSARTS, Ferdinand DENIS, DESPREZ, Alexandre DUMAS, baron DE LA DOUCETTE, membre de la Chambre des députés; Ernest FOUINET. Auguste FABRE, GUIZARD, directeur des bâtimens civils; le baron Alexandre GUIRAUD, de l'Académie française; Jules JANIN, JULLIEN de Paris, JULIA DE FONTENELLE, DE LAMARTINE, de l'Académie française; Paul LACROIX, Antoine DE LATOUR, DE L'ECLUSE, Charles LAFONT, le baron DE LAMOTHE-LANGON, Auguste DE LABOUÏSSE, MOLLEVAUT, de l'Institut; MONMERQUÉ, MIGER, Justin MAURICE, DU MERSAN, Albert DE MONTÉMONT, Xavier MARMIER, DE MONGLAVE, Charles NODIER, de l'Académie française; Camille PAGANEL, membre de la Chambre des députés; PERROT, Charles ROMEY, le comte DE RIPPER-

FIGURE 7-2: "Table alphabétique," Alfred de Montferrand, *Biographie des femmes auteurs contemporaines françaises* (Paris: Armand-Aubrée, 1836). Bibliothèque nationale de France, Paris.

TABLE ALPHABÉTIQUE

DES NOTICES CONTENUES DANS CE VOLUME.

———•———

FIN DE LA TABLE.

The idea "in the air" had taken hold; throughout the 1830s, periodicals appeared in which women were the major if not sole contributors and women's writing received special emphasis. Former Saint-Simionian Eugénie Niboyet took the *JDF* as inspiration for her weekly Lyons-based *Conseiller des femmes* (1833–34).[26] The monthly *Citateur féminin* (1835), devoted to ancient and modern women's literature, introduced and reviewed the work and lives of authors from Sappho to a number of *JDF* writers such as Clémence Robert, Eugénie Foa, and Mélanie Waldor. Several *JDF* contributors also wrote for the *Gazette des femmes* (1836–38), notorious for both its legislative petitions and its male cofounder, Herbinot de Mauchamps, none other than the author of many fashion articles for Richomme's *JDF*.

Michèle de Riot-Sarcey describes the early 1830s as "times of liberty, a short, paradoxical time, in the middle of which women signified their will to be and spoke of equality."[27] The story of Richomme's *JDF* is equally paradoxical. As a "women's magazine," its "nonpolitical" status marked it as unthreatening and ephemeral. However, in its time, the *JDF* became an important if momentary touchstone for women's writing and literary engagement. Indeed, the various transformations of Richomme's periodical—both those generated from within and those imposed from without—demonstrate that developing journalistic space for "women only" was not neutral ground no matter how "juste-milieu" its political tenor. This was born out by the fact that as the *JDF* became an important agent in shaping female literary identities, it did not remain a no man's land during these formative years of the mass press. By the mid-1830s, the euphoric moment for a community of women writers in the press seemed to have passed, as advertising and men appropriated their medium and its capital. Coincident with this turn, fashion and literature moved into the new daily press, giving rise to newly gendered spaces such as Constance Aubert's fashion column in the *Siècle* and Delphine Gay de Girardin's weekly column, an amalgam of fashion, society, and sociopolitical commentaries.[28]

Although fashion periodicals akin to Champeaux's 1836 version of the *JDF* flourished and became more specialized, women more interested in what "women say and do rather than what they wear" continued their journalistic work in various publications until the next wave of aggressive feminist journalism in 1848 subordinated the question of women's authorship to women's political rights.[29] In this post–1836 light, the *JDF* played a galvanizing role in a transitional moment when it seemed possible that "Balzac's little sisters" might fare better than he in creating a press of their own.[30]

If the 1840s saw attempts by Balzac, Daumier, Janin, Soulié, and others to pin down, if not arrest, the seemingly ubiquitous *femme-auteur* in her un-fashionable *bas-bleus* (bluestockings), the early 1830s show us examples of actual writing women who were neither exceptional in the manner of George Sand nor faceless members of the "sexe en masse" Sainte-Beuve heard scribbling away in 1833.[31] Their first steps into journalistic space may not directly follow those of the early *flâneur* or the dandy[32] but they do provide more than a fleeting glimpse of women taking up positions in the developing modern press in Paris. As male writers turned their gaze onto the city to create human comedies, numerous female writers negotiated uneasy alliances with fashion-related journalism in order to publish. The over-looked attempt of the *JDF* to advocate a woman-centered, literary journal-ism provides an early, telling example of the subtle ways in which the rhet-oric of *chiffons* denied a name to French women of "privilege" in the press, especially when they were writers with professional designs.

Notes

1. In "Making Sex Public: Félicité de Choiseul-Meuse and the Lewd Novel," Kath-ryn Norberg states that Choiseul-Meuse died in 1824 (*Going Public: Women and Publish-ing in Early Modern France,* Elizabeth C. Goldsmith and Dena Goodman, eds. (Ithaca, N.Y.: Cornell University Press, 1995), 163. While this changes understanding of how Choiseul-Meuse's piece and others by her got into *JDF* (its appearance there now explained by an editorial selection), it still speaks to writing women's growing aware-ness of the changing gendered terms of the print culture.

2. The *roman de femme* usually refers to the novels of feeling by women (such as Adèle de Souza, Claire de Duras, and Sophie Cottin) in the first decades of the nineteenth century. Michel Raimond describes this form as a "pale imitation" of *Werther* or *La Nouvelle Héloïse* in *Le Roman depuis la révolution* (Paris: A. Colin, 1981), 12; Marguerite Iknayan contends that even the best work of these women was "tiresome" and "monotonous," *The Idea of the Novel in France: The Critical Reaction, 1815–1848* (Ge-neva: Droz, 1961), 53.

3. References to the twelve volumes of the collected issues of the *Journal des femmes* (May 1832–December 1835) and to the two volumes of the second series (January 1836–January 1837) appear parenthetically in the text with the appropriate volume and page numbers. The abbreviation *JDF* will be used in the text to refer to the periodical.

4. Richard Terdiman, *Discourse / Counter-Discourse: The Theory and Practice of Symbolic Resistance in Nineteenth-Century France* (Ithaca, N.Y.: Cornell UP, 1985), 129. For further discussion of the role of the press in 1830s print culture, see Walter Benjamin, *Charles Baudelaire: Un poète lyrique à l'apogée du capitalisme,* Jean Lacoste, trans. and pref. (Paris:

Payot, 1974); James Smith Allen, *Popular French Romanticism: Authors, Readers, and Books in the Nineteenth Century* (Syracuse, N.Y.: Syracuse University Press, 1981); and Roland Chollet, *Balzac journaliste: Le tournant de 1830* (Paris: Klincksieck, 1983).

5. Nancy K. Miller, *Subject to Change: Reading Feminist Writing* (New York: Columbia University Press, 1988), 72.

6. Quoted in Iknayan, *The Idea of the Novel in France,* 64. Iknayan cites 1832 as the year the novel was "near the crest of its popularity and of critical acclaim," 61.

7. See also Priscilla P. Ferguson, "The *Flâneur:* The City and Its Discontents," *Paris as Revolution: Writing the Nineteenth-Century City* (Berkeley: University of California Press, 1994), 80–114.

8. See Janet Wolff, "The Invisible *Flâneuse:* Women and the Literature of Modernity," *Feminine Sentences: Essays on Women and Culture* (Berkeley: University of California Press, 1990), 34–50; and Anne Friedberg, " 'Les Flâneurs du Mal (l)': Cinema and the Postmodern Condition," *PMLA* 106 no. 3 (May 1991): 419–31.

9. Roddy Reid, *Families in Jeopardy: Regulating the Social Body in France, 1750–1910* (Stanford: Stanford University Press, 1993).

10. In his *Etudes critiques sur le feuilleton-roman,* 2 vols. (Paris: Perrodil, 1845–46), Alfred Nettement accused Delphine Gay de Girardin of stripping daily newspapers of "la franchise de leurs allures" [their straightforwardness] and "la netteté de leur ligne" [clarity of line]. He also condemned her use of the masculine pseudonym that "vicomte de Launay" as a filmy pretext, "transparent et assez semblable à ces gazes qui n'ont l'air de cacher que pour mieux attirer le regard sur les objets qu'elles enveloppent sans les couvrir" [transparent and rather like those gauzy veils which only seem to hide all the better to steer our gaze to objects they envelop but do not cover], 1: 4.

11. For example, a table of geologic layers, a phrenologic map, a sewing pattern, an art lesson on perspective, various place scenes to accompany travel sketches, and a table explaining how to take reading notes.

12. Volume 1, twenty-two women, thirteen men; volume 6, forty-seven women, no men. Toward the end of the first year it was decided that men would write the book reviews, since women could not be "judges and judged."

13. Evelyne Sullerot, *Histoire de la presse féminine en France des origines à 1848* (Paris: Armand Colin, 1966), 164.

14. Nina Rattner Gelbart, *Feminine Opposition Journalism in Old Regime France: "Le Journal des dames"* (Berkeley: University of California Press, 1987), 36. See Gelbart for discussion of the three female editors, 95–207; see also Suzanna Van Dijk, *Traces de femmes: Présence féminine dans le journalisme français du XVIIIe siècle,* (Amsterdam, APA Holland University Press, 1988).

15. The "call to women" launched by Enfantin became a slogan for the Saint-Simonian-owned *Globe* (1831–32). In the *Femme libre* (1832–34) the Saint-Simonian women made their own "call to women" and privileged their "word." Richomme's use

of the same formulas in a more literary context further complicates contemporary discursive battles over the figure and uses of "woman."

16. A note on the bottom of the page explains that Robert's article was presented as a paper on 24 September 1833 before the "Society on Teaching Methods" as a response to the topic question: "What are the means to further the great intellectual movement of women?"

17. See Margaret Waller, *The Male Malady: Fictions of Impotence in the French Romantic Novel* (New Brunswick, N.J.: Rutgers University Press, 1993).

18. Naomi Schor, "Feminism and George Sand: *Lettres à Marcie,*" *Feminists Theorize the Political,* Judith Butler and Joan W. Scott, eds. (New York: Routledge, 1992), 51.

19. Recalling Betty Friedan's early work, Carolyn Heilbrun reminds us that "privileged" women, most often married and financially secure, nonetheless experience problems for which there are no names in "Non-Autobiographies of 'Privileged' Women: England and America," *Life Lines: Theorizing Women's Autobiography,* Bella Brodzki and Celeste Schenk, eds. (Ithaca, N.Y.: Cornell University Press, 1988), 62–76.

20. In its specialized sense, *"juste-milieu"* was the term used to describe Louis-Philippe's moderate July Monarchy government. Richomme's use of the term to describe her middle-of-the-road position vis-à-vis radically opposed viewpoints on women's legal rights allowed her to take no sides and appease her readers.

21. Jeanne Veret, *La Femme libre,* 8 October 1832 and "Marie-Reine," *La Femme libre* 15 October 1832.

22. *La Perle, ou les femmes littéraires* (Paris: L. Janet, 1832) and *Les Heures du soir: Livre des femmes,* 6 vols. (Paris: Urbain Canel, 1833) are two examples of such publications. Canel's *Heures du soir* included stories by ten *JDF* contributors.

23. Principal publisher of *Almanachs* that included fashion illustrations from as early as 1802 and throughout the Restoration, among them *L'Empire de la mode* (1817), *Paris et ses modes* (1821), *Les Modes et les belles* (1822), *Le Règne de la mode* and *Le Miroir des modes parisiennes* (1824). In 1834 he also published *L'Album de la mode,* a collection of twelve fashion plates.

24. Sullerot, *Histoire de la presse féminine,* 168–74 and 140–41. According to the *Gazette des femmes* (10 July 1836), Paul Simon also owned the *Gazette des salons* and the *Miroir des dames,* which Champeaux directed. After Simon was condemned for debt in mid-January 1836, their ownership probably went to Champeaux who later edited *La Fashion* (1839–41) and *L'Oriflamme des modes* (1840–44). See also Raymond Gaudriault, *La Gravure de mode féminine en France,* Michel Mellot, pref. (Paris: Editions de l'Amateur, 1983), 147, n. 39.

25. Alfred de Montferrand, ed., *Biographie des femmes auteurs contemporaines françaises,* Charles Nodier, intro. (Paris: Armand-Aubrée, 1836).

26. Clémence Robert, Sophie Dudrezène (Uliac-Trémadeure), Aimée Harelle, Emilie Marcel, Mélanie Waldor, and Anaïs Ségalas contributed to Niboyet's paper.

27. Michèle Riot-Sarcey, *La Démocratie à l'épreuve des femmes: Trois figures critiques du pouvoir, 1830–1848* (Paris: Albin Michel, 1994), 43.

28. See Cheryl A. Morgan, "Les Chiffons de la M(éd)use: Delphine Gay de Girardin, journaliste," *Romantisme* 85, no. 3 (1994): 57–66.

29. Thus Eugénie Foa, in a summer 1843 issue of the second *Gazette des femmes* (1841–44), reported on the activities of the Académie des femmes, a female French academy and writers' society rolled into one and sponsored by Jules de Castellane. Mentioned as participants in this "great work" were Foa herself, George Sand, Virginie Ancelot, Delphine Gay de Girardin, Mme de Bawr, Clémence Robert, and Anaïs Ségalas, many of whom were at that time publishing material in another *Journal des femmes* (1840–51). See also "Les Académies de femmes en France" by "Une Vieille Saint-Simonienne," *Revue des revues* (15 December 1899): 557–74. Neither the *Gazette des femmes* nor the *Journal des femmes* of the 1840s were directed by women. The *Journal des femmes* claimed to unite "the most honorable and literary names of our time" (20 September 1840). The *Gazette des femmes* more closely resembled Richomme's periodical—even to the point of recycling some *JDF* pieces—although it was noticeably more geared to society life.

30. Although the phrase acknowledges Christine Planté's *La Petite Soeur de Balzac: Essai sur la femme auteur* (Paris: Seuil, 1989), I am more interested in women's journalistic practices in their own right.

31. C.-A. Sainte-Beuve, Rev. of *Lélia, Portraits contemporains,* New edition, 5 vols. (Paris: Calmann-Lévy, 1881) 1: 495–96.

32. In chapter 6 of *The Dandy: Brummel to Beerbohm* (New York: Viking Press, 1960), Ellen Moers examines the dandy who went "to press" in 1830.

8 Between Seeing and Believing

Representing Women in Appert's *Crimes de la Commune*

It is hardly possible to write a history of information separately from a history of the corruption of the press.
— *Walter Benjamin, "Paris of the Second Empire in Baudelaire"*

To speak of gender and revolutionary imagery in nineteenth-century France is to find oneself, inevitably, in the company of Eugène Delacroix. His *Liberty Leading the People* provided the century with one of its most durable allegories of the revolutionary impulse that rocked the nation periodically from 1789 until its final convulsions in 1871 (fig. 8-1). *Liberty* is nothing if not history painting conceived on a grand scale. In its juxtaposition of gritty resolve and grim corpses, it is meant to account for both the reality of experience on the barricades on 28 July 1830 (significantly, the title of the painting often includes this "dateline"), but it also came to stand for something more: the enduring, unfinished struggle of the people for freedom.

Crucially, what is real about this painting and what is allegorical turns on the female figure standing atop the barricade, breast bared and tricolor held aloft. Delacroix's Liberty is both particularly described and testimony to the artist's revolutionary investment in the believable concreteness of the visible. Not a goddess condescending to mix with mere mortals, she is a woman arrested in the process of transcending her own mortality to become a sign (and this incomplete process of transcendence is perhaps best thematized in the awkward transition between the flattened, almost archaic rendering of her head and the fully rounded muscularity of her body).[1] In her composite character and her commanding materiality, her irresolvability (is she a vision or a person?) and her total authority, Liberty not only embodies the promise of revolution, she also stands for a changing sense of history and one's access to the past. Scholars have often noted that insofar as Liberty functions as allegory, she derives a good deal of her allegorical authority from conventional iconographic representations of History.[2] While Delacroix may have exchanged History's pen and opened book for the revolutionary's

FIGURE 8-1: Eugène Delacroix, *Liberty Leading the People,* oil on canvas, 1830, Musée du Louvre, Paris. © Photo RMN H. Lewandowski.

rifle, he kept Liberty's leading foot firmly planted on the quadratic stone that, in images of History, had long stood for the "uncorrupted truth." Moreover in *Liberty,* the "uncorrupted truth" is not merely represented as a symbolic square of rock. Truth also takes the form of a meticulously painted, on-the-spot reportage: the sturdy washerwoman's arms of Liberty herself, the cravat and black topcoat of the bourgeois bearing his rifle to the ready, the torn uniform of the dead national guardsman fallen in the foreground. Revolution, such descriptive work attests, is above all history-in-the-making; allegory is to be literally a part of the here-and-now.

By 1871, despite such a well-established prototype (*Liberty* had been publicly exhibited in 1831, 1848, and 1855, and engravings of her and after her were readily available), it seemed impossible to conceive any such confident rendering. No significant history painting was to be produced out of the events of the *année terrible,* nor of the barricades raised to defend Paris both from Prussian attack during the siege of 1870–71 and from the Versaillais troops who later flooded the Communard-controlled city to return it to a centralized French rule. Instead, the memory of Delacroix's *Liberty* echoed most convincingly not in paint, but in the mass press, where her allegorical value had turned to caricature more often than not.[3] And she tended to appear less often as the virtuous embodiment of revolutionary freedom, than as the vulgar incarnation of insurrection (of course, such vulgarity had always been a part of *Liberty*'s power and her continued currency). Transformed (or "inverted") into the *pétroleuse,* or female arsonist, she was meant to represent those women blamed for willfully setting fire to much of Paris during the desperate days of the *semaine sanglante,* the bloody week of street fighting and massive casualties that brought the Commune to an end in May 1871[4] (figs. 8-2 and 8-3). Explicitly "of the people" and yet not quite human, meant to be more sensationally particular than in any way "universal," cruel images of the *pétroleuse* as a torch-bearing harridan on the barricades or a shrieking "emancipated woman" in the streets argued that Liberty's latest Communard incarnation was fueled not by ennobling sentiment but by fever-pitched emotion; she was not the wellspring of revolutionary fervor but the catalyst of popular hysteria.[5]

As for Delacroix's easy union of the authority of bodily presence and the effect of allegorical transcendence, by 1871 painting had largely ceded the force of that claim to photography. Since its simultaneous invention in France and England in 1839, photography had been celebrated as *the* definitively transparent, dumbly mechanistic mode of reproducing the real (indeed, it might not be too much to suggest that certain passages of Delacroix's *Liberty* dream of photography *avant la lettre*). Photography was nature's "pencil" or "mirror," but it was also culturally invested with a mysterious excess that rendered it a peculiarly revealing trace. Photographed objects seemed almost inevitably to appear as themselves and also something more: a tantalizing clue in a detective story, an eloquent souvenir of an absent lover, a piece of hard evidence introduced into a court of law. Moreover, photography not only provided the nineteenth century with an image of history experienced as fragmentary, concrete, immediate, but also immediately a representation, real but also really nothing without interpretation (the caption or archive or narrative to which it was all too tenuously bound). Photography was also the preferred metaphor for a broad cultural investment in visible reality, which is to say it was not simply a medium but a system of meaning, whose mere invocation could signal a range of effects dealing with authenticity, truthfulness, the persuasiveness of the factual, the inevitable authority of the natural, the excitement of the modern.[6] In this sense, photography resides at the nexus of a convergence between the ideological power of the real allegory as one means by which modern society increasingly embodied its beliefs and a range of media of mechanical repro-

FIGURE 8-2: Bertall, "La Barricade," lithograph, *Types de la Commune,* c. 1871, McCormick Library of Special Collections, Northwestern University Library.

La Femme, émancipée, répandant la lumière sur le monde.

FIGURE 8-3: Lecerf, "La Femme émancipée répandant la lumière sur le monde" [The Emancipated Woman Shedding Light on the World], 1871. Musée Carnavalet, Paris. © Photothèque des Musées de la Ville de Paris.

duction no less ideological in function that packaged those beliefs for dissemination and consumption. These media would include the mass press, whose mass appeal was predicated in no small part upon its transformation from an instrument of opinion (largely political) to one of information dissemination (largely quotidian and sensationalist, a montage of crimes, celebrity sightings, political scandals and natural catastrophes, the you-were-there assurances of the *actualité,* the distractions of the *faits divers,* and the democratic come-ons of the commercial advertisements that subsidized the entire enterprise).[7] Even before the mass press could accommodate photographs in its pages, it invoked photography as the mode (and model) of objectivity most well-suited, ideologically if not yet technologically, to the requirements of a modern, information-based society.[8] And such invocations worked both ways, since photography, I will suggest, had already recognized its journalistic future.

What does this have to do with the *pétroleuse?* As visibility took on a central role in articulating *and* substantiating beliefs about modern life, photography answered to this requirement by becoming the ultimate guarantor of visibility. Yet the *pétroleuse* was, by definition, problematically outside the visible: a revolutionary woman who stalked the streets furtively and alone, not perched atop the barricades as if they were a theatrical set (or knitting before the guillotine in the same theatrical manner), but lurking in the shadows, slipping beyond the spectacle, armed with the silent yet voracious power of incendiary materials. Caricature, which relies upon the exaggeration and transformation of already visible traits in order to produce meaning, was hard put when it came to the *pétroleuse,* and its shrilly over-the-top, obsessively repetitive range of solutions was an indication of the degree to which it found itself overburdened with its descriptive project.[9] Moreover, it was not simply that the *pétroleuse*'s activities were invisible for all intents and purposes; the *pétroleuse* herself was largely mythic. Notwithstanding the blackened monuments that marred the center of Paris in the Commune's aftermath, and the public trials of five women incendiaries in particular, there was a conspicuous lack of hard evidence for the *pétroleuse*'s existence.[10] Nevertheless, she remained a crucial ideological tool in the campaign to discredit the Commune and a strong argument for the suppression of revolutionary Paris.[11] Her unverifiability was perhaps all the more reason to crank up the visual machinery and keep her image incessantly before the public. But what happened, I want to ask, when one of the most powerful imaginary constructions of the Commune encountered the technology that had the potential to make her real?[12] If French society needed to see the *pétroleuse* in order to believe in her, then what *would* they see when she was brought before the camera?

Take, for instance, Eugène Appert's composite photographs of the pivotal events of spring 1871, marketed as a series entitled *Les Crimes de la Commune*. A Parisian portrait photographer specializing in images of government officials and royalty, Appert remained active well into the 1880s. Several times previously, most notably during the French war with Prussia, he had tried his hand at recycling these portraits into a more topical product, producing such novelties as an image of Louis-Napoléon and his generals at Châlon by cutting and pasting their heads onto a staged scene of the military encampment, and then rephotographing and printing the result.[13] Appert fabricated the approximately twelve composite images associated with the *Crimes de la Commune* in a similar manner. Their production spanned a period of several months, with the first images of the series entering a lively market in Commune memorabilia in September 1871; in time they would appear in a variety of formats including *carte-de-visite* postcards and deluxe prints.[14] Although obviously not able to compete with the scale of history painting, Appert, who advertised himself as a *peintre-photographe,* doubtless had history painting's ambitions in mind. The *Crimes de la Commune* was by far the most complicated project the photographer had ever mounted; it marked Appert's most sustained engagement with the composite technique, his greatest commercial success, and his most significant attempt to intervene in the imaging of contemporary life. Perhaps as a result of its popularity, Appert produced at least one more related image the following year: a composition of Maréchal François-Achille Bazaine staring glumly at the guard mounted outside the house at Versailles where he was detained while awaiting trial for treacherous acts on the battlefields of Metz in 1870.

As will quickly become obvious, it would be too easy a task to simply align the *Crimes de la Commune* with the prevailing modes of female identity in play in the press and elsewhere during the period of the Commune. The significance of Appert's images, I would suggest, stems not so much from their ideological originality as from the peculiar power of their ideological restatements. Nor, in the end, will the *Crimes de la Commune* offer much help in extracting the real experience of women from the photographic traces they left behind—although photography's "indexical" status as an image almost akin to a fingerprint often tempts the pursuit of such a project.[15] Instead, I propose to focus on the positioning of female characters as significant presences and as signifying elements within Appert's composite dramas; to focus on them, explicitly, as *photographic* representations whose force of reality and fragmentary character, concreteness and semiotic volatility were all part of the way they intersected with a lexicon of types and physiognomies that was itself all too quickly established.[16] Tucked in and among Appert's stiffly staged scenes of Communard atrocities and executions, pictured gathered together en masse after their arrests, or presenting a straight little row of backs in the spectator's gallery at the military tribunals of Versailles: if women were to allegorize the Commune's threat, to visualize both its power and, ultimately, its containment, then how might photography itself inflect that process of allegorization? Such a question would seem to allow a different look at images that have often been bluntly dismissed as "mere" propagandistic attempts to justify the brutal suppression of the "criminal" Commune.[17] However important it is to take their propagandizing gambits seriously, privileging gender as a determining category of analysis might offer the possibility of saying something historically specific about the deep structure of the *Crimes de la Commune* as a series; it might also entail examining the limits of its propagandistic value as well as its particular persuasiveness. Hence, my interest in locating Appert's representations of women at the nascent juncture between photography and contemporary journalism, two modes of meaning with historical points of encounter with propaganda, in particular to the degree that their persuasive power is dependent upon their appearance of being unmediated (their "transparency") and disinterested (their "objectivity"). But that said, my aim is not to position Appert's production in such a way as to confirm (yet again) the coercive uses of photography and its disciplinary role in a modern society in which power and visibility are closely joined.[18] Instead my concern is to probe the weaknesses and possible blindspots of the medium in its emergent journalistic form, to begin to understand, in sum, the constraints Appert's mode of representation may have placed upon his message. The *Crimes de la Commune* would seem a particularly interesting test case in this regard, not only for what it might reveal concerning nineteenth-century practices of photography as such, but also for how it registers the pressures of an event-driven conception of the mass press to which photography would make an increasingly large contribution.

Taken as a whole, the *Crimes de la Commune* is important for a number of reasons: it foreshadows the shift from portraiture, landscape, and still life to current events and "instantaneous" reportage as one of the defining concerns of modern photography; it reveals the technical inadequacies of the photographic medium at that transitional moment—its cumbersome slowness and inability to capture the "action" as it unfolded; and it also offers a

FIGURE 8-4: Charles Soulier, *Hôtel de Ville incendié,* composite photograph, c. 1871,
Bibliothèque historique de la Ville de Paris.

glimpse of photography's possibilities—not the least in its unsurpassed ability to concentrate and distill the essence of an event into a single, significant moment. However, it does not do to overlook the obvious: although the *pétroleuse* held a nearly unshakable grip on the imagination of post-Commune Paris, and despite her obvious marketability, Appert staged no scenes in the *Crimes de la Commune* of *pétroleuses* caught in the act. Nor, for that matter, does the series include any representations of the fires that raged throughout Paris during the *semaine sanglante.* Appert left it to other photographers to fashion such images—and several of them did, although admittedly with less than perfect success. Like Appert, they had to rely upon the composite technique—stitching together a whole scene from bits and pieces of scenery and isolated figures and then retouching and rephotographing the result. One such image of the burned-out Hôtel de Ville, pictorially reignited so that the "fires" might be quenched one more time for the camera, suggests just how clumsy the results could be (fig. 8-4). What viewer, however naive or inattentive, could overlook the incongruous contrast between the completely gutted building and the billowing clouds of hand-painted smoke, or reconcile the blurry shapes of the bystanders in the foreground with the sharply defined but undersized figures of the collaged firemen fighting the blaze? It may seem easy to discount these bungled attempts out of hand, but

FIGURE 8-5: Eugène Appert, "Monseigneur Darboy, Archevêque de Paris, dans la cellule no. 23," [Monsignor Darboy, Archbishop of Paris, in cell no. 23], composite photograph, *Les Crimes de la Commune,* 1871. Collection of the author.

their existence remains important in at least one way. For while it is tempting to credit Appert's limited themes to the insurmountable technical difficulties that might have been posed by re-creating the sensational acts of the *pétroleuses* and the lurid atmospheric effects of Paris burning, these images would suggest that such practical considerations may not, of themselves, have constituted sufficient deterrents.[19] So from the outset we need to frame Appert's selection of scenes as purposeful, and his omissions as deliberate.

If not rampaging *pétroleuses,* then what? Appert focused largely on scenes of public execution and retribution; at times they seem designed to form matched sets or "miniseries." One coupling, for example, might place the deaths by impromptu firing squad of Generals Clément Thomas and Lecomte that marked the Commune's beginnings against the official execution of Communard leaders Ferré, Rossel, and Bourgeois on the Satory plain

PRISON DES CHANTIERS, LE 15 AOÛT 1871.
VERSAILLES

INTÉRIEUR DE LA PRISON DES CHANTIERS

FIGURE 8-6: Eugène Appert, "Intérieur de la prison des Chantiers," [Interior of Chantiers Prison], composite photograph, *Les Crimes de la Commune,* 1871. Collection of the author.

after the Commune fell. Another grouping might compare the hastily organized deaths of Republican journalist Gustave Chaudey, or Archbishop Darboy of Paris, with the formal pomp of the trials of accused Communards in the months following the Commune's defeat. On at least two occasions, Appert "expanded" the place of an event within the series by framing it with more explicitly portrait-like tableaux whose iconic value seems deliberately greater than their narrative content: a "reunion-like" gathering of the monks who escaped slaughter at Arceuil (to complement an image of those who succumbed in the massacre on May 25), for example; or a peepshow staging of Monsignor Darboy calmly passing the final hours of his life in cell number 23 at La Roquette prison, the carceral setting combined with the word *"surveillant"* stenciled on the adjacent cell door placing in play the disciplinary paradigm of the camera as panoptic device with stunning clarity (fig. 8-5). (The "series" also included an image of the bodies of Darboy and his colleagues being removed from the execution site.) The pictorial conceit of the composite-style portrait gallery shows up yet again in another possible pairing: the "massacre" of Commune-held hostages in the rue Haxo during the heated confusion of Bloody Week, and the mass roundup of female Communards displayed in the detention camps at Versailles (figs. 8-6 and

FIGURE 8-7: Eugène Appert, "Assasinat de 62 otages, Rue Haxo," [Assassination of 62 Hostages, Rue Haxo], composite photograph, *Les Crimes de la Commune*, 1871. Collection of the author.

8-7). In most cases, Appert preferred to stage his images within the formal settings of institutionally administered force: the executioner's wall, the prison, the court—whether under the control of the Commune or the Versailles government. And this would seem one indication of Appert's responsiveness to his medium, for as frames these settings themselves signified events that could and were meant to be watched and witnessed: public spectacles in which action and exhibition-value were closely joined—in marked opposition to the stealthy activities of the *pétroleuses*. But, as these last two images begin to suggest, the presence of women was central to such spectacles as well.

Both its supporters and detractors commented upon the high-profile visibility of women during the Commune in terms that, despite their more obvious polemical differences, could be at bottom remarkably similar.[20] "Women everywhere," exulted Jules Vallès, "What a great sign!" "Quand les femmes s'en mêlent, quand la ménagère pousse son homme, quand elle arrache le drapeau noir qui flotte sur la marmite pour le planter entre deux pavés, c'est que le soleil se lèvera sur une ville en révolte"[21] [When the women get mixed up in things, when the housewife gives her husband a push, when she snatches the black cloth covering the stewpot and plants it like a flag between two paving stones, it means the sun will rise on a city in revolt]. (Unless otherwise noted, all translations in this chapter are my own.) While Communards such as Vallès celebrated the presence of everyday women whose participation they took, sadly and mistakenly, as the greatest guarantee of the Commune's ultimate success (that is to say, Vallès valued the women both symbolically *and* pragmatically—as both representations of victory and the much-needed motive force behind their laggard spouses), anti-Communard voices tended to emphasize the extraordinary ferocity and tenacious demeanor of the women who fought during the *semaine sanglante*. But like Vallès, Maxime du Camp, among others, still remarked upon the profound influence that "women," and then he corrected himself, "females" had on their male counterparts, especially during the last, desperate days of May: "Là, comme dans toutes les tueries de la dernière heure, les femmes donnèrent l'exemple. Pendant ces tièdes journées de mai, au renouveau, la femme,—la femelle,—exerça sur les mâles une influence extraordinaire [There, as with all the butchery that took place during the final hours, women set the example. During those mild May days of spring, the woman— the female—exercised an extraordinary influence over the males].[22] Du Camp's last shift, from the social role of the *femme* to the biological relation-ship of the *femelle* to her mate is deeply telling, for time and again it was as if the women of the Commune had exerted an almost instinctual pull over their male counterparts (as if revolutionary fervor could be equated with being "in heat"). *Le Monde illustré* put the social threat posed by the Com-mune just this way, detecting in the "dirty" and "sordid" aspect of the imprisoned *Communardes* the dimmed sex appeal of those "viragos" who in inciting the passions of their "socialist Don Quixotes" had also schemed for the emancipation of women.[23]

Such fundamental consensus across partisan boundaries brings me to my second point concerning Appert's choice of themes. As spectacles, they represented eminently social events, but as social events they brought the particular bind of women participants into acute focus. On the one hand, this consensus assumed a conception of society as thoroughly saturated with the feminine (indeed, such a conception almost went without saying, for it was held in tension with the connection between masculinity and individu-ality).[24] On the other hand, it dramatized the potential for falling out of the rightful social order of any woman claiming an active role in that society.[25] Such a bind might be extended from the woman participant to the Com-mune itself, for it typified the widespread perception of the Commune as feminized—woman-defined and woman-perpetuated—while serving to rationalize its brutal suppression (because such an aberration as a society constituted in no small part by "females" was always already outside the Law).

The events leading to the so-called massacre on the rue Haxo place us at the heart of the matter. On the afternoon of May 26, as the *semaine sanglante* was drawing to a close, a group of fifty hostages chosen nearly at random (among them Parisian guards, *gendarmes,* police informers, and clerics) was taken from La Roquette prison and paraded through the streets to the twentieth arrondissement, to Belleville, the quarter that *Le Figaro* characterized as "that sinister breeding ground of riots."[26] A barely controllable crowd had gathered by the time the convoy reached the rue Haxo, and it called loudly for the hostages' execution. Officials of the Communard government, among them Jules Vallès, tried, unsuccessfully, to intervene. The hostages, in groups of three and four, one group following hard upon another, were put to death in a furious onslaught of rifle fire and bayonet thrusts. The entire incident was said to have spanned a little over fifteen minutes.

Women figured luridly and almost folklorically in nearly every contemporary account of the events that took place on the rue Haxo that day—that is, they made their appearance through a series of well-established tropes put into play by those on both sides of the partisan fence.[27] Predictably, such official mouthpieces as Maxime du Camp and Jules Claretie reveled in the most ghastly anecdotes: rumored instances of women stomping on the bloody corpses; sightings of women repairing to a café to refresh themselves with strong drink once the mayhem was over; and tales of their bragging—especially the claim made by one young woman that she had tried to rip the tongue from a dead curate's mouth. The most notorious figure, however, was cut by a young *cantinière* sporting a red *képi* and mounted upon a white horse. In the midst of the efforts to calm the crowd, it was she who reportedly gave the command to open fire.[28] Further, it is worth noting that although only one woman was ever brought to trial in connection with the events on the rue Haxo, Vallès himself confirmed such reports, albeit couched in more sympathetic terms.[29] In *L'Insurgé,* he takes pains to explain that one of the blood-stained women at the café was avenging her sister who had been corrupted by a priest. The *cantinière* who gave the command to fire did so as revenge for her father's incarceration and death in prison at the hands of police spies.[30] Viragos or victims—the stories amounted to much the same thing.

Appert's representation of the afternoon on the rue Haxo frames the moment of high drama just as the executions were about to begin (see fig. 8-7). The mounted *cantinière* raises her sword; her steed appears to rear back on his hind legs, lifting her above the crowd. The hostages await their fate with dignity and resignation. A crush of both male and female Communards make ready to fire; indeed the women outnumber the men in the foreground plane. To heighten the impact of the scene and to capitalize upon its scale, Appert masses all of the victims and all of the perpetrators together in one image, despite reports that the hostages were shot in smaller groups and in spite of the fact that this compositional decision has the unfortunate result of causing the tightly packed group of Communards to appear in danger of shooting each other.

The liberties Appert took in compressing the massacre of the rue Haxo into a single image may seem to militate against its value as an eyewitness representation—the value that would seem most specific to photographic representations in general. But such liberties were common in the illustrated press, from which Appert no doubt took his cue. More than one image from the *Crimes de la Commune* suggests that Appert relied not only on textual accounts of these "crimes," but more crucially on engraved representations that had already appeared in such periodicals as *L'Illustration*. Appert's reconstruction of the "Executions of Generals Clément Thomas and Lecomte" provides a case in point, and it takes advantage of a similar narrative device— for these two representatives of the Versailles government, who met their fate after the army's bungled attempt to confiscate the cannons of Montmartre on March 18, were shot not side by side but one after another, the hapless Lecomte forced to stand next to the already dead Thomas; and according to *L'Illustration,* neither was felled in a single volley of gunfire, but rather each rifleman took his turn, one after the other, in the style of military executions (figs. 8-8 and 8-9).[31] Yet *L'Illustration*'s engraving, with the two generals standing side by side to face their executioners, was presented to the journal's readers as an accurate rendering of the incident, precise in its details as to protagonists and setting, and indeed *L'Illustration*'s market niche was as a purveyor of *actualités*—crisply topical accounts of current events, whose claim to objectivity was in no small part secured by the presence of visual "evidence." To a great degree, Appert relied upon these images to invest his own compositions with the authority of ostensibly "straight" reportage; in turn, this reliance placed his photographic products in direct competition with such "documentary" engravings.[32]

In the case of the execution of the two generals, Appert's most significant departures from his engraved "model" consisted in pulling back slightly from the overall scene and inserting a ragged little group of spectators into the background. These departures doubly exploited photography's all-encompassing and minutely detailed ability to capture reality, for while they

FIGURE 8-8: "Mort des généraux Clément-Thomas et Lecomte," [Death of Generals Clément-Thomas and Lecomte], engraving, *L'Illustration*, 25 March 1871, 164. Courtesy of Doe Library, University of California, Berkeley.

require exchanging the up-close immediacy of the draftsman's sketch for the panoramic comprehensivity of the photographic view, they do so without any sacrifice of descriptive texture, providing, if anything, more (*more* particulars of costume, physiognomy, setting) to look at. Indeed, this sense of "seeing more" is what the spectators seem placed there to enact. As in other images, the group comprises both men and women, and its addition has much to do with the overall impact of Appert's project as I see it. For insofar as it is possible to construct a master narrative for such a fragmentary (and sometimes oddly arbitrary) collection of images, that narrative would seem to concern conceptualizing the performative value of looking; modeling the various positions for viewing the Commune-as-visual spectacle; and aligning these viewing positions with polemical positions regarding the Commune itself. Could it be merely accidental that more than one image requires the viewer to take the position of executioner, looking down the barrel of a gun, only to place that same viewer in the spectators' gallery at the public trials? Such pictorial decisions make visible the degree to which the activity of exhibiting Communard Paris might be just as contested as the barricades themselves. Moreover, they conspire to stage the suppression of the Com-

ASSASSINAT DES GÉNÉRAUX CLÉMENT THOMAS & JULES LECOMTE
Rue des Rosiers 6 à Montmartre
DANS LA JOURNÉE DU 18 MARS 1871

FIGURE 8-9: Eugène Appert, "Exécution des généraux Clément-Thomas et Lecomte," [Execution of Generals Clément-Thomas and Lecomte], composite photograph, *Les Crimes de la Commune,* 1871. Collection of the author.

mune as a narrative of realignment and reordering, a story of returning ownership of that exhibitionary power to the ruling class.[33]

Certainly images of the Commune as spectacle filled the pages of the illustrated press both during the spring of 1871 and well into the summer. Two typical engravings, for example, split their attractions between the panorama and the close-up, the one taking a mapmaker's long view of the *guerre civile,* and the other proposing that not even the least fragment of ruined Paris was beneath notice. The first appeared in *Le Monde illustré* the week of May 6 (fig. 8-10). In the background stretches the field of engagement to the south of Paris, between the Communard-held forts along the Parisian perimeter and the onslaught of the Versailles troops, where the fighting had been fiercest in the weeks leading up to the *semaine sanglante.* The foreground is occupied by a parade of spectators clambering to the rooftops of their houses on the *rive gauche* the better to take in the view of the fires and

FIGURE 8-10: Sellier and Vierge, "La Guerre civile—vue panoramique de toutes les positions du sud de Paris," [The Civil War—Panoramic View of All Positions to the South of Paris], engraving, *Le Monde illustré,* 6 May 1871, 280–81.

explosions that dot the landscape; several even use telescopes and binoculars to enhance their vision. It is a mixed crowd—of men, women and children, some men in top hats, others in workers' caps and smocks, some women with neatly bonneted heads, others protected only by a loosely knotted kerchief—and indeed this social mixture was the Parisian crowd most often on view while the Commune held sway.[34] Moreover, not only is the rooftop crowd varied in terms of gender, age, and class, we might speculate that it was also divided in terms of its sympathy to the Commune itself, for the *arrondissements* of the Left Bank were the quickest to capitulate when government soldiers finally gained access to the city center.

The second image, published in *Le Monde illustré* the week of June 24, displays the devastation wrought by the *semaine sanglante* safely transformed into a touristic ruin to be scrutinized by residents and visitors alike, with binoculars, magnifying glasses, and even, in the upper left-hand corner of the image, a camera (fig. 8-11). The aftermath of Communard Paris had to be seen to be believed, the engraving argues, and every available device for enhancing that view—from hand-held, personal optics to published drawings and photographs—was to be pressed into service with that aim in mind. Indeed, in both images, I would suggest that the picturing of such devices as binoculars and magnifying glasses is more than merely anecdotal. Rather, these devices mark the places in the images where the argument is most urgently put that the engravings themselves are equivalent to such optical devices; they are also mechanisms to be seen through, framing and mediating the spectacle of the Commune with a sense of immediacy and enhanced visual mastery meant to assure the consumers of *L'Illustration* and *Le Monde*

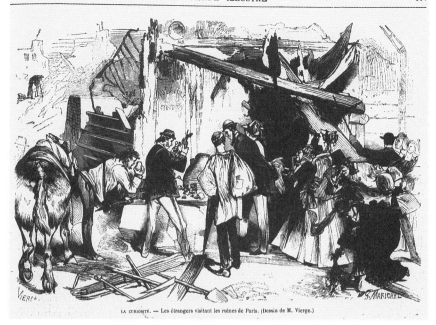

LA CURIOSITÉ. — Les étrangers visitant les ruines de Paris. (Dessin de M. Vierge.)

FIGURE 8-11: Vierge, "La Curiosité—les étrangers visitant les ruines de Paris," [Curiosity—Foreigners Visiting the Ruins of Paris], engraving, *Le Monde illustré,* 24 June 1871, 397.

illustré that to hold the magazine in their hands constituted a special purchase on contemporary events.

Of course, at some level these images simply affirm that, in the nineteenth century as it would be in the twentieth, the pleasurable practice of rubber-necking was nearly universal. People like to look, especially upon disaster—this is, after all, the truism that the illustrated presses of the nineteenth century (not to mention the producers of today's reality-based media) counted upon. But it is more than that, for the vision of spectatorship framed by these images has specific implications for our historical under-standing of the thematics of idle public looking and spectacle-gazing as a privileged pastime limited to the Parisian, bourgeois male—to the *flâneur* as he was so famously called.[35] In this respect, I would suggest that the pres-ence *of women* spectators is crucial to such images as those appearing in *Le Monde illustré;* that is, these women were there to confirm the status of Communard Paris as spectacular *by their looking,* which was as much at issue as the status of being constantly available to view that was the presumed lot of any woman who passed through the public spaces of the city.[36] And by restoring that look to certain types of women—the fashionably dressed, properly escorted women who gazed, transfixed, upon ruined Paris—these images sought to confirm that order had been restored to the city (and the nation) at large. This is where Appert also comes in.

Before expanding upon that point with respect to the *Crimes de la Commune,* let me make one last observation regarding the photograph of the rue Haxo (see fig. 8-7): Appert's image may be framed by the visual dialogue between his work and the engraved *actualités* appearing in such journals as *L'Illustration* and *Le Monde illustré,* but it also represents a significant departure. Interestingly, the Haxo incident was *not* widely featured in the illustrated press. The executions of Chaudey and the Archbishop of Paris must have seemed more urgently newsworthy at the time. Judicial authorities, however, later commissioned Appert to photograph the area around the rue Haxo as part of the process of evidence gathering for the Communard trials.[37] Clearly, Appert must have recognized his unique opportunity to break new ground in representing the Commune's "criminal" acts, and he exercised his visual and entrepreneurial skills to the utmost in its realization. As one of his most elaborate productions, the Haxo composition reportedly necessitated a call for actors "from all the theaters of Paris."[38] In one sense, the appeal is obvious: taking on the project of representing the events of the rue Haxo offered him the irresistible opportunity to one-up the illustrated press, supplying an image that outclassed their own product—it is Appert's version of an "exclusive." But more than just another scene of Commune-perpetrated horror, it also offered him a way to tap into the most potent threat of the Commune on his own terms, offering visual confirmation that women participated publicly and collectively (rather than secretly and alone) in the disorder of the Commune. This the illustrated press did not do, for by and large women were *not* widely featured in the scenes of executions and streetfighting that filled its pages.

If the "Massacre on the rue Haxo" provided consumers of the *Crimes de la Commune* with eyewitness-style evidence of women's prominent involvement in Communard atrocities, then Appert's view of the women's quarters at the makeshift prisons of Versailles can only be seen as its inevitable pendant (see fig. 8-6). The post-Commune call to order demanded that an image of female participation be matched by one of female incarceration. No need to wait for a trial: Appert's view of "The Interior of Chantiers Prison," where many of those women accused of participation in the insurrection were detained, places these women on public display, identifying them generally as "*Pétroleuses,* Ambulance Workers, Canteen Workers, etc. etc.," and then naming particular names—often incorrectly—in two long columns of text. Their photographic visibility was meant to be part of their punishment (the ignominious fate of wives and daughters who had, against the codes of propriety, dared to claim a role in public life), but it was also a vital part of society's "cure." Among many other bourgeois gawkers, Dumas *fils* made the pilgrimmage to the detention camps at Versailles, justifying the excursion in typically positivist fashion: "J'ai été à Versailles *pour voir;* voir c'est savoir, savoir c'est prévoir" [I went to Versailles *to see;* to see is to know; to know is to be able to foresee].[39] Once there, however, he found the spectacle of post-Commune Versailles almost *un*seeable, floating beyond his optical grasp:

> A la surface flottait cette population molle, incolore et huileuse qui surnage au dessus des civilisations excessives, qui se déplace selon les courants et qui tache partout où elle touche, incapable de se fixer d'ailleurs et ne reflétant jamais rien, si bleu que soit le ciel et si profondes qui soient les vagues.[40]

> [To the surface floated this indolent, colorless, and oily population that survives on intemperate civilizations. It is displaced according to the currents; it soils everywhere it touches, incapable of settling anywhere and never reflecting anything, no matter how blue the sky and how dark the waves.]

Shifting and colorless, fluctuating and light-absorbing, a free-floating jumble of surfaces lacking contrast and edge: Dumas's inability to perceive the contours of the mass of humanity gathered at the nation's "new" temporary capital seems to cry out for a photographic fix. Less literary but more pragmatic, *Le Figaro* diagnosed just this solution to Dumas's (all too temporary) sensation of post-Commune disorientation when it expressed the widely shared wish that the hordes of prisoners could be photographed and so studied at leisure, particularly by residents of the provinces who may well have wondered how "*ces fantastiques théories*" could have held Paris in check for so long.[41]

Appert seized the chance to give *Le Figaro*'s "fantastic theories" material form, for luck and a knack for knowing an opportunity when he saw one had placed him in a particularly good position to do so. After dutifully fulfilling the commission for views of the rue Haxo, Appert used his position as an already semiofficial government photographer to negotiate with both the state and the Communard prisoners for permission to photograph the detainees at Versailles. The state was overwhelmed by its own policy of mass arrest and saw in photography a potential means to process its suddenly swollen prison population more efficiently.[42] For their part, the Communards seemed to have welcomed any chance to leave a photographic memento to their families in the wake of the death they believed certain. For most of the working-class prisoners, Appert's offer, sweetened with the promise of unlimited complimentary prints, would have provided a rare opportunity indeed—access to the portrait studios of the *grands boulevards* was usually beyond their economic reach.[43] Small wonder that both Appert's state patrons and his Communard "clients" readily agreed to the plan.

Rigging an open-air portrait studio from a chair and a plain backdrop, Appert photographed hundreds of the accused Communards, and these images, over which the photographer retained exclusive rights, provided the fodder and much of the visual fascination and concreteness of the *Crimes de la Commune*. In their memoirs of the Commune, both Marc-Amédée Gromier, a shopkeeper and secretary to Communard leader Félix Pyat, and the Communard activist Louise Michel, reported having their portraits made by Appert.[44] The photographer's inventory also included images of the notorious *pétroleuses* Eugénie Suétens and Elizabeth Rétiffe, publicly tried and condemned to death for their supposed roles in the torchings of the Légion d'honneur and the rue de Lille (the sentence was later commuted to deportation and hard labor) (figs. 8-12 and 8-13).[45] Both women are pictured seated solemnly, in conventional portrait poses, as groomed as they could manage under extraordinarily abject prison conditions. And both women turn up in Appert's composite view of the prison yard; they are featured prominently in the right foreground in a group of *Communarde* celebrities that also included Louise Michel (standing, arms folded, to the right of Rétiffe).

Moreover, such deliberate grooming and posing were typical of Appert's prison portraits in general, although decorum and propriety were not always their intent (poses of defiance were equally possible and sometimes assumed). It is worth remembering that the conventions of police photography were still evolving in 1871, and such "mugshots" as those produced by Appert required not only the simple consent but indeed the active complicity of both State and sitter: how else to accommodate ourselves to the poignant strangeness and tender formality of Appert's double portrait of the Clémence sisters, the hands of one sister folded neatly on the shoulder of the other, both soberly presenting a three-quarter view to the camera (fig. 8-14). Brought before the camera's disciplinary gaze, this image seeks to document the sisters "as they were," but it also stages them as they most

LÉONTINE SUÉTENS
(Condamnée à mort. Commutation.)
D'après une photographie faite à la prison
des Chantiers, à Versailles.

ISABELLE RÉTIFFE
(Condamnée à mort. Commutation.)
D'après une photographie faite dans la prison
des Chantiers, à Versailles.

FIGURE 8-12: Eugène Appert, *Léontine* [sic] *(Eugénie) Suétens, carte-de-visite* photograph, 1871. *Paris sous la Commune par un témoin fidéle: La Photographie* (Paris: Charaire et cie., c. 1895), McCormick Library of Special Collections, Northwestern University Library.

FIGURE 8-13: Eugène Appert, *Isabelle* [sic] *(Elizabeth) Rétiffe, carte-de-visite* photograph, 1871). *Paris sous la Commune par un témoin fidéle: La Photographie* (Paris: Charaire et cie., c. 1895), McCormick Library of Special Collections, Northwestern University Library.

wanted to appear; it was destined not only for their police dossier, but also for their family album, as well as for Appert's composite image, where the sisters can be glimpsed tucked into the last row on the upper right. This instability—of destination, of compositional convention and meaning—was an essential component of photographic practice at the time and had specific ramifications for the representations of women in Appert's *Crimes*.

The first thing that should be said about Appert's image of the women's quarters at Versailles is that it is framed and enabled by the positivist belief in the science of physiognomy—the conviction that deviancy is legible on the faces of the deviant—and the general recognition that photography was eminently suitable to furthering such physiognomic study.[46] Moreover, it conspires in the belief that the causes of the Commune could be detected in

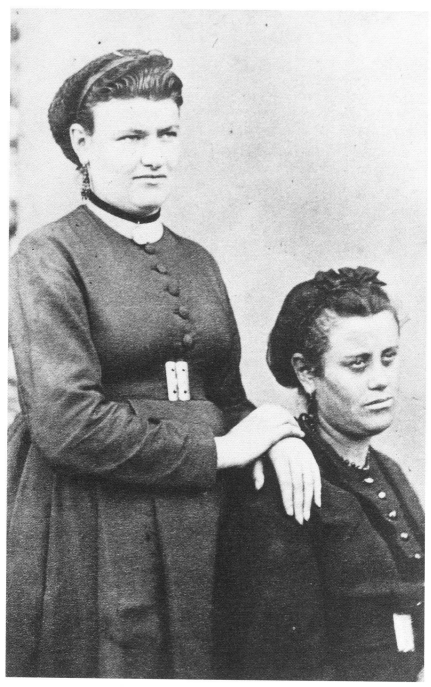

FIGURE 8-14: Eugène Appert, *Les sœurs Clémence [The Clemence Sisters], carte-de-visite* photograph, 1871. McCormick Library of Special Collections, Northwestern University Library.

the physiognomic study of its women in particular, and it panders to the voyeuristic interest in subjecting lower-class women to salacious scrutiny that was so often physiognomy's other half. Such beliefs and interests were given frequent voice in the press. Maxime du Camp served up a taxonomy of these lower-class types: "the vacationing boarders of Saint-Lazare; the natives of little Poland and greater Bohemia; the vendors of *modes à la tripe de Caen* [*sic*]; the gentlemen's seamstresses; the gentlemen's shirtmakers; the teachers of grown-up schoolboys; the maids-of-all-work"—the list goes on.[47] In its account of the convoys of captured Communards on the march to Versailles, *Le Figaro* took special pains to describe the bedraggled appearance and unrepentant demeanor of the women, reporting that it was the female insurgents, above all, who captured the attention of the crowd eager "to devour them with its eyes."[48]

The illustrated weeklies also featured images of the women prisoners, and these answered to public demand by featuring close-up, descriptive renderings that were at pains to be individually specific. An engraving that appeared in *L'Illustration* the week of June 24 offered a view of a group of accused *pétroleuses;* they ran the gamut from young and muscular to old and cronelike, from feminine attire to trousers, from expressions of remorse to resignation to an irrepressible sensuality (exhibited by the figure posed as an upright odalisque at the extreme left) that was widely thought the source of the *pétroleuse*'s power (fig. 8-15).[49] In contrast, the pendant image (on the same page), providing *L'Illustration*'s readers with a view of the quarters where the most dangerous male suspects were held, was far less concerned with such graphic detail (fig. 8-16). Panoramic in scope, it emphasized the containing frame of the prison itself, the heavy guard, and the undifferentiated, crowdlike crush of detainees—indeed, the soldiers are more carefully drawn than the prisoners. The difference in the descriptive value of the two images, and their comparative weight as "primary" or "supplementary" representations becomes even more compelling when one reads the accompanying essay by Jules Claretie. After providing a detailed physiognomic account of the various types of male prisoners (the *intéressants,* the *compromis,* and the *dangereux*), the author states that he himself had not had the opportunity to make a close-up study of the women incendiaries, "these new species of shrews for whom it was necessary to create a new word: '*les pétroleuses*'." Faced with the admitted insufficiency of his mother tongue, Claretie instead refers his readers to Darjou's sketch, which, he maintains, renders the *pétroleuses* in real life, "in all their insolence and cynicism."[50] On the one hand, the two engravings taken together suggest that their pictorial decisions—close-up or establishing shot, impression by physiognomic spec-

LES PRISONNIERS A VERSAILLES. — Les *Pétroleuses.*

FIGURE 8-15: A. Darjou, "Les Prisonniers à Versailles—Les Pétroleuses," engraving, *L'Illustration,* 24 June 1871, 360, Courtesy of Doe Library, University of California, Berkeley.

ificity or broad generalization, the titillation of face-to-face contact with the *Communarde* threat incarnate, or the more reassuring vision of a safely policed distance between that (faceless) threat and *L'Illustration*'s customers—posed necessarily either/or propositions for the draftsmen. On the other hand, Claretie's decision to defer the task of describing the *pétroleuse* entirely to the engraver seems a particularly revealing move. It breaks the heretofore seamless thread of Claretie's eyewitness narrative, which up to that moment reads like nothing so much as a *flâneur*'s trajectory through the prison camps, a bit of panoramic literature tossed off to reconnect traumatized Parisians with the more familiar narrative practices of the Second Empire. By abruptly requiring the reader to transform him/herself into a viewer (by substituting the practices of showing for telling), it also trades the *flâneur*'s narrative seductiveness for the enhanced exhibitionary value of the visual image-as-*actualité* with its ostensible transparency and status as the proverbial "picture worth a thousand words." Such a trade-off seems nothing less than strategic: if the engraving's function was objectively to render, its ability to present the *pétroleuse* as if she were simply there and true is invoked precisely at the moment when the vitriol characteristic of many accounts might have strained belief in Claretie's pose as a professionally disinterested guide.

Appert's image also means to capitalize upon the perceived insufficiency

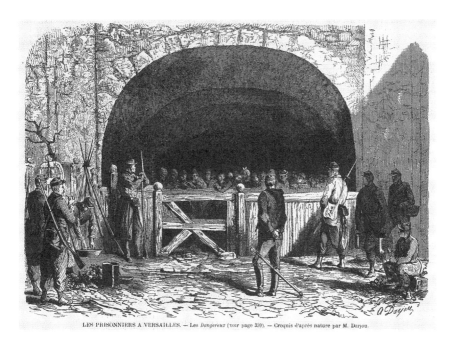

LES PRISONNIERS A VERSAILLES. — Les *Dangereux* (voir page 359). — Croquis d'après nature par M. Darjou.

FIGURE 8-16: A. Darjou, "Les Prisonniers à Versailles—Les Dangereux," engraving, *L'Illustration,* 24 June 1871, 360, Courtesy of Doe Library, University of California, Berkeley.

of textual accounts. And while the *Crimes de la Commune* contains no comparable image of the male quarters, Claretie's account begins to suggest a compelling reason: the men were an easier study, their actions and demeanors more easily accounted for; they were of no particular interest photographically speaking. The women, however, presented a different opportunity. Like his representation of the rue Haxo, Appert's image of the women's prison banks on the convergence between the ideological persuasiveness of objectivity as a trademark of the journalistic *actualité* and photography's greater ability to deliver the sheen of the real, its voracious propensity for detail and vividness. (For Appert could hope to display to his viewers both an epic panorama of the female threat contained *and* its particular face; unlike the dilemma faced by Darjou in his engravings of the men's and women's quarters, there was no need for him to choose.) But like Darjou, Appert had to reach past the functional distinctiveness of his particular medium in order to produce an image of the *pétroleuse* as both mythic and real.

The problem might be put this way: at the moment in Darjou's engraving in which the *pétroleuse* might seem most fully incarnated as sensual, threatening, still defiant—something more compelling than a sad victim or an old crone (the moment in which she takes the form of the odalisque reminiscent of contemporary iconographic representations of Marianne, symbol of the French Republic, her bare arms also recalling Delacroix's Liberty)—the engraving falls out of the realm of reportage into allegory. It becomes something more evocative of contemporary caricatural production, which was habitually rendered not by engraving's precise economy of etched lines and sharp cross-hatching, but by the limber fluidity and unruly improvisational cursiveness of the lithographic crayon. (It was through this alternative mode of visual reproduction that the illustrated newsweeklies like *L'Illustration* and *Le Monde illustré* maintained their functional distinction—as objective purveyors of *actualités*—from caricatural weeklies such as *Le Charivari* and *Le Grelot,* who supplied satirical, opinionated "entertainments.")[51] The surface of Darjou's engraving is ruptured by this allegorical intervention (the *pétroleuse*-as-debased-Marianne stands alone in the foreground; she seems to occupy a separate spatial capsule from her lineup of counterparts), just as the seamlessness of Claretie's narrative is ruptured by reference to the image.

Moreover, this effect of rupture has even more dramatic consequences in Appert's photomontage, where Hortense David's arms are wrenched up not merely to primp her hair, but to lift a collaged bottle of strong drink to her lips, or where Clémence Martel's folded hands are pried apart to hold a wine glass (both women are featured in the left foreground). Nor was Rétiffe's unfeminine, splayed-leg pose part of Appert's *carte-de-visite* portrait of her. Allegations of public drunkenness and licentiousness were common currency in the caricatural output hostile to the Commune, and Appert went to considerable effort to supply photographic confirmation of the same in his image of the prison yard. To no small degree, photographic montage constituted Appert's effort to naturalize his caricatural interventions, the better to allow his audience the seductive pleasure of consuming their fictions *as if* they were real. Such an attempt gained greater force (and no doubt offered greater viewing pleasure) by tapping into two powerful ideological constructions: that of the indexical "nature" of the photographic sign and that of the "natural" plasticity of the female body as a caricatural signifier.

Of course, photography's affinity for physiognomic study had long placed it in proximity to the art of caricature, whose investments in the conventions of the *portrait charge* and the signifying devices of exaggeration, distortion, and diminishment were extensions of the belief that inner character was legible in particular configurations of physical features. It was no coincidence that the great portrait photographer Nadar turned from caricature to the camera in midcareer; as I have already suggested, Appert also claimed

FIGURE 8-17: Nadar, *Panthéon Nadar,* lithograph, 1854. Bibliothèque nationale de France.

some artistic training. In this respect, Appert's image of the women's prison bears more than a passing family resemblance to such caricatural productions as Nadar's 1854 *Pantheon* of contemporary luminaries (fig. 8-17). Indeed, if Dumas *fils* referred to the spectacle of humanity placed on view in the makeshift prisons at Versailles as "cette zoologie de révolutionnaires," implying a sort of Grandvillean menagerie of outlaw types and ultimately exclaiming, "Quelle galerie!" then Appert offered up just such a rogue's gallery of the notable and notorious: from the hard-drinking and dissipated but youthful and coifed *démi-mondaines* seated in the left foreground to the most conspicuous women celebrities of the Commune grouped on the right—including not only Michel, Rétiffe, and Suétens, but also Eulalie Papavoine (pictured with arms crossed over her chest, at the extreme right), a dress-maker and builder of barricades, whose "massively brutal head" merited amazed attention in a description of her photograph in *La Vie Parisienne.*[52]

It would be too easy to dismiss Appert's prison image as one more bone-chilling instance of the crass sensationalism that dogged the women of the Commune. But how women were represented in such forums as the mass press and the burgeoning market in Commune memoirs and picture souvenirs (photographic and otherwise) did crucial ideological work in building consensus in support of the treatment they would receive at the hands of

French justice. If one measure of the respectful attention with which the Commune leadership received the input of its organized women supporters was the near total absence during the Commune of the Daumier-style bluestocking caricatures that had commonly depicted women activists, then the especially vicious pitch of post-Commune representations of the *Communardes* might lead us to suspect what has been confirmed by archival research.[53] Women prisoners received such unusually harsh sentences that recent scholars have been prompted to observe that "men were punished for threatening the state order; women were punished for being *women* who threatened the state order. The cultural difference is stark."[54]

The post-Commune judicial process (not to mention the more summary judgments executed during the *semaine sanglante*) indeed marked a situation where normative nineteenth-century attitudes of chivalry toward women were all but suspended; but it should be quickly added that this suspension depended for its legitimacy on effecting certain representational transformations of gendered identities within the cultural field.[55] In his article on the Versailles prisoners, Claretie remarks of the women: "Ce qui frappe dans leur aspect, c'est l'opposition de leur contenance bravache et grossière avec l'hébétude ou le silence souvent digne et triste des hommes. La femme n'est femme que dans la vertu. Dans la folie ou dans le crime, elle est plus horrible que l'homme" [What is most striking about their appearance is the contrast between their vulgar and bullying demeanor and the bewilderment or often dignified and sad silence of the men. A woman is only a woman when she is virtuous. When she is crazed or criminal, she is more horrible than a man].[56] Women into female animals; social revolution into madness and crime; the misguided, but repentant Communard men (who had, in the end, for reasons both economic and social to be repatriated as Frenchmen) and the "new species of shrew" who had incited them and were now to be the expendable scapegoats—like a caricature (but also, in the end, I want to claim, unlike it), Appert's image of the *Interior of Chantiers Prison* was poised to operate like a device of optical intensification; it was positioned, like some infernal combination of magnifying glass and cruel fun-house mirror, to allow its consumers to see the *Communardes* through the lens of their beliefs.

But look again at Appert's photograph. The pictorial quandary it poses might be put differently than that of Darjou's drawing, for it *begins* from the premises of montage and discontinuities of space and scale, rather than lapsing into them. For Appert, photomontage signified the willful attempt to stitch his fictions together, not the moment at which they fall apart. And these fictions are potentially undone not by the liberties taken by Appert in physically cutting through the integrity of the photographic surface, but by photography's own stubborn propensity for realistic, naturalized description. If the intent of Darjou's image to deliver up the *pétroleuse* as a safely consumable visual spectacle splits apart at the moment in which the "Marianne"-figure suggests that the subversive power of the *pétroleuse* remained unquenched and potentially uncontainable, the rupture in the surface of Appert's image occurs on the grounds of its very banality, within the thrall of photography's everyday eye. Look once: Appert's image of the women's quarters at Versailles forces the *pétroleuse* into the realm of photographic visibility. Look again: Appert's image does nothing so effectively as document the disappearance of the *pétroleuse* (as an imaginary construction) into the mundane, factual detail of photography itself: the careful adjustment of a lace shawl, the neat tying of a ribbon necklace, the stewpots, lines of clean laundry, and other clutter of everyday life that domesticate the prison space. Seen according to this light, Dumas was right to express uncertainty when he looked upon the spectacle of post-Commune Versailles, for such explicitly visual uncertainty *was* the paradox of the *pétroleuse:* the more one desired to *see* her, the more she seemed to slip from view. While Dumas evoked her resistance to visualization by allowing the *pétroleuse* to dissolve into the fog, *incolore et huileuse,* that characterized the crowd, Appert's image engages the same paradox in its free fall from sensationalism into ordinariness.

Such free fall places us at the crux of what Walter Benjamin terms the "tiny spark of accident, the here and now" that the photograph compels us to seek.[57] That spark was, and remains the grounds for, its indexical appeal (as well as its status as visual authority or legal evidence), and it resonates as much with Benjamin's conception of the photograph as allegory as with something like Roland Barthes's conception of the photographic *punctum*— the detail that pricks or wounds, that involuntarily widens the focus of the photograph to something beyond itself.[58] Where might Barthes have located the *punctum* in Appert's photograph? Not in the wine bottle, for example, that merely confirms what the viewer already suspects of the *pétroleuse* as a female type (this Barthes would term the photograph's *studium*), but perhaps in the demurely crossed hands of Mlle Clémence, highlighted against her sister's dark shoulders—a gesture-out-of-place whose right-angled intersection suggests another possible frame for this image. This is (one of) the photograph's telling moments, and what it proposes to tell is not the popular myth of the *pétroleuse.*

This semiotic ambiguity would seem to require yet another prop, or at least one was proposed in one of the terminal images of the *Crimes de la Commune* (fig. 8-18). If women figure in Appert's images as the sign of

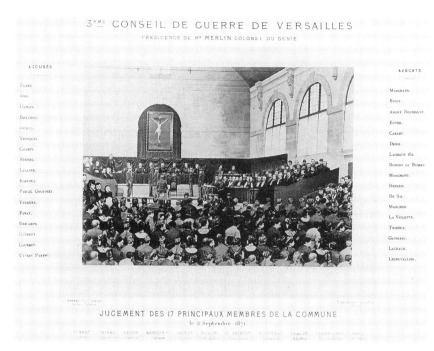

FIGURE 8-18: Eugène Appert, "3eme Conseil de guerre de Versailles, Jugement des 17 principaux membres de la Commune," [3rd Council of War at Versailles, The Judgment of the 17 Principal Members of the Commune], composite photograph, *Les Crimes de la Commune,* 1871. Collection of the author.

disorder, so that their bodily presence at various sites in the history of the Commune allowed them to stand in for a whole host of metaphors related to the lapse into chaos of modern society, then they also might be said to be crucial to Appert's project of reordering and returning society to its proper configurations. In Appert's image of "The Third Council of War at Versailles," women appear as spectators at the spectacle of the post-Commune military tribunals. Present but not to be seen, their function to direct the view without wholly submitting to its scrutiny, the difference of these women from the female Communards was signaled not only by their decorous anonymity, but by their utilitarian sameness. (As opposed to the individual particularity of each woman's face featured in "The Interior of Chantiers Prison," one woman's back could do repeat duty in filling the spectator's gallery at the Third Council of War.) This unremarkable, nonspecific presence would seem to be the rebuttal to contemporary accounts of the sensational behavior of the bourgeois women at Versailles, which threatened to garner almost as much attention as the hated *pétroleuses.*

In chronicling the enforced marches by which the Communard prisoners were driven from the *grands boulevards* of Paris to the detention camps of Versailles, Gaston da Costa offered a typical account of the veritable gauntlet of well-to-do women who queued up to gawk at the hapless insurgents, to poke and prod them, to pelt them with stones and heap upon them verbal abuse:

> [A]près les avoir lentement promenés sur nos grands boulevards, afin de les mieux exposer aux regards et aux insultes des boursiers revenus, ils les avaient dirigés sur Versailles. . . . A Versailles, devenu le boulevard de Gand de la réaction féroce, ce fut pis encore: les belles madames, ou lorettes, ou duchesses, ou riches bourgeoises au bras d'officiers insolem-ment triomphants, lapidaient et frappaient les malheureux prisonniers exténués par une marche de 20 kilomètres sous les coups de crosse des fantassins et les coups de plat de sabre des cavaliers.[59]

> [After having paraded them along our great boulevards, in order to better expose them to the view and the insults of the speculators newly returned to Paris, [the soldiers] led them toward Versailles. . . . At Versailles, upon turning onto the Boulevard de Gand, the ferocious reaction became even worse: the kept women, or *lorettes,* or duchesses, or the rich bourgeois women on the arms of insolently triumphant officers, stoned and struck the hapless prisoners who were already worn out by a twenty kilometer march under blows from the foot soldiers' rifle butts and from the flat sides of the calvarymen's swords.]

Such bourgeois women occupied a significant place in the social imagination of post-Commune Paris, and they exemplified a dangerous, potentially de-stabilizing loss of feminine decorum and control across the boundaries of class and belief.

Of course, one might have expected such an account from da Costa, who had paid his dues as a Communard, but even Dumas *fils,* while admitting to having succumbed to the (feminized) crowd's excesses once, backed away from its blood lust.[60] Like many bourgeois foes of the Commune, Dumas would have it both ways: while advocating the purges of the *semaine sanglante* as a necessary sort of civic triage, he also wanted to console his conscience by taking the higher ground and expressing distaste for reprisals conducted outside the law. Smoothing over this double requirement of the "enlight-ened" bourgeoisie was no small motivation in the pageantry of the post-Commune military tribunals at Versailles. In the end, Appert's series also sought to answer such a requirement by attempting to reestablish and rein-force the division between *femelles dangereuses* and *femmes bourgeoises* that had been crossed and recrossed during this revolutionary period. It was not enough that the women of the Commune, the "females," were to be brought under the punitive scrutiny of the camera and the law, exhibited as a *galerie "zoologique"* of biological specimens and forcibly remanded from the position they had all too temporarily assumed as possessors of the look and fashioners of their own representations and destinies. The women of Versailles, the *"femmes,"* properly speaking, had also to be restored to their proper roles, from which they too had threatened to slip, too easily susceptible to infection by the "hysteria" of May 1871.[61] The task was made no less urgent by the recognition that if the *pétroleuse* might lapse into an undisciplinable ordinariness, the very ordinariness of these women spectators might conceal the potential to turn into something else: was she or wasn't she? *femelle dangereuse* or *femme bourgeoise?* In the end, the woman in public could never be perceived as anything less than a threat.

It may seem, perhaps, that I have come a long way from my original question as to why Appert represented no *pétroleuse* caught in the incendiary act in his *Crimes,* but her ungovernability in the face of the disciplinary gaze of the camera also sets the stage for her absence. In one way, my aim has been to implicate Appert's images in the substantial costs women paid not only for their involvement in the Commune, but for their simple existence *as women* in the Commune's aftermath. Myth or not, the *image* of the *pétroleuse* made the forcible remanding of women to the private sphere an urgent priority of the early Third Republic.[62] But in another way my concern has been to challenge the apparently inevitable claim of panopticism ceded to the camera, and to begin at least to explore the functional limits of its intimate counterpart, a *presse d'information.* My interest has been as much in what evades photographic vision as in what is arrested before it, as much in what conventions of journalistic objectivity preclude as in what they allow.

In such a vein I would suggest that the status of the *pétroleuse* vis-à-vis Appert's series be framed in this way: in no trivial sense, we might say that, fully incarnated, the *pétroleuse* was "always-already" a caricature. She was made to bear the full weight of caricatural excess, she was the ultimate overproduction, charged with sustaining the bourgeois fear and fascination with the "female" threat to propriety and property at its most extreme pitch. Very soon after the *semaine sanglante,* her never-more-than-caricatural status had to be admitted even by such vindictive foes of the Commune as du Camp and Claretie.[63] And, as wholly grounded within the caricatural domain, visualizing her caught in the incendiary act would have overburdened Appert's project to the point of breaking. In one respect, this seems to me the most compelling power of the *pétroleuse* as a subversive construction; for an all too brief moment woman's terrifyingly imaginary character rendered her a force to be reckoned with. And this is, fundamentally, the threat behind the all-too-real animosity against women in the Commune's aftermath. But in another way, these concerns also expose the *pétroleuse* as an obsolete allegory—old-fashioned and caught in a semiotic stall, ill-fitted to a society in which ideology and objectivity are closely bound, a society in which the relationship between visibility and surveillance was finding in photography a new set of possibilities. Appert's project is worked not only within a sense of photography's potentials as a manipulatable medium (and these potentials were very much a part of normative photographic practice at this time), but also under the self-policing pressures of photography's graphic claims to the real; it demanded a certain circumspection in its alignment of the feminine and the fabricated story (in contrast, circumspect is what caricature is not).[64] This seems to me the critical significance of the *Crimes de la Commune:* not its propagandistic lies (which are too easily undone), but its ability to offer a precious view onto a moment of historical disjuncture (rather than con-juncture), a moment when history itself might be glimpsed breaking down into fragments, when newly adopted practices of historical representation were only incompletely capable of sustaining society's most potent ideologi-cal myths.

To put it another way: ultimately, I think, the *pétroleuse* belonged more properly in the realm of the old-fashioned epic story than in that of the contemporary journalistic narrative, more in the realm of the *Salon des beaux-arts* than in the realm of the photographic album (she was an allegory in need of a history painting—and no Delacroix was waiting in the wings). If there was a place for her in the press, it was certainly more comfortably framed by the tactics of sensationalism that seem (still) the ambivalent, often denied other half of an "objective," "legitimate" press. At a moment in which the emphasis on information made local verifiability an absolute requirement (a moment at which the mere fact of the contemporary had to suffice for the mythic), the *pétroleuse* became an image-out-of-place, disconnected (save in the realm of caricatural embellishment) from the stories that would have sustained her.[65]

Objectivity and visibility, the needs for authentication and documenta-tion as commercial requirements of the mass press: in the end, the *pétroleuse* was fit for none of this. Was there any other image of the Commune that might suffice, then, as its real allegory? I think it revealing that the only engraving published on the austere front page of *Le Figaro* in 1871 was an image of the Ministry of Finance destroyed during the fires of the *semaine*

FIGURE 8-19: "Ruins of the Ministry of Finance," engraving after photograph by Alphonse Liébert, *Le Figaro* (17 June 1871), front page. Photo: A.C.R.P.P., Paris.

sanglante, an image, not coincidentally, based upon a photograph by Alphonse Liébert (figs. 8-19 and 8-20). Widely admired as the most aesthetically satisfactory of the demolished buildings left in the wake of the Commune, *Le Figaro* compared its broken arcades and piles of crumbled stone to the picturesque remains of the Roman Colosseum. After this momentary lapse into a connoisseur's pleasure, however, the newspaper's interest in photography continued in a more practical vein, claiming that "La photographie a une exactitude qui ne peut se compléter que par les chiffres d'un constat, que par les termes d'un procès-verbal" [Photography possesses an exactitude that can only be matched by figures in a certified report or by the terms of a police report].[66] What followed was a detailed accounting of the expense of rebuilding the city's lost monuments and private residences—31,000,000 francs for the Hôtel de Ville (whose exact replication was completed in 1884), an estimated 27,000,000 francs for the Tuileries Palace (which would never be rebuilt), etc.[67] As more than one writer reminded readers, these buildings were not merely damaged architectural structures; instead they represented the very history of the city writ in stone.[68] The concrete and costly spectacle of Paris destroyed by fire not only provided a

FIGURE 8-20: Alphonse Liébert, "Ruins of the Ministry of Finance," albumen photograph from *Ruines de Paris et de ses environs* (Paris: Photographie américaine, 1871). Collection of the author.

richer, more ideologically governable image of revolutionary terror than the *pétroleuse;* it also helped to displace the memory of the more than twenty thousand Communard dead left in the wake of the retaliatory measures of the *semaine sanglante.* Surely the state recognized the efficacy of this displacement (buildings for bodies, the real cost of reconstruction versus the potentially incalculable loss of human life) when in 1872 it outlawed from view all images related to the Commune—even Appert's—save those of *Paris incendié.*[69] Fragmentary, material, as factual as the lines in an accountant's ledger, as styleless as the words in a police dossier: photographically speaking, the debris of Communard Paris could appear as contemporary as today's headlines, as timeless as the artifacts of ancient Rome.[70] As Benjamin so powerfully reminded us, the real allegories of modernity appear more often than not in ruins.[71]

Notes

Research support for this project was provided by a National Endowment for the Humanities Summer Stipend and a J. Paul Getty Postdoctoral Fellowship in the History of Art and the Humanities. I owe special thanks to Robin Greeley, Gay Gullickson, Melissa Hyde, Jenny Shaw, and Marcus Verhagen for their comments on earlier drafts of this essay.

1. On Delacroix's *Liberty,* see Werner Hofmann, "Sur la Liberté de Delacroix," *Gazette des beaux arts* 86 (1975): 69. On female allegory and the French Revolution, see Maurice Agulhon, *Marianne into Battle: Republican Imagery and Symbolism in France, 1789–1880,* Janet Lloyd, trans. (New York: Cambridge University Press, 1981); Madelyn Gutwirth, *The Twilight of the Goddesses: Women and Representation in the French Revolutionary Era* (New Brunswick, N.J.: Rutgers University Press, 1992); Marina Warner, *Monuments and Maidens: The Allegory of the Female Form* (New York: Atheneum, 1985).

2. See, for example, Heinz-Dieter Kittsteiner, "The Allegory of the Philosophy of History in the Nineteenth Century," *Walter Benjamin and the Demands of History,* Michael P. Steinberg, ed. (Ithaca, N.Y.: Cornell University Press, 1996), 44.

3. On caricature and the Commune, see James Leith, "The War of Images Surrounding the Commune," *Images of the Commune/Images de la Commune* (Montreal: McGill-Queen's University Press, 1978): 101–50; Adrian Rifkin, "Cultural Movement and the Paris Commune," *Art History* (June 1979): 201–20; Adrian Rifkin, "No Particular Thing to Mean," *Block* 8 (1983): 36–45. These articles point the bibliographic way to larger collections of Commune imagery.

4. Gay L. Gullickson identifies representations of the *pétroleuse* as "inversions" of Delacroix's Liberty. See *Unruly Women of Paris: Images of the Commune* (Ithaca, N.Y.: Cornell University Press, 1996), 218–19. Gullickson's is the most current study of the roles and representations of women during the Commune. Other useful essays include Eugene Schulkind, "Le Rôle des femmes dans la Commune de 1871," *1848. Révue des révolutions contemporaines* 42, no. 185 (February 1950): 15–29, and David A. Shafer, "*Plus que des ambulancières:* Women in Articulation and Defense of Their Ideals during the Paris Commune" (1871), *French History* 7, no. 1 (1993): 85–101.

5. On the *pétroleuse* and the nineteenth-century pathology of hysteria, see Janet Beizer, "Hystericizing History: The Commune According to Maxime du Camp's *Les Convulsions de Paris,*" *Ventriloquized Bodies: Narratives of Hysteria in Nineteenth-Century France* (Ithaca, N.Y., and London: Cornell University Press, 1994), 203–26.

6. For more on the nineteenth-century taste for reality, see Vanessa R. Schwartz, *Spectacular Realities: Early Mass Culture in Fin-de-Siècle Paris* (Berkeley: University of California Press, 1998).

7. Not to mention the descriptive pleasures of the *roman-feuilleton*—the novel-in-installments whose ability to create an imaginary world was also, in the hands of Balzac, Sue, etc., predicated upon claims to objective reportage. On the mass press and the relationship between commercialization and discourses of objectivity, see Walter Benjamin, "Paris of the Second Empire in Baudelaire," *Charles Baudelaire: A Lyric Poet in the Era of High Capitalism,* Harry Zohn, trans. (New York: Verso, 1983), 27–34;

Siegfried Kracauer, "Photography," *The Mass Ornament: Weimar Essays,* Thomas Y. Levin, trans. (Cambridge: Harvard University Press, 1995), 57–59; Richard Terdiman, "Newspaper Culture: Institutions of Discourse; Discourse of Institutions," *Discourse/Counter-Discourse: The Theory and Practice of Symbolic Resistance in Nineteenth-Century France* (Ithaca, N.Y., and London: Cornell University Press, 1985), 117–46; as well as other contributions to this volume, most particularly those by Dean de la Motte and Maria Adamowicz-Hariaz.

8. Photographic illustrations, produced by transferring photographic images directly onto wood engraving plates, first appeared in the pages of the mass press in 1891. For a discussion of the old and new technologies of reproduction used by the illustrated press, see the excellent article by Anne-Claude Ambroise-Rendu, "Du dessin de presse à la photographie (1878–1914): Histoire d'une mutation technique et culturelle," *Revue d'histoire moderne et contemporaine* 39 (January–March 1992): 6–28.

9. These solutions were also largely recycled products, derived from such revolutionary chestnuts as the *tricoteuse* and the *furie de guillotine,* believable not so much because they named a new threat, but because they keyed into existing beliefs about feminized revolutionary terror. See Gullickson, *Unruly Women,* 69. Such a coupling of old and new was perhaps put most neatly in the mean-spirited pages of *La Vie Parisienne,* from whence the following *bon mot* was culled: "Les femmes de la Commune—Les fricoteuses de la guillotine" *La Vie Parisienne* (12 August 1871): 819. However, such recourse to revolutionary tradition was not always couched in the negative. Most recently, Martin P. Johnson has argued the importance of such gendered revolutionary traditions as the women's march on Versailles in 1789 in mobilizing support for the Commune. See "Memory and the Cult of Revolution in the 1871 Paris Commune," *Journal of Women's History* 9, no. 1 (Spring 1997): 39–57.

10. Edith Thomas's passionate account of *Les Pétroleuses* (Paris: Gallimard, 1963) is largely an exposé of their imaginary character. Translated into English as *The Women Incendiaries* (New York: Braziller, 1966). All following citations are from the English edition. A more recent discussion of the myth of the *pétroleuse* is Patricia-Pia Célérier, "Les Pétroleuses de la Commune de Paris ou le mythe terroriste," *Romance Quarterly* 44, no. 2 (Spring 1997): 93–98.

11. See Gullickson, *Unruly Women,* 159–60.

12. The other compelling scapegoat of the Commune, less studied in recent years but no less ripe for a revisionist deconstruction of its representations than the *pétroleuse,* was the International Working Men's Association, which occupied a privileged place in the French imaginary, far out of proportion to either its pervasiveness or allegations as to its omniscient power during the Commune. A fundamental text in English on the involvement of the Internationale in the Commune remains Edward S. Mason, *The Paris Commune: An Episode in the History of the Socialist Movement* (New York: Macmillan, 1930; reprinted New York: Fertig, 1967). See also the important work of

Jacques Rougerie: "Les sections françaises de l'Association internationale des travailleurs," *La première Internationale à Paris pendant la Commune* (Paris: C.N.R.S., 1968) and "L'A.I.T. et le mouvement ouvrier à Paris pendant les événements de 1870–1871," *International Review of Social History* 17 (1972): 3–102. Of course, as Eugene Schulkind reminds us, the two categories, woman and socialist activist, could overlap. See "Socialist Women during the 1871 Paris Commune," *Past and Present,* 106 (1985): 124–63.

13. For a reproduction of this image, see Georges Bourgin, *La Guerre de 1870–71 et la Commune* (Paris: Flammarion, 1971), 59.

14. On the publication history of the *Crimes de la Commune,* see Donald English, "Photography and the Paris Commune: Symbol, Myth, Censorship, and Identification," *The Political Uses of Photography in the Third French Republic, 1871–1914* (Ann Arbor: University of Michigan Research Press, 1984), 31–46. See also English's article on Appert, "Political Photography and the Paris Commune of 1871: The Photographs of Eugène Appert," *History of Photography* 7, no. 1 (January 1983): 31–42.

15. Much has been written on the indexical character of the photographic sign. A fundamental essay is Rosalind Krauss, "A Note on Photography and the Simulacral," *October* 31 (Winter 1984): 49–68.

16. For another view of the relationship between photography and gender during the Commune, see Gen Doy, "Women, Class, and Photography: The Paris Commune of 1871," *Seeing and Consciousness: Women, Class and Representation* (Oxford and Washington, D.C.: Berg, 1995), 82–106.

17. Such dismissals have generally taken the form of pointing out the propaganda value of Appert's images and then immediately pointing to inaccuracies and inconsistencies in their production, as if the distastefulness and dishonesty of the message were somehow revealed within the inept fakery of its expression. Claude Nori thus identifies Appert as among the first to exploit the propagandistic potentials of the medium, his "ignoble" example contrasted to that of the photographer most often named as a hero of the Commune, Bruno Braquehais. See *French Photography from its Origins to the Present* (New York: Pantheon, 1979), 21. Jean-Claude Gautrand does the same, adding that it supposedly took years to discern the falseness of certain images. See "Les Photographes et la Commune," *Photo-Ciné Revue* (February 1972): 57–59. Gen Doy is at pains to point out the static, obviously posed quality of the photographs and their impossible lack of blurriness, while speculating that even these defects would not deter a public predisposed to accept these images as "factual." See "The Camera against the Paris Commune," *Photography / Politics: One* (Terry Dennett and Jo Spence, eds. (London: Comedia Publishing Group, 1979), 19–21.

18. Such discussions generally stem from Michel Foucault's seminal discussion of Bentham's panopticon in *Discipline and Punish: The Birth of the Prison,* Alan Sheridan, trans. (New York: Random House, 1979), 195–228. For specific applications of the

Foucauldian concept of panopticism, see, for example, John Tagg, *The Burden of Representation: Essays on Photographies and Histories* (Amherst: University of Massachusetts Press, 1988).

19. I also find it significant that doctored images related to the burning of Paris (and I know of at least three) use the composite technique to display the restoration of order rather than to re-create Paris in the grip of the Communards—that is, they use the composite technique to bring on the firemen, rather than to catch the *pétroleuse* in the act.

20. Most recently, David Barry has argued that the Commune represented a significant increase in both the number of women involved in revolutionary insurgency and the level of refinement of their activism (that is, he maintains that that feminine insurgency was more ideological and less opportunistic than during previous revolutionary moments). See *Women and Political Insurgency: France in the Mid–Nineteenth Century* (New York: St. Martin's Press, 1996), 105–54.

21. Jules Vallès, *L'Insurgé* (Paris: Gallimard, 1975), 156.

22. *Les Convulsions de Paris,* 4 vols. (Paris: Librairie Hachette et Cie., 1878): 1:300.

23. "Pour le sexe faible, qui s'est montré si féroce dans les derniers jours de l'émeute, pour les pétroleuses, les cantinières intraitables, les Théroignes de Méricourt de la Commune, on a eu plus d'égards. Ces viragos ont été enfermées dans le hangar situé dans le cour à droite. Il y a des portes et des fenêtres. Elles peuvent s'abriter du vent et de la pluie. Leur aspect n'a rien à seduisant et ces créatures n'ont de la femme que le nom. Un grand nombre renonçant aux habits de leur sexe, se sont fabriqué des costumes militaires où l'immodiste lutte avec le grotesque. Ce sont des pantalons de drap à bandes rouges, des tuniques d'uniforme à parements rouges démesurés. Et tout cela est sale, sordide. . . . Il y a en a parmi ces communeuses qui demandaient l'émancipation de la femme, qui la prêchaient dans les églises profanées. Leur aspect d'aujourd'hui n'est pas fait pour enflammer le zèle des Don Quichotte socialistes qui auraient pu rompre des lances en leur honneur." *Le Monde illustré* (1 July 1871): 11.

24. On the "permeation" of society with the feminine, see Denise Riley, *"Am I That Name?" Feminism and the Category of "Women" in History* (Minneapolis: University of Minnesota Press, 1988), 15.

25. As Joan W. Scott has shown, this was no less acutely the case for the female worker than the female Communard. See her " 'L'ouvrière! Mot impie, sordide . . .': Women workers in the discourse of French political economy, 1840–1860," in *The Historical Meanings of Work,* Patrick Joyce, ed. (Cambridge and London: Cambridge University Press, 1987), 119–42.

26. *Le Figaro,* 31 May 1871.

27. As Edith Thomas has noted, the vicious harpies hallucinated by the enemies of the Commune, and the honest housewives and heroic *citoyennes* conjured by its sup-

porters, were more often than not one and the same—these cardboard constructions were nearly indistinguishable when applied to the real women who took up arms in the streets. *The Women Incendiaries,* 56. Moreover, such bloodthirsty constructions resonate with gendered accounts of revolutionary terror during the dangerous year (1793–94). See Gutwirth, *Twilight of the Goddesses,* 309–11. Recent histories of the Commune include Steward Edwards's *The Paris Commune, 1871* (London: Eyre & Spottiswoode, Ltd., 1977) and William Serman's *La Commune de Paris, 1871* (Paris: Fayard, 1986). On the events of the rue Haxo, see Edwards, 336–37 and Serman, 515–16.

28. Maxime du Camp, *Les Convulsions de Paris:* 1, 429. Jules Claretie, *Histoire de la révolution de 1870–1871* (Paris: Aux bureaux du journal l'Eclipse, 1872), 696–98.

29. In the end, 1,051 women appeared before the Councils of War, but only one, Pauline Lise Séret, wife of a sculptor, was charged with, among other "crimes," inciting the mob to murder the hostages and brutalize their corpses. See Edith Thomas, *The Women Incendiaries,* xiii. On Pauline Lise Séret, see Thomas, 194–95. Recent histories of the Commune have suggested that it was not a woman at all, but a Colonel Bénot who initiated the executions. See Serman, *La Commune,* 516.

Somewhat surprisingly, given her notoriety, Mme. Séret is not listed among the women whose portraits were included in Appert's image of the "Intérieur de la prison des Chantiers." However, two other women condemned for their roles in the execution of four hostages at the Place de la Roquette (one on very slim evidence), Marie Cailleux (Cayeux) and Marie Wolff (*femme* Guyard), were prominently featured. On Cailleux and Guyard, see Thomas, *The Women Incendiaries,* 195–96 and Kathleen B. Jones and Françoise Vergès, "Women of the Paris Commune," *Women's Studies International Forum* 14, no. 5 (1991): 498–501.

30. Jules Vallès, *L'Insurgé,* 319. P.-O. Lissagaray wrote that Versailles soldiers taken as prisoners of war had been marched through Belleville without incident over the preceding two days, "but these *gendarmes,* these spies, these priests, who for fully twenty years had trampled upon Paris, represented the empire, the bourgeoisie, the massacres under their most hateful forms." See his *History of the Commune of 1871,* Eleanor Marx Aveling, trans. (New York and London: Monthly Review Press, 1967), 372.

31. "Nos gravures," *L'Illustration* (25 May 1871): 170. Philibert Audebrand recounts the execution in much the same way. See *Histoire intime de la révolution du 18 mars: comité central et Commune* (Paris: E. Dentu, 1871), 57. For an excellent deconstruction of the role of women in the events of March 18, see Gullickson, *Unruly Women,* 24–56.

32. For more on this particular pair of images, see Jeannene M. Przyblyski, "Moving Pictures: Photography, Narrative and the Paris Commune, 1871," *Cinema and the Invention of Modern Life,* Leo Charney and Vanessa Schwartz, eds. (Berkeley: University of California Press, 1995): 253–78.

33. On the Commune as a radical intervention in the domain of the symbolic (that

is to say, as a revolution of the spectacle rather than of the governmental infrastructure), see Guy Debord, Attila Kotányi, and Raoul Vaneigem, "Theses on the Paris Commune" (1962), especially theses nos. 2, 4, 7, and 10 [reprinted in the *Situationist International Anthology,* Ken Knabb, ed. and trans. (Berkeley: Bureau of Public Secrets, 1981), 314–17] and Henri Lefebvre, "La Commune: Dernière fête populaire," *Images of the Commune,* 33–45.

34. One might consult the barricade photographs made on and around March 18, or even more tellingly, the many images of the crowd that gathered to witness the toppling of the Vendôme Column on May 16.

35. The literature on the *flâneur* continues to increase. Most relevant to the point at hand would be Janet Wolff, "The Invisible *Flâneuse:* Women and the Literature of Modernity," *Feminine Sentences: Essays on Women and Culture* (Berkeley and Los Angeles: University of California Press, 1990): 34–50 and Griselda Pollock, "Modernity and the Spaces of Femininity," *Vision and Difference: Femininity, Feminism, and the Histories of Art* (London: Routledge, 1988), 50–90. See also the recent anthology edited by Keith Tester, *The Flâneur* (London and New York: Routledge, 1994).

36. A growing body of work is being done on the status of female looking in nineteenth-century Paris. See, for example, Jann Matlock, "Censoring the Realist Gaze" in *Spectacles of Realism: Gender, Body, Genre,* Margaret Cohen and Christopher Prendergast, eds. (Minneapolis: University of Minnesota Press, 1995), 28–65.

37. *Gazette des tribunaux* (29 October 1872): 1049–50. Cited in Donald English, *The Political Uses of Photography in the Third French Republic,* 34.

38. Bourgin, *La Guerre de 1870–71 et la Commune,* 373.

39. Alexandre Dumas fils *Une Lettre sur les choses du jour* (Paris: Michel Levy, 1871), 1.

40. Dumas *fils, Une lettre sur les choses du jour,* 8. Dumas's description conforms to typical nineteenth-century images of the threatening crowd. See Susanna Barrows, *Distorting Mirrors: Visions of the Crowd in Late Nineteenth-Century France* (New Haven: Yale University Press, 1981).

41. "Les derniers prisonniers faits aux combats de la Villette, de Belleville et de Père-Lachaise, continuent d'affluer à Versailles. Je voudrais qu'il fut possible de photographier ces fantastiques théories pour montrer aux gens de la province, aux ruraux comme les appelaient dédaigneusement les fédérés, les horribles figures qui ont tenu deux mois la civilisation française en échec." *Le Figaro* (2 June 1871): 1.

42. The Commune, as Maxime du Camp noted approvingly, marked the beginnings of police photography in France. See *Convulsions de Paris,* 2:327–28.

43. On this point, see André Rouillé, "Les Images photographiques du monde du travail sous le Second Empire," *Actes de la recherche en sciences sociales,* no. 54 (September 1984): 42.

44. See Marc-Amédée Gromier, *Journal d'un vaincu* (Paris: V. Havard, 1892): 217, and Louise Michel, *La Commune* (Paris: Stock, 1898): 305.

45. On the trial of the pétroleuses, see Edith Thomas, *The Women Incendiaries,* 172–82.

46. On the relationship between photography and physiognomic study, see Allan Sekula, "The Body and the Archive," *October* 39 (1986): 3–64.

47. *Les Convulsions de Paris,* 2:61.

48. "Les convois d'insurgés," *Le Figaro* (2 June 1871): 1.

49. I am particularly indebted to Gay Gullickson, who challenged me to think more deeply about this particular figure, and whose insights I draw upon here and in what follows.

50. "Les Prisonniers à l'Orangerie de Versailles," *L'Illustration* (24 June 1871): 362.

51. On this point, see Terdiman, *Discourse / Counter-Discourse,* 152.

52. *La Vie Parisienne* (14 October 1871): 969.

53. On the correlation between iconographic "types" and the receptivity of the Commune government to women's participation, see Eugene Schulkind, "Socialist Women During the 1871 Paris Commune," 137.

54. Kathleen Jones and Françoise Vergès, " 'Aux citoyennes!': Women, Politics, and the Paris Commune of 1871," *History of European Ideas* 13, no. 6 (1991): 725.

55. For more on the discursive transformation of women into "monstrous" females, see Barry, *Women and Political Insurgency,* 147–48.

56. Jules Claretie, "Les Prisonniers à l'Orangerie de Versailles," 362.

57. In his essay on "A Short History of Photography," Walter Benjamin aligns the photograph with his conception of allegory: "All the artistic preparations of the photographer and all the design in the positioning of his model to the contrary, the viewer feels an irresistible compulsion to seek the tiny spark of accident, the here and now. In such a picture, that spark has, as it were, burned through the person in the image with reality, finding the indiscernible place in the condition of that long past minute where the future is nesting, even today, so eloquently that we looking back can discover it. It is a different nature which speaks to the camera than speaks to the eye, so different that in place of a space consciously woven together by a man on the spot there enters a space held together unconsciously." "A Short History of Photography," Phil Patton, trans., *Artforum* (February 1977): 47.

58. Roland Barthes, *Camera Lucida: Reflections on Photography,* Richard Howard, trans. (New York: Hill and Wang, 1981): 25–27.

59. *La Commune vécue, 18 mars–28 mai 1871,* 3 vols. (Paris: Ancienne Maison Quantin): 3:191.

60. Dumas fils, *Une lettre sur les choses du jour,* 8.

61. Gullickson makes a similar point. See *"La Pétroleuse:* Representing Revolution," *Feminist Studies* 17, no. 2 (Summer 1991): 255.

62. See Barry, *Women and Political Insurgency,* 151–54. On the implications of the defeat of the Commune for French feminism, see Claire Goldberg Moses, *French*

Feminism in the Nineteenth-Century (Albany: State University of New York Press, 1984), 193–94, and Joan Wallach Scott, *Only Paradoxes to Offer: French Feminists and the Rights of Man* (Cambridge: Harvard University Press, 1996), 96–103.

63. On the mythic status of the *pétroleuse,* see Maxime du Camp, *Les Convulsions de Paris,* 2:286–87. Claretie, while addressing the "legend of the *pétroleuse,*" warned of it being replaced by a potentially more dangerous myth—that of the "martyrs of May." Instead, he laid blame for the fires of the *semaine sanglante* squarely upon the Commune leadership. See *Histoire de la Révolution de 1870–1871,* 682–88.

64. On the early history of composite photography and combination printing, see James Borcoman, "Notes on the Early Use of Combination Printing," *One Hundred Years of Photographic History: Essays in Honor of Beaumont Newhall,* Van Deren Coke, ed. (Albuquerque: University of New Mexico Press, 1975), 16–18 and Robert A. Sobieszek, "Composite Imagery and the Origins of Photomontage," *Artforum* (September 1978): 58–65; (October 1978): 40–45.

65. On the connection between information, verifiability, and the demise of the art of storytelling, see Walter Benjamin, "The Storyteller," *Illuminations: Essays and Reflections,* Hannah Arendt, ed. (New York: Schocken, 1969), 89.

66. A. Duplessis, "Paris incendié," *Le Figaro* (17 June 1871): 1.

67. On the political uses of ruined Paris, see Kirk T. Varnedoe, "The Tuileries Museum and the Uses of Art History in the Early Third Republic," *Saloni, gallerie, musei et loro influenza sullo sviluppo dell' arte des secoli XIX e XX,* Francis Haskell, ed. (Bologna: CLUEB, 1981), 63–68. On the painted response to ruined Paris, see Albert Boime, *Art and the French Commune: Imagining Paris After War and Revolution* (Princeton: Princeton University Press, 1995), 46–76.

68. For example, Louis Enault wrote, "La première fois que je vis les ruines de ce noble monument, qui fit si longtemps l'orgueil et la joie des Parisiens, dont chaque partie était comme une page de leur histoire sculptée dans la pierre vive, dont l'ensemble racontait une longue période de gloire, de luttes, de revers, de triomphes, de catastrophes et des fêtes, c'était la nuit." *Paris brûlé par la Commune* (Paris: Plon, 1871), 188.

69. See "No 882: Instructions relatives à la publication et à la vente des gravures, estampes, emblèmes, etc., Paris le 25 novembre 1872," *Recueil officiel de circulaires émanées de la Préfecture de Police, 1849–1880,* 2 vols. (Paris: Chaix, 1883), 2:289–92. Cited in English, "Political Photography and the Paris Commune," 40. The international market, however, remained lively.

70. In his essay accompanying Liébert's images of ruined Paris, Alfred d'Aunay perhaps put it best when he remarked of this same image of the Ministry of Finance, "Rien de beau, rien de grandoise comme les ruines du Ministère des Finances . . . en photographie." Alphonse Liébert, *Les Ruines de Paris et de ses environs,* 2 vols. (Paris: La Photographie américaine, 1872), 1:9.

71. On Benjamin's early conceptualization of the relationship between allegory and ruin, see *The Origin of German Tragic Drama,* John Osborne, trans. (New York: Verso, 1990), 177–82. Benjamin is quoted most famously as stating, "Allegories are, in the realm of thoughts, what ruins are in the realm of things." (*Origins,* 178). Such conceptualization is reworked in Benjamin's study of Baudelaire—see, in particular, Benjamin's discussion of Baudelaire's poem, "Le Cygne." *Charles Baudelaire: A Lyric Poet in the Era of High Capitalism,* Harry Zohn, trans. (New York: Verso, 1983), 81–90. Richard Terdiman discusses this poem in detail with respect to the demolition of old Paris under the auspices of Baron von Haussmann. See *Present Past: Modernity and the Memory Crisis* (Ithaca, N.Y.: Cornell University Press, 1993), 106–50. On the centrality of the allegory-as-ruin to Benjamin's analysis of modernity in the *Arcades Project,* see Susan Buck-Morss, *The Dialectics of Seeing: Walter Benjamin and the Arcades Project* (Cambridge: MIT Press, 1990): 159–201. Also relevant is Peter Bürger, "Benjamin's Concept of Allegory," *Theory of the Avant-Garde,* Michael Shaw, trans. (Minneapolis: University of Minnesota Press, 1984), 68–73.

9 The Language of the Press

Narrative and Ideology in the Memoirs of

Céline Renooz, 1890–1913

Not long ago poststructuralists began to historicize theory.[1] They no longer claimed the imperious autonomy of language. Structuralism's challenge to Marxism is in fact now considered a problematic project, one with profound implications for subordinate populations defined by class, of course, but also by race and gender.[2] In the politics of discourse, pace Roland Barthes and Michel Foucault, the author is not dead, but a figure determined to resist its discursive erasure in both theory and praxis. This lesson rings true for various renegade voices, past and present, that have contested the hegemonic elision of their subjectivity and agency. Reinscribed at the center of language, the knowing self of marginal figures especially is seen to challenge the mechanistic system of signs and their apparently elusive referents.[3] Some feminist theorists on autobiography, for example, have addressed the existential and ontological issues raised by theory's exclusive textuality, and they have defined instead a more contextualist dialectic.[4] Like theoretically related studies of discursive resistance, the resulting work on language's conflicting ideologies has quite logically turned to the historical moment in order to (fore)ground these conflicts.[5]

I want to explore this development in literary theory and criticism, using the unpublished memoirs of a passionate figure in nineteenth-century France: Céline Renooz (1840–1928). Her "Prédestinée: l'autobiographie de la femme cachée," written intermittently between 1890 and 1913, is now at the Bibliothèque Historique de la Ville de Paris. Like their author, the memoirs are of particular interest for the light they shed on the role played by contesting discourses in an ideologically driven narrative. For Renooz was an ardent, indeed a combative individual who left a detailed account of her differences with other writers: fellow activists, scholars, and journalists. But her writing demonstrates much more; it also represents the historical features inherent in discursive practice, particularly in the press whose ideological assumptions she borrowed and confronted in her autobiographical *récit*. What my examination seeks, in effect, is a historically grounded reassessment of the way actual as well as textual spaces provided the sites for clashing ideologies in the modern news.[6]

For this reassessment, my analysis of the ideological and narrative elements of Renooz's memoirs suggests a more historicist approach. Rather than examining the press itself as a text, I have preferred to study its discursive presence in the autobiography of an assiduous reader and writer of newspaper prose. Ineluctably, almost inevitably, the press intruded into her most intimate reflections as well as her most polemical positions. Renooz's historical situation ensured that the press's ideological conflicts would appear in her personal story because she insisted, as a self-conscious woman, on redefining these conflicts in her sacred mission to write the Truth. By contrast, but also by example, the press provided Renooz with the material she needed to construct her subjectivity, her agency—in effect her identity—in writing the memoirs that she saw neither to completion nor to publication. Her obscurity, then as now, is no more an accident than the obscurity of the newspapers whose language she both appropriated and challenged in her autobiography. Like their literary and historical significance, the contesting voices in her work, I argue, are fundamentally interdependent, intertextual, but above all dialectical in context. History, as both a narrative and the past itself, has a presence in her language, just as language finds its place in moments other than its own.[7]

Who was Céline Renooz?[8] Born and educated in Liège, she married an engineering student from Spain in 1859 and moved with him to Madrid where they had four children. But their marriage was so unhappy that she left her husband and moved to Paris in 1875 to pursue her interests in natural history, feminist organization, and polemical journalism. Because Parisian publishers refused to consider her work without subvention, Renooz founded the Société néosophique in 1897; this small but faithful coterie of friends raised the money necessary to promote her controversial views on science and religion. In all, Renooz published more than a dozen volumes on evolution, cosmology, and the history of Western religions. In addition to this work, she sponsored conferences and maintained an extensive correspondence with allies and adversaries alike. After a brief illness Renooz died at age eighty-seven, leaving behind the personal papers that were eventually acquired by Marie Louise Bouglé for her archival collection on the history of the women's movement in France.[9] Renooz's long life of serious intellectual engagement is well documented by her publications and many boxes of letters, newspaper clippings, and manuscripts, including her unfinished memoirs.

Renooz's ideas—her entire raison d'être—progressed across three disparate but related fields that were developing rapidly in the nineteenth century: evolutionary embryology, scientific epistemology, and visionary feminism.[10] Her earliest interests actually developed in response to Charles Darwin's *The Origin of Species,* translated into French by Clémence Royer in 1862; Renooz's first book, *L'Origine des animaux* (1883), critiqued Darwin's theory of evolution because she found its method "inconciliable avec les exigences rigoureuses de la science" [incompatible with the rigorous demands of science].[11] (Unless otherwise specified, all translations in this chapter are mine.) Instead of tracing the origin of species by the established conventions of natural history—Darwin's approach—Renooz proposed examining evolution in light of recent work in embryology. The results, she felt, were conclusive:

> Les formes traversées par l'homme et les animaux aériens, au commencement de leur évolution, sont des formes végétales (lesquelles sont reproduites fidèlement dans les premières phases de la vie embryonnaire actuelle—celles de la végétation primitive). Mais que le monde végétal actuel—qui recommence une évolution lente—est *renversé* par rapport aux animaux actuels, c'est-à-dire que, dans la station végétale, l'extrémité céphalique est en bas et l'extrémité caudale en haut.[12]

> [The structures developed by humans and flying animals at the beginning of their evolution are vegetable structures, forms that are faithfully reproduced in the first phases of present-day embryonic life resembling primitive vegetation. But in its slow replication of evolution, the vegetative world is just the *reverse* of that for present-day animal life. In other words, in the vegetative phase of animal gestation, the cephalic extremity is inverted, while the caudal extremity is on top.]

For Renooz nothing could be more obvious: the vital center of life in the plant is located in its lowest extremities, its roots, while the most important extremity of the human being is the head, which appears upside down in the fully formed fetus. Embryologically the head develops in the same relation to the body that roots already have to the plant. Renooz thus echoed Ernst Haeckel—ontogeny recapitulates phylogeny both within and across species—but with one critical difference: animal evolution, she believed, occurs only after plants have developed sufficient structures for animals to replicate in their earliest stages of life.

One significance of this argument, based on creative analogy drawn from biology, is Renooz's rejection of a principal feature of Darwin's theory: the differentiation of species by natural selection. Writes Renooz,

> L'origine végétale nous ramène à la fixité des espèces, mais [aussi] nous conduit à l'évolution dans chaque espèce. Elle nous les montre toutes, suivant chacune son évolution, tranquillement, sans conflit avec ses voisines, et perpétuant à travers les âges les caractères spéciaux à chacune d'elles.[13]

> [The vegetable origin of animal life leads us back to the fixity of species, but (it also) leads us to the evolution of each species. It shows us that all of them follow their respective evolution tranquilly, coexisting without conflict with their neighbors and perpetuating across the ages the special characteristics for each one of them.]

In short, her version of evolution was symbiotic and functional rather than competitive and conflictual. Nature for her was not animals fighting for survival but plants cooperating in harmony. But this quasi-ecological critique of Darwin's struggle for existence had another significance; Renooz's early anti-Darwinism was at the heart of a new scientific epistemology, one of many similar critiques of nineteenth-century positivism.[14]

The failure of Darwinians to recognize the obvious—to acknowledge the utility of embryology in the study of evolution—is owed, Renooz felt, to fundamental flaws in the scientific method. Therefore, she argued, the basis of all true scientific knowledge cannot be empiricism, the pervasive positivist model for all fields including literary studies at the end of the nineteenth century.[15] Rather, science as knowledge must become intuitive; it must adopt a woman's (nonessentialist, Bergsonian) immediate recognition of truth as a formal manner of knowing.[16] Renooz assumed as a personal responsibility the promotion of this new epistemology—hence her inspiring statement of principles for the journal that she founded in 1888, *La Revue scientifique des femmes:*

> Il faut refaire la science pour montrer à l'homme ce qu'il est et ce qu'il doit être. C'est à la femme qu'incombe cette tâche. C'est elle qui, à l'aide de cette faculté que lui reconnaissent les hommes, mêmes les plus injustes: *l'intuition,* doit rendre, au vieux monde, la lumière qui fera renaître la vie intellectuelle.[17]

> [Science must be recast in order to show men who they are and what they ought to be. It is to woman that this task is entrusted. With the help of

the power that even the most obstinate of men recognize in them—intuition—women can bring to the old world the light that will re-create intellectual life.]

Once science was established on new epistemological foundations, all knowledge, indeed all morality logically derived from it, would ensure a more creative and peaceful existence for everyone—thanks to female intuition.[18]

Thus it was a series of small steps in Renooz's thinking that eventually took her all the way from embryology to epistemology to feminism. Other French women in science, like Madeleine Pelletier and Clémence Royer, followed similar paths.[19] By the time she began writing her memoirs in 1890, Renooz was already interested in women's issues, especially in higher education and scholarly research. But she was even more concerned with elaborating, through a new cosmology of both physical and spiritual forces that she outlined in *La Nouvelle Science* (1890–1920), a feminist vision of universal harmony: "Espérons que la génération nouvelle franchira avec nous l'étape qui sépare le vieux monde du monde nouveau, qui sera basé sur la VERITE ABSOLUE, simple et grandiose comme la Nature au sein de laquelle nous sommes nés" [Let us hope that the coming generation will take the next step that separates the old world from the new one that will be based on the ABSOLUTE TRUTH, a great and simple truth like Nature itself, at the heart of which we are born].[20] In its turn this Saint-Simonian conception rested on yet another, much larger project tracing the origins of patriarchy in Western society. The establishment of a new cosmology, Renooz asserted, required an understanding of its historical roots reaching back to the ancient world when, according to J. J. Bachofen, men had usurped women as divine agents.[21] This insight led her to write a six-volume study, her magnum opus, *Ere de vérité* (1921–33), on the original role of women—and their displacement—in religious practice.

Renooz's passionate commitment to feminist action was therefore complemented by an equally passionate exploration of its necessity: to redress the primal injustice done to women's original divinity that she claimed to have rediscovered and felt compelled to reestablish (notwithstanding the prior claims of the utopian socialists).[22] Accordingly, the end of her life was devoted to explaining and promoting woman's special calling:

> Nous avons donc, pour compléter notre oeuvre historique, à faire l'histoire de cette Renaissance dont les . . . premières étapes sont déjà accomplies. La dernière seule reste à réaliser. Elle est attendue, et c'est son auteur qui sera le Vrai Messie des temps nouveaux, le *nouveau instructeur* [*sic*] de l'humanité.[23]

[In order to finish our historical efforts, we have thus written the history of this Renaissance whose . . . first stages have already been completed. The last stage alone remains to be realized. It is much awaited, and its animator will be the True Messiah of the new world, the *new teacher* of humanity.]

Renooz's ideas during a lifetime of creative work were concerned with a particular view of woman placed at the center of a harmonious cosmos. Here nature was not red in tooth and claw like a wild jungle, but peaceful and symbiotic like a well-tended garden. Here knowledge was not mere power but social morality. Here woman was not a victimized object, but an active subject in an orderly universe ultimately of her own making. That Renooz often confused women's causes with her own is, of course, no reason to dismiss her vision. Its language and context are well worth study in themselves.

One obvious reason for interest in Renooz's work is its special place in the history of ideas.[24] It reflects earlier intellectual movements, especially messianic romanticism and utopian socialism; but it also shares in subsequent challenges to the ideologies of positivism and rationalism. Like the romantic idealists Alphonse de Lamartine and Edgar Quinet, for instance, Renooz developed a prophetic vision of social justice and spiritual renewal. This Rousseauesque conception of a better world returned a benign, indeed beneficent nature to its rightful place in a society that had been corrupted by men. More in tune with the natural, Renooz believed, women would inspire men to achieve true social harmony, just as the Saint-Simonian activist Prosper Enfantin and his devoted followers had argued they would. And yet Renooz also participated in the fin-de-siècle's reassessment of experimental science and political liberalism. For her, progress and materialism were pernicious myths. Not having read either the neo-Kantians, the syndicalists, or the avant-garde—the French counterparts to Nietzsche, Marx, and Freud—Renooz still recognized the limits to reason in the scientific method and the rational individual, pillars of Western self-confidence and patriarchal hegemony on the eve of the twentieth century. In this way, like many early feminist thinkers, Renooz actually shared in the many currents and crosscurrents of ideas among her contemporaries.[25]

Within this remarkable synthesis of European ideas, however, Renooz's real significance lies in her complex expression of multiple, often conflicting discourses. And her lengthy memoirs, in particular, offer the best site to overhear these voices in her work. Despite its forthright chronological organization, "Prédestinée" incorporates the features of several different texts—

private diary, personal correspondence, scientific scholarship, polemical journalism, utopian vision, and feminist debate—instances of which are even attached to the manuscript where Renooz's retrospective narrative plays off of them.[26] Rusty pins hold in place fragments of her childhood journal, letters she received and copies of those she sent, articles clipped from scholarly reviews and various newspapers, and pages torn from her other writings (see fig. 9-1). As an operative technique, this curious collage physically embodies and thereby suggests the contrasting discursive practices at work in Renooz's self-consciously intertextual writing. At one point, citing Albert Kölliker's *Embryologie* (1882), she remarks how "je n'avais qu'à y ajouter des citations prises dans l'ouvrage . . . pour donner plus d'autorité à mon travail" [I had only to add some citations here and there . . . in order to lend more authority to my writing], even though Renooz had more subversive purposes in mind.[27] A close reading of Renooz's memoirs suggests just what these purposes were.

Richard Terdiman's *Discourse / Counter-Discourse: The Theory and Practice of Symbolic Resistance in Nineteenth-Century France* (1985) provides perhaps the most appropriate approach to the discursive contrasts in Renooz's text. For not only does her ideologically driven narrative attempt to explain and justify her resistance to dominant discourses, but it also adopts those voices because they are so pervasive and so inescapable, because they are essential to all historical conflict. "Nineteenth-century intellectuals," writes Terdiman, "experienced their struggle almost as if they were living the dialectic of history itself, an intricate and continuous interplay of stability and destabilization which produces the social world for all of its actors."[28] As an instance of counter-discourse—like those of Marx, Flaubert, Baudelaire, and Mallarmé that Terdiman studies—Renooz's autobiography expresses the uncanny operation of the dominant within such deliberate challenges to it. The contending voices in Renooz's personal narrative thus share in a discursive struggle of historical proportions.

Throughout "Prédestinée" Renooz responds to other texts, most often the ones she has pinned to the manuscript. For instance, the correspondence she cites is not simply historical documentation that her readers can use, like footnotes, to verify the truth value of her narrative—though Renooz certainly had this purpose in mind, too. Rather, the letters are also sounding boards for her own ideas; they are voices for her to interpret, to correct, or to refute, including the ingenuous letters written by her childhood friends that often clutter the pages and the narrative of her memoirs. Writes Renooz,

En copiant les lettres de mes amis, je constate qu'en parlant de moi elles vantent continuellement *ma bonté*. Cela semble n'être qu'une formule épistolaire. Ah! bien non, c'est qu'en réalité la bonté était la caractéristique de la famille Reno[o]z, et je tiens de mon père par là, lui il était le type parfait de la bienveillance.[29]

[In copying my friends' letters, I declare that in speaking of me they were continuously praising *my kindness*. That seems to be only an epistolary convention. But, no, in reality kindness was characteristic of the Reno(o)z family, and I consider my father just that. He was the embodiment of kindness itself.]

For Renooz no correspondence is transparent or innocent. The discursive significance of every missive must be assessed and contested for the sake of the sacred mission entrusted to her, that only she understands and can express.

Renooz's memoirs also challenge the books they quote. Every scholarly text here receives the same critical treatment. Darwin's *The Origin of Species* is only the most obvious manifestation of this habit. There are dozens of others: Ernest Renan's *La Vie de Jésus* (1863), René Descartes's *Discours sur la méthode* (1637), Jules Michelet's *Bible de l'humanité* (1864), Jean-Jacques Rousseau's *Confessions* (1781–88), and more, all by men, of course. But where Renooz found ideas of value, she adopted a less confrontational style, even if her contestatory purposes remained the same. In reference to Antoine Fabre d'Olivet's *La Langue hébraïque restituée* (1816), a work central to her interpretation of the Old Testament, she remarks parenthetically how she must always read "entre les lignes avec cette intuition que je possède et qui me fait apercevoir des choses que les autres ne voient pas" [between the lines with this intuition of mine that enables me to apprehend some things that others do not even see].[30] In time Renooz quotes or cites fewer and fewer books by other authors, because she wanted to free her work from contaminating influences. Renooz found it increasingly burdensome to critique everything that challenged her clearly defined vision: "Que je trouve les littérateurs petits, que je trouve mesquin leurs oeuvres, que d'idées fausses que la science rectifiera, et comme cette éternelle glorification de la force et de l'amour de l'homme me fatigue" [How petty I find literati, how paltry I find their work, how false are the ideas that science will rectify, and how this eternal glorification of men's force and love tires me].[31]

Renooz was perhaps the most combative in her accounts of conferences. After 1890, during an intense period of intellectual activism, she was particularly assiduous in attending and giving public lectures on issues of imme-

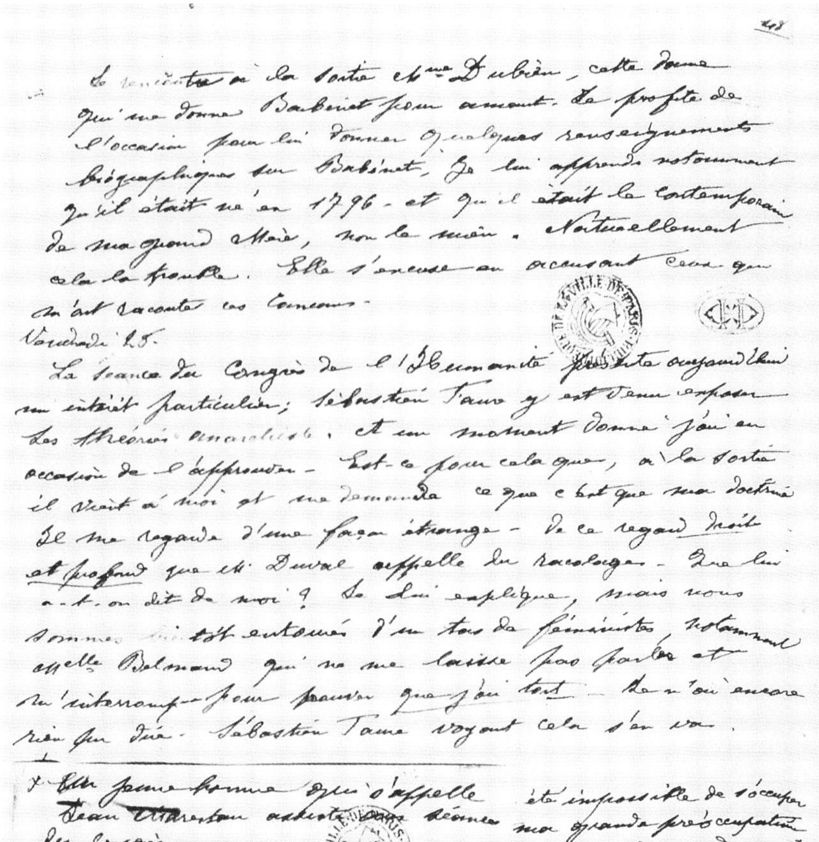

Je rencontre à la sortie Mme Dubien, cette dame
qui me donne Babinet pour amant. Je profite de
l'occasion pour lui donner quelques renseignements
biographiques sur Babinet. Je lui apprends notamment
qu'il était né en 1796 – et qu'il était le contemporain
de ma grand mère, non le mien. Naturellement
cela la trouble. Elle s'excuse en accusant ceux qui
m'ont raconté ces [illegible].
Vendredi 25.
La séance du Congrès de l'Humanité présenta aujourd'hui
un intérêt particulier; Sébastien Faure y est venu exposer
les théories anarchistes. Et un moment donné j'ai eu
occasion de l'approuver – Est-ce pour cela que, à la sortie
il vient à moi et me demanda ce que c'est que ma doctrine
Il me regarde d'une façon étrange – de ce regard droit
et profond que Mlle Duval appelle du racolage – Que lui
a-t-on dit de moi? Je lui explique, mais nous
sommes bientôt entourés d'un tas de féministes, notamment
Mlle Belmont qui ne me laisse pas parler et
m'interrompt pour prouver que j'ai tort – Je n'ai encore
rien pu dire – Sébastien Faure voyant cela s'en va.

FIGURE 9-1: Céline Renooz, *Prédestinée, l'autobiographie de la femme cachée, 1890–1913,* d. 1900., f. 408r. Bibliothèque Historique de la Ville de Paris.

diate concern to her. And her memoirs provide deliberately polemical reports of these face-to-face exchanges. To promote her own ideas, she found, "je commençais à comprendre combien il est difficile aux lecteurs de s'assimiler toutes les idées que j'expose si elles ne sont pas présentées sous forme d'un enseignement oral, suivi de conversation et de discussion" [I began to understand how difficult it is for readers to digest all of my ideas if they are not presented in the form of oral instruction, followed by conversation and discussion].[32] As for the ideas of others, Renooz had few flattering things to say. In March 1892 during a meeting of the Solidarité des femmes, Marie Pierre openly called on Renooz to document her assertions by references either to recognized authorities or to scientific experimentation. In response to this charge, Renooz wrote, "On me dit: vous ne faîtes pas d'expériences et d'observations—alors que je ne fais que cela. On me dit: vous faîtes la *spéculation* philosophique—alors que c'est justement cela que je combat" [I am told, "you do not perform experiments and gather data," while I do just that. I am told, "you are engaged in philosophical *speculation*," while I am fighting precisely that].[33] In this way Renooz's memoirs become a locus for public debate.

But the principal focus of Renooz's "Prédestinée"—and most of her other personal papers—is on the press. More than four boxes of her personal papers are devoted to newspaper clippings on various subjects, most of them concerning her interests in women and their destiny, including articles on divorce, prostitution, and domestic violence. Moreover, after 1890, Parisian newspapers became her primary source of information and reference. Her memoirs mention more than a dozen different dailies—most often *Le Matin, Le XIXe Siècle, Le Figaro, La Petite République,* and *Le Temps*— whose accounts of her ideas and activities she scrupulously followed. Nearly an obsession, the press offered her the publicity and the medium that she needed for her work, just as it provided her with the positions and the discourse that she sought to contest. The polemical edge to her efforts at explanation and justification in her memoirs is obviously derived from the newspapers she read, mimicked, and opposed. The most important public forum for Renooz's ideas was the press; and her memoirs are filled with its rhetorical gestures and its discursive practices, despite her opposition to everything that the press represented.

When the first story of the Dreyfus Affair appeared in print, for example, Renooz immediately perceived its personal significance. "Moi, en lisant cela, je compris tout de suite—dès le premier article—que c'était une machination diabolique et que cet homme n'était pas coupable" [In reading that, I understood right away, from the first article, that this was a devilish intrigue and that this man was not guilty].[34] She then drew explicit parallels between Alfred Dreyfus and herself: both were social pariahs and victims of unjust persecutions, she felt. And she wrote the Dreyfus family to offer her assistance.[35] By 1903, in deliberate imitation of Emile Zola's famous open letter originally published in *L'Aurore*, Renooz drew up her own list of accusations. "Après l'Affaire Dreyfus et le Manifeste de Zola, j'ai aussi écrit mon 'J'accuse'" [In the manner of the Dreyfus Affair and Zola's manifesto, I too made public my indictments], identifying eleven specific charges against the scholars who had obstructed her mission on behalf of suffering humanity.[36] She never published her list, maybe because she had already adopted the appropriate pose in her memoirs. Either to dispute or to corroborate, Renooz's prose invariably resorts to the press.

Two other instances of Renooz's selective challenge to and appropriation of this dominant discourse deserve attention. One concerns her theory of radiant energy which, she felt, made climatic conditions at the north and south poles particularly dangerous. In the first volume to *La Nouvelle Science,* Renooz had asserted the primacy of oxygen as a force in the universe.[37] The inordinate consumption of oxygen by the sun in particular made its rays the primary source of physical and spiritual animation on earth. But when the sun's rays hit the earth tangentially, as they do at the poles, the result is a turbulence unmediated by the earth's absorption of their energy. "Il en résulte que tous objets libres, sur ce point de la sphère, doivent être mis en mouvement par la radiation tangentielle et entrainés avec elle dans les profondeurs de l'espace" [The consequences of this are that all unfixed objects on this part of the globe must be caught up by the movement caused by tangential radiation and swept by it into the depths of space].[38] The winds at the poles, Renooz warned, preclude any possibility of exploration there. For this reason, then, Renooz wrote to the editor of *Le Matin* explaining the failure of the polar expedition by balloon undertaken by S. A. Andrée in 1897; a similar fate, she stated, awaited this Swede's foolhardy imitators.

In light of Renooz's theories, based as they were on her intuitive epistemology, this view made perfect sense. Its expression in the eight newspaper articles she clipped and saved for her memoirs, however, was much less sensible. The published responses to her warning were unequivocally cruel.[39] Several journalists made fun of her, while other writers, like Elysée Réclus, flatly contradicted her: "Les épouvantables rafales dont parle Nansen n'a rien de plus épouvantables que d'autres mouvements aériens observés dans les régions tropicales" [The frightful storms that Nansen (one of Renooz's sources) discussed are no more frightful than other storms in the tropics].[40] But Renooz was unmoved. Her original article, she noted in her memoirs, had been travestied by the press; its scientific language had been deliberately reformulated to make her look absurd. As M. Dautherive, the editor of *Le Matin,* admitted in a letter to Renooz, "Il me paraît impossible qu'un journal élucide des problèmes aussi ardus. Les lecteurs ne possèdent pas un langage scientifique tel que le vôtre, Madame" [It seems impossible to me for a newspaper to clarify such difficult problems. Readers do not possess language as scientific as yours, Madame].[41] Renooz's counter-discursive practice had to be translated into the dominant discourse in order to make her views intelligible. In this case Renooz failed because she had not fully resorted to the press's polemical strategies.

This clash of voices in Renooz's memoirs appears in another, less overt guise. By 1905, in the face of such opposition, she had despaired of seeing her work accepted, a pessimism reflected in the final pages of her manuscript. For the next eight years Renooz's autobiography lapses into annual summaries of fruitless activity, frustrated predictions, and extended lamentations. But Renooz does express some hope in her project, albeit indirectly, by the unusual attention she pays to Louise of Saxony's "Histoire de ma vie." This sensational story was serialized by *Le Matin* in September 1911 and carefully preserved in Renooz's dossiers of press clippings. Unhappily married into the Saxon royal family, Louise left her husband and three children in 1907, the princess wrote, to escape the misery of her circumscribed life in Dresden, notwithstanding the scandal that her abrupt departure created. Her memoirs, like Renooz's, are an extended apology: "Je me suis efforcée de montrer le vrai monde de la cour tel qu'il existe à Dresde, sans partialité et avec exactitude et de faire ressentir tout ce que j'ai souffert du fait d'ennemis acharnés et sans scrupules. . . . Maintenant j'ai plaidé ma cause" [I have strived to show the real world of the court just as it is in Dresden, impartially and exactly, and to make manifest all that I have suffered in fact from tenacious and unscrupulous enemies. . . . Now I have pled my case].[42]

Even though Renooz's memoirs make no mention of Louise of Saxony, the two women shared a common subtext: they were both targets of public misunderstanding and unjust persecution. Renooz's failure to complete her memoirs owes to many different causes, but one of them must be the same discourse of defiant failure that Louise adopts in her own attempt to justify herself after having given up her children and married unhappily for the second time. For example, Renooz marked what for her must have been a significant passage in Louise's memoirs about the latter's Saxon in-laws:

> Telle était la famille royale dans laquelle j'étais destinée à vivre. Il y eut dès le commencement un antagonisme mutuel. Je fus comme le coucou dans

un nid de moineaux ou comme la seule personne de goûts artistiques ou originaux au sein d'une brave famille bourgeoise. J'oubliais que *l'originalité et l'imagination sont les seuls péchés qui ne se pardonnent pas.* On me le rappela. Me plaçant à ce point de vue, je me rends compte maintenant que je dûs jeter le trouble et faire scandale pour ce que *je ne m'estimais pas satisfaite d'être simplement une princesse.* Chaque manifestation de *mon esprit d'indépendence* fut reçue avec *colère* et soupirs.[43]

[Such was the royal family with whom I was fated to live. From the start there was a mutual antagonism. I was like a cuckoo in a nest of sparrows, or like the sole person of artistic or original taste in the midst of a proper middle-class family. *I forgot that originality and imagination are the only unpardonable sins.* I was reminded of it. In retrospect, I confess now that I had to make trouble and create a scandal because *I did not consider myself satisfied merely with being a princess.* Each indication of my independent mind was received with *anger* and gasps.]

Renooz felt and gave voice to precisely these sentiments of natural superiority—beyond even that of a princess—thanks to her originality, imagination, and independence of mind. Here both women express their mutual consternation over the uncomprehending, unjustifiable ire of their contemporaries. Their memoirs are sustained gestures in opposition to the dominant discourse that defined women's intellect and comportment in society. In both instances, however, the women still rely on the very discursive agency that had so sternly condemned them in the first place: the press. With the publication of her memoirs in *Le Matin,* Louise of Saxony's reliance is more overt than Céline Renooz's, whose unpublished autobiography only imperfectly shares its language.

This unsuccessful appropriation suggests another, more profound reason why Renooz never completed or published her memoirs. Ultimately, her discursive resistance to dominant voices everywhere, but especially in the press, was simply overwhelmed. Unlike nineteenth-century texts that have since become canonical, Renooz's memoirs neither adapted nor rejected the discourse they sought to oppose; their rhetorical strategies relied on neither re/citation (subversive appropriation) nor de/citation (deliberate exclusion) to contest the language of men.[44] Renooz must have realized this. After 1905, her memoirs seem preoccupied with self-exculpation and accusation. Claiming the same martyrdom as Captain Dreyfus and Louise of Saxony, Renooz sees enemies to her mission behind every obstacle, from publishers refusing her manuscripts to hecklers disrupting her lectures. In her view there can be no other explanation for the ineffectiveness of her voice.

The source of all these woes, Renooz claims repeatedly, was Mathias Duval, a professor in the Paris faculty of medicine and an honored member of several scientific associations. In 1887 this Darwinian transformationist had told Renooz to her face that she was demented.[45] The memory of this encounter, and many others like it, cast a long shadow over Renooz's memoirs.[46] It is a leitmotif of her work. When Duval died in March 1907, for instance, Renooz remarks melodramatically: "Par sa lutte colossale contre la Femme, il a réalisé la figure terrifiante et satanique de l'antichrist, qui n'est pas un personnage fatidique et imaginaire mais une réalité. . . . Duval a été *le vandale de la science*" [By his colossal struggle against Woman, he embodied the terrifying and satanic figure of the antichrist, which is not prophesized or imaginary but a reality. . . . Duval was *the vandal of science*].[47] In good newspaper form, she includes a large photograph of her nemesis. Her memoirs express a bathos of persecution worthy of the daily tabloids whose uncritical language Renooz adopts and whose pervasiveness finally quells her opposition. The rest of her manuscript recounts mechanically her activities month by month until like the press it loses all coherent narrative form. By the end of 1913, her memoirs finally fall silent.

I need not dwell on this silence. In the long history of women's subordination to men, it is all too easy to understand. But the theoretical implications of Renooz's life and language deserve further consideration here. Above all, I think, her work demonstrates how the personal becomes political, or as Terdiman might put it, how the discursive becomes historical. Renooz's memoirs and the frustrations they represent are firmly rooted in painful experience, beginning with her unsuccessful marriage to Angel Muro: "Il paraît que je devais faire ce triste apprentissage de la vie" [It seemed that I had to undergo this sad apprenticeship in life], she wrote in 1892. "La haute destinée qui m'était réservée en étant de près il me fallait connaître les hommes, c'est-à-dire souffrir, pour trouver, un jour, la cause du mal qui mine la société et son remède. Quinze années de souffrance m'ont donnée cette science" [The lofty fate that was reserved for me required that I know men intimately, that is, to suffer in order to discover one day the roots of evil that undermine society and its salvation. Fifteen sorrowful years gave me this knowledge].[48] Renooz's existence informed her representation of it. The historical dialectic between self and other, between individual and society, ultimately between language and context appears clearly in Renooz's writing.[49] Although her work is easily dismissed by a triumphant positivism, it assumes a singular significance of its own in the complex relations between literary theory and women's history.

Very much the same may be said about Renooz's stout resistance to gender roles, and more, to the discourse that defined those roles. Her memoirs mark a serious effort to challenge the values and language of a sexist society, especially in her improbable claims for women's redeeming mission in the world. But more modestly and more realistically, as in her scholarly work on natural history and epistemology, Renooz's autobiography sought to establish a discursive base to women's creative agency in the world. Her writing asserted a knowing and active subject, an independent voice capable of defining a new language and a new vision appropriate to it. This self-conscious discursive presence in her work in effect suggests a more constructivist perspective on women, not as passive automata whose fate is already scripted for them either by their bodies or by men, but as effective agents in their own right whose future rests on the control of language on their own behalf. Thanks to this assertion of subjectivity, then, Renooz's work rejects, implicitly at least, the essentialist positions of her contemporaries, but also ironically those at the heart of her own discursive practices.[50] In both her science and her memoirs, Renooz borrows the very language she uses to contest its control of herself and other women. This ideological ambivalence is in fact one result of the dialectic between history and language. Nevertheless, or perhaps even consequently, Renooz's apparent disenchantment with embryology and autobiography moved her to complete a history of women in Western religion, a more successful demonstration of her agency in both language and the world.

Renooz's work lends credence to Gerda Lerner's argument in *The Creation of Feminist Consciousness* (1992). It is easy to see how, like the women Lerner studies, Renooz "transformed the concepts and assumptions of male thought and [none too] subtly subverted male thought so as to incorporate women's cultural knowledge and viewpoint." Renooz's memoirs actually mark a culmination in a "tradition of women's long-range resistance to patriarchy and the factors which have brought about changes in women's consciousness of their own situation."[51] Although Lerner emphasizes the explicit manifestations of this consciousness in the West from the medieval writer Hildegard of Bingen to the African-American evangelist Sojourner Truth, I want to suggest that Renooz's distinctive contribution to this history lies in her understanding of language and its power in male hands. She identifies men's discursive control of women everywhere, especially in institutions like the Napoleonic Code, the university, the scientific method, the religious beliefs and practices of Christianity, the study of history, and the spaces of modern journalism. But "Prédestinée" also goes further, at least initially, in reasserting a woman's historical agency in writing itself. As Renooz says at the very beginning of her memoirs,

Je ne veux pas abandonner ma personalité à la fantaisie romanesque des étourdis, ou à la calomnie des envieux. Je veux, en même temps, faire connaître les circonstances très extraordinaires qui m'ont amenée à faire un travail sans précédent dans l'histoire des sciences. Il ne me suffit pas de montrer ce que j'ai fait—je veux aussi dire [ce] que je suis.[52]

[I do not mean to abandon my personality to the novelistic fantasies of bigots, much less to the slander of the envious. On the other hand, I do want to make known the rather extraordinary circumstances that led me to unprecedented work in the history of scholarship. I will not do myself justice simply to show what I did, I also want to say who I am.]

For with the power of even borrowed language, Renooz implies here, comes women's identity, their sense of self, their very existence.

The lesson of Renooz's memoirs is thus historical as well as discursive, its textual and contextual elements perhaps always already linked. Literary theorists, I think, can recognize in her work the role played by context, especially in the dialectic between experience and language. That much is obvious. It clearly underlies her grand but no less sincere expression of a harmonious world re-created by women. This feminist vision is based not solely on the autonomy of its language, but also on the prolonged and intense personal pain of its author—the misery of her marriage, the opposition to her science, the frustration of a public sphere closed to women. In her life Renooz experienced first-hand, and contested the ideologies inherent to, an essentialist conception of gendered language.[53] While she claimed a transparently natural and authentic status for a woman's intuition in scientific inquiry, she also recognized its power to oppose the institutionally sanctioned positivist conception of knowledge—the prevailing epistemology that was widely used against her—because it was seen as the only basis for modern, progressive science. It was against precisely this Kuhnian paradigm, one embraced by the Third Republic's scientific community, that Renooz posited another of her own, however indebted her science was to its opposition, however much she endured and suffered in the humiliation of its rejection.[54]

But still closer to the point are the subjectivity and agency of women suggested in the dialectical context that Renooz's memoirs manifest. Perhaps in spite of her deep fears and personal pain, but more surely because of them, Renooz gave voice to her identity in and through her writing primarily as an act of self-assertion and ultimately of human dignity. Thanks to insuperable obstacles to her efforts, Renooz remains obscure, but posterity's cruel judgment is derived from the phallocentric world that she sought to combat. All her life she resisted the objectifying and marginalizing effects of patriarchy, in its institutions, and more, in its language. Renooz was not alone in her discursive resistance, however derivative that resistance actually was from the dominant voices represented by the press. For this reason, at least, Renooz's work and that of many women like her deserve close analysis.[55]

Consequently, Richard Terdiman's insightful perspective requires elaboration. His correction of structuralism's ahistorical bias itself falls prey to another ahistoricism, not in its conception of hegemony and resistance, but in its omission of patriarchy as a crucial feature of that hegemony. Terdiman's dialectic is most obviously indebted to Antonio Gramsci's *Prison Notebooks* (1927), which fundamentally reassesses the passive role of culture in Marx's dialectical materialism. But Gramsci's project—by implication Terdiman's as well—gives primacy to one context in particular, that of class conflict, aside from its complex presence in language. But there is at least one other set of oppositions, that of gender relations and their discourses in patriarchal society. A careful reading of Renooz's memoirs suggests the historical significance of this gendered dialectic that is neglected in Terdiman's consideration of clashing social voices in nineteenth-century France. As Renooz's work amply demonstrates, besides the texts by men that Terdiman studies, some French women developed critical discursive practices of their own.

In this latter conflict the modern press looms equally large. Since at least the eighteenth century, women themselves have read and written for newspapers most often but not always in the guise of men. Evelyn Sullerot has already shown the importance of the first periodicals for and about women.[56] As for female journalists in France, Madame Roland, George Sand, and Rachilde are the best known, but not necessarily the most important. Despite Renooz's withering appraisal of their efforts—"N'est-il pas douloureux de voir des femmes inconscientes prendre fait et cause pour les hommes?" [Is it not painful to see unconscious women take men's side?]—the all-female staff of Marguerite Durand's *La Fronde* also served women's interests at an important moment in the French suffragist movement before World War I.[57] The presence of women in literate life grew with the rapidly rising rates of female literacy; and a larger discursive space for women opened in the press by the end of the century for the likes of Céline Renooz.[58] Given its pervasiveness in both dominant and subversive contexts before the appearance of electronic media, the newspaper embodied the most controverted features of language as a historical and a literary phenomenon.

Ultimately, then, posterity's judgment of Renooz and her ideas does not matter. Marginal, eccentric, paranoid—whatever the adjective—Renooz was

no more so than many of her better-known contemporaries. Just a generation earlier these same terms apply to Auguste Comte, for example, whose
colleagues at the Ecole polytechnique disdained him, whose spiritualist visions he systematized, and whose erratic behavior required institutional
treatment.[59] And yet Comte was no Renooz. Rather the latter is forgotten
while the former is not, even though Renooz too had devotees who raised
the money necessary to support her work. In her own time, notwithstanding
what seem like crackpot ideas, she was more widely regarded than she is
now. Her language, like that of the press, was perhaps too much a product of
her times, and it passed with them. But the dialectic of her experience and
her language makes Renooz interesting, at least historically. Studying her
memoirs elucidates the nature of readers and writers like her in all their rich
discursive historicity.

Notes

1. E.g., see Louis Montrose, "New Historicisms," *Redrawing the Boundaries: The
Transformation of English and American Literary Studies,* Stephen Greenblatt and Giles
Gunn, eds. (New York: Modern Language Association of America, 1992), 392–418;
and more provocatively, Cary Nelson, *Manifesto of a Tenured Radical* (New York: New
York University Press, 1997), 23.

2. For a survey of this work, see also *Redrawing the Boundaries,* Greenblatt and Gunn,
eds., esp. 320–48, 437–65; and *Marxism and the Interpretation of Culture,* Cary Nelson and
Lawrence Grossberg, eds. (Urbana: University of Illinois Press, 1988), esp. 271–313,
347–60.

3. Cf. Gerda Lerner, *The Creation of Feminist Consciousness from the Middle Ages to
Eighteen-Seventy* (New York: Oxford University Press, 1993); and Paul Ricoeur, *Oneself
as Another,* Kathleen Blamey, trans. (Chicago: University of Chicago Press, 1992).

4. Cf. *Life/Lines: Theorizing Women's Autobiographies,* Bella Brodzki and Celeste
Schenk, eds. (Ithaca, N.Y.: Cornell University Press, 1988); *De/Colonizing the Subject:
The Politics of Gender in Women's Autobiography,* Sidonie Smith and Julia Watson, eds.
(Minneapolis: University of Minnesota Press, 1992); and Françoise Lionnet, *Auto-
biographical Voices: Race, Gender, Self-Portraiture* (Ithaca, N.Y.: Cornell University Press,
1989).

5. Cf. Fredric Jameson, *The Political Unconscious: Narrative as a Socially Symbolic Act*
(Ithaca, N.Y.: Cornell University Press, 1981); Richard Terdiman, *Discourse/Counter-
Discourse: The Theory and Practice of Symbolic Resistance in Nineteenth-Century France* (Ithaca,
N.Y.: Cornell University Press, 1985); and James C. Scott, *Domination and the Arts of
Resistance: Hidden Transcripts* (New Haven: Yale University Press, 1990).

6. See Michel Foucault, *The History of Sexuality,* vol. 1: *Introduction,* Robert Hurley, trans. (New York: Pantheon Books, 1981), esp. 135–59.

7. Note the rethinking of history among historians discussed in Lynn Hunt, "Introduction: History, Culture, and Text" in *The New Cultural History,* Hunt, ed. (Berkeley: University of California Press, 1989), 1–24. For the purposes of my essay, however, history is distinguished by its contextual emphasis, its dialectical character, and its experiential basis. By contrast, language tends to the textual, the functional, and the theoretical. Where these two disciplines intersect in Renooz's writings is of primary interest here.

8. A fuller treatment of Renooz and her work—on which the present essay is based in part—is James Smith Allen, "Science, Religion, and Feminism: The Utopian Signs of Céline Renooz, 1840–1928," *Worldmaking,* William Pencak, ed. (New York: Peter Lang, 1996), 163–84.

9. See Maïté Albistur, *Catalogue des archives Marie Louise Bouglé* (Paris: Bibliothèque Historique de la Ville de Paris, 1982), photocopied typescript. To avoid unnecessary repetition here, all my references to Renooz's personal papers in the Bouglé collection will provide just the box number, the dossier title, and the folio number. I will omit the specific information required on the *bulletins* used to order this material at the BHVP: "Fonds Bouglé/Papiers Renooz."

10. See the useful discussion of late nineteenth-century European intellectual trends in Eric Hobsbawm, *The Age of Empire, 1875–1914* (New York: Vintage Books, 1987), 243–61.

11. Céline Renooz, *L'Origine des animaux. Histoire du développement primitif. Nouvelle théorie de l'évolution réfutant par l'anatomie celle de M. Darwin* (Paris: J. B. Baillière et fils, 1883), 1:5. Cf. Yvette Conry, *L'Introduction du Darwinisme en France au XIXe siècle* (Paris: Presses Universitaires de France, 1974).

12. Renooz, "Une révélation," *La Religion laïque et universelle* (15 May 1888): 267.

13. Renooz, *L'Origine des animaux,* I:6.

14. See H. Stuart Hughes, *Consciousness and Society: The Reorientation of European Social Thought, 1890–1930* (New York: Vintage Books, 1958), 33–66.

15. Renooz anticipates the controversy in France sparked by literary historian Ferdinand Brunetière's repudiation of science's positive role in knowledge, society, and morality. See René Wellek, *A History of Modern Criticism 1750–1950,* vol. 4: *The Later Nineteenth Century* (Cambridge: Cambridge University Press, 1983), 58–71; Harry W. Paul, "The Debate over the Bankruptcy of Science in 1895," *French Historical Studies* 5, no. 2 (Autumn 1968): 299–327; and Renooz, "Prédestinée," BHVP box 17, d. 4me étape, fols. 99–105.

16. Renooz defined her notion of intuition as "cette faculté extraordinaire de l'Esprit, qui a la puissance de déchirer subitement le voile qui nous cache la vérité et

ouvre devant nous un horizon nouveau en nous donnant la connaissance soudaine" [this extraordinary mental ability that has the power to rip away the veil that hides the truth from us and (that) opens before us a new horizon by providing us unexpected knowledge]. It was not essentialist; she claimed this manner of knowing for children as well as women; in patriarchy men lost this otherwise innate capacity (quote from Renooz, "Prédestinée," BHVP box 16, d. Ma vocation scientifique, fol. 4). Cf. the definition of intuition in Henri Bergson, *The Creative Mind,* Mabelle L. Andison, trans. (New York: Philosophical Library, 1946), 190: "the *sympathy* by which one is transported into the interior of an object in order to coincide with what there is unique and constantly inexpressible in it" (Bergson's emphasis).

17. Renooz's emphasis and phrasing. Renooz, "Régénération morale par la science," *La Revue scientifique des femmes* 1, no. 2 (June 1888): 49.

18. Note how this apparently essentialist view of gendered knowledge is itself open to challenge, as recent constructivist feminist theory has argued. See implications of this shift discussed and applied in Judith Butler, *Gender Trouble: Feminism and the Subversion of Identity* (New York: Routledge, 1990); Personal Narratives Group, *Interpreting Women's Lives: Feminist Theory and Personal Narratives* (Minneapolis: University of Minnesota Press, 1989); and *Writing Women's History,* Michelle Perrot, ed., Felicia Pheasant, trans. (Oxford: Basil Blackwell, 1992).

19. See Felicia Gordon, *The Integral Feminist: Madeleine Pelletier, 1874–1939* (Oxford: Polity Press, 1990); and Joy Harvey, *"Almost a Man of Genius": Clémence Royer, Feminism, and Nineteenth-Century Science* (New Brunswick, N.J.: Rutgers University Press, 1997). Cf. Londa Schiebinger, *The Mind Has No Sex? Women in the Origins of Modern Science* (Cambridge, Mass.: Harvard University Press, 1989), 265–77.

20. Renooz, *La Nouvelle Science,* vol. 1: *Les Forces cosmiques. Synthèse des lois de l'univers, l'évolution des astres, principes d'une nouvelle physique,* 3d ed. (Paris: Librairie Nationale, n.d.), 187. See similar utopian views discussed in Frank E. Manuel, *The Prophets of Paris: Turgot, Condorcet, Saint-Simon, Fourier, and Comte* (Cambridge, Mass.: Harvard University Press, 1962), esp. 1–10.

21. See J. J. Bachofen, *Myth, Religion, and Mother Right,* Rudolf Marx, ed., Ralph Manheim, trans. (Princeton: Princeton University Press, 1967), 69–207. Cf. Stella Georgourdi, "Bachofen, le matriarcat et le monde antique. Réflexions sur la création d'un mythe," *Histoire des femmes en occident,* vol. 1: *L'Antiquité* (Paris: Plon, 1991), 477–92.

22. Despite obvious similarities, Renooz denied any influence of the Saint-Simonians on her work. See Renooz to M. Poignand, 12 February 1902, BHVP box 10, d. 1902, no. 34, in which she praises the utopian socialists but criticizes their emphasis on economic rather than moral reform.

23. Renooz, *Ère de vérité,* vol. 6: *Le Monde moderne* (Paris: Marcel Giard, 1933), 738.

24. See Allen, "Science, Religion, and Feminism"; Christine Bard, *Les Filles de Marianne. Histoire des féminismes 1914–1920* (Paris: Fayard, 1995), 106–16; and more

generally, Claire Goldberg Moses, *Feminist Thought in Nineteenth-Century France* (Albany: State University of New York Press, 1984), 229–37.

25. See *Feminisms of the Belle Epoque: A Historical and Literary Anthology,* Jennifer Waelti-Walters and Steven C. Hause, eds. (Lincoln: University of Nebraska Press, 1994).

26. The editor of the Fonds Marie Louise Bouglé, Maïté Albistur, has organized Renooz's memoirs in six sections of unequal length: 1) Souvenirs d'enfance et de jeunesse, 1840–75 (504 folios); 2) Temps intermédiaire entre la vie familiale et la vocation scientifique, 1875–78 (101 folios); 3) Histoire d'une découverte, 1878–95: Feu dévorant (512 folios); 4) Histoire d'une découverte, 1896–1900: Persécution, Dévastation (229 folios); 5) 1901–08 (272 folios); and 6) Mémoires à partir de 1909–13 (165 folios).

But Renooz notes in her memoirs on at least two occasions that her autobiography falls more naturally into four parts: her early years in Belgium (1840–59), her married life in Spain (1859–75), her intellectual creativity in Paris (1875–90), and the active promotion of her ideas, also in Paris (1890–1913). Despite the archival outline and yet another version based on the headings in the text itself, the logic of Renooz's narrative seems to support best the latter organization, discussed in her preface, BHVP box 16, d. Souvenirs d'enfance, fols. 1–2.

27. Renooz, "Prédestinée," BHVP box 17, d. 1re étape, fol. 44.

28. Terdiman, *Discourse/Counter-Discourse,* 13.

29. Renooz's emphasis. Renooz, "Prédestinée," BHVP box 16, d. Souvenirs d'enfance, fols. 169–70.

30. Renooz, "Prédestinée," BHVP box 18, d. 1890, fol. 365.

31. Ibid. fol. 329.

32. Ibid. fol. 377.

33. Renooz's emphasis. Ibid. fol. 416.

34. Renooz, "Prédestinée," BHVP box 17, d. 4me étape, fol. 97.

35. Renooz to Mme Alfred Dreyfus, 6 January 1895, BHVP box 10, d. 1895, no. 12; and Renooz to Mme Alfred Dreyfus, 17 November 1898, BHVP box 10, d. 1898, no. 9.

36. Renooz, "Prédestinée," BHVP box 17, d. 1903, fol. 4.

37. Renooz, *La Nouvelle Science,* vol. 1: *Les Forces cosmiques,* 127–28.

38. Paraphrased in W. de Fouvielle, "Au Pôle nord. Le Ballon d'Andrée et les courants solaires—La Théorie de Mme C. Renooz—Une expédition impossible," *Le Matin* (31 August 1900). Cf. Renooz, *La Nouvelle Science,* vol. 1: *Les Forces cosmiques,* 106.

39. See articles in BHVP box 20, d. 1900.

40. Cf. version of letter from Elysée Réclus to Renooz, 24 March 1898, in "Prédestinée," BHVP box 18, d. Ostracisme, fol. 248, with the original, 7 April 1898, BHVP box 3, d. 1898, no. 48. For more about climatic conditions at the North Pole,

see Renooz's source, Fridtjof Nansen, *Vers le pôle,* Charles Rabot, ed. and trans. (Paris: Ernest Flammarion, [1906]), 158, 171, 421–22.

41. Letter from Mr. Dautherive to Renooz, 11 September 1900, in BHVP box 3, d. 1900, no. 11.

42. Louise de Saxe, "Histoire de ma vie: La Princesse de Saxe et le maestro Toselli," *Le Matin* (25 September 1911) in BHVP box 24, d. Histoire de Louise de Saxe.

43. Renooz's underscorings in Louise de Saxe, "Mémoires de Louise de Saxe: Chapitre 4. Ma belle-famille," *Le Matin* (5 September 1911) in BHVP box 24, d. Histoire de Louise de Saxe.

44. "De/citation" and "re/citation" are terms Terdiman uses to describe two counter-discursive practices in nineteenth-century France. See Terdiman, *Discourse/Counter-Discourse,* 279–80.

45. Renooz quotes Duval—"Ce que vous faîtes c'est l'aliénation mentale"—in "Prédestinée" BHVP box 17, d. 3me étape, fol. 191.

46. See Clémence Royer to Mme [Avril] de Ste. Croix, June 1897, in Bibliothèque Marguerite Durand, d. Céline Renooz, no. 6: "Cette pauvre folle de Céline Renooz . . . "; and Renooz to M. Vaughan, 10 October 1899, BHVP box 10, d. 1899, no. 15, concerning Paule Mink's having called her "une folle."

47. Renooz's emphasis. Renooz, "Prédestinée," BHVP box 19, d. 1907, fol. 5.

48. Renooz's, "Prédestinée," BHVP box 17, d. Souvenirs d'enfance, fol. 188.

49. Cf. the position of Ricoeur, *Oneself as Another,* 1–26, 113–68; and that of Joan W. Scott, "The Evidence of Experience," *Questions of Evidence: Proof, Practice, and Persuasion across the Disciplines,* James Chandler et al., eds. (Chicago: University of Chicago Press, 1994), 363–87, 397–400. I do not feel that Scott has engaged Ricoeur's challenge on the irreducibility of actual experience as expressed by the likes of Renooz.

50. See the survey of (and response to) the conflicting claims of essentialist and constructivist feminists in Denise Riley, *"Am I that Name?" The Category of "Woman" in History* (Minneapolis: University of Minnesota Press, 1988), esp. 96–114.

51. Lerner, *The Creation of Feminist Consciousness,* 12, 13.

52. Renooz, "Prédestinée," BHVP box 17, d. Souvenirs d'enfance, fols. 1–2.

53. See, e.g., a long, vicious review of Renooz's *Psychologie comparée de l'homme et la femme* (1897) in Théodore Joran, *Autour du féminisme* (Paris: Bibliothèque des "Annales Politiques et Littéraires," 1906), 129–217.

54. On the contested place of positivism in nineteenth-century biology, see Harry W. Paul, *From Knowledge to Power: The Rise of the Science Empire in France, 1860–1939* (Cambridge: Cambridge University Press, 1985), 60–92.

55. This interest is developed at greater length in my recently completed monograph, entitled "Poignant Relations: Three Modern French Women."

56. See Evelyn Sullerot, *Histoire de la presse féminine en France des origines à 1848* (Paris: Armand Colin, 1966).

57. See Renooz to unknown correspondent, 10 July 1917, in Bibliothèque Marguerite Durand MS. 091 REN No. 2. On the suffragists, see Laurence Klejman and Florence Rochefort, *L'Egalité en marche: Le Féminisme sous la troisième République* (Paris: Presses de la Fondation nationale des sciences politiques, 1987), 127–37. See Mary Louise Roberts, "The *Frondeuse:* Gender Identity and Journalism in Fin-de-Siècle France" in this volume.

58. On female literacy rates, see Allen, *In the Public Eye: A History of Reading in Modern France, 1800–1940* (Princeton: Princeton University Press, 1991), 58–59.

59. See Mary Pickering, *Auguste Comte: An Intellectual Biography, Volume 1* (Cambridge: Cambridge University Press, 1993), 362–403, 477–504.

10 Subversive Copy

Feminist Journalism in Fin-de-Siècle France

Only one man worked at *La Fronde*. Founded in December 1897 by the journalist Marguerite Durand, this daily newspaper for women was modeled after the mass dailies of the period. Sometimes called "*Le Temps* in skirts," *La Fronde* boasted a circulation of fifty thousand, embraced republicanism, covered politics, debated social questions, and ran serialized literature.[1] But one important thing distinguished it from all other dailies: the paper was edited, written, and even typeset exclusively by women. Men were categorically denied collaboration, with the exception of the night janitor, who as Alexandre Hepp of *Le Journal* hotly put it, was called upon to be "a specimen of great authenticity so as to embody as best possible the usefulness and honor of the sex which, in a century, has produced only a Napoléon and a Hugo."[2]

Marguerite Durand once defended such a position by arguing that if even one man had been employed by *La Fronde*, doubters could claim that it was really written by men, not women. To produce the paper, Durand gathered around her an extraordinary circle of women. Among them were Clémence Royer—a scholar, the translator of Darwin into French, and the first woman to give a course at the Sorbonne; Séverine (Caroline Rémy), who at the time already had a national reputation as a reporter and journalist; Daniel LeSueur (Jeanne Lapauze)—a playwright and novelist, and one of the first women named to the French *Légion d'honneur*; Jeanne Chauvin, a lawyer and nearly the first woman admitted to the bar in Paris; Blanche Galien, the first female pharmacist in France; and Melle Klumke, the first woman astronomer to enter the Paris observatory. *La Fronde*'s headquarters were the newly decorated offices on 14 de la rue Sainte-Georges, where women in crisp green uniforms typeset the paper in elegant gray-blue surroundings. Durand insisted on paying her female typographers the same wage as their male counterparts, and she was forced to work around labor legislation that forbade women to work at night.[3]

Durand herself was known throughout Paris as a former actress and "one of the prettiest *parisiennes* of our era," as Maurice Barrès put it.[4] (Unless otherwide noted, all translations in this chapter are my own.) "The gold, frothy halo" of Durand's hair, in particular, became the object of fetishistic attention.[5] She debuted at the Comédie française in 1882 at the age of seventeen and enjoyed a great success there until her marriage to the young deputy Georges Laguerre three years later. When Laguerre became deeply involved in the Boulangist movement, Durand emerged as the driving force behind its primary propaganda organ, *La Presse*. After the collapse of the Boulanger campaign, Durand divorced Laguerre and continued her career as a journalist at *Le Figaro* beginning in 1891. In 1896 she became a self-avowed feminist and the following year she founded *La Fronde*.[6] As for the paper's finances, rumor had it that Gustave de Rothschild, a wealthy and prominent Jewish banker, was secretly funding Durand's paper with a "tidy sum of a million."[7] Appearing only weeks before the publication of Zola's "J'Accuse," *La Fronde* was hounded by accusations that it was nothing more than a Dreyfusard rag. More than once, Durand and her *frondeuses* engaged in verbal and legal skirmishes with Edouard Drumont of *La Libre Parole*.[8] Indeed, the links joining *La Fronde,* the Affair, anti-Semitism, and the construction of the "Jew" at the fin de siècle are so multiple and complex as to deserve their own detailed treatment elsewhere.[9]

In the weeks before the first edition rolled off the presses, *La Fronde* became the thing to talk about, both in France and throughout the world.[10] Most of the buzz concerned not how it would be funded, but who would write and produce it. Parisian journalists ostentatiously worried over how a group of women, left to their own resources, would possibly produce a newspaper. The title of the paper, *"La Fronde,"* for example, provoked a melodramatic display of concern. Translated literally as "the slingshot," it linked the paper with the *frondeur* tradition of journalism that had originated in the seventeenth-century uprising against Mazarin, and that distinguished itself by belief in the right of marginal groups to participate in debate on serious matters.[11] Clearly Durand wanted to give historical weight to her demand that women, too, move in from the margins and speak.[12] But to her male colleagues in the press, this "bellicose" title was nothing but "the intention to declare war on men" and an advance sign that "the most resolute amazons of militant feminism, with their unpleasant and rebellious ways" were on the rise.[13] The "*avant-garde of the female army*," the *frondeuses* were rumored to be "skillfully us[ing] the slingshot that it has adopted as its weapon" and "attacking the doors [of society] with blows of stone."[14] Georges Duval dubbed *La Fronde* "David in skirts" and Emile Goudeau wept for the masculine Goliath who, "hit in the face by *La Fronde*'s projectiles, bites the dust on the plain of repentance."[15] "Will the masculine Goliath get a stone in the face from the David of feminism?" wondered one journalist as the first edition finally arrived in the kiosks of Paris.[16]

Yes and no. As the paper actually began to appear, it did more to confuse than to assault its male readers. According to a *Le Temps* article published two weeks after *La Fronde*'s debut, the "unanimous criticism" of the paper was that it "doesn't seem to have a perfectly defined doctrine" and lacked a "distinctive physiognomy." While one day an article demanded political rights for women, the next day a second article declared these rights useless. In this way, observed *Le Temps*, *La Fronde* was no different from any other paper that kept its readers abreast of feminist issues but did not act as a *journal de combat*.[17] And the paper was confusing in still another way. According to *Le Temps*, the other observation that "everyone had made" was that "this paper edited by women in order to serve women's interests is in reality not very feminine at all." The new daily, it had been hoped, would bring to journalism "those particular feminine qualities" that made the letters of Madame de Sévigné so charming, and thus lead to "a renaissance of light-heartedness and delicate grace" in French culture. But, "if you hadn't been warned, if you were not paying attention to the by-lines, you would believe that these long and conscientious, well-informed and often very edifying articles were written by austere scholars."[18]

These last remarks reveal long-held aesthetic preconceptions. In modern France, as Naomi Schor has shown, the "detail" characterized a feminine aesthetic. In visual representation, the detail took the form of decoration and ornament. In female writing such as that of Madame de Sévigné, it was translated as "light-heartedness and delicate grace" in contrast to a more "austere" masculine style. The feminine detail was considered beautiful but insubstantial; ultimately it expressed nothing of value. In this way, the detail was linked in the popular imagination to the censure of woman as frivolous and inconsequential.[19] Hence one male contemporary confessed his expectation that *La Fronde* would be "more gracious, more powdery, more feminine than what was given us."[20] *La Revue* compared the *frondeuses* unfavorably to seventeenth-century women writers "with their admirable gifts of coquetry, *mondanité*, occult powers."[21]

In addition, *La Revue* sneered, unlike their seventeenth-century counterparts, the *frondeuses* were hardly inventing anything new. "Let's not go so far as to see innovators in these new female journalists! Not in the least. They are content to imitate their galant elders."[22] Journalists were certainly justified in noting that *La Fronde* had the style of any other paper covering the news of the day, the prices of stock, and the results of the races. In this sense, they concluded, the paper was edited in a "virile form," and written "with a vigor that is very masculine."[23] For the journalist Maurice le Blond, the belligerent tone of the paper belied the fact that its editors were still "submitting to our domination on one point—that you do not cease to borrow our pace and tone. Despite yourselves, you write in a male style.[24] The *frondeuses* would not have disagreed that they were mimicking journalistic forms and styles of rhetoric. Durand, for example, was proud of the paper's nickname as "*Le Temps* in skirts."[25] But did the *frondeuses* consider that act of mimicry as mere "submission" to male "domination," as Maurice Le Blond would have it?

Three facts throw this interpretation into doubt. First, the *frondeuses* drew on a long history of feminist journalism in France. According to historians, from the eighteenth century onward, women journalists in France had used the newspaper "to counter misogynistic attitudes" and "to transform the image of the woman at all social levels."[26] Second, such a tradition would have been particularly attractive to the *frondeuses* during the 1890s, when an intense debate was waged in France concerning the nature of female identity. For many contemporaries, new professional and educational opportunities for women as well as the emerging feminist movement threatened to overturn conventional gender relations.[27] While the discursive sites for this fight were complex and heterogeneous, the Parisian newspaper played a crucial role. During these years, the "new woman" emerged as a subject of heated discussion in the press. Women teachers, journalists, doctors, lawyers, scientists, and feminists were portrayed as *hommesses* who scorned marriage and children in order to pursue a career.[28] Because the *frondeuses* pursued conventionally male professions, and because *La Fronde* was part of the press, it lay at the center of contests concerning gender in fin-de-siècle France. Finally, work by feminist critics over the past decade has emphasized, in Nancy Miller's words, "the irreducibly complicated relationship women have historically had to the language of the dominant culture."[29] According to these critics, complex acts of appropriation and revision allowed women writers to confront dominant systems of representation (such as journalism) and the ideologies of gender produced within them.[30] To see *La Fronde*'s mimicry as a gesture of submission would be to overlook this important contestatory element of women's writing.

Furthermore, we have already seen a key piece of evidence indicating that the *frondeuses* were using the paper to resist dominant ideologies of gender: its own *cultural illegibility*. Historically, female journalism in nineteenth-century France had been either "feminine" or "feminist." *La Fronde* was neither, according to male contemporaries. The paper disoriented them because they could not read it clearly in terms of gender conventions; it did not mirror conventional ideologies of gender in such a way that, as *Le Temps* put it, its "physiognomy" became clear. For example, Durand intentionally made the paper's feminist content quite ambiguous. Although prominent leaders such as Maria Pognon and Hubertine Auclert published articles in *La Fronde*, Durand insisted that "our paper will be the organ of all French women." Her chief editor, Madame Fournier defined it as "the instrument of a sex and not of either any one element nor of any feminist sect."[31] But neither was the paper "feminine" according to male readers. And if we are to believe Séverine, the *frondeuses* also took up a "virile," "austere" style as a conscious choice. "We have exaggerated our seriousness?" she asked, addressing her critics. "Without a doubt."[32]

But if *La Fronde* was neither feminist nor feminine, what was it? In the enigma of the paper lay its recalcitrance to received ideas concerning female identity. Cultural legibility was the measure of collusion with such ideas; illegibility, a sign of the decision to fly in the face of them.[33] And if male readers seemed to be unnerved rather than relieved by the lack of discernible feminist bias in the paper, this was probably because for them feminism was the only culturally available narrative in which women confronted ideologies of gender. The conspicuous lack of feminist discourse discomfited them because it left the paper's subversive elements unaccounted for within conventional discursive boundaries.

If *La Fronde*'s reproduction of a daily newspaper cannot be seen simply as a gesture of submission, as Le Blond argued, how precisely was its mimicry subversive? And why copy journalistic styles and forms of rhetoric in particular? What were the attractions and dangers of this system of representation? What did the *frondeuses* hope to achieve? Previous work on *La Fronde* has seen the paper as an important fin-de-siècle forum for feminist views on a variety of issues, among them, politics, education, female wage work, and trade unionism.[34] By contrast, I am interested in how the *frondeuses*, while keeping their readers abreast on matters of politics, the economy, and sports, also launched a radical critique of how gender identity had been produced in French culture. I have paid particularly close attention to the first six months of *La Fronde*, when its circulation and thus its cultural impact were at their highest. In these first few months, the *frondeuses* not only mimicked the conventions of journalism, but also the notion of *mimesis* itself that lay at the heart of fin-de-siècle journalism—the professional discourse that shaped journalism as the literal reproduction of the "real" world. As we shall see, such mimicry allowed them, in turn, to challenge ideologies of gender.

Mad Criminals and Courtesans: La Crise de la Presse

If we are to understand what made *La Fronde* subversive copy, we must first examine fin-de-siècle journalism as a system of representation. In choosing the daily paper as the medium for all-female self-expression, Marguerite Durand could not have trespassed on a more culturally dangerous— and pivotal—discursive territory. Through her early career as a Boulangist, Durand had become acutely aware of journalism as a powerful force. "Once a vehicle of ideas—particularly political ideas—at the service of only a certain class," she argued, "the newspaper today has become the indispensible 'thing' for all classes."[35] Delivered from the threat of government censorship in 1881, bolstered by technological innovations and a burgeoning literacy rate, the Parisian mass press almost tripled its circulation between 1880 and 1914.[36] Beginning at midcentury, papers such as *Le Petit Journal* became mass cultural commodities by lowering prices, using new advertising methods, and emphasizing *faits divers,* which covered crime, domestic quarrels, and other events of everyday life.[37] The results were spectacular. The fin de siècle became the "golden age" or the "apogee" of the French press due to both its prevalence and its influence.[38]

But the newspaper also acted as a screen upon which was projected a litany of fin-de-siècle fears. These fears were rising to a fevered pitch just as the first edition of *La Fronde* rolled off the presses in December 1897. At precisely this time a major survey of views concerning the so-called *crise de la presse* appeared in the weekly *La Revue bleue.* The survey provides an excellent source for understanding the cultural construction of the press at the time Durand's paper made its debut.[39] The survey continued for several weeks and, according to the review's director, Henry Bérenger, had a "national impact" inasmuch as it brought to the surface growing anxiety about the power of the press.[40] Among the readers of *La Revue bleue,* there existed a widespread consensus that the press "had fallen into a deplorable state . . . and no longer acts as anything but an agent of moral disorganization."[41] Press corruption was attributed to fierce competition, the economic dependence of editors on financiers and advertisers, political extortion, and a general decline in morality, among other things.[42] The newspaper came to bear responsibility for political and financial scandal, for violence, and for so-called moral degeneracy in a democratic, commodity-oriented society.[43] In short, "*la crise de la presse*" was a master narrative of fin-de-siècle anxiety, a rival of "the depopulation crisis" at century's end.

Also at stake in *la crise de la presse* were fears related to the discovery of unconscious forces working in the human mind. Research in this era concerning such phenomena as hysteria, hypnosis, and suggestion heightened public awareness of unconscious mental "domination." The inspiration for the *Revue bleue* survey had come from an earlier article in the same journal by Alfred Fouillée, in which he had blamed newspapers for inciting juveniles to violence by reporting crimes in vivid detail.[44] The survey began with this acknowledgment of the power of the press:

> Chaque jour, un Français ou une Française, même dans les basses classes, lit un journal au moins, le plus souvent deux. . . . Comme la poussière et comme le vent, il s'insinue dans les consciences les mieux fermées, il balaie incessamment les plus ouvertes, il crée une atmosphère sociale d'où personne ne peut s'évader.[45]

> [Each day, a French man or woman, even in the lowest classes, reads at least one paper, often two. . . . Like the dust and the wind, it insinuates itself in even the most closed mind, and in short order sweeps the most open; it creates a social atmosphere from which no one can escape.]

Fouillée's concerns had, in fact, expressed a widely held fear: that the social role of the press had undergone a monstrous transformation, so that although it once served to educate and enlighten the French, it now catered to their instincts and manipulated their thoughts.[46] Knowledge of such domination was threatening to the public inasmuch as it called into question the Enlightenment notion of a rational, autonomous self.[47]

The notion of mimicry lay at the heart of this anxiety concerning unconscious forces. In his earlier article, Fouillée drew on popular psychological theory concerning suggestion to conclude that young people, being "at an age when imitation prevails over personal responsibility," found irresistible the temptation to mimic sensational crimes reported in the papers. Fouillée's cry of alarm joined a growing chorus of voices dismayed by gruesome reportage and panicked by soaring rates of crime and juvenile delinquency.[48] In a culture preoccupied with Jean Charcot's work on suggestion, Fouillée was not the only one to caution the French concerning their susceptibility to the power of the printed image.[49] Throughout the 1890s, the prominent psychologist Séverin Icard had deplored the particular "vulnerability" of women, especially during periods of menstruation or menopause, to images in the paper of murder and suicide. Drawing on an old discourse concerning the dangers of women reading novels, Icard reasoned that because so many women "have chosen a home on the frontier of madness," reading the wrong article could "bring them instantaneously into the territory of mental derangement."[50] The notion of unconscious mimicry was again central to Icard's concern. Using the *journaux intimes* of female criminals as evidence, he argued that "the instinct to imitate"—present in all humans but undeterred by reason in the young and the feeble—had driven these women to murder and suicide after they had read of similar crimes.

Because in the popular imagination women were thought to lack a rational, autonomous self to begin with, they served as a convenient symbol for the newly recognized power of irrational drives. Icard's half-mad female criminals illustrate how woman became a projection for fears concerning the manipulation of unconscious forces by the press. In 1897 the Baron Tanneguy de Wogan agreed that his "worst" fear about the press was "the woman who reads" because in doing so she "becomes completely indifferent to evil, even if she does not commit it."[51] Zola feared that the newspaper "held the nation" in a "state of nervous excitation" so that it became "similar to those nervous women that jump at the slightest noise."[52]

Similarly, anxiety about the moral corruption of the press was organized around another female image—the prostitute selling herself to the masses.[53] In the *Revue bleue* survey, Bérenger warned his readers that although they thought the press was free, "Each of you democrats is a king surrounded by courtesans: your newspapers allow you to know only the truth they want you to know." The "total power" of newsprint lay in the fact that "it never commands but always suggests."[54] For Bérenger, the press had become an insidious female force seducing and enslaving its readers and thus eating away at democracy. In a metaphor common to the French nineteenth century, woman represented the power of instinctual drives—this time, sexual temptation—that overwhelmed the human capacity to reason. Also in *Revue bleue,* Anatole Leroy-Beaulieu condemned the press that "makes itself the courtesan of the masses, and like a good courtesan, fears above all to be boring, repulsive. . . . For it is, alas, much easier to attract men and masses by catering to their appetites or passions than by talking to their reason or conscience."[55]

The press-as-prostitute also served as a symbol of fin-de-siècle fears about a bourgeoning commodity culture.[56] Since Baudelaire, the prostitute—as "saleswoman and wares in one" to use Walter Benjamin's phrase—had represented the commodification of human behavior in France's growing consumer society.[57] In the fin-de-siècle debate on the press, the image of the prostitute helped the French to express anxiety that the newspaper, now a mass cultural commodity, was both a polluted and a polluting force. "Hasn't [the press] prostituted itself to money only in order to corrupt the damned masses even more?" Bérenger asked his readers.[58] "A street, a public place, that's all the press is today!" lamented the journalist Maurice Talmeyr.[59]

For many of the French, the newspaper epitomized a trend toward democratization in new mass forms of culture. Once again, the prostitute— perceived to be everywhere in the newly Haussmannized Paris—symbolized the social mixing and "leveling" of pleasures that distinguished the new commodity culture. For Leroy-Beaulieu, the press as courtesan was the new "press of democracy," sharply contrasting with the old "elite press, serious, worthy of its high mission." This view of French journalism was hardly new—as, for some time, its practitioners had been viewed as a shady group. Throughout the modern period, critics had dismissed the honor of the press as compromised by party politics and private interest.[60] But as Philip Nord has argued, the struggle between the old entrepreneurial and the new mass consumer forms of capitalism during this period found its parallel in the intellectual world, where journalists who catered to a mass readership increasingly supplanted an older literary elite.[61] Hence one *Revue* reader perceived the journalist as "a man without conviction or scruples who sells his services to the highest bidder. . . . a prostitute of literature."[62]

The image of the newspaper as courtesan was also common in the wider literature on *la crise de la presse*. In 1895, for example, the dramatist Jules Case described the press in this way: "Popular with the masses, she seems old, worn out, like an aging coquette who dresses up and puts on makeup, calling on every artifice to prolong her failing popularity.[63] Finally the image was expressed visually. A series of allegorical postcards from the era feature scantily clad women whose dress and demeanor suggest a less-than-respectable profession (figs. 10-1, 10-2). The names of the various newspapers they represent are often strategically draped over their pelvic area. An important exception here is the female representing *La Fronde,* who, it could be argued, appears to be *reading* rather than erotically *displaying* her newspaper (fig. 10-3). As such, she acts as a reading subject rather than as a sexual symbol of the press. Unlike most of the other figures, she is dressed in male garb, linking mimicry to cross-dressing. Because the *frondeuses* were women mimicking a male profession, their paper is symbolized by a woman dressed as a man.[64]

Even this brief glance at the discourse on *la crise de la presse* reveals how anxiety about the production and consumption of newsprint was organized around common, late nineteenth-century images of women such as the mad reader and the prostitute. The appearance of pejorative female images in the press follows a general pattern at the turn of the European century, when as

Andreas Huyssen has argued, "aesthetic discourse . . . consistently and obsessively genders mass culture and the masses as feminine, while high culture, whether traditional or modern, clearly remains the privileged realm of male activities."[65] Critics have surmised that such a construction of mass culture was political in nature, that it was coincidental with the rising threat of the masses—in particular, the first major women's movement in Europe.[66] From the prostitutes of the barricades to the *petroleuses* of 1871 to the crowds of Zola and Gustave Le Bon, the threat of the masses had been described in feminine terms.[67] As Huyssen argues, "the fear of the masses in this age of declining liberalism is always a fear of woman, a fear of nature out of control, a fear of the unconscious, of sexuality, of the loss of identity."[68] Clearly these same fears suffuse the debate on la *crise de la presse*.

Gender also lay at the heart of crucial discursive changes taking place in the field of journalism during the fin de siècle. The "new journalism" that gained credence and popularity in this period can also be seen in gendered terms—as an effort to "re-virilize" the profession, to make the press more "manly" and thus more honorable. Historians agree that toward the end of the century, reportage, with its Anglo-American emphasis on information and the detached observance of public life, remade journalism in its name.[69] The movement away from the early nineteenth-century *presse d'opinion*—in which a paper argued in favor of a particular party—and toward the more neutral *presse d'information* had been underway for a while.[70] But by 1892 Eugène Dubief was calling newspapers "information offices" and by 1894, Zola was able to write that "information . . . has transformed journalism."[71] In this transition a new cadre of professional journalists replaced an older more bohemian literary elite. As Hugues Le Roux put it in 1889, "the *chroniqueur,* the brilliant old man of witticisms and words about this and that, has been dethroned by a writer less anxious to shine but better informed about the subjects he treats: the reporter.[72] The new emphasis on information enabled journalists to pump up the truth value of their product so that it might rise from the moral quagmire into which it had fallen. Precision was to be the saving grace of journalism. "For a long time, the press has been a pulpit," wrote the journalist Yves Guyot in 1901. "It will more and more become an inquiry office and a laboratory.[73]

The popularity of reportage represented only part of the French public's "new and marked taste for reality," as the historian Vanessa Schwartz has put it. The phenomenon was obvious both in such "high" cultural movements as naturalism and such "low" cultural trends as public visits to the morgue and the opening of the wax Musée Grévin.[74] The fin-de-siècle "taste for reality" relied on a technology of vision. As one journalist described the fad

FIGURE 10-1: "Les Journaux de Paris," allegorical postcards of the Belle Epoque. René Livois, *Histoire de la presse française,* vol. 2 (Paris: Les Temps de la Presse, 1965).

FIGURE 10-2: "Les Journaux de Paris," allegorical postcards of the Belle Epoque. René Livois, *Histoire de la presse française,* vol. 2 (Paris: Les Temps de la Presse, 1965).

LES JOURNAUX DE PARIS !

FIGURE 10-3: "La Fronde," "Les Journaux de Paris," allegorical postcards of the Belle Epoque. René Livois, *Histoire de la presse française,* vol. 2 (Paris: Les Temps de la Presse, 1965).

for reportage, "abstract notions, discussions of principle, the search for the absolute, fictions and tales no longer suffice to satisfy or charm our spirit." The French, he continued, "are willing to believe only what they see with their eyes.[75] In this way, the public "taste for reality" became inseparable from the "spectacular" culture taking shape on the boulevards of Haussmannized Paris—where to see and be seen in the streets, theater, and cafés became a social imperative.[76]

The technology of vision guaranteed reality's truth value, which lay in the unmediated relation between the observer and the observed. Journalists relied on this technology to define their craft.[77] The reporter was an *eye* witness whose copy was nothing more than that—an undistorted mirror of the real world. "They will retrace what they have seen, nothing more, nothing less," was how a spokesperson for the *Ecole de journalisme* described the reporter's job in 1899.[78] To see, to reproduce transparently what one has seen—that was the journalist's task. Paul Pottier called reportage "the art of seeing" and Clovis Hugues described the reporter as "the eye that sees everything.[79] "Le reportage, c'est la chose vue," as the historian Bernard Voyenne put it succinctly.[80] Reporters often cited Victor Hugo's two-volume *Choses vues* (1887) as an important model.[81] When the prominent journalist Arthur Meyer set out to write his memoirs just before the war, he called it *Ce que mes yeux ont vu;* similarly, the journalist Jules Huret titled his memoirs *Tout Yeux, tout oreilles.*[82] The mirror was also a symbol of this mimetic quality in journalism. Of the journalist Henry Fouquier, Jules Lemaître once wrote: "He is a sentient mirror open wide to the world and to life.[83] This image of the reporter was in turn projected onto the newspaper itself. In 1892, the journalist Eugène Dubief described the daily paper as "a magical turning mirror, an active, speaking mirror.[84] These images of the press as a mirror shielded journalists from angry criticisms, as the words of Max Nordau, the author of *Degeneration* (1895), illustrate: "Recognize yourself in the figure of the press's reflection," he admonished his readers, "If this figure horrifies you, be ashamed of yourself. It is all too easy to blame the press for your own vices and faults.[85]

In relying on metaphors of vision and reflection to define their craft, journalists drew on a modern aesthetic that was construed in terms of pure visuality. Impressionists such as Monet, naturalists such as Zola, and voyeurs such as Marcel Proust all relied on an aesthetic that privileged observation of the visual surface.[86] As the French filmmaker Jean-Louis Comolli has written, "the second half of the nineteenth century lives in a sort of frenzy of the visible.[87] But Nordau's remarks also reveal how journalists could use the metaphor of vision as literal transparency in order to ward off accusations of bias and corruption. Accused of inventing the facts and distorting the news to fit their own political or private aims, journalists appealed to the authority of a "real" world. A. de Chambure's dramatic sketch of a reporter seeking employment in an editor's office involves his confession that "I've never known myself to have any imagination at all" but "I have . . . eyes that can see fifteen-hundred meters away.[88] An eyewitnessed reality became the essential reference in journalistic narrative because it served as its own justification for speaking and it imposed its own laws. "I obey only one law—the news," professed a reporter for *Petit journal,* "the news alone guides me.[89] Because the "real" world was given uncontested power, accident governed the reporter's technique. The journalist Fernand Xau claimed to report only on those men and events "that the wind of current events pushes toward the light.[90]

The trend toward reportage can also be seen as a response to the assault on empiricism and Enlightenment rationalism in fin-de-siècle intellectual circles.[91] As we have seen, it was widely believed in this era that the social role of the press had been changed from one of purposeful instruction to one of insidious mental domination. This transformed image of the press was only one element in a larger fin-de-siècle pattern, in which Enlightenment notions of rationality and the autonomous subject were challenged by popular psychology, Bergsonian "intuitionism," and symbolist poetry.[92] By drawing on metaphors of vision and light, and by framing their project in rigorously empirical terms, as the passive collection of information, these reporters reconstructed the meaning of journalism once again in traditional Enlightenment terms—as the imparting of objective knowledge for pedagogical purposes. But this claim to radical empiricism camouflaged the inevitably selective discursive practices that reporters drew on in order to produce their "copy."[93] While journalists presented their *faits-divers* as graphic, "real-life" stories of crime, they were consistently accused of turning violence into a "*pièce de théâtre*" and daily events into a "spectacle."[94]

Journalists also attempted to disguise such practices by making sharp distinctions between reportage and literature. Strong links had always existed between journalism and literature as systems of representation. Aspiring writers began their careers as journalists who were considered part of a bohemian literati.[95] Given the emphasis on observation and documentation in fin-de-siècle literary movements such as naturalism, one could argue that the journalistic and literary were closer than ever. In 1889 Zola compared his own work as a novelist with that of a reporter: "we proceed in the exact same manner as the journalist studying current affairs, meeting the personalities of the day, publishing only reports of events."[96] But by the beginning of the new century, the new reporter-journalist began to define his profession in *opposition* to literature. "Journalism," argued the reporter in Charles Fenestrier's novel *La Vie des frelons* (1908), "has nothing in common with literature."[97] Not all journalists were happy about this new opposition. "This hideous reportage," railed Adolphe Brisson, "these cold, banal, impersonal accounts, from which all emotion, verve, and fantasy are excluded!"[98] Papers continued to serialize novels but reportage and literature became mutually exclusive categories. In 1901 Edmond Pilon predicted that "newspapers are the masters of the future." Literature, he warned, was "succumbing under the daily invasion of these formidable mountains of paper."[99]

By defining "reportage" as a choice of "reality" over "fantasy," the reporter buttressed the truth value of the new journalism. In fact, of course, the sharp dichotomies upon which the new journalism rested—the "real" versus the "fantastic," literature versus reportage—were highly unstable. Many reporters still harbored literary aspirations. The fictitious journalist above, who won employment by claiming to have good eyes and no imagination, celebrated his new job by having cards printed with "J. Furet, homme de lettres" on them.[100] In addition, the "selling" of the news depended upon inscribing it in a narrative and embellishing it in such a way that it became interesting. In his manual for journalists, the Baron Tanneguy de Wogan urged his readers to write reportage in this way: "Be careful to put a little fantasy into your work. Information can only serve as your guide; depart from this starting point if you can."[101]

Gendered meanings helped to support the unstable dichotomy between the "real" and the "imaginary" upon which reportage was based. In 1892 the journalist Fernand Xau fretted that "the desire for rapid, plain, hard information" would not completely satisfy French readers. Literary sections were necessary because, as Xau put it, "we need something more. . . . Businessmen and politicians are not the only ones reading the paper. Writers and artists also do so, as well as women who are not particularly interested in banal, brutal information."[102] Xau's remark reveals the way in which contemporary notions of gender and journalism were imbricated in each other. Rapid, plain, hard, and brutal (as opposed to insidious) reportage was clearly masculine discursive terrain; women and feminine types, such as writers and artists, could hardly appreciate it. The association of literature with the emotional, irrational, and inferior sex—stuck at the stage of imagination, according to Rousseau—encouraged the repression of literary elements in the new journalism.[103] "*Le grand reportage* is the king of journalism," agreed Paul Pottier.[104] "In contemporary journalism, the reporter reigns as the master" agreed *Le Peuple*.[105]

If one considers these gendered metaphors as a response to Bérenger's earlier comment concerning the press as a "courtesan" enslaving democrat-kings, we can conclude that the deployment of reportage was an attempt to re-virilize journalism—to achieve the virile status granted to "higher" literary forms. In 1897 the Baron Tanneguy de Wogan argued for reportage in this way: "It is news, information more than imagination, that we need; it is statistics, figures, facts, and not womanizing that seduces the public."[106] Armed with plain, hard information, the male reporter could swear off the forbidden fruit of corruption and become his own master again.

Mimicking Reporters: Rebels with Ink on Their Fingers

But what about the female reporter? Given the degree to which anxiety concerning the press was organized around cultural images of women—mad readers, prostitutes, effeminate *chroniqueurs*—what did it mean for women such as the *frondeuses* to practice the new journalism?

Combining low moral prestige with wide cultural authority, the daily newspaper provided the *frondeuses* with an unparalleled opportunity for cultural visibility. Critics have argued that the nineteenth-century woman writer, afraid of public exposure or intimidated by "high" literary forms, often gravitated to genres that were marginal (diaries, travelogues) and hence less likely to be judged rigorously according to literary standards.[107] As the "prostitute of literature," the mass-circulation newspaper gave women the chance to write with little pretension but potentially wide effect. This mix of low literary expectation with high cultural impact made journalism attractive to feminists and other so-called new women trying to lead unconventional lives. As one contemporary put it, the new women, in general, were nothing more than "rebels with ink on their fingers."[108]

But in terms of the new journalism, the *frondeuses* were not rebels at all: they copied rather than challenged the established terms of the genre. The *frondeuses* embraced the terms of a recently "virilized" journalism; they engaged the same binary oppositions—real versus abstract, factual versus literary, masculine versus feminine—that organized reportage as a discursive field. The *frondeuse* Marie-Louise Néron, for example, once described the older *chroniqueurs* in feminine terms as "the dispossessed, those who have been brutally chased from pleasant positions where they had become accustomed to lounging, conversing for the reader, stringing together high-sounding words and splitting hairs." Frivolous hairsplitters, chatterers, and lounge lizards, the old literary types had clearly received a well-deserved (albeit brutal) comeuppance from their more virile colleagues, the reporters. "Reportage reigns, governs; it is a conquerer," concluded Néron.[109] The well-known *frondeuse* Séverine made the same distinction between literary journalism and reportage, referring to the former as "journalisme assis" [armchair journalism] and the latter as "journalisme debout, courant, alerte, s'assouplissant à l'actualité" [journalism on its feet, up-to-date, alert, responsive to the events of the moment].[110] Séverine once distinguished between previous women writers "ne se mêlant à la vie normale contemporaine que dans le domaine de l'abstraction ou de l'observation" [engaging in normal contemporary life only in the domain of abstraction], and her own generation who "entre résolument dans la carrière dépourvue d'aînées; s'en prend aux faits" [were resolutely entering the career forbidden their elders and taking on the facts/events].[111]

Despite the fact that the *frondeuses* mimicked rather than challenged the terms of the new journalism, Séverine's comment provides a first clue as to why such mimicry, far from being submissive, might be subversive. The double meaning in French of "*fait*" as both "event" and "fact" summarizes neatly the double challenge to conventional ideologies of gender that Séverine set forth by "posing" as a reporter. As we shall see, by taking on the events, Séverine challenged female domesticity. And by taking on the facts, she defied female frivolity. Séverine could be a reporter *but not quite,* because she was also a woman. That ambiguity was the key to her subversion of traditional gender roles.[112]

First, by "taking on the events"—by their insistence on engaging in contemporary public life—the *frondeuses* had to violate the conventional domestic enclosure of woman in the private realm.[113] Being a reporter, unlike being a female novelist, required a woman "to leave her house, to see, hear, and observe beyond the constraints of the family circle," to use Marguerite Durand's definition.[114] Because the visible was privileged as the origin of knowledge in the new journalism, the reporter spent less time in the office and more time as an eyewitness to events. According to Léon Daudet, reportage arose at the same time as a new need for on-the-spot observation.[115] At great expense the globetrotting, adventurous reporter—"Le Sieur de va-partout" or "Monsieur tout-le-monde," as he was called—traveled the world as a foreign correspondent.[116]

But throughout the nineteenth century, activity outside the home was deemed shameful for the single middle-class woman, who was often not allowed to venture out unchaperoned. The public element of the reporter's job exposed the *frondeuses* to a storm of ridicule. In one journalist's mock recreation of the goings-on at Durand's paper, she tries to send one of her journalists to report on a fire in progress in Belleville. "Not another bad *quartier!*" the reporteress complains, "I'll never get the chance to meet a *monsieur.*" When Durand insists, the reporter leaves but then repeatedly comes back, first for her lipstick, second because her garter breaks, and finally because she has discovered that in the meanwhile the fire has been put out.[117] This farce reveals what was at stake for women in journalism: the entry of women reporters into new public spaces threatened the boundaries of the conventional female role—to look pretty, stay at home, and find a husband.

A woman who ventured out in public was culturally intelligible to contemporaries mostly as a prostitute. In this way, the public nature of the *frondeuses*'s job called into question their respectability. The journalist Georges de Dubor feared that the *frondeuse* on her beat late at night at the Gare de Lyon would most likely be "confused with a prostitute."[118] Another male journalist called *La Fronde* "*Le Moniteur de Saint-Lazare*" after a Parisian prison for prostitutes.[119] The critic Hans Ryner sarcastically praised the *frondeuse* Séverine for being "the most sensible of merchants," and accused her of having prostituted her beliefs in order to sell a maximum amount of copy.[120] When *La Fronde* ceased publication in 1903, one male journalist confessed that what he had found most disturbing about the paper was "the sight of the "*reporteress*" at the Chamber, the Municipal Council, the Palais, in street demonstrations, in short, everywhere that one had seen only a "*reporter.*" It goes without saying," he noted tartly, "that they made a great couple."[121] The veiled reference here to illicit sex again shows how the *frondeuses* were vulnerable to charges of immoral behavior. In this way, the *frondeuse* became a literal embodiment of Bérenger's image of the press as the insidious courtesan.

Against the backdrop of this formula, which equated women's presence outside the home with prostitution, *La Fronde* created a new public identity for women. By taking up the subject matter of the mass daily, Durand's paper produced an image of woman as knowledgeable about and involved in the conventionally masculine spheres of politics, jurisprudence, and high finance. Daily newspapers chronicled a public world from which women were excluded in fin-de-siècle France—the stock market, the Parliament, the Ministry, the courtroom. Similarly, the pages of *La Fronde* were filled with eyewitness *compte rendus* of sessions of Parliament, reports from the courts, the stock market, the *Elysée* palace, and interviews with major political figures such as Georges Clemenceau. The paper was openly republican in political orientation. In order to cover events in these areas, Durand had to get permission for women to enter—for the first time ever—the stock market, the senate, the chamber, the municipal and departmental councils.[122] The newspaper genre, then, allowed the *frondeuses* to make claims for inclusion in conventionally male public spaces.[123] Through mimicry of the newspaper genre, these women validated their presence as republican citizens in the public world.

But at the same time, this mimicry of a paper's topical coverage only threw into relief women's marginal status in relation to power. Even as the newspaper authorized women's claims for inclusion, it marked their exclusion. Women reporters had access to the centers of power in France—*but not quite,* simply because they were women. When the *frondeuses* reported on this world, implying their own presence within it, they exposed the contradiction between women's marginal place in the Third Republic and the republican ideals (including freedom of the press) that afforded citizens access to social and economic institutions of power. The feminist articles appearing in *La Fronde* served to justify explicitly the silent infractions made by the paper's act of mimicry. The effect of *La Fronde* was to call into question both the knowledge of politics and the politics of knowledge. What did knowledge of political affairs mean for women when they could not vote or run for office? Why did they have the right to learn about republican politics but little power to act on such knowledge? And what claims for inclusion did women make by seizing the power to impart and receive that knowledge?

Were the *frondeuses* aware that their paper was "subversive copy" in this way? Did they consciously set out to expose the contradictions of republican ideology in the Third Republic? It is hard to say, but also hard to believe that Durand and her colleagues were not aware of the ironic effect of their paper when they reported on political and economic events. As Joan Scott has shown, a major strategy on the part of feminists throughout the nineteenth century was to point to inconsistencies and contradictions in republican ideology.[124] In any case, Durand quite clearly set out to educate women in political matters and to give them a civic identity. She allowed no men on the editorial board, she claimed, because she wanted to prove that "women . . . were capable of doing all the rubrics" of a newspaper, including politics and finance.[125] If we are to believe the long-time reader, Madame Cadet, the impact of *La Fronde* fulfilled Durand's ambition. Cadet once wrote Durand that due to the paper, she had overcome her "long-held belief that politics were not for women."[126] Durand also reveled in the access her reporters gained into political and financial institutions of power. Citing the examples of Briand, Poincaré, and Viviani, Durand once defined journalism as an entryway into politics.[127] Women such as Jane Misme and Maria Vérone, who began their careers at *La Fronde* and went on to become prominent interwar feminists, again proved Durand right.

As we have seen, then, by first "taking on the events," Séverine and the *frondeuses* challenged the constraints of female domesticity. Second, by "taking on the facts," the woman reporter signaled her frustration with a life of novelistic fantasy. To be real reporters, the *frondeuses* had to venture out into the brave world of facts, leaving their imaginations behind. In doing so, they defied the widespread nineteenth-century notion of women as creatures of whimsy rather than reason.[128] One male journalist later recalled "the almost universal feeling that greeted the debut of *La Fronde*" in this way: "What . . . women directing a paper?! Literature and novels are one thing (a matter of imagination, that!), but to meddle in civic affairs, to give one's opinion on such and such a deputy, candidate, senator, good God—that is enough to make you laugh out loud!"[129] It was the idea of a woman reporter, not of a woman writer, that raised eyebrows in 1897.[130] Imagination was one thing, but reality was another. Male contemporaries such as Francisque Sarcey could only express astonishment when they found the content of *La Fronde* truly journalistic: "these women pride themselves on being serious to an extent that you cannot imagine."[131] If the *frondeuse* as she took on the events was read as a prostitute, the *frondeuse* as she took on the facts was beyond what Sarcey could even imagine. Her cultural *illegibility* once again signaled a challenge to received ideas concerning female identity. Clearly disappointed at the skill of the *frondeuses'* mimicry, male journalists repeatedly criticized the paper as "austere," "dense," "solid," "heavy, severe" or "just as boring as those produced by men."[132] "Evidently, the *frondeuses* fear the reproach of frivolity," a more astute reader noted. "But since the proof has been made, and more than made . . . they need not worry in giving free rein to their fantasy."[133]

But the *frondeuses* did have to worry—about the widespread prejudice that they would not surmount their own imaginations, their "fantastic" and "frivolous" way of writing as women. As we have seen, Séverine claimed that seriousness was a conscious strategy "to prove that if we really applied ourselves, we could in a pinch write as austerely as men. Has that happened? Yes, since you proclaim it. Hence, we have succeeded. The step was necessary."[134] With playful insouciance, Séverine waved away lingering fears that in a pinch women could not write in an austere male style. In doing so, she also airily dismissed the prejudice that imagination and fantasy—the makings of a devalorized feminine aesthetic—were the only means of self-expression available to women.

Séverine's response to the charge that the *frondeuses* were overly serious demonstrates again how their mimicry could be subversive. The philosopher Luce Irigaray has argued that mimicry as a rhetorical strategy allowed a woman writer to resubmit herself to systems of representation that repressed the feminine without, in doing so, being completely reduced to them. The effect of mimicry was to repeat playfully these systems in such a way that women writers gained some distance from them. By being good mimics, women writers proved that "they also remain[ed] elsewhere"—an elsewhere from which they could point to their own exploitation within language.[135] In the same way, Séverine and the *frondeuses* were able to playfully repeat the austere style (as well as the format and subject matter) of journalism—a representational form in which women had been largely invisible either as authors or as subject matter. But as Séverine reveals in her comments, the *frondeuses* were also able to put distance between themselves and an overly serious style by declaring it a necessary step toward respectability. Such a distance allowed them, in turn, to critique the narrow and restrictive way in which they had been perceived, not only as writers but as women.

The *frondeuses* took on the facts as a subversive gesture in still another, perhaps even more important way. Like all new journalists, they adopted as a general standard the notion of journalism as an unproblematic reflection of reality. But with this standard of realism, they went on to denounce as fantasy the way in which men had constructed female identity in French culture. Again and again they used the word "*fantaisiste*"—meaning both fanciful and eccentric—to describe the representation of women in literature and the press. For example, "Chevreuse" complained on December 22 that a female association called the "Ladies' Club" had been "presented to the public by the masculine press in a rather fanciful way, motivating the author to re-present it to her readers "in its *real* light."[136] Three days later she again accused the press of responding in a fanciful way to the question of whether or not an *institutrice* should ride a bicycle.[137] Similarly, "J. M." accused the journalist Georges Duval of citing "examples of high fantasy" to support his contention that women writers were neurasthenic and insane.[138]

In this way the *frondeuses* used the new emphasis in journalism on mirroring "reality" to challenge male views of women. Literary writers were critiqued on the same basis, so that the distinctions between journalism and literature were erased in a way that might discomfit reporters. Alexandre Dumas, for example, came under fire by Urgèle for creating a "fantasy mold" of woman into which he poured his own "antipathies, bitterness."[139] With dripping sarcasm, Marie Anne de Bovet complained of how Guy de Maupassant had declared woman feeble and limited to love by "basing his argument on the experience of centuries." How ironic, she sneered, that women formed his primary reading audience: "that is called firing on your own troops."[140] Proudhon, notorious coiner of the phrase "housewife or harlot," was trounced for his lies, insults, and platitudes about women.[141] And Judith Cladel took all writers to task for creating in literature the woman who "dwells in his imagination" as "a phantom" and a "sweet chimera" rather than "a terrestial creature" he meets in real life.[142]

In self-conscious contrast to such "examples of high fantasy," the *frondeuses* presented in-depth "copy" on various aspects of female experience. Maria Pognon provided figures on just how many women and children were working in the *ateliers* "in order to give some idea of the importance of the work produced by women in our dear country where one speaks only of a woman's grace, of her charm, her seductions, and other silly things."[143] Similarly, Pauline Kergomard urged the mother "to raise her children in the reality of things and not in a sort of artificial mysticism."[144] Long investigative articles revealed the low pay and often dangerous conditions of women working in the *ateliers de couture* and factories of all kinds.[145] The same week that *La Fronde* was sarcastically crowned *"Le Moniteur de Saint-Lazare,"* Ghénia Avril de Sainte Croix brought her readers into the fabled prostitute's prison, exposing it in grand reporter-style as a lugubrious house of horrors.[146] Dismissing as hypocrisy the conventional image of the prostitute as depraved, Avril de Saint Croix represented her as a "slave," and a "victim of misery."[147] It was hardly a coincidence that prostitution—the female profession that had suffered more fantastic male representation than any other—was among the first topics that the *frondeuses* took on as reporters.[148]

Of course the *frondeuses* were no more neutral than any male reporters. But like these reporters, they appealed to the authority of a "real" world as a way of promoting the truth value of their own point of view. In their critique of the production of sexual difference, the *frondeuses* also focused on the metaphor of vision so fundamental to the contemporary notion of *reportage.* While for male journalists, the image of the mirror expressed their transparent reproduction of the real, for the *frondeuses,* it measured the distortion between the male construction of woman and the real woman herself. Referring to Dumas's literature, Urgèle spoke of "the truncated, false image [of women] that this unfaithful mirror reflects" so that they say to themselves: "But this is not us; we do not recognize ourselves."[149] Daniel LeSueur saw the mirror as representing the invisibility of all women who lay outside the male-defined erotic economy that constructed female identity: "Ugly girls, neglected wives, old women—creatures toward whom men do not direct their desire. . . . They are forbidden to recognize their existence in the imagination of others, as all reflection of their being is erased from the mirror of hearts."[150] If the visible was privileged as the origin of knowledge in reportage, invisibility described women's own relation to representation. Unconventional women, who found no model of themselves within the boundaries of representation, were reduced to a spectral existence: "If a woman no longer loves men, no longer inspires or feels passion," argued the *frondeuse*

Paule Vigneron, she "has no choice but to die or else wander like a sorry phantom among the living."[151]

In a world where the French public was clamoring for an eyewitnessed reality, the *frondeuses* called attention to the ways in which vision was politicized: who was being seen and not seen? how were women being seen? Paule Vigneron, for example, denounced the absolute control that men had over the production of gender identity:

"Depuis si longtemps qu'il y a des hommes," et qui écrivent . . . et qui parlent, ils ont entassé les parchemins et les livres, semé dans l'air les mots, les conférences et les chansons pour dire leur pensée sur nous; pensée créée souvent par leur imagination de poètes, toujours par les passions égoïstes de leurs vies d'hommes. Ils ont fait de nous des anges gardiens comme Antigone, des flirteuses comme Pénélope, des traîtresses comme Dahla. . . . Ils nous ont traitées de pas grand'choses dans les fabliaux, de perverses au temps du romantisme, de détraquées dans les romans contemporains, d'esprits faibles et bornés presque toujours. Ils ont dit que nous étions fausses, ô Machiavel, ô Talleyrand; poltronnes, ô Goethe . . . nerveuses, ô Musset.—Ils ont même dit que nous étions bavardes, eux qui ont inventé les parlements, les meetings, les tribunaux où ils se réservent de parler tous seuls, les cercles et les cabarets. Bavardes! quand l'histoire n'est remplie que de leurs phrases et les journaux de leurs discours! Mais au contraire, nous sommes les "grandes muettes." . . . La femme, être vivant, pensant, aimant, a presque disparu submergée sous les mots: *Words, Words!*[152]

[As long as there have been men who write and talk, they have heaped up their parchments and books, sprinkled the air with their words, lectures, and songs in order to pronounce their opinion of us, an opinion constructed most often from their poet imaginations and always from the egotistical passions of their lives as men. They made us guardian angels like Antigone, flirts like Penelope, and traitors like Delilah. . . . They treated us as nonentities in fables, as perverts in the era of romanticism, as lunatics in contemporary novels, and nearly always as weak and limited in spirit. They have said that we were false, oh Machiavelli, oh Talleyrand; cowardly, oh Goethe . . . nervous, oh Musset! They have even said that we were chatterboxes—they who invented parliaments, meetings, tribunals, clubs, cabarets, where they reserve for themselves the right to speak. Chatterboxes! When history is filled with only their sentences and their discourses! On the contrary, it is we who are "the great silent ones." . . .

The woman—a living, thinking, loving being—has nearly disappeared, drowned by words: *Words, words!*]

Vigneron's image of woman slowly drowning in a sea of male words blended metaphors of the visual and the auditory. The historical silence and invisibility of women justified her own project: to posit the reality of women's lives as opposed to the fantasy version that had sprung from the imaginations and egotistical passions of men. It would take all the columns of all the newspapers for several centuries to respond to such *bêtises,* conjectured Vignernon, but she was willing to settle for a few lines in *La Fronde.*

By appropriating the principles of the new journalism—the authority of the "real" world, the metaphors of vision, speech, and a mirrored reality—the *frondeuses* were able to set forth a radical critique of how female identity had been produced in French culture. Whether such an appropriation was intentional or not, we can never know. But *frondeuses* such as Vigneron and Marguerite Durand were quite conscious of the power of their paper to shed new, more accurate light on women's lives. The mass press, Durand believed, could serve to correct false images of women and produce new ways of imagining the female self. Up until now, she complained, "women [were] given such a small and meager part in the masculine press." The female journalist had been allowed to write little more than literary chronicles. In using a pseudonym as "a visible way to figure her desire to hide herself," she had presented herself only when "well-veiled or even hidden behind fans." In this way, women had made visible nothing more than their desire for invisibility.[153] But, Durand promised, *La Fronde* presented the opportunity "to dare to write, to dare to talk, to dare to act without the cover of a mask or a fan."[154] With *La Fronde,* the French woman could become her own eyewitness reporter.

Mimicking Real Women: David in Skirts

Besides correcting the false male views of women that were created by writers and journalists throughout history, the *frondeuses* produced their own images of female identity. The results were sometimes surprising. Despite their own break with social convention, these women consistently cast themselves in traditional female roles. For example the editors celebrated their first Christmas in operation by throwing a party for the children of Paris. "Children hold a special place in a woman's heart," they explained, "hence it is natural that the first party given by *La Fronde* was a party for children."[155] Motherhood was extolled as woman's highest calling, sometimes in even bizarre ways.[156] A case in point is how the *frondeuses* reported the *faits-divers*—the spectacularized crime stories that spiced up all daily papers of the era. On December 12, for example, the paper reported in gruesome detail the story of a mother who had killed her child and herself by asphyxiation. While the woman could have been condemned as cold and heartless, *La Fronde* excused her by citing her desperate poverty. When the police arrived, "the arms of the dead one held her child so closely to her breast that it was necessary to break them in order to separate her from the baby." In this way even an infanticide became an excuse to romanticize and praise maternal love.[157]

In various ways, the *frondeuses* also emphasized the conventional female roles of wife, housekeeper, and charity worker. When in January 1898 an *Illustration* reporter requested a group picture of all the *frondeuses,* one of them said: "My portrait in *Illustration?* . . . I do not know if I could. . . . I need to ask my husband and he is not here. A wife owes obedience to her husband."[158] A column on "Le Home" provided helpful advice about all aspects of cuisine and household maintenance. Strong pleas were made for the protection of children against physical abuse through support of pending senate legislation.[159] One *frondeuse* proclaimed that the time had come for women to unite in a religion of humanity so "that the rallying cry be put forth by those who are ready for any kind of devotion, forgetting themselves in order to think only of others."[160] Similarly, Avril de Sainte Croix reported on American women who had given relief to the Irish, thus showing how "the place of the modern woman . . . is on the side of the oppressed, not the victor."[161] On 1 January 1897, Manöel de Grandfort made this New Year's Day plea for the poor: "I am only an ignorant, frivolous assembler of words incapable of saying by what means this ardent hope would be realizable," she began. Nevertheless, she pleaded: "I demand, I solicit, I implore bread, bread for those who lack it."[162]

How can we reconcile these images of the *frondeuses*—as obedient, self-sacrificing, ignorant, and frivolous—with others in which they appear to be confident reporters knowledgeable about all aspects of the public world? These examples illustrate the sometimes incongruous ways in which female identity was produced in *La Fronde* during its first six months. By shifting abruptly between "manly" and "womanly" concerns, the *frondeuses* appeared to be both "new women" and "real women" at the same time. In this sense, the observation of *Le Temps* that *La Fronde* lacked a distinctive physiognomy takes on another meaning. The paper was culturally illegible not only in its politics and style but also in its scramble of often diametrically opposed gender identities.

No one pulled off this feat better than Séverine, whose "Notes d'une frondeuse" was the paper's most important daily feature. "A woman crushing a dragon with her naked foot, and holding a small child in her arms"— this was the visual icon Séverine once used to describe the new woman.[163] The image neatly delineates her approach to journalism. A fierce polemicist who used her daily column to expose the lies and evasions of anti-Semitic politicians involved in the Dreyfus Affair, she was also nicknamed "Notre Dame de la larme à l'oeil" for her staunch defense of the poor. "Notes d'une frondeuse" was a stormy denunciation one day, a lullaby the next. Respected by her male colleagues as one of the toughest, most truthful journalists of her day, she once urged her female readers "whose small hands were made to ease suffering and dress wounds" to "remain womanly, very womanly, in the role assigned to us by nature."[164] Séverine's fusion of the dragon-fighter and the mother epitomized *La Fronde's* editorial policy generally. By constantly shifting their self-representation as political actors—from feminists to altruists, from trade unionists to charity workers—the *frondeuses* tried to teach women how to merge republican politics with more traditional forms of female power. To imagine a uniquely female republicanism, they drew on an old, often inconsistent stock of images. Their republican citizen was as much Virgin Mary as she was Marianne.[165]

But the simultaneous embrace of conventional and unconventional womanhood was not as contradictory as it might first appear. As the example of Séverine shows, this approach allowed the *frondeuses* to contest a much-touted real woman–new woman divide. In the popular imagination of the fin de siècle, the "new woman" was pitted against the "real" or womanly woman as two ways of conceiving the female self. According to the feminist journalist Jane Misme, writing in 1901, the new woman and the real woman were "in conflict and the world is fighting over them."[166] The belief that the new women, preoccupied with their careers, could not possibly be able to fulfill their more conventional roles as loving wife and mother, sparked widespread anxiety. To conceive of new female powers within a conventional set of aims (defense of children, the poor) would calm fears that women were changing rapidly and/or for the worse.

The *frondeuses* plainly intended to address such fears. Séverine, for example, reassured her readers that "the woman made robust by writing and the virile female citizen ready to desexualize herself completely—these remain the exceptions to the rule."[167] Similarly, the *frondeuse* Anne Lorraine dismissed the view that in professional careers a woman "will lose her natural gifts, her family virtues, so that the charm of the home will be broken and corrupted." The aspirations of the new woman, she promised, "include nothing that can frighten you."[168] *La Fronde*'s embrace of conventional womanly traits reflected a general trend among moderate bourgeois feminists, who were attempting to erase their public image as abrasive eccentrics. According to the historians Laurence Klejman and Florence Rochefort, the feminist Ligue française pour le droit des femmes (LFDF) "chose to seduce rather than to shock and to make 'feminine charm' one more asset to the struggle for women's rights."[169] It was bad enough that the *frondeuses,* as reporters, practiced a "virile" form of journalism. All the more necessary, then, that they present themselves in a way acceptable to the French public. "The stones flung by *La Fronde* had the sweetness of a fan's caress" recalled one journalist in 1903 when the paper stopped publication.[170]

Once again the question arises: can we interpret this strategy—the display of obedience to one's husband, the column Le Home, the appeal to female self-effacement—as mere submission to the domestic ideal? In fact a critical distance separated the *frondeuses* from such an ideal. That distance was both obvious and subtle. Séverine could be a "real" woman *but not quite,* because she was a reporter, just as she could be a reporter *but not quite,* because she was a woman. Real women certainly did not write columns in newspapers, particularly those that excluded men and attacked male politicians. *Frondeuses* like Séverine were no more than mimics of the conventional women they played in the pages of *La Fronde.* Even though they submitted themselves to the conventions of the real woman, their reenactment of this identity opened up a space of difference that was subversive. By the very act of working outside the home and writing for a newspaper, they disavowed themselves as conventional women. And so in espousing these female roles, they also exposed their essential artifice—as roles that could be staged even in the most unconventional of lives. By enacting the real woman, the *frondeuses* also contested her fixity and naturalized status.

Two examples from *La Fronde,* both dated January 1898, must suffice to show how this type of mimicry could be subversive. Both involved conscious attempts by the *frondeuses* to insert themselves in the debate on *la crise de la presse* examined above. More specifically, both involved attempts to destabilize the two images of woman—the mad reader and the prostitute—that organized anxiety concerning the press in the *Revue Bleue* survey. The first example is a parodic commentary by "Pug" on an article written by M. le Comte de Vogüé in response to the survey. Like Alfred Fouillée and Séverin Icard, Vogüé has warned his readers of the potentially "terrifying" and "deplorable" effects of newspaper reading on the human brain, its ability to confuse and overwhelm even the author himself. As we have seen, women were singled out in the literature as particularly vulnerable to such cerebral shock.

But in Pug's commentary, men, not women, were the vulnerable readers on the frontiers of madness. She describes the hapless Vogüé as "a witty academic whose head I would have believed to be more solid." She ostentatiously laments his having read the "toxic" morning paper, which rendered him "incapable of all serious intellectual work for the rest of the day." With feigned worry, she contrasts her own example of sturdiness: "Oh! My head, my poor head! When I think that for so many years, I've read a dozen papers upon waking, without even counting the reviews!" She then continues:

> Mes soeurs, ne permettons plus à nos maris la lecture du journal, qu'après le diner. . . . Et encore, la digestion, mon Dieu! La digestion! . . . Que trois heures au moins après le dîner. Puis, le lit tout de suite, le sommeil réparateur, après une tasse d'infusion de tilleul additionnée d'eau de fleurs d'oranger. . . . Peut-être ainsi pourrons-nous atténuer les effets néfastes de la lecture des feuilles publiques sur les cerveaux qui nous sont chers![171]

> [My sisters, let us no longer permit our husbands to read the paper until the dinner hour. . . . But then, there's digestion! My God! Digestion. . . . not until three hours after the dinner hour. Then to bed right away for some restorative sleep after a tissane of lime-blossom tea fortified by orange water. . . . Perhaps in this way we will be able to minimize the harmful effects on the brains that are dear to us of reading public papers.]

While Pug evokes the concerned, nurturing wife here, she is mimicking the role. First, Pug's sarcasm puts distance between herself and the loving wife she pretends to be. This is a parody of conventional femininity.[172] Second, the context in which this parody occurs—on the front page of a newspaper in which women are the sole authors—further secures a critical distance between the domestic role and Pug's own reenactment of it. She is no "normal" housewife.

That distance is critical in two senses. First it is critical in the sense of necessary, because it allows Pug to locate herself as removed from and resisting conventional femininity. Second, it is critical in the sense of being censorious, because it allows her to point to her own position as an individual exploited through language—in this case the prevalent conception of woman as irrational and feeble-witted. Pug is a loving wife *but not quite,* because she is also a journalist intervening in a wider debate on the press, one in which she has some very disparaging things to say. At the article's end, she makes sure to remind us of her journalist status by protesting as an interested party the censure of morning papers, of which *La Fronde,* of course, was one. By parodying a conventional role, Pug achieves a transgressive end: to refuse the male/female, rational/irrational binarisms around which so much of the press debate was organized.

The second example of subversive mimicry concerns a *frondeuse* who challenged the other anxiety-provoking female image cited in the *Revue bleue* survey: the prostitute. In this article Clothilde Dissard referred to Albert Fouillée's "brilliant" censure of an immoral press and lamented "the many hatreds it has instigated" in the Dreyfus Affair. "Shouldn't we consider our task to be a true apostolate?" she asked her female readers. The press had "lost its dignity" but, Dissard promised, *La Fronde* would "become the remedy of all these faults," by taking a stand against polemicists such as Edouard Drumont and "all the passions they awaken." In the absence of formal restraints on the press (a topic of fierce debate in the survey), women alone could exercise a "salutary and beneficial" influence, introduce "that tender pity that [the press] too often lacks" and "institute a journalism that is serious, truly impartial and exempt from the hatred and obstinacy of political parties."[173] (Dissard here appropriates the image of the rational individual at the heart of republican ideology in order to condemn the new nationalist right as well as to counter the view of herself and other women as creatures of irrational drives.)

Like Pug, Dissard evokes a conventional female identity—the woman as "naturally" the more compassionate, moral sex. By representing women journalists as disciples marching fearlessly on an "apostolate" to clean up the seamy male world of journalism, Dissard made *La Fronde* intelligible within the terms of nineteenth-century gender roles. She also challenged the image of woman as prostitute that defined journalism symbolically. Reenacting a conventional role allowed her to reconfigure the gender imagery in the press debate: here woman symbolizes a moral and rational, rather than an immoral force, a *religeuse* on an apostolate rather than a *courtesan* on her beat. Once again, Dissard used traditional imagery in order to imagine a female republican role. Far from losing their own respectability, the *frondeuses* would bring it *to* journalism as they fought these threats to the Republic.

But Dissard's moral missionary, like Pug's loving wife, was largely an act of parody. Her claim to be a journalist-apostle was, at least in part, sincere. But that claim must also be understood in light of Dissard's original purpose in writing here, which was to respond angrily to condescending critiques of *La Fronde* by the journalists Charles Maurras and E. Ledrain.[174] At first appearance, Dissard commented, these critiques seemed to be "veiled" in the "most exquisite courtesy." But, she fumed, such courtesy was ultimately undercut by the authors' sarcastic tone, which revealed not only their "misogyny," but also their cheap insincerity. Comparing the two men to butterflies (a sobriquet in French for a fickle person), Dissard charged that they had cheapened journalistic courtesy by using it to veil their disdain.[175] Her anger here is important because it contradicts her tone in the rest of the article—in particular, her own sincerity and "tender pity." That contradiction, in turn, suggests that Dissard was herself a butterfly, who used a conventional female identity to veil her anger and get her revenge. Her parody of the female missionary enabled her both to take the moral high ground against male arrogance and, once again, to point out the condescending manner in which women writers were judged.

This interpretation finds further evidence in Dissard's parting shot. Once again, her imagery merges the republican and the biblical; the *frondeuses* are at once Davids striking at the Goliath of male privilege, and revolutionaries storming the Bastille.

> Nous dévions déjà, à l'autorité de votre tutelle, d'être devenues bonnes, douces, charmantes, telles en un mot, que vous nous désiriez. Non pas telles, puisque vous avez eu la fantaisie de fronder même notre faiblesse. A cela nous devons le désir d'être moins faibles, et c'est encore vous qui aurez porté les premiers coups à l'édifice de vos privilèges.[176]

> [We are already in your debt for having become good, sweet, charming, in a word, all that you desire. But not all, since you have had the fantasy of attacking even our weakness. To that attack we owe our desire to be less weak, so thus it is you yourself who have struck the first blows against the edifice of your privileges.]

In referring to women journalists as moral apostles, Dissard has here gone to great lengths to portray herself as the all that she claims men want "good, sweet, charming" women to be. But in the end she puts distance between herself and that all by exposing it as something women are in debt to men for—something artificial and imposed rather than natural and innate. All, but not all; good, *but not quite*. By attacking *"la fantaisie de fronder"* on the part of men, Dissard joined her colleagues in condemning the fantastic male construction of female identity.

In addition, Dissard reveled in the vulnerability of language. The male fantasy of female weakness, according to her, had become the first stone thrown against male domination, as women strove, in response, to become less weak. What Dissard refers to here—the reenactment of Goliath's language against Goliath himself—describes precisely *"la fronde"* of *La Fronde.* Whether it be the loving wife, the moral missionary, or the impassioned defender of the poor, the *frondeuses* parodied the all that men wanted them to be—in order both to veil the violence of the battle and to fling stones at that Bastille itself.

Conclusion: We Have the Right Not to Resemble Each Other

As we have seen, in the first six months of its existence, *La Fronde* was preoccupied with questions of language—in particular, the way in which notions of female identity were produced in French culture. But if we are to believe the *frondeuses* who addressed these issues, their ultimate aim was not to arrive at one "true" or "real" notion of womanhood. "A woman is both more and less than the books have wanted to make her," Paule Vigneron argued, "we have the right, like you, not to resemble each other, to have different ideas and feelings."[177] As we have seen, Vigneron demanded the right to respond to centuries of male fantasy concerning women. But ultimately her attack focused on the category of gender itself—the attribution of any universal characteristics to the female sex. She was not the only *frondeuse* to argue in this way. Some days before, her colleague Marie Anne de Bovet questioned the notions of the "eternal feminine" and "feminine mystery." "One never hears of an 'eternal masculine,'" she quipped. "There is certainly the mystery of each woman, but this is not an essential mystery, proper to one's sex."[178] Judith Cladel argued in the same vein: "Just as you, a woman is free to say what she pleases, from great thoughts to complete nonsense." The danger, she warned, was when women grew up "under the hand of bad gardeners" who treat them "without regard for their difference and variety."[179]

If *La Fronde* acted as a "David in skirts," as so many male journalists at first believed, their Goliath was not simple misogyny, but the category of gender itself as an essentialized way of understanding individual women. The goal was not to render one "true" meaning of woman clearer, but to make women visible in all their rich diversity. In light of this goal, which is often made explicit in the pages of *La Fronde,* the tendency of the *frondeuses* to scramble gender ideologies by embracing both conventional and unconventional roles can also be seen as a more conscious strategy for undermining the category of gender. To present an image of woman that was internally contradictory, was to reject all notions of the eternal feminine and to produce a female self that resisted fixed meaning. What I have been calling the cultural illegibility of the paper provides evidence of its effort to make woman, in Vigneron's words, "both more and less than the books have wanted to make her." This notion of endless difference was the reality of women's lives.

Here, once again, the *frondeuses'* mimicry of the daily paper was key to their subversion. Unlike a novel or treatise, its format—six columns and five to eight separate articles per page—allowed for the juxtaposition of texts displaying competing gender identities. On the pages of *La Fronde,* articles voicing "womanly" concerns for the poor and children could jostle with those reporting on the Municipal Council or on labor conditions and with those speaking out for women's political rights. For example, the December 10 issue of *La Fronde* placed side by side the news of a meeting of Parliament and a law enabling women to witness civil acts (both implying a fully developed civic identity for women) with a Ballad of Pardon that urged women to forgive even those who had done them harm (thus reinforcing a more passive image). The paper's easy juxtaposition of "hard" news with articles on "female" concerns, such as philanthropy or children, had the effect of challenging the conventional opposition between male and female activity. More important, as a genre that was both multitextual and multivocal, the newspaper provided the *frondeuses* with a format in which conflictual notions of femininity—religious and republican, Mary and Marianne—could be expressed simultaneously without canceling each other out.

In short, the paper was a veritable playground of gender identity. What resulted was a composite image of woman that exposed the artifice of each competing gender identity while remaining subversively unclear. In this sense, the paper's layout repeated a feature of the paper that has often puzzled historians. The front-page headline of *La Fronde* always gave the date in four different calenders: the Republican, the Russian, the Protestant, and the Jewish. December 10, for example, was at once the 20 Frimaire; 28 November; the day to read Philippe III, verse 3; and 15 Kislev, year 5658. The multiplicity of calendars was unabashedly republican and aligned the paper with the world of Dreyfus and other marginal groups. It also suggested that a phenomenon as seemingly fixed as time was in fact arbitrary and subjective. By the logic of extension, the calendars pointed to the artifice of another seemingly essential phenomenon: female gender identity.

In the hands of the *frondeuses,* the standard format of the daily paper became a revolutionary weapon. Again, whether or not the *frondeuses'* appropriation of this format was intentional, we can never know. But the effect was the same. If the cultural illegibility of *La Fronde* is any measure, the daily newspaper as a genre helped to raise questions concerning gender in fin-de-siècle France. Journalism, a profession that had excluded women in every way, "struck the first blows" against the edifice of its own privilege.

The *fronde* of *La Fronde,* then, can tell us much about the diverse and subtle ways in which women at the turn of the century challenged ideologies of gender. To do so, the *frondeuses* took on available cultural identities such as the male reporter, the moral missionary, and the loving wife. Their tendency to "perform" identity in this way can be best understood against the background of an increasingly commodified urban French culture. As Roger Shattuck has argued, due to Haussmannization, "Paris had become a stage, a vast theater for herself and all the world" by the fin de siècle; "living had become increasingly a special kind of performance presided over by fashion, innovation, and taste," and even politics had become a form of "low comedy."[180] At the heart of this new theater stood Parisian journalism, intent on documenting the "spectacle" of modern life in the most dramatic, entertaining, and lucrative way possible. In this world of *faits-divers,* voyeuristic reporters, and pseudonymous writers, role-playing and performing became acceptable forms of behavior.

As such, journalism permitted the *frondeuses* literally to act out the instability of gender identity and thus to refashion themselves as women in new ways. In addition, the "performative" strategies of the *frondeuses* can be linked to the fin-de-siécle crisis of bourgeois subjectivity. As we have seen, in relating the findings of Salpêtrière experiments with hypnotism and suggestion, social thinkers such as Alfred Fouillée depicted a new vision of selfhood to the French mass public. The old notion of a rational, autonomous, willing self was replaced by another, at once more mercurial and subterranean, disaggregated and performative. Fouillée himself described the human mind as a kind of psychic theater, where a "troupe of different, multiple actors enacted an interior drama."[181] In the fin-de-siécle imaginary, women symbolized these newly "discovered" irrational drives. As Séverin Icard's half-mad female criminals illustrated, women were thought to be born mimics, to lack a rational, autonomous self from the start. Hence in mimicking conventional female identities, the *frondeuses* were only playing up an old, familiar role as imitators *par excellence.* And in demonstrating the artifice of such identities—as roles to be played rather than as essentialized selves—the *frondeuses* exploited the contemporary critique of rational, bourgeois subjectivity. By constructing woman as an irrational mimic, male social thinkers such as Séverin Icard had once again "struck the first blows" against the edifice of male privilege. At the same time, to embrace this image was tricky for the *frondeuses,* as it defied the notion of the rational individual at the heart of their republican beliefs.

While feminist historiography has often emphasized the exceptional and pioneering qualities of women such as the *frondeuses,* in fact, these women were clever manipulators of more conventional gender identities rather than wholesale inventors of new ones. In this sense, *La Revue* had it right when it sneered that far from being innovators, the *frondeuses* were "content to imitate their gallant elders.[182] Nevertheless, mimicry alone had its own seditious power. The *frondeuses* were reporters, but not quite, because they were real women; they were real women, but not quite, because they were reporters. Their reenactment of conventional identities opened up a space of difference that was disruptive. That space of difference, that "elsewhere" of illegibility, allowed the *frondeuses* to challenge how they were defined as women and writers. The subversive copy of *La Fronde* thus helps us to understand how change occurred in bourgeois women's lives at the fin de siècle. This group of women broke with the domestic ideal and began to construct unconventional identities by exploiting the internally contradictory, dynamic nature of language.

Notes

For their editorial comments and suggestions, I would like to thank Keith Baker, Edward Berenson, Steven Kaplan, Kathryn Norberg, Jeannene Przyblyski, Bryant T. Ragan Jr., Paul Robinson, Joan Scott, Karen Sawislak, Vanessa Schwartz, Debora Silverman, the New York Area History Group, the Cornell University European History Group, and the UCLA European History Workshop.

1. In its first week of publication, an impressive 200,000 copies of the paper were sold per day, and by February its daily circulation held steady at 50,000. For these figures, see Odile Welfelé, "*La Fronde:* Histoire d'une entreprise de presse" (Thèse, Ecole de Chartres, 1982), part 3, chapter 1. These figures are modest compared to *tirages* of *les quatres grands,* for example, *Le Petit Parisien* at 1,400,000 copies per day or *Le Petit Journal* at 835,000 per day in 1910. But the circulation of *La Fronde* looks respectable next to that of other smaller papers in 1910, for example, *Le Figaro* (37,000) *Le Gaulois* (30,000), *Intransigeant* (70,000), *Humanité* (72,000), *Le Temps* (36,000), and *La Libre parole* (47,000). See Claude Bellanger et al., *L'Histoire générale de la presse française* (Paris: Presses Universitaires de France, 1972), 3: 296. Unfortunately, *La Fronde* was not able to sustain this circulation. By the end of 1899, it was 14,660 and by 1902, only 2,250. It is difficult to understand precisely why, although many papers failed at this time due to decline of interest in newspaper-reading after the end of the Dreyfus Affair. Also hard to determine is how widespread sales of *La Fronde* were outside Paris. But *La Fronde* did have a reputation as *the* daily of the *institutrices* throughout France.

See Irène Jami, "*La Fronde* (1897–1903) et son rôle dans la défense des femmes salariées" (Paris: Université de Paris I, Mémoire de Maîtrise, 1981), 45.

2. Alexandre Hepp, "La Bataille de dames," *Le Journal,* 7 December 1897, Articles Parus sur La Fronde (hereafter APSF), Bibliothèque Marguerite Durand (hereafter, BMD). For the single-sex orientation of *La Fronde,* see also Annie Dizier-Metz, *La Bibliothèque Marguerite Durand, Histoire d'une femme, mémoire des femmes* (Paris: Mairie de Paris—Agence culturelle de Paris, 1992), 10.

3. The male typographers' union condemned Durand for her wage policies, but it refused to admit women in its ranks. In response, Durand founded the *Syndicat des femmes typographes* in 1899, and donated one thousand francs to secure its financial future; the next year saw the legal creation of a cooperative society of female typographers. Durand also did this, in part, to avoid trouble with the law. Since *La Fronde* was a morning paper, the typographers had to work late, thus breaking a Law of 1892 that forbade women to work at night and that was immediately invoked by the Chambre syndicale des hommes typographes. According to the Société coopérative de femmes typographes, women became *patronnes associées* who could work when and how they wanted. See Dizier-Metz, *La Bibliothèque Marguerite Durand,* 14.

4. Cited in Jeanne Landre, "Une feuille féminine," no periodical or date (1898), APSF. See also "L'Actualité: La Fondation d'un journal exclusivement féminine," no place, no date, APSF, BMD.

5. "Portraits de femmes," *Carnet mondial de Jocelyne,* 31 March 1898, APSF, BMD. For more on Durand, see my "Acting Up: The Feminist Theatrics of Marguerite Durand," *French Historical Studies* 19, no. 4 (Fall, 1996): 1103–38.

6. The biographies of Durand are: Jean Rabaut, *Marguerite Durand (1864–1936): "La Fronde" féministe or "Le Temps" en jupons* (Paris: L'Harmattan, 1996); and Sue Helder Goliber, "The Life and Times of Marguerite Durand: A Study in French Feminism" (Ph.D. Diss., Kent State University, 1975).

7. See *L'Eclair,* 4 October 1897, APSF; Landre, "Une Feuille féminine." For the rumors about Rothschild, see also Dossier Marguerite Durand, Bibliothèque historique de la ville de Paris. In this dossier are some notes claiming that Rothschild gave Durand seven million francs to make *La Fronde* a Dreyfusard paper. *La Libre parole* frequently made the same sorts of accusations. In fact, the issue of how *La Fronde* was financed will never be clarified, in large part because Durand destroyed the financial records of the paper. In any case, the expense of running a paper of *La Fronde's* circulation was about Fr 500,000 a year. (Based on estimates given in Alexandre Guérin, *Comment on devient journaliste* [Paris: Publications Universelles Illustrées, 1910], 24.) According to Jami, "*La Fronde,*" page 13, Durand began *La Fronde* with a capital of Fr 500,000 divided into 5,000 *actions* of which she owned 2,000. Since Durand had no other source of income and she was not independently wealthy, she probably did

accept money from another party. On this point, see Laurence Klejman and Florence Rochefort, *L'Egalité en marche: Le Féminisme sous la Troisième République* (Paris: Des femmes, 1989), 130, where the authors suggest that Durand did accept Gustave de Rothschild's money based on recorded gifts from this name in her diary. See also Steven Hause with Anne R. Kenney, *Women's Suffrage and Social Politics in the French Third Republic* (Princeton: Princeton University Press, 1984), 290.

8. See, for example, the nasty exchanges between Gaston Méry and Marguerite Durand in the pages of *La Libre parole* and *La Fronde* throughout December of 1898. Two libel cases against *La Libre parole* resulted, one filed by Durand alone when this paper failed to publish a letter she wrote in response to the editor Gaston Méry (published in *La Fronde* on December 20), and one filed by Durand and her editors together for libelous remarks made on 22 December 1898 by Méry. Durand lost the first suit on February 1 but won the second on 15 March 1898. Fines totalling Fr 1000 were imposed on Méry, the manager Millot, and *La Libre Parole,* and Durand was able to insert announcement of the court judgment in ten papers of her choice, to be paid for by *La Libre Parole.* When Durand received the fine money, she donated it to a *syndicat* of women typographers that she was organizing.

9. See my "Bad Performances: Gyp, Séverine, and the Dreyfus Affair," in "Great Performances: The New Woman, Journalism, and Theater at the Fin de siècle," in progress.

10. On 23 January 1898, the *London Times* declared *La Fronde* "a great success" and "the best all-around print in Paris"; its articles were "quite as brilliant as *Le Figaro.*" *La Fronde* was the subject of comment in the presses of Finland, Germany, Italy, Spain, the Netherlands, Belgium, Switzerland, the United Kingdom, as well as the United States and Thailand. See APSF, BMD for a sampling of these international voices.

11. Nina Gelbart, *Feminine and Opposition Journalism in Old Regime France: Le Journal des dames* (Berkeley: University of California, 1987), 19.

12. Ibid. 29–30. Gelbart herself makes the connection between Old Regime women journalists and the *frondeuses* on pages 295–96.

13. *L'Evénément,* 5 December 1897, APSF, BMD; "Ce que pensent les hommes de la Fronde," *La Fronde,* 23 December 1897.

14. *"La Fronde,"* no periodical, 24 December 1897, APSF.

15. Georges Duval, "Journalistes en jupons," no periodical or date [1897], APSF; Emile Goudeau, "Les Quat'z'arts," no periodical or date [January 1898]. I have guessed at the dates of these two articles based on the chronological ordering of the APSF and their positioning within groups of dated articles.

16. Jules Clarette, "La Vie à Paris," *Le Temps,* 9 December 1897, APSF, BMD.

17. "Ce que pensent les hommes de *La Fronde,*" *Le Temps,* 25 December 1897, APSF.

18. Ibid.

19. Naomi Schor, *Reading in Detail: Aesthetics and the Feminine* (New York: Routledge, 1987), particularly chapter 1, "Gender: In the Academy."

20. "La Fin de la Fronde," *Phare de la Loire,* 3 September 1903, APSF.

21. Raoul Deberdt, "Les Femmes journalistes," *La Revue des revues,* 15 January 1898.

22. Ibid.

23. L. M., *La Fronde,* no periodical or date [December 1897] APSF.

24. Maurice le Blond, "Etudes sur la presse," *Revue naturiste,* Avril 1900, Archives *La Fronde* (hereafter ALF), BMD. The view that the *frondeuses* had adopted a conventional style of journalism became the occasion for much jocular self-criticism. See, for example, Louis Schneider, "Au Jour le jour: Un Journal de femmes," Le Soleil, 25 November 1897, APSF. Le Journal féministe, *Le Nord,* 31 October 1897, ALF, BMD, Raoul Ponchon, *Gazette Rimée, Le Courrier français,* 1 December 1897, APSF, BMD.

25. See Marguerite Durand, "Les Femmes dans le journalisme," Manuscripts, vol. 3, BMD, 31.

26. Gelbart, *Feminine and Opposition Journalism,* 293; Laure Adler, *A L'aube du féminisme: Les Premières journalistes, 1830–1850* (Paris: Payot, 1979), 75. Similarly, Evelyne Sullerot has described the feminine press in the early nineteenth century as "the expression of a rise in collective consciousness . . . concerning the female world." See her *Histoire de la presse féminine en France, des origines à 1848* (Paris: Librairie Armand Colin, 1966), 211, and also Pamela Langlois, "The Feminine Press in England and France, 1875–1900" (Ph.D. Diss., University of Massachusetts, 1979); Bernard Voyenne, *Les Journalistes français* (Paris: CFPJ-Retz, 1985), 214–22.

27. In her "Chronique féministe," *La Fronde,* 27 March 1898, Camille Belilon lists the increase in the number of women in various professions between 1870 and 1890. Since Belilon does not cite the source of her figures, it is impossible to have any idea of their accuracy.

28. The phenomenon of the "new woman" was in great part due to legislation such as the Camille Sée Law of 1880, which established secondary education for women. The number of lycée degrees obtained by women jumped from 4,300 to 13,000 in the years 1885 to 1900. For the "new woman," see Debora Silverman, *Art Nouveau in Fin-de-Siècle France: Politics, Psychology, and Style* (Berkeley: University of California Press, 1989), chapter 4, and "The 'New Woman,' Feminism, and the Decorative Arts in Fin-de-siècle France," in *Eroticism and the Body Politic,* Lynn Hunt, ed. (Baltimore: Johns Hopkins University Press, 1991); Jo B. Margadant, *Madame le Professeur: Women Educators in the Third Republic* (Princeton: Princeton University Press, 1990); Annelise Maugue, *L'Identité masculine en crise au tournant du siècle* (Paris: Editions Rivage, 1987).

29. Nancy Miller, "Emphasis Added: Plots and Plausibilities in Women's Fiction," *PMLA* 96 (1981), 38.

30. See Elizabeth Abel, "Introduction," in *Writing and Sexual Difference,* Elizabeth Abel, ed. (Chicago: University of Chicago Press, 1982), 2.

31. "Le Feu à *La Fronde,*" *Le Gil Blas,* 7 December 1897, APSF. As *Illustration* put it, La Fronde wanted to offer women "not feminist theses, but exclusively feminine opinions on politics and the news of the day." "Chez les frondeuses," *L'Illustration,* 15 January 1898, ALF, BMD. Jami, *"La Fronde,"* 109–11, 114, has calculated "the number of columns and percentage of printed surface dedicated" to various subjects during two weeks in June and December throughout the life of the paper. The percentage for *"vie de femmes, féminisme"* is surprisingly "weak," ranging from 8 percent in December 1897 to 3 percent in June 1899 and June 1903. She agrees with the readers of *Le Temps* that *La Fronde* is *"un journal d'information"* before being *"un journal militant."*

32. Séverine, "Notes d'une frondeuse: Réponse à Ponchon," *La Fronde,* 21 December 1897.

33. In thinking about the cultural illegibility of *La Fronde,* I have been helped by Nancy Miller's notion of "plausibility" in "Emphasis Added."

34. See Sylvie Cesbron, "Un Journal féministe en 1900: *La Fronde* (1897–1903)" Mémoire dactylographié, BMD; Jami, *"La Fronde";* Welfelé, *"La Fronde."*

35. Durand, "Les Femmes dans le journalisme," 3.

36. The law of 29 July 1881 created a very liberal set of rules for the press and put an end to a long history of the repression of republican ideas. See Jean-Marie Mayeur and Madeleine Rebérioux, *The Third Republic from its Origins to the Great War, 1871–1914* (Cambridge: Cambridge University Press, 1987), 82; Langlois, "The Feminine Press," 65; Henry Avenel, *Le Monde des journaux en 1895* (Paris: L'Annuaire de la presse française, 1895), 3–7; René de Livois, *Histoire de la presse française* (Lausanne: Editions SPES, 1965), vol. 2, 325–26, 342–43; René Mazedier, *Histoire de la presse parisienne* (Paris: Editions de pavois, 1945) 155–56.

37. The literature on the history of the press is sizeable, but these three works have been the most helpful: Bellanger et al., *L'Histoire de la presse;* Thomas Ferenczi, *L'Invention du journalisme en France. Naissance de la presse moderne à la fin de XIXè siècle* (Paris: Plon, 1993); Michel Palmer, *Des petits journaux aux grandes agences* (Paris: Aubier, 1983). Also useful is Richard Terdiman, *Discourse / Counter-Discourse: The Theory and Practice of Symbolic Resistance in Nineteenth-Century France* (Ithaca, N.Y.: Cornell University Press, 1985).

38. Bellanger et al., *Histoire générale,* call the period between 1880 and 1914 "L'apogée de la presse française." See also Livois, *Histoire de la presse,* 393. In the year 1897, Tanneguy de Wogan counted 2,327 papers in Paris and 3,493 in the provinces. See his *Manuel des Gens de lettres* (Paris: Librairie de Paris, 1897), 15.

39. "Les Responsabilités de la presse contemporaine," *La Revue bleue,* 4 December 1897–22 January 1898. For references to the *Revue bleue* survey in *La Fronde* itself,

see Séverine, "Réponse à Ponchon"; Pug, "Pourquoi?" *La Fronde,* 4 January 1898; Clothilde Dissard, "Le Rôle de la presse féminine," *La Fronde,* 12 January 1898.

40. For Bérenger's notes about the survey's impact, see installment of 4 December 1898, page 707. For mention of the survey in the historiographic literature, see Voyenne, *Les Journalistes français,* 152; Mazedier, *Histoire de la presse,* 157; Livois, *Histoire de la presse,* 391–92, and most important, Ferenczi, *L'Invention,* chapter 7.

41. Remarks of Gabriel Monod, *Revue bleue,* 15 January 1898, 71. This view was widespread in literature on *la crise de la presse* outside of the survey. See for example, Charles Fenestrier, *La Vie des frelons* (Paris: Société nouvelle, 1908); Joseph Mallat, *La Presse et les lectures populaires* (Paris: Librairie de la société bibliographie, 1887), 11–13; Anatole Leroy-Beaulieu, *Les Responsabilités de la presse* (Paris: Comité de defense et de progrès social, 1898), 4, 8–9. The imagery of the press as a sewer or a disease was common. See, for example, the remarks of Henry Maret in Henri Avenel, *La Presse française au vingtième siècle* (Paris: Flammarion, 1901), and the remarks of Henry Maret in "Enquête de la presse," *Revue naturiste,* March 1900, 232. For a Catholic condemnation of the press, see Paul Soleihac, *Le Grand Levier ou de la presse et de son influence politique et social à notre époque* (Paris: Librairie Blériot, 1906); Abbé Augustin Lemann, *Un Fléau plus redoutable que la guerre, la peste, la famine* (Lyon: Librairie Catholique Emmanuel Vitte, n.d.); Msr. Touchet, *La Presse* (Orleans: Gout et Cie, 1906). For the Catholic campaign against the press (propaganda, almanacs, circulating libraries), see Mallat, *La Presse et les lectures populaire,* 22–23; L'Abbé Elie Blanc, *Le Journalisme contemporain: Nécessité d'une organisation populaire et chrétienne* (Paris: Librairie de P. Lethielleux, 1904), 8–10. For a different view, see Edouard Drumont's "Le Rôle de la presse," *La Libre parole,* 10 December 1897, where he argues that the newspaper is the last defense against a corrupt republican government and a morally decaying society. In the secondary literature, see Patrick Brantlinger, "Mass Media and Culture in Fin-de-siècle Europe," in *Fin de Siècle and its Legacy,* Mikulás Teich and Roy Porter, eds. (Cambridge: Cambridge University Press, 1990), 105.

42. The best explanation of the relationship between newspapers and the world of high finance is to be found in Henry du Roure, *La Presse d'aujourd'hui et la presse de demain* (Paris: Au Sillon, 1908), 25–29.

43. "Les Responsabilités de la presse," *La Revue bleue,* remarks of Jean Jaures (4 December); Max Nordau (4 December), Georges Clemenceau (11 December), Maurice Barrès (11 December), Leroy-Beaulieu (18 December), Georges Renard (25 December), Pierre Baudin (1 January), Alfred Fouillée (8 January). See also Alfred Meyer, *Ce que mes yeux ont vu* (Paris: Plon, 1914), 408–9, 411–12; Robert de Jouvenal, *Le Journalisme en vingt leçons* (Paris: Payto et Cie, 1920), 106–7; Eugène Dubief, *Le Journalisme* (Paris: Hachette, 1892), 310.

44. Alfred Fouillée, "Quelques réflexions sur la criminalité et le socialisme," *La*

Revue bleue, 30 October 1897, 550. Beginning in the 1880s, Fouillée wrote many articles about recent "discoveries" in psychological or neurological research. See Silverman, *Art Nouveau,* 90–91; Ferenczi, *L'Invention,* 213–14.

45. Bérenger, *La Revue bleue* 4 December 1897, 706–7. For statements on the cultural power of the press outside of the *Revue bleue* survey, see Docteur Séverin Icard, *De la contagion du crime et du suicide par la presse* (Paris: Edition de la nouvelle revue, 1902); Dubief, *Le Journalisme,* 307–8; Meyer, *Ce que mes yeux,* 363.

46. See also in the survey the remarks by l'Union pour l'action morale, 25 December 1897, 807. For the traditional pedagogical role of the press, see Ferenczi, *L'Invention,* 215.

47. Silverman, *Art Nouveau,* 76.

48. Alfred Fouillée, "Quelques réflexions," 550. For the worried concern about crime during this period, see Eugen Weber, *France Fin de Siècle* (Cambridge, Mass.: Harvard University Press, 1986), 40–50.

49. Silverman, *Art Nouveau,* 83–91.

50. Icard, *De la contagion du crime.* Icard was a member of the Institute and the Academy of Medicine. For the discourse on the dangers of women reading, see Jann Matlock, *Scenes of Seduction: Prostitution, Hysteria, and Reading Difference in Nineteenth-Century France* (New York: Columbia University Press, 1994), chapters 6 through 8, and particularly 212–13.

51. Tanneguy de Wogan, *Manuel,* 66, 168.

52. Zola, "Le Journal," *Les Annales politiques et littéraires,* 22 July 1894, 51. The Dreyfus Affair alienated Zola from the French press.

53. For prostitution in France, see Alain Corbin, *Les Filles de noce: Misère sexuelle et prostitution* (Paris: Flammarion, 1978); Jill Harsin, *The Policing of Prostitution in Nineteenth-Century Paris* (Princeton: Princeton University Press, 1983); Charles Bernheimer, *Figures of Ill Repute: Representing Prostitution in Nineteenth-Century France* (Cambridge, Mass.: Harvard University Press, 1989); and most recently, Jann Matlock, *Scenes of Seduction.*

54. Bérenger, *La Revue bleue* 4 December 1897, 707. See also the remarks of Max Nordau, same issue, page 716; Gabriel Monod, 15 January 1898, 71. For a similar description of the press outside of the survey, see L'Abbé Coubé, *La Bonne et la mauvaise presse* (Paris: Bureau de la ligue eucharistique, 1905). In his *The Trial of Madame Caillaux* (Berkeley: University of California Press, 1992), 211, Edward Berenson has adopted this view of the press as a subtle but insidious force.

55. Leroy-Beaulieu, *La Revue bleue* 18 December 1897, 770. See also his *Responsabilités de la presse,* 6. For the same argument, see also the remarks of Jules Case, *La Revue bleue* same installment, 774; Auguste Sabatier, *La Revue bleue* 1 January 1898, 11.

56. In the secondary literature, see T. J. Clark, *The Painting of Modern Life: Paris in the Art of Manet and His Followers* (New York: Alfred Knopf, 1984), 103–4; Vanessa Schwartz, "The Public Taste for Reality: Early Mass Culture in Fin-de-Siècle Paris,"

(Ph.D. Diss., University of California at Berkeley, 1993), 24. See also Schwartz, *Spectacular Realities: Early Mass Culture in Fin-de-siècle Paris* (Berkeley: University of California Press, 1998).

57. See Walter Benjamin, "Paris, Capital of the Nineteenth Century," *Reflections: Essays, Aphorisms, Autobiographical Writings* (New York: Schocken, 1969), 157.

58. Bérenger, *La Revue bleue,* 4 December 1897, 707. See also the remarks of Georges Renard, 25 December 1897, 804; L'Union pour l'action morale, same installment, 806.

59. Talmeyr, *La Revue bleue,* 4 December 1897, 717. For other references to prostitution (some more direct than others), see also the remarks of Canivet, *La Revue bleue,* 11 December 1897, 739; Zola, *La Revue bleue,* 18 December 1897, 772; of Emmanuel Vidal, *La Revue bleue,* 15 January 1898, 72; L'Union pour l'action morale, *La Revue bleue,* 24 December 1897, 807. For similar images of the press as prostitute beyond the survey, see Paul de Ritter, *Quelques vérités: Les Journaux, les femmes et la politique, romans et théâtre* (Libourne: Impr. régionale), 8; "Enquête sur la presse," *La Revue naturiste,* remarks of Sylvain Pitt, 236; Tanneguy de Wogan, *Manuel,* 67.

60. Leroy-Beaulieu, *La Revue bleue,* 18 December 1897, 770. See Robert Darnton's description of the eighteenth-century French "hack" journalist in *The Literary Underground of the Old Regime* (Cambridge, Mass.: Harvard University Press, 1982), 115–16. For the early nineteenth century, see William Reddy's important article: "Condottieri of the Pen: Journalists and the Public Sphere in Postrevolutionary France," *American Historical Review,* 99 (December 1994), 1546–70.

61. Philip Nord, *Paris Shopkeepers and the Politics of Resentment* (Princeton: Princeton University Press, 1986), 448–49, 460–62. "If we are witnessing the death throes of the literature of elites," Zola declared in 1894, "that is because the literature of our democracies is about to be born." See "Le Journal," *Les Annales politiques,* 52.

62. 15 January 1898, 72–73. For the negative view of journalists, see also the remarks of Vidal, Moulier, Brazillier, and Bérenger in the same installment as well as the remarks of Auguste Sabatier, 1 January 1898, 10. For the same view beyond the survey, see Henry du Roure, *La Presse d'aujourd'hui,* 25–29; Jouvenal, *Le Journalisme,* 105; Livois, *Histoire de la presse,* 387–88; the remarks of Hugues Destrem and Pierre Camo in "Enquête sur la presse," *La Revue naturiste.*

63. Jules Case, "La Presse contemporaine," *La Nouvelle revue,* 1 April 1895.

64. For cross-dressing, see: Majorie Garber, *Vested Interests: Cross-dressing and Cultural Anxiety* (New York: Routledge, 1992); Richard Ekins, *Blending Genders: Social Aspects of Cross-dressing and Sex-changing* (New York: Routledge, 1996); Julia Epstein and Kristina Straub, "Introduction" to *Body Guards: The Cultural Politics of Gender Ambiguity,* Epstein and Straub, eds. (New York: Routledge, 1991).

65. Andreas Huyssen, *After the Great Divide: Modernism, Mass Culture, Postmodernism* (Bloomington: Indiana University Press, 1986), 47.

66. Huyssen credits Stuart Hall as well as himself for making this argument, ibid.

67. See Neil Hertz, "Medusa's Head: Male Hysteria under Political Pressure," *Representations* 4 (Fall 1983); Gay Gullickson, "La Petroleuse," *Feminist Studies,* 17, no. 2 (Summer 1990); and Gullickson, *Unruly Women of Paris: Images of the Commune* (Ithaca, N.Y.: Cornell University Press, 1996); Susanna Barrows, *Distorting Mirrors: Visions of the Crowd in Late Nineteenth-Century France* (New Haven: Yale University Press, 1981).

68. Huyssen, *After the Great Divide,* 52.

69. See Ferenczi, *L'Invention,* 35–36; Bellanger et al., *Histoire générale,* 278; Voyenne, *Les Journalistes français,* 144. See also Berenson, *Trial of Madame Caillaux,* 211. Obviously the Dreyfus Affair tested this new conception of journalism as politically neutral. But as Ferenczi points out, the Affair was also a struggle to establish the truth, a battle for a good "scoop"—the latest fact or information. See *L'Invention,* 178–79, 208.

70. Many historians trace the shift from "opinion" to "information" back to the great early nineteenth-century journalist-genius, Emile de Girardin. See Terdiman, *Discourse / Counter-Discourse,* 130–31; and Voyenne, *Les Journalistes,* 148–49, 156. Voyenne argues that Delphine de Girardin, the wife of Emile de Girardin and a famous journalist in her own right, was among the first reporters. In addition, Voyenne argues that the word "reporter" was imported into the French language in 1829 by Stendahl, and also figured in the 1869 Larousse dictionary. (By contrast, Livois, *Histoire de la presse française,* 351, argues that "reportage" was still not officially admitted into the French Academy as a French word in the 1890s.)

71. See Dubief, *Journalisme,* 245. Zola, "Le Journal," 51. See also Eugène Tavernier, *Du Journalisme: Son Histoire, son rôle politique et religieux* (Paris: H. Oudin, 1902), 300; "Enquête sur la presse, *La Revue naturiste,* the remarks of Paul Alexis and Léon Balzagette.

72. *Le Temps,* 22 February 1889. Cited in Bellanger, *Histoire générale,* 279, n. 2. See also Nord, *Paris Shopkeepers,* 460–61; Voyenne, *Les Journalistes,* 143; and A. de Chambure, *A Travers la presse* (Paris: Th. Fert, Albouy et Cie, 1914).

73. Quoted in Henri Avenel, *La Presse française,* x. See also Paul Pottier, *Professions et métiers. Les Journalistes* (Paris: Action populaire, 1907), 4; J. Jaouën, *Les Spécialistes de la presse: Brillants Pamphlétaires et fougeux polémistes* (Paris: Chamuel et Cie, 1901), 1.

74. See Schwartz, "The Public Taste for Reality."

75. "Le Reporter," *Le Peuple,* 11 March 1889.

76. See Clark, *The Painting of Modern Life.* See also Jeannene M. Przyblyski's essay in this volume.

77. See Stephen Heath, "Realism, Modernism, and 'Language-consciousness' " in *Realism in European Literature,* Nicholas Boyle and Martin Swales, eds. (Cambridge: Cambridge University Press, 1986), 105, where he argues that realism means, in general, that creative attention will be given to the visible over the invisible.

78. Adolphe Brisson, "Promenades et visites: L'Ecole du journalisme," *Le Temps,*

3 November 1899, Dossier Ecole du journalisme, BMD. See also Palmer, *Des petits journaux aux grandes agences,* 70, 101; Paul Pottier, *Professions et métiers. Les journalistes* (Paris: Action populaire, 1907), 11, 13.

79. Pottier, *Professions et métiers,* 19; Clovis Hugues, *Paris vivant: Le Journal* (Paris: F. Sahure, 1890), 23; Fernand Xau, "Le Reporter," *Le Voltaire,* 12 January 1881; "Le Reporter," *Le Peuple;* and Tavernier, *Du Journalisme,* 302; Tanneguy de Wogan, *Manuel,* 134, 156.

80. Voyenne, *Les Journalistes,* 161. Voyenne sees a natural relationship between reportage and photo journalism that began to develop precisely in this period. For the same argument, see also Daudet, *Bréviaire du journalisme* (Paris: Gallimard, 1936), 44.

81. Daudet, *Bréviaire,* 23; and Palmer, *Des petits journaux,* 279, n. 78.

82. Arthur Meyer, *Ce que mes yeux ont vu* (Paris: Plon, 1914). See his statement, page 364; "We are often only reflections and agents of transmission." Jules Huret, *Tout yeux, tout oreilles* (Paris: Bibliothèque Charpentier, 1901).

83. Quoted in Ferenczi, *L'Invention,* 121.

84. Dubief, *Du Journalisme,* 71.

85. Max Nordau, *La Revue bleue,* 4 December 1897, 714.

86. See *Modernity and the Hegemony of Vision,* David Michael Levin, ed. (Berkeley: University of California Press, 1993).

87. Quoted in Martin Jay, *Downcast Eyes: The Denigration of Vision in Twentieth-Century French Thought* (Berkeley: University of California Press, 1993), 149. See chapter 3, in particular, for the visual preoccupations of modernists during this period.

88. Chambure, *A Travers la presse,* 446–47.

89. Quoted in Palmer, *Des petits journaux,* 25.

90. Palmer, *Des petits journaux,* 70.

91. See Leo Loubère, *Nineteenth Century Europe: The Revolution of Life* (New York: Prentice-Hall, 1994), 321.

92. See Silverman, *Art Nouveau,* chapter 5.

93. Helpful to me in thinking about "reality" in this context were Roland Barthes, "The Reality Effect," in *The Rustle of Language* (New York: Hill and Wang, 1986), particularly 146; Michel de Certeau, "History: Science and Fiction," in *Heterologies: Discourse on the Other* (Minneapolis: University of Minnesota Press, 1986), 199–221; George Levine, *The Realistic Imagination: English Fiction from Frankenstein to Lady Chatterley* (Chicago: University of Chicago Press, 1981).

94. Fouillée, "Quelques réflexions," 550.

95. For the links between journalism and literature, see Ferenczi, *L'invention,* chapters 1 and 2; Nord, *Paris Shopkeepers,* 462.

96. Quoted in Palmer, *Des petits journaux,* 87. See also "Le Reporter," *Le Peuple.* In the secondary literature, see Jay, *Downcast Eyes,* 171–86.

97. Fenestrier, *La Vie des frelons,* 74.

98. Brisson, "Promenades et visites." For a similar use of the notion of "fantasy," see Henry de Roure, *La Presse d'aujourd'hui et la presse de demain* (Paris: Au Sillon, 1908), 17, 21–22.

99. Edmond Pilon, "Evolution du journalisme française," *La Nouvelle revue,* 1 September 1901, 128. On this point, see also "Enquête sur la presse," *La Revue naturiste.*

100. Chambure, *A Travers la presse,* 448.

101. Wogan, *Manuel,* 162. See also Robert de Jouvenal, *Le Journalisme en vingt leçons,* 81; Jaouën, *Les Specialistes de la presse,* 63; Marcel Schwob, *Moeurs de diurnales: Traité du journalisme* (Paris: Editions des cendres, 1985; orig. pub. by Mercure de France, 1903); "Enquête," *Revue naturiste,* 210, remarks of André Beaunier.

102. Quoted in Palmer, *Des Petits Journaux,* 89. For another statement that women are primarily interested in the newspaper's serialized novel, see also Dubief, *Le Journalisme,* 308.

103. For Rousseau's view on women and imagination, see Michèle Crampe-Casnabet, "A Sampling of Eighteenth-Century Philosophy," in *A History of Women: Renaissance and Enlightenment Paradoxes,* Georges Duby and Michelle Perrot, eds. (Cambridge, Mass.: Harvard University Press, 1993), 328–31.

104. Pottier, *Professions et métiers,* 19. For the same image, see also Dubief, *Du Journalisme,* 246; Hugues, *Paris vivant,* 22.

105. "Le Reporter," *Le Peuple.*

106. Wogan, *Manuel,* 72. For a similar image, see the novel by Paul Brulat, *Le Reporter* (Paris: Perrin, 1898), 221.

107. See Sarah Mills, *Discourses of Difference: An Analysis of Women's Travel Writing and Colonialism* (London: Routledge, 1991), 41.

108. M. Reader, "La Position de la femme en France," 10 November 1892, Dossier féminisme, XIXe siècle, BMD. See also "Nouvelles de féminisme," *Le Temps,* 4 September 1903, ALF, BMD.

109. Marie-Louise Néron, *Notes et impressions d'une Parisienne* (Paris: Librairie Alphonse Lemerre, 1914), 136. For a caricature of the literary journalist that precisely fits this image of a lounge lizard, see Reddy, "Condottieri of the Pen," 1565.

110. Séverine, "Notes d'une frondeuse," *La Fronde,* 7 January 1899. See also Durand, "Les Femmes dans le journalisme," 6. In *Feminine and Opposition Journalism,* 36–37, Gelbart also makes the same general distinction between "*journalisme assis*" and "*journalisme debout.*" Similarly, Barbey d'Aurevilly called the newspaper "*la lecture debout*" as opposed to "*la lecture assise*" because many people read it standing up in the streets and along the boulevards. Quoted in Terdiman, *Discourse / Counter-Discourse,* 131.

111. Séverine, "Le Journalisme féminin," *Le Journal,* 5 August 1899, Dossier Journaliste, BMD. See also "Une Belle déclaration de Séverine sur les femmes et le journalisme," cited erroneously as from *La Fronde,* 1895 in Catherine Trespeuch, *Un Étre*

asexué: La Femme journaliste, (Paris: Université de Paris II, 1981). For Séverine as a "new" journalist, see Ferenczi, *L'Invention,* 83–84, 99–100; Voyenne, *Les Journalistes,* 217.

112. See Homi Bhabha, "Of Mimicry and Man: The Ambivalence of the Colonial Discourse," most recently published in Bhabha's collection of essays, *The Location of Culture* (New York: Routledge, 1994). In this essay, Bhabha explores the mimicry of conventions of race, whereas I am more interested in ideologies of gender. On mimicry and women, see Luce Irigaray, *This Sex Which Is Not One,* Catherine Porter with Carolyn Burke, trans. (Ithaca, N.Y.: Cornell University Press, 1985), 76.

113. The literature on women and domesticity is vast, but a sampling of the most important works would include Bonnie Smith, *Ladies of the Leisure Class: The Bourgeoises of Northern France in the Nineteenth Century* (Princeton: Princeton University Press, 1981); and Smith, "The Domestic Sphere in the Victorian Age," *Changing Lives: Women in European History* (Lexington, Mass.: D. C. Heath, 1989); Anne Martin-Fugier's *La Bourgeoise* (Paris: Bernard Grasset, 1983).

114. Marguerite Durand, "En Cinq ans," *La Fronde,* 15 December 1902.

115. Léon Daudet, *Bréviaire,* 23. See also Dubief, *Du Journalisme,* 72.

116. See Palmer, *Des petits journaux,* 68–69, 93–96. Another name for the reporter was "*Le Sieur de Va-Partout*" after a book by Pierre Giffard (1880) concerning his travels around the world. See Chambure, *A Travers la presse,* 448, 455; Voyenne, *Les Journalistes,* 158; Brulat, *Le Reporter,* 18.

117. "Enfin seules," no title or date [1900], APSF, BMD.

118. Georges Dubor, "Chronique: Journal féministe," *La Paix,* 3 October 1897, APSF, BMD. See also Candide, no title, *Le Rapide,* 6 December 1897, APSF.

119. See Séverine, "Réponse à Ponchon." For accusations of prostitution, see Edmond Deschaumes, "Le Plat de lentilles," *Le Journal,* 30 April 1898; "La Femme sauvée par la femme," *Le Journal,* 30 May 1898; and Ponchon, "Gazette Rimée," all APSF, BMD.

120. Hans Ryner, *Le Massacre des amazones: Etudes critiques sur deux cents bas-bleus contemporaines* (Paris: Chamuel, 1899), 164–65.

121. "La Fin de la Fronde," *Phare de la Loire,* 3 September 1903, APSF.

122. See Dizier-Metz, *Bibliothèque,* 14.

123. For the notion of inclusion that I am using here, see Jacques Rancière, *Les Noms de l'histoire: Essai de poétique du savoir* (Paris, Seuil, 1992), 61.

124. Joan Scott, "Rewriting the History of Feminism," *Western Humanities Review* 58, no. 3 (Fall 1994); *Only Paradoxes to Offer: French Feminists and the Rights of Man* (Cambridge, Mass.: Harvard University Press, 1996).

125. See her "Les Femmes dans le journalisme," 1–2, 7, 30.

126. Durand, "Enquêtes de La Fronde," ALF, BMD.

127. Durand, "Les Femmes dans le journalisme," 1–2, 36.

128. For the debate concerning women's rational powers in the contemporary literature, Jules Allix, "Chronique féministe," Extrait du journal *Bulletin bimestrial de la société pour l'amélioration du sort de la femme,* 15 November 1897; Daniel Riche, no title, *Littoral,* January 1898; Georges Duval, "Journalistes en jupons," no title or date [1897–98]; Marie Dutoit, "A Travers le féminisme," no title or periodical, July 1899, all APSF, BMD. In the secondary literature, see Stephane Michaud, "Science, droit, religion: Trois Contes sur les deux natures"; Yvonne Knibiehler, "Le Discours médical sur la femme: Constantes et ruptures," both in *Romantisme,* no. 13–14 (1976).

129. Tigrane Tchaian, "La Fronde," No periodical or date [1899], APSF, BMD.

130. Some commentators were still against the idea of a woman writer altogether. See, for example, Maurice Dumoulin, "La Fronde," no periodical, 17 March 1899, APSF; Duval, "Journalistes en jupons."

131. Quoted in Clothilde Dissard, "Prétendues victoires," *La Fronde,* 18 December 1897.

132. "Ce que pensent les hommes," *Le Temps;* Merlin, "Opinion de ces dames," *Avenir de Blaye,* 19 April 1898, APSF; "La Fin de la Fronde" *Phare de la Loire;* Camille Belilon, "Conférence de M. le Comte de las Cases," *La Fronde,* 19 December 1897; Charles Maurras, "Les Matriarches," *Le Soleil,* 1 January 1898.

133. "Ce que pensent les hommes," *Le Temps.*

134. Séverine, "Réponse à Ponchon."

135. Irigaray, *This Sex Which Is Not One,* 76.

136. Emphasis mine. "Au Ladies' Club," *La Fronde,* 22 December 1897.

137. "Les Institutrices et la bicyclette," *La Fronde,* 25 December 1897.

138. J. M. [Jeanne Marni?], "Réponse," *La Fronde,* 12 December 1897.

139. Urgèle, "Les Femmes d'Alexandre Dumas," *La Fronde,* 17 January 1898.

140. Marie-Anne de Bovet, "Ménagère ou courtisane"? *La Fronde,* 9 December 1897.

141. Ibid. See also Thécla, "Les Femmes dans la science," *La Fronde,* 3 February 1898; Urgèle, "Les Femmes d'Alexandre Dumas."

142. Judith Cladel, "Les Aimées," *La Fronde,* 24 January 1898.

143. Maria Pognon, "Loi du 2 November 1892 sur le travail des enfants, des filles mineures et des femmes dans l'industrie," *La Fronde,* 12 December 1897.

144. Pauline Kergomard, "A Travers l'éducation," *La Fronde,* 11 December 1897.

145. See, for example, the series by Aline Valette, *La Fronde,* 24 December 1897; 1 and 9 January, 1898.

146. Savioz [Ghénia Avril de Sainte-Croix], "Les Femmes à Saint-Lazare" *La Fronde,* 15 December 1897.

147. Savioz, "La Serve," *La Fronde,* 21 January 1898.

148. See Matlock, *Scenes of Seduction.*

149. Urgèle, "Les Femmes d'Alexandre Dumas."

150. Daniel LeSueur, "Nos Idylles," *La Fronde,* 10 December 1897.

151. Paule Vigneron, "Si nous leur répondions?" *La Fronde,* 25 December 1897.

152. Ibid.

153. Allix, "Chronique féministe." Paul Lafage, "Souvenirs de Frondeuse," no periodical, no date [1903], ALF, BMD. In "L'Eternel féminin," *La Fronde,* 22 December 1897, Marie-Anne de Bovet uses this same image of veiling and hiding behind fans. The *frondeuses* were also interested in giving women visibility in history. See, for example, Camille Belilon, "Chronique féministe," *La Fronde,* 2 February 1898; Jeanine, "Une Historienne au XIVe siècle," *La Fronde,* 15 February 1898.

154. Durand, "En Cinq ans." Nevertheless, several of the *frondeuses* did use pseudonyms.

155. "La Fête de la Fronde," *La Fronde,* 26 December 1897.

156. In "Un Journal féministe en 1900," 65, Cesbron argues that motherhood and marriage remained sacred institutions to the *frondeuses.*

157. "S," "Navrant Suicide," *La Fronde,* 12 December 1897.

158. "Chez les frondeuses," *Illustration.*

159. J. Herter-Eymond, "Enfin, l'on pense à eux!" *La Fronde,* 24 March 1898.

160. "Les Mères," *La Fronde,* 6 February 1898.

161. Savioz, "Les Irréducibles," *La Fronde,* 2 February 1898.

162. Manoël de Grandfort, "Chronique: A Propos du premier jour de l'année," *La Fronde,* 1 January 1898.

163. "La Sainte Marguerite," *La Fronde,* 21 July 1899. As Gay Gullickson has shown, the famous *communarde* and *"vierge rouge"* Louise Michel had much the same public image—as both "warrior and nurturer." See *Unruly Women of Paris,* 154.

164. Séverine, "Notes d'une frondeuse: "L'Attitude à prendre," *La Fronde,* 19 December 1897. See also Jean Deslettres, "Ballade du pardon," *La Fronde,* 10 December 1897.

165. On the virgin Mary, see Michael Carroll, *The Cult of the Virgin Mary* (Princeton: Princeton University Press, 1986). On Marianne, see Maurice Agulhon, *Marianne au pouvoir: L'Imagerie et la symbolique républicaines de 1880 à 1914* (Paris: Flammarion, 1989).

166. Jane Misme, "La Femme dans le théâtre nouveau," *La Revue d'art dramatique,* October 1901, 608. After the war, Misme became one of the most prominent feminists in France and editor of the feminist *La Française.* Like many others of her generation, Misme's early career as a journalist and feminist was bolstered by her presence on *La Fronde*'s staff.

167. Séverine, "Notes d'une frondeuse: Galante réforme," *La Fronde,* 25 December 1897.

168. Anne Lorraine, "Les Conquêtes de la femme," *La Fronde,* 16 February 1898. See also Camille Belilon, "Chronique féministe," *La Fronde,* 18 February 1898. Some of her colleagues were not so patient. Henriette Marchal, for example, fumed: "Il a

peur! De quoi? d'être effaće, anéanti! C'est enfantin!" [He is afraid! Of what? Of being eclipsed, overwhelmed? How childish!]. See her "Le Féminisme inconnu," *La Fronde,* 26 February 1898. See also Dissard, "Le Rôle de la presse."

169. Klejman and Rochefort, *L'Egalité en marche,* 101. For late nineteenth-century feminism, see Hause with Kenney, *Women's Suffrage;* Jean Rabaut, *Féministes à la Belle Epoque* (Paris: Editions France-Empire, 1985).

170. P. B., "La Fronde disparait," *La Petite Gironde,* 3 September 1903, ALF, BMD.

171. Pug, "Pourquoi?" *La Fronde,* 4 January 1898.

172. According to Irigaray, to mimic femininity is to "assume the feminine role deliberately. Which means already to convert a form of subordination into an affirmation, and thus to begin to thwart it." See *This Sex Which Is Not One,* 76.

173. Clothilde Dissard, "Le Rôle de la presse." For other condemnations, see Séverine, "Notes d'un frondeuse," 26 December 1897; and Marcelle Tinayre, "La Nostalgie de la mort," *La Fronde,* 23 January 1898. For male journalists who felt that women should play this role, see Jaouën, *Les Specialistes de la presse,* 63, and Msr. Antolin Lopez Pelaez, *La Femme et la presse* (Poitiers: Société française d'imprimerie, 1902).

174. Judging from the date of Dissard's article, I have guessed that the critique by Charles Maurras was "Les Matriarches." I was unable to find the critique by E. Ledrain.

175. Dissard, "Le Rôle de la presse."

176. Ibid.

177. Vigneron, "Si nous leur répondions?"

178. Marie Anne de Bovet, "L'Eternel féminin." See also her "Ménagère ou courtisane."

179. Judith Cladel, "La Rentrée," *La Fronde,* 10 January 1898.

180. Roger Shattuck, *The Banquet Years: The Origins of the Avant-Garde in France, 1885 to World War I* (New York: Vintage Books, 1955), 4–6.

181. Silverman, *Art Nouveau,* 90. I am grateful to Debora Silverman for bringing this quote to my attention.

182. Deberdt, "Les Femmes journalistes."

Afterword: Reading the News

Je ne comprends pas qu'une main pure puisse toucher un journal sans une convulsion de dégoût. [I do not understand how an uncorrupted hand could touch a newspaper without a shudder of disgust.]
—*Charles Baudelaire, "Mon coeur mis à nu"*

Paris-Midi *annonce qu'un professeur allemand a été mangé par les cannibales au* Congo.
C'est bien fait
L'Intransigeant *ce soir publie des vers pour cartes postales. . . .*
—*Blaise Cendrars, "Crépitements"*

Nothing is deader than yesterday's news. So why this book on old newspapers? In our age of CNN in 140 countries and the World Wide Web on-line, what justifies a collection preoccupied with periodicals out of date by more than a hundred years, publications that might seem the journalistic doubles of what Monty Python memorably styled a "late parrot"?

Today the technological and social intensification of our access to the news—or its access to us—makes the print productions of the nineteenth century seem quaintly antique. How should we understand this apparent obsolescence? We sense, or are continually told, that we are at a turning of epochal developments in information collection, transmission, and processing. The buzz is that in our contemporary world *the news itself is new,* that the innovations that bring it to the screens of our TVs and PCs (and soon to our palmtops and personal communicators) have transcended the journalistic institutions of the nineteenth century. Then, newspapers and other periodicals were just beginning to organize themselves as daily experiences for large numbers of people. Today, they have become so integral to the way our lives are produced for us that any comparison with the period this volume discusses might seem an egregious mistake. In the face of such representations of a technological and epistemological break in the development of the

---

*Unless otherwise noted, all translations in this chapter are my own.

"news," how should we analyze our relation to the nineteenth-century cultural material that *Making the News* records and reexamines?

Today people reluctant to credit the transforming leaps that are said to define our presumed postmodernity are often dismissed as disreputable Hegelians or unenlightened historicists. But I put myself on the side of these latter skeptics—both in general and with particular regard to the technologies and practices of the news. Despite postmodernist disdain, there are a lot of us who cannot sign on to the notion of a present abruptly broken off from the past. We are convinced that historical time is mostly continuous, and that the present derives developmentally from the past. However, we do not think of history as some blithe and easy glide toward the future. We acknowledge that disruptions—even revolutions—happen, and that in culture almost nothing gets transmitted unproblematically. But we believe transmission happens anyway. For this reason we think that the poststructuralist notion of rupture is a barrier to analysis, rather than an enabler. This is because the notion of rupture, in its denial of mediations across the chasm it figures, offers no understanding about what might connect the past to the present, and hence what might help us make sense of the past from our perspective today. As against such a figuration of history, in the face of all the revolutions of the last two hundred years and more, we still note—and I believe we must still draw important methodological conclusions from—the astonishing longevity of "habitus"[1] and the seemingly insuperable persistence of homeostasis. In social existence the quotidian changes with excruciating slowness. Human beings generally practice the same routines on both sides of the divides that are said to define contemporaneity. As Julia Kristeva once put it, "notre siècle vit encore sur la lancée du XIX⁰ siècle" [our century is still living on the nineteenth century's momentum].[2]

So I think that we need to maintain a healthy skepticism concerning claims of radical transformation, and that we ought to credit breaks in culture only in the rarest and most extraordinary circumstances. The compliance of language makes such claims of rupture easy to advance—you can *say* anything you like. But most often the materiality of existence and the refractoriness of human time and memory render such claims more fanciful than real. From this perspective, allegations of a break between the practices of the present and those of the past can seem more devices for marketing modishness than registers of an authentic disjunction of *now* from *then*. Indeed—to radicalize the claim in the context of this Afterword to a volume on nineteenth-century media—journalism itself might stand as an emblem and a test case of the stubborn conservatism of social forms and practices once they are instituted in culture. Then in its recurring constancy, journalism's very object—the *quotidien,* the newspaper—could represent the defining, eponymous element of our dailiness. It has been around for nearly two hundred years, and we still read it every day.[3]

Consequently representations of a break between contemporary practices of most things and their nineteenth-century analogues seem to me inflated. Such claims appear most often to be examples of modernism's chronological chauvinism, its vocation—driven diversely by the most exalted notions of genius and the most tawdry practices of merchandising—to project the present as unique.[4] The tactic has been familiar since the period under analysis in this volume. Its objective is to hypostatize change as difference, and innovation as discontinuity. Overall, the argument can get pretty theological.

But in the case of journalism the basis for claims of such a break seems weak. It might sell quantities of high-priced gear today—*check out our new model!*—to argue that our contemporary information technology propels us beyond the frame of past practices and forms of news experience. But the evidence is thin. As I write this essay, an article in the *New York Times* examines what it concludes is a persistent but mistaken contemporary myth: that the velocity of technological acceleration is greater today than it has ever been. But pace those whose job is hyping upgrades, the historians of technology agree that the period of the most intense and consequential technological—and cultural—change in our history was the very one *Making the News* centers on, the second half of the nineteenth century.[5]

I think a better argument would focus our attention not so much upon the equipment and the technology through which information and images are transmitted, but on the distribution and marketing practices by which they are purveyed, and particularly on the phenomenology of our reception, the consumption practices by which we take them up. With regard to the former, our own century has redefined the hardware and extended the network remarkably. But concerning the latter, the sometimes misprized nineteenth century still seems astonishingly advanced. A few years ago Whittle Communications caused a flap by pushing an educational television service called Channel One. They supplied TVs, VCRs, and current events programming to schools for free. In return, students were required to watch the commercials broadcast over the system.[6] Or, in a parallel development, through the lure of instantaneous access to the news, Pointcast and similar "push technologies" are trying right now to put streams of similarly "free" advertising on the screen of your PC. Contemporary merchandising thus seeks ways of colonizing for commerce the information space created by the new technologies. But this is old news. The nineteenth century may not have had the circuit boards we have, but they had *selling* wired already; they had naturalized merchandising. We can read the success of their conflation of distributing the news and flogging products in the double meanings of words like "article" and "commercial."[7] In light of the institutionalization of these patterns during the last hundred and fifty years, it may seem that today's innovations are doing no more than playing catch-up with what the last century had already defined for us as a constitutive "habitus" of the mercantile.

The story of journalism's pioneering role in this process is familiar. In July 1836 in Paris, Émile de Girardin brought out a new daily, *La Presse,* at a subscription rate that undercut by half the going price for newspapers. His calculation was simple: to make up in advertising revenue what he lost on subscription income—or, putting it more crassly, to increase the proportion of the paper's cost borne by advertising and consequently the proportion of space in the paper devoted to it. While Girardin charged subscribers half as much as his competitors, he billed his advertisers at the same rates. And they were willing to pay him because he could promise them wider distribution at no increase in cost.[8]

Then in 1863, in a second leap in the development of this journalistic "massification" and commercialization, Moïse (Polydore) Millaud launched *Le Petit Journal,* for the first time selling the newspaper by the individual copy, and consequently forcing himself, by the logic of the operation, to focus his attention on making each issue of the paper desirable for a mass audience. With *Le Petit Journal,* the meaning of the "daily" takes on its still-familiar resonance. While the distribution of Girardin's *La Presse* in the thirties and forties had never risen higher than 22,000, by 1880 Millaud's paper was selling 600,000 copies.[9] This astonishing increase in the perfusion of the social field by journalism coincided with what is generally seen as the golden age of consumer capitalism in France under the Third Republic.[10]

Increasing literacy; growing disposable income and leisure time among a rising consumerist middle class; innovative forms of the marketing of consumer commodities; the extension of the franchise and of electoral politics; even the fascination of a world coming under the sway of European imperialism and commercial domination—these are among the conditions that made this leap in the circulation of newspapers possible. But it was changes in the character of *what* Girardin, Millaud, and their imitators published that transformed the typical faction newspaper of the 1820s—the sectarian organ of one or another political fragment or interest group—into the increasingly neutral and "objective" general circulation daily of the sixties and after.[11] So the mass-circulation newspapers projected a new form of readership with whom their relation was to be one of objective purveyor of an increasingly desirable (if increasingly colorless) commodity—*information*—whose circulation in these innovative forms, however, entailed the increasingly skillful and successful merchandising of distinctly less metaphorical commodities.

Dominant accounts of nineteenth-century French journalism have regularly emphasized the development of a pervasive and increasingly centralized publication technology and information economy, an increasing homogenization and massification of the press, in a familiar pattern of capitalist concentration and market domination. This depiction of growing control of the field of journalism by increasingly consumerist mass circulation dailies remains accurate in general. But *Making the News* revises our sense of the overall climate and complex of practices in which such developments must be seen. Readers of the current volume who have gotten as far as this Afterword will already be convinced that the collection's striking contribution toward renewing our understanding of the news in nineteenth-century France is its demonstration of the vibrant *variety* of periodical publication in a historical conjuncture that has regularly been portrayed as monolithic. In particular, as my co-contributors demonstrate, the trend toward massification and homogenization of the journalistic field distinctly did *not* exclude the existence and indeed the flourishing of a variety of dissident or heterodox publications. They stretch from the anarchist working-class daily *Père Peinard* directed by Emile Pouget (examined in Howard Lay's fine article) to Marguerite Durand's feminist *La Fronde* (as Mary Louise Roberts's remarkable essay discusses).

Making the News thus enriches and complicates our sense of the newspaper's place and scope in nineteenth-century life—and hence, given the ubiquity of the daily and its allied publications, of the character of such life to begin with. The evidence for the development of massification seems to me incontestable, as my brief summary earlier of Girardin's and Millaud's innovations suggests. The mass press *was* increasingly defining and taking over the field, and it *was* increasingly driven by a commercial logic whose overt crassness was bitterly deplored by the partisans of an elite or politically or socially engaged press. The dispiriting pessimism about mass media and dominant discourses that we associate variously with the members of the Frankfurt School or with Foucault thus has considerable empirical and cultural warrant. Yet such patterns was far from determining everything that was happening in the period. Given this heterogeneity, how should we make sense of French journalism in this formative time?

We need theory when the surface of things camouflages their meaning. An often-repeated maxim reminds us that what is closest to us is what we most forget.[12] Indeed, it was the nineteenth century that promulgated this doctrine. The period made a methodological axiom of the suspicion of appearances.[13] But in connection with *Making the News,* it is worth noting that our perception is probably the most mystified when something seems to carry its reality on its face. Thus one of the conditions that can most mislead us is the very *banality* of an object, the constancy of its presence in the network of our practices. This issue is particularly pertinent when it comes to journalism, when we seek to make sense of newspapers. The newspaper calls for investigation beyond its quotidian banality precisely *because of* its quotidian banality. Like the commodity in Marx's *Capital,* it only *seems* a simple thing. By shifting our vision from the blind spot of contemporary dailiness, by inducing us to see the present anew through its homologies with the network of cultural representations and interpretations that were being devised and fought over a century and more ago, *Making the News* helps us read ourselves just as it renews our understanding of the protohistory of modern journalism and information distribution.

I want therefore to briefly consider how contemporary scholarship has represented the field of nineteenth-century journalism and what can be learned from the pattern of this research to which *Making the News* now makes the most recent contribution. Let us begin with the scholarly *doxa.* Journalism—particularly its nineteenth-century French avatar—has had bad press. In the wake of a virulent critique on the part of canonical modernist and avant-garde writers of the degradation of cultural values that journalism both reflected and fostered,[14] scholars and critics in our own period have examined the increasing ideological hegemony of the mass-journalistic developments that pervaded the field in the nineteenth century. Inevitably this examination of dominant trends scanted the diversity of journalistic activity in the period that *Making the News* now restores to view. To begin with, the shift of scholarly attention away from the most degraded and meretricious journalistic forms, and toward more marginal or heterodox expression, can easily be justified on simple grounds of empirical completeness, of filling out a map in which a significant portion of the territory had generally been ignored. But I think it is fair to suggest that the motivation for this rebalancing effort has been overdetermined by considerations of cultural politics in our own time. Surely our sensitivity to the expressions of dominated or disenfranchised groups, such as those studied in *Making the News* by a number of my co-contributors, has been increased as a result of liberation movements in our own time. The effort to give counter-discursive representations—whether in the last century or in our own—their due, then, honors our commitment to a cultural history, and to a politics, that will value *all* individual and collective contributions and aspirations.

But as we seek the egalitarian rebalancing that both the objectivity of our scholarship and the passion of our politics mandate, we need to ask ourselves how we should best understand the functioning and the bearing of all the diverse discourses that compose the internally conflicted social field—but perhaps most crucially those that do *not* dominate it and the social effects it determines. What is the realm of effectiveness of the heterodox and the dissident? For (to return to the material of *Making the News*) it is not enough to rediscover the existence of a heretofore-forgotten dissident newspaper, however valuable in itself that archival retrieval may be. The deeper problem is to decide what such dissident expression *meant* in its cultural setting, to determine its effectivity in the face, in the space, of dominant adversaries. This implies that we must conceive the discursive field as a site of contention, in which it is not enough that my counter-discursive paper *exists* (though that is already significant). For despite the falsely egalitarian ideology of the market, itself so powerfully developed and marketed in the nineteenth century, publications do not enter commerce on equal terms simply by virtue of being present on the racks. Anyone with experience of social existence under market capitalism knows that the latter idealization wildly falsifies the picture. The underground weekly and the *New York Times* do not stand on the same footing in the cultural field—no more than *La Fronde* and *Le Petit Journal* did in their own period. Just check the advertising rates.

Mass forms draw attention to themselves and produce their social and cultural effectiveness by virtue of their very ubiquity. That is why most history is the history of the victors. With great energy and scholarly inventiveness, *Making the News* seeks to overturn such marginalization of marginality and to rebalance what might otherwise seem the univocal hegemony of dominant forms. History from below, or from the margins, thus fruitfully contests the appearance of the self-evidence and omnipresence of dominant practices by restoring the loci in which their domination was resisted or contested. But (as the French say), *faut pas exagérer:* it is important to carefully assess, and not to overinflate, the meaning of such a fact.

By recovering and displaying a series of alternative voices and voicings in the field of nineteenth-century journalism, *Making the News* gives us the chance to think through again how the dominant discourses in this (or any) social field relate to the heterogeneous and heterodox counter-discourses that resisted absorption or subsumption in them. Scholars sometimes stage this remapping as if it were an ethical struggle, as if the domination of the dominant (or our depiction of it) were somehow a shameful capitulation to power, rather than a reflection of the reality of power itself. The battle then takes the form of a contention whose structure appears identical to the one linking—and opposing—the counter-discourses active in any cultural situation to the discourses and practices that dominate them and the social field as a whole. This battle suggests an affective identification with the objects of our scholarly attention. Should you write about—and thus arguably reproduce and reinforce—the dominant? Or should you not rather contest it today by writing about what contested it in its own period? Then the scholarly problem of making sense of the past can seem to transform itself into the question of which side you are on.

A dispute along these lines has been frequent in recent decades as efforts to recover the cultural production of formerly ignored, misprized, or marginalized groups have redrawn our map of numerous periods, regions, and realms of social activity. At first glance the critical and disciplinary struggle over such a remapping can appear to be an atemporal argument about method and focus, pitting attention to dominant forms of expression against concern with the dissident or marginal counter-discourses that press against them. Each side of the disciplinary struggle then vies for critical and analytic priority. And, as in the notorious battle over the canon that has exercised literary and allied disciplines over the past ten years or so, a considerable amount of academic blood can get spilled.

But despite its obvious political resonances and determinants, this contest between canonical and anticanonical critical objects might rather be represented as a regularly evolving disciplinary narrative, as a normal paradigm. The election of our research object at any moment is not *just* a voluntaristic choice. It is diagnostically constrained. The social field is complex and heterogeneous, but representations of the practices and discourses that compose it are *not* all equally available at any time. Rather, ideology functions to make certain social facts easier to see and say, and others more difficult to detect or to represent. If it did not, ideology—here I am understanding by this term the foundational and often preconscious belief systems and cognitive mechanisms that organize our interaction with the world—would cease to function.

The pattern of this contention reaches into a gentle dispute in *Making the News*. What should be studied in the diverse and heterogeneous field of nineteenth-century French journalism? A number of contributors to the volume generously refer to my own earlier work on newspapers of the period. This scholarship goes back fifteen years, and today I can see it with some dispassion. So I am delighted when writers in *Making the News* (particularly in the interesting essays by Jeremy Popkin and James Smith Allen) point to my neglect, in that earlier account, of the social and political *diversity* of journalistic production in the period. It is surely accurate to say that I focused on dominant trends, on the rise of mass journalism and on the ideological and technological inflections that made such new institutions of the news possible. Consequently, like most scholarship done on the period at that time, my account slighted publications that diverged from what was emerging as the hegemonic journalistic and media market form—the ones, in other words, upon which *Making the News* largely and productively focuses.[15] The present volume thus corrects my, and our, image of nineteenth-century media in the most salutary way.

It may be, however, that the rectification of such neglect in the scholarly tradition follows a law in our representation of the past that can itself be usefully disengaged—the evolving narrative and normal paradigm I referred to earlier. Methodologically speaking, accounts of dominant discourses probably must precede those of the marginal or counter-discursive forms that contest or seek to subvert them. There is thus a predictable (by which I do not mean a necessary) order of discovery. This would suggest that the study of dominant discourses and the study of the counter-discourses that oppose or resist them ought not to be thought of in opposition to each other, but rather in terms of complementarity.

We can see this if we try to imagine a counter-discourse abstracted from the dominant discourse. It is of course evident that the character of the concept of a counter-discourse makes such isolation logically absurd. But crucially, in this case, the logical form of the concept seems only to mirror the structure of social experience. In our perception as in our discourse, we *feel* the pressure of the *doxa,* of dominant practice and expression. Before we begin to look or to write, and whether we acknowledge it explicitly or not, we have already internalized the differentials of cultural power and social effectivity that make a mapping of the discourses in any period possible to begin with. These are the factors that assign centrality or marginality, effectiveness or powerlessness, to cultural objects and practices according to their coincidence with or divergence from the forms we experience as dominant. If this is so in general, the fact of such differential power, and the consequent pattern of such priority in the developing historical narrative, express themselves and make sense precisely in the evolving pattern of our scholarly attention. It derives from a different form of precedence, not now temporal but *social,* that inscribes in the tale we tell about our past a reality of power. It is important for this to register if we are not to lose grounding in the materiality of existence and in the constraints that ideology and dominant "habitus" exercise upon our vision and our knowledge.

As Foucault put it in the title of his Collège de France inaugural lecture, social discourses are almost always *ordered* in this way.[16] Consequently their coexistence in any period can almost never be conceived as an absence of normative structures.[17] Discourses may be heterogeneous, but they are not random. The rich diversity of journalistic effort in the nineteenth century, reflecting commitments to the broad variety of group, class, and gender politics that *Making the News* chronicles and illuminates, only makes sense if we construe the contention such practices instantiate against the implicit hierarchy that orders them. For dominant discourses *dominate*. In social life this is what they really and materially *do*. Then, discursive contention is not the neutral and abstract confrontation of opposing notions logically arrayed against each other, as it were, horizontally and on equal terms. The hard facts of real inequality underlie almost every form of difference we encounter. So however complex their heterogeneity, such situations inscribe and are constrained by a *hierarchy* of discursive power and effectivity.

Because we have always already internalized the experience of such differential power, counter-discourses never mistake themselves for dominant ones. Of course they wish and they may strive to achieve predominance. But precisely at the moment that they are produced and propagated, they *know* their subordination through the pressure they feel exerted against them by the settled assumptions and the default expectations of the discursive field within which they seek to achieve their effectiveness. This pressure is always present like the current in a river: it is rare for rowers to be uncertain about whether they are proceeding upstream or down. *The current tells them.*

Yet it is also the case that critical analysis of a period's dominant discourses presupposes at least the beginning of a disengagement from them and their ideological self-evidence. Representation of the dominant thus is not simply its reproduction, still less its automatic affirmation or solidification. Such representation is only possible when critique opens an internal distance in the ideological transparency of dominant practices. So rather than opposing attention to counter-discursive forms such as the ones *Making the News* mainly considers, our critical accounts of the dominant discourse lie on a demystificatory continuum with them.

To be sure, some—I might say much—scholarship functions as apologia for dominant power and its hegemonic ideological forms. Even leaving aside the question of venality,[18] it should not be surprising that the university turns out such echoes and reflexes of domination, since despite the self-congratulatory image it often constructs of itself, the academy is no more disjoined from society than the locutors within it are disjoined from the ideologically inflected language that everybody speaks. But it would be as much a mistake to think that scholarly or critical accounts of the institutional, linguistic, and practical elements (by which the domination of any social form propagates and reproduces itself) flat-footedly solidify these processes as to believe that an analysis of the ideology-producing effects of newspapers since the nineteenth century will inevitably become captured and canceled in the force field of these effects themselves.

Methodologically we need to appreciate what critique can and cannot do. Critique on its own does not revolutionize reality. It is unable to lift the weight of the constituted power whose depiction it seeks and whose mechanisms it aims to deconstruct. *Deconstruction* (an intellectual and conceptual counterideological act) is not *destruction* (a material and potentially violent revolutionary act). Since action of the latter kind seems distinctly suspect today at a time when some version of liberal politics appears to have gained an extraordinary hegemony (in the West at least), we need an even more focused and functional understanding of what ideological critique can do—and indeed what, under present conditions, it ought to be even more urgently called upon to do. Why is it hard to see this? Again, it is an effect of ideology, of the domination of our minds by domination itself.

In its ideal projection, liberal ideology—particularly in its American forms—wants to imagine society as a tabula rasa. No previous contents, no constraints or established hierarchies are supposed to burden the production of any new initiative. Liberalism shows a peculiar blindness to power. In the consecrated figure, it asserts that the playing field is level—this at least is the normative image, and anything that subverts it is construed as derogation, as noise. But this assessment seems to get the normal situation backward. In real existence the field of play is never horizontal; verticality and hierarchy are inscribed in *everything social*. This is why the liberal model, purging from its effectiveness in any moment the burden of practices and of habits that give form to any present, cannot capture the way people experience their experience. Liberal ideology functions to blank out ideology itself; it projects ideology's end in a fantasy that frees us and our institutions from history. We might take this dream as a truncated, particularly perverse and perverting reflection of Enlightenment notions of liberation—but crucially missing the Enlightenment's careful analytic dismantling of the mechanisms by which, in real societies, such liberation is forestalled and resisted. In practice the liberal dream of equal access to power is never actionable and leads only to deeper enmeshment in the hegemonic network of domination that it functions to deny.

What has come along as an alternative is a complex of doctrines of "social construction." Such theories seek to recover that *other* side of Enlightenment insight, the one erased by contemporary liberalism—that is, the side that sought to detect and to display how power is created and organizes itself, and how it propagates not only its effectiveness but even more crucially its invisibility. Perhaps we might see in the functioning of journalism itself a protoimage of such theories, as every day the newspaper purports to give us an account of how our world is put together. Yet the limitations of such a vision are visible in this comparison. The newspaper reports the "news"— that is, according to the canons of objectivity that dominate American journalism, it gives us a description of what has happened. But "happened" on what level? What is missing is an active practice of "critique" in the depiction that we give of how any element of social reality functions. For simply restating the mechanisms that we can observe in such functioning produces no gain in efforts to decenter or denaturalize them. What such accounts unaccountably leave out is a sense of the "value accent" that inflects any social practice, the interests that it serves—which for good and determinate reason are usually nowhere visible in narratives of its mechanism.[19]

This tendency to constrain analysis to the restatement of "what happened" is a reflex of the contemporary slippage of social constructionism toward the status of orthodoxy. We need to be alert to the reduction or deadening that *any* orthodoxy brings with it. Methodologically, the "construction" thesis has helped to reinvigorate social theory by demystifying the naturalness of all tradition or constituted practice—and, as I suggested earlier, it has been doing so since its inception in Enlightenment attacks upon the irrational sanctity of custom. Traditional indenture to a supposedly fixed set of legitimate institutions and social practices has thus given way to the notion that everything social is contingently determined. But in the period of its own hegemony today, what risks fading from such a conception is *the work of determination itself*: the protracted and circumstantial narrative of the mechanisms by which social practices are in fact produced—and particularly of the interests that drive this production. We would not require that critique achieve such knowledge if restatement of what can be seen of them by inspection could really penetrate their mystery. But social structures are not like watches, and we cannot understand them by breaking them down into their component parts. Marx put this point strikingly in volume 3 of *Capital:* "Science would be unnecessary if the form of appearance of things and their essence directly coincided."[20] A critical hermeneutics would thus seem indispensable for any analytic that seeks to understand social life or any of its multifarious registers.

Without this hermeneutic narrative, the doctrine of social construction that prescribes the contingency of social facts risks becoming just as mystical or idealist as traditional notions according to which the forms of existence were divinely decreed. We ought not to allow the concept of social construction, which has been so effective in subverting a priori visions of reality, to devolve into an unexamined a priori. When the narrative that underlies the labor by which any practice was constructed fades precisely because everyone *presumes* it, then the rich materialist notion of "construction" withers, and it contracts into a trendy synonym for the serendipity of chance.

It would be wonderful if things gave us their meanings effortlessly, in an epiphany that entailed no work of demystification, no translation. But what has in the past been "constructed" of our social existence appears in the present without the plans and blueprints, without the false starts and groping redesigns, that were indispensable to its development. It comes to us, in other words, absent the whole *history* of its production and the determinations that drove this process. Like scaffolding, these are relegated to oblivion once the work is done. For this reason the processes of social life, the institutions that compose and determine it, cannot automatically be read from the present in a way that reveals the long narrative of conflict, confusion, and revision that has shaped their current appearance of stability and self-consistency. We cannot take things at their word because language is always inflected by ideology. In this sense the antihermeneutic poststructuralist doctrine of "depthlessness" abdicates a fundamental analytic responsibility—with political consequences that, or such is my suspicion, only those in positions of advantage could possibly fail to see.

Now I want to return to newspapers and ask how journalism relates to these issues. The ties are multiple, complex, and revealing. Let me begin with the relationship between journalism and ideology. The newspaper reads how ideology works because powerful ideological elements take form and function within it. But it does not necessarily explain this to us in its own pages. This is where our critique of its practices becomes indispensable. How do people know how to conceive their world? Much comes from their experience. But in modern societies, in a world much more complicated than can be mastered by any individual, experience is mediated by a shifting range of processes. A great deal of our information comes to us through institutions: family, school, religious organization, and *media*—precisely those institutions that diverse strains of the theory of ideology have identified as its principal and most socially effective bearers. Of course, "ideology" means something different from false consciousness or overt deception. It is the constructed and structured pattern of how we live in and interpret the world. We know that this pattern is mutable, yet durable. But we also know that it does not explain itself to us in some benign self-demystification.

In our age of revolutions since the repeated upheavals of the nineteenth century, we have seen ideology's evolution over time and experienced its remarkable refractoriness to change. Journalism has played its own role in this pattern of—sluggish—transformation. But what has remained constant beneath the shifting patterns of news preoccupation is a relation to the news itself that the daily both instantiates and induces in its consumers. Such a structure of relation bears different contents within it—for one example, every daily paper in the United States has a *business* page, but you will not find a single one with a *labor* page. These elements of format and organization carry messages that are all the more effective because they are nowhere explicitly stated. The heart of the process is the creation of a durable "habitus," the form through which the daily portion of new information served up in the morning paper comes to represent for readers a formative metonym of the world.

This process of meaning-creation began in earnest during the period chronicled in *Making the News*. This was when newspapers and allied publishing institutions became a principal source not only of information but of modern structures of consciousness. In an increasingly stressed temporal and perceptual economy, newspapers motivated the focusing—or the re-focusing—of social and individual attention. They served as shortcuts to experience, they *mediated* it. This means that someone else's history—or interests—preceded the formulation and provision of our own. Thus the question of *politics*—which the mass dailies of the period were marginalizing in service of the astonishing increases in circulation spoken about earlier in this essay—returns at a different level and with a striking pertinence. But if we look closely at the political effectiveness and range of these publications, it becomes possible to see a stratification in the stakes in information distribution and control that, for the first time since the decline of the church as an organized form of social structuring, could be imagined to be reinvested in a single institution.[21]

With these stakes, it becomes obvious that the impetus was great in the period *Making the News* considers for the diverse groups in an increasingly vocal and heterogeneous society to seek to create and utilize an organ of opinion-formation and expression: *their* newspaper. The periodicals that emerged from the dozens of presses pressed into the service of factional or group politics were remarkably varied, as *Making the News* convincingly demonstrates. Along the dimension of content and political position there was no unity in the nineteenth-century press, as a number of the contributors clearly argue in this volume. But the Press with a capital *P* must still be conceived as an institution whose coherence asserted itself at a different—and I would argue an even more consequential—level than that upon which party or group disputes played out, even in a century as fractious as the one under consideration here.

So whatever the specific political or social bearing of the periodicals that emerge from it, on another level the Press and its productions constitute a seminal cultural discourse, a structured and instrumental social practice, whose increasingly widespread and increasingly formative effects upon our consciousness and our perceptual habits do not arise simply in the specific contents of any particular paper. To put it crudely, whichever party, group, or faction it may have explicitly supported, one paper looked pretty much like another. And whatever position it took on whatever issues a publication may have taken most to heart, the complex of reading habits—how one encountered, how one assimilated, how one processed the information, opinions, and even the merchandise it proffered—that one brought to and found reinforced in it broadly resembled those learned from and active in the reading even of periodicals whose explicit politics were diametrically opposed. At a certain level of the creation of "habitus," of the experience of practice, form swamps content. And that is how the dominant exercises its domination—not in imposing allegiance to any specific political party or program, but in subtly enforcing a pattern of experience, a structure defining the quotidian. In that sense, for modernity, the daily constructed dailiness.

Thus while we celebrate the recovery in this volume of the history and orientation of a variety of counter-discursive publications, it would be a methodological mistake to allow this attention to the dissident and counter-discursive to erase the overarching, *meta*-discursive effects of the daily—of whatever explicit political or ideological stripe—on the infrastructural "habitus" of *reading the news* that the journalism of the period was fashioning for, and propagating to, an increasingly broad spectrum of people. The nineteenth century was learning to draw a growing quota of their vision of the world from this medium—and willy-nilly they were simultaneously apprenticing themselves to the ambiguous "article" (with all its attendant perceptual habits and acquisitive seductions) in their daily commerce with the press.

A provocative image of this metadiscursive level, on which differences of content become canceled and enfolded into congruence in social *form,* occurs in John Barbaret's article in this collection. He considers Balzac's "Illustre Gaudissart," a short story that chronicles the failure of the traveling salesman Gaudissart to make a success of selling newspaper and magazine subscriptions. (Curiously, in view of its subject, and unlike many of Balzac's texts, this one was not first serialized.) But as Barbaret points out, Balzac transforms this anecdote of commercial fiasco into an economic *victory: his novel sells Gaudissart's failure* to sell the same commodity. The medium thus demonstrates a bewildering capacity to achieve an effectiveness that diverges from and functions *against* its own explicit content.

This is the point at which it becomes possible to see how we might better understand the methodological and ideological tension between scholarly focus on dominant discourse and scholarly focus on its counter-discursive antagonists, considered earlier in this essay. As *Making the News* strikingly demonstrates, the nineteenth-century journalistic field had room for both, was indissolubly composed of both. But what were the inner articulations of this diversity? We can get at this problem in the following way. The creation of the mass daily and its self-assertion as hegemonic journalistic form in the nineteenth century simultaneously—and indivisibly—fostered the rise of the dissident publications that the contributors to the current volume illuminate. In effect the mass daily *produced* the opportunity for marginal voices to be sounded and propagated. We may not be happy to discover our dissidence yoked inescapably to what it opposes. But in social life that scandal is what almost always occurs. In the case of journalism it happened, first of all, because the cost of newspapers inexorably dropped during the seventy-or-so years from Girardin's invention of *La Presse* to the end of the century. Moreover, this decline in cost represented an absolute reduction in the daily's price accompanied by the remarkable rise in personal income to which I have already alluded (see n. 10), hence to a parallel diminution in the effective cost of reading the paper. But perhaps most significantly, the rise of diverse publications happened because the mass daily created the expectation that reading the news was central to daily existence.

The effect of this revolution in the "habitus" was to lower the economic and social entry cost into journalism for a whole variety of publications that aimed at narrower and more specifically defined class, gender, professional, or political factions than the mass dailies ever sought to target. The capital required to start a paper had not become negligible. But it became possible to imagine making a go of a publication with a readership composed, *not* of the moneyed readers who alone could pay the elevated subscription costs of papers before Girardin so dramatically lowered the price, but of less advantaged people who could identify with the political or ideological orientation of specific dissident papers, and whose concerns these papers articulated. These counter-discursive niche markets were thus an unintended but systemic consequence of the industrialization of journalism and the sophisticated coupling of advertising with information-gathering and distribution. So the mass daily *created* the conditions for its counter-discursive competitors and its dissident antagonists.

This is precisely what we would expect to find underlying an internally heterogeneous but ultimately hierarchical discursive field. For one sort of investigation the journalistic field is a horizontal one, with all papers published at any time equally available and bearing within themselves the potential for comparable social effectiveness. But from a different perspective, emphasizing the commercial and ideological organization of the market, and the inevitable power differentials dividing its seeming homogeneity, it is always the dominant discourse that sets the frame and establishes the conditions in which counter-discursive competitors must function. This is what happened here.

We can see this demonstrated in the analyses in this volume. As examples, let me choose the two essays in *Making the News* that bear most directly on women, the group most of us would probably designate as most excluded from or marginalized in the canon of the previous generation. The pieces in this volume by Cheryl A. Morgan on *Le Journal des femmes,* and by Mary Louise Roberts on *La Fronde,* deal directly with newspapers that were designed to be produced by women and to be about women.[22] From its Enlightenment origins, and for good political reasons, social-constructionist thinking has mostly taken *dominant* practices and objects as its focus. The objective of such a method was to displace the self-evidence of hegemonic forms. But if we conceive the field of cultural discourses as an internally heterogeneous but ultimately linked and mutually determining structure, then we must consider with equal attentiveness the construction of *counter-discursive* objects, whatever our sympathy for their dissident positions. Morgan's and Roberts's essays provide the chance to test such a methodology. To begin with, the dailies they examine spent considerable time *situating* themselves in relation to dominant male-run and male-oriented papers. Questions of women's authorship, preoccupations, and insights arose repeatedly in the intense and even anxious self-reflection that Morgan and Roberts chronicle in the case of the female contributors to these publications.

Tongue slightly and sympathetically in cheek, we might term this effect the "second city" phenomenon. I refer to a celebrated (if now anachronistic) designation of Chicago, nervously situating itself in relation to New York's indifferent hegemony. Or we might think of Herb Caen's amused realization years ago that while San Franciscans worried obsessively about Los Angeles, Angelenos hardly bothered to think about San Francisco at all. It is bad enough when someone is located above you; it is particularly galling when they do not even notice you. But these examples only show us the comical corner of a deadly serious structure of social constraint. In this much more consequential mode, consider the following perception from a recent study of attitudes about race in America: "A black person [in the United States] cannot go very long without thinking about race."[23] Crucially the nexus that determines that preoccupation is not imagined to function—and no doubt does not function—in the same way for whites. Whether these dissymmetries index the grievous inequalities of my last example or only detect the anodyne differences of the earlier ones, they are the internalized registers of hierarchy to which I referred earlier in this essay. They record the capacity of domination to determine a seemingly irresistible flow of power (running from the side of the hegemonic to that of the counter-discursive) and, reciprocally, of preoccupation (running predictably in the reverse direction).

There is no need to conceive of these hierarchically determined flows as completely rigid. Ideology does not work so mechanically. Dominant publications could not entirely ignore their dissident cousins. Rather, at a certain point, they acted to co-opt them. So for example at a certain moment in their evolution, the nineteenth-century mass dailies typically established a fashion rubric (to the point that much later in the century Mallarmé could found and publish a periodical—entirely composed by himself—called *La Dernière Mode*). But one does not have to be feminist to sense in such innovations the scant recognition of the sorts of feminist *programmatic* concerns that had led Richomme to found the *Journal des femmes* or (in more modulated ways) Durand to establish *La Fronde*.

But flowing powerfully—almost inexorably—in the other direction, we can feel the influence of dominant institutions, ideologies, and commercial forms on these counter-discursive examples. Let me first consider the *Journal des femmes*. After Richomme took ownership in 1834, she cut the paper's subscription price in half (reproducing the logic that had been driving Girardin's journalistic and commercial innovations, as Dean de la Motte explains in his article in this volume). And she sought to increase the circulation and no doubt the influence of her paper by targeting a readership broader than "elegant society," extending it to women of "all educated classes." What happened? Whether the reason was entirely financial is not clear from Morgan's account. But a year later, in 1825, Richomme fused the paper with another periodical to create *La Revue fashionable*. The change, however, involved more than the name. The women who had produced the *Journal des femmes* no longer exclusively staffed the new publication; soon a male editor had taken it over. In 1836 the old title returned, but the paper was now under male direction, and it announced an explicit program of banishing (feminist) "politics" from the paper.

The *Journal des femmes* thus began with a counter-discursive ideological edge. But its programmatic feminist politics and practice were dulled and undermined as the magnetic influence of merchandising—of the dominant journalistic discourse—induced a retreat from engagement with women's issues in favor of capitalization of the sorts of concerns that, for more than a century to come, the mass dailies would complacently segregate to the safety of the "women's page." The commercial *mode* thus trumped the intellectual one; fashion won out over politics; and the image of "women's" place in the journalistic field was comfortably recontained in the world of the ideologically dominant through a tolerance so hegemonic that (as we might say remembering Marcuse) it felt no need to be "repressive" at all.

Mary Louise Roberts's remarkable analysis of *La Fronde* enables us to understand the complex dialectic of dominant power and counter-discursive impulse at a much later and more developed stage in periodical journalism and feminist consciousness in France. What fascinates in the story Roberts has to tell is how insidious and pervasive are the effects of dominant discourse even in the face of conscious analysis of such effects on the part of those who experience them. *La Fronde* was not conceived as some microcirculation sectarian sheet. On the contrary. It aimed at the kind of currency and influence that had at that point become institutionalized for the male-dominated mass circulation dailies. Its readership attained fifty thousand, and it covered the same full range of topics as its competitors. But it was run by women.

Where can we sense the difference that *that* difference made? Roberts makes a persuasive claim: even when you model your institution after the dominant one, your divergence from it—in the case of *La Fronde,* foregrounding the fact that *your* daily is produced without a single male collaborator—inevitably changes the effect of what might otherwise seem no more than "mimicry." The effect is uncanny. It resembles the difference between dressing and *cross*-dressing (the image is explicit in Roberts's discussion, as in some of the textual and visual sources upon which she draws). The former is the unproblematic and unmarked case; the latter, however, is inevitably (if however subtly) disorienting because it cannot be comfortably read in terms of any accustomed "habitus."

This decentering is familiar to us when it is produced through the representational exaggerations of satire and caricature, by the overloading of recognizable features that pull representation beyond uninflected reproduction and toward a critique of, or an intervention in, our assessment of the real. But in the case of *La Fronde,* a daily that Roberts reports was slyly dubbed "*Le Temps* in skirts," it is not the *content* of the expression that is subtly "off," but rather the locutors themselves who do not comfortably "fit" the paradigm of utterance that they mimic and exploit, and in whose tonality they thus induce a Heraclitean slippage. The same words your antagonist uses sound *different* when you use them yourself.

What in Roberts's analysis becomes the inevitable (if subtle) focus of such discursive *dépaysement* is the construction of discourses of gender—and their inevitable, if subtle, critique. This is what made the "politics" of *La Fronde* so fascinating. With an artful will to *reproduce* the practices and modes of the dominant papers, with a programmatic determination not to challenge these on the level of overt expression, *La Fronde* shrewdly torqued and twitted them nonetheless.[24]

Without specifics regarding the social and hierarchical parameters of a speech situation, the reenactment of dominant discourse never can tell you by itself whether you are deepening its hold on consciousness or cannily subverting it. Reaching a conclusion depends on who is perceived as speaking, on who is present or projected as audience, and on the character of the links that join them—in particular, whether the latter fall into accustomed and unquestioned patterns of the "habitus," or whether an utterance and its reception subtly *bend* these in the direction of one or another protocritical deviation. Whence what Roberts, in her analysis, terms the "seditious power" of mimicry (p. 336).[25]

"Tout cela ne va pas trop mal," as Montaigne says at the conclusion of "Des Cannibales" (*Essais,* Book 1, chapter 31)—that is all very well. And Roberts's subtle detection of the counter-discursive potential of *La Fronde* is persuasive. Yet at the same time our analysis must take cool measure of the *constraints* upon any counter-discourse. For despite a seductive tendency in some quarters of academic criticism to transfer the project of overturning the dominant from the arena of mass to that of cultural politics, subversion is not so easy to achieve through language alone.[26] This becomes clear in what I might term the *other* side of the story Roberts herself has to tell about *La Fronde.* We must, therefore, look at the amount of power hegemonic forms retained even in the construction of *La Fronde*'s subversion (as Roberts projects it) and despite the remarkable ingeniousness of her analysis. For the entire structure of the paper's projected social effectiveness still relied, and indeed entirely depended, upon the forms and structures of a commercial institution whose power could to some degree be turned to one's own use, but never entirely displaced or mastered—particularly in the ideological effects that are always reproduced when they are deployed, even when the intention is explicitly parodic or subversive.

As I argued earlier, ultimately the dominant dominates. It creates and it controls the frame in which the forms of counter-discursive practices can be essayed and deployed.[27] To be sure, domination is always porous to some degree, and there is almost always (in Ross Chambers's fine phrase) "room for maneuver."[28] But as a variety of modern theories of the ideological have helped us to understand, the power of domination tends to *increase* as the hand that enforces it becomes less violent, less overtly onerous.[29] So as we consider the variety of feminist, working-class, and other dissident publications in the field of nineteenth-century journalism, it seems methodologically essential to avoid any form of romanticism concerning their social effectivity. We tend to term such publications "marginal," a word that resonates with our current fascination with "marginality" in all its diverse forms. Perhaps such a language might be questioned in the context of this volume. I am tempted to suggest the substitution of an imagery of "zones of effectiveness." For the diversity of the media that *Making the News* brings so strikingly to light makes it clear that, for significant populations in nineteenth-century France, publications like *Le Père Peinard* and *La Fronde* were not marginal at all.

Rather, we might find it helpful to talk about diverse "modalizations" of the political, cultural, and social effects of dominant and counterdiscursive media. Their expressions would then be modalized, would then sound, feel, and function somewhat differently: dominant discourses tending to work infrastructurally, forming almost unnoticed the perceptual and practical habits that organize our intercourse with the world; counter-discourses, on the other hand, functioning more consciously in a mode of programmatic confrontation. Of course it is precisely the latter "second city" effect that recognizes and expresses the hierarchy of power in which social discourses are always inscribed.

Through the uncircumventable infrastructural effects that defined the mass dailies and their dissident imitators, nineteenth-century journalism (and the related mechanisms of dissemination that this volume examines) transformed what we mean by "the public." The newspaper, the advertisement, the photograph, the scientific or technical periodical, later the cinema—these media might reasonably be said to have devised and defined crucial structures of life in the modern period. "The public" will always remain an elusive abstraction. But it can be read in what is *published*—produced, distributed, and digested—within a society. Deep enigmas and contradictions of modernity live in this wordplay between the ideality of the "community" the nineteenth century was learning to imagine and the materiality of its common and increasingly generalized practices.

Markets and products form each other. In the nineteenth century, the codetermining power of these social elements—new mass public, new mass publications—reads like a paradigm of how everyday life gets made. Disseminated, decentralized, diverse (whatever the dreams of individual press barons to dominate the social sphere at one or another moment may have been), this is a system with no identifiable author or victim. Yet—increasingly as the century advances—it involves an entire society. It precipitates an image—perhaps the *first* such image with wide social circulation—of that centerless, automatic, ubiquitous mechanism by which modern dailiness has been propagated and naturalized.

In the image of the daily paper, gone in twenty-four hours, the media participates in a paradox. Each number of a daily may be fleeting. But its power to form social consciousness and practice extends far beyond its ephemeral existence. This power has proven astonishingly durable. It arises uncannily through evanescence. News publications are not just consumed. We read them; but they form us. We discard yesterday's paper, but our habit of doing so only reinforces our practice of reaching for this morning's delivery. It deepens our quotidian anticipation of the *quotidien,* our daily expectation of the "news."

Notes

1. I borrow the term "habitus"—the habitual, patterned, and relatively stable ways of understanding, judging, and acting that arise from, and define our position in, the social structure—from the work of Pierre Bourdieu. See particularly his *Outline of a Theory of Practice,* Richard Nice, trans. (Cambridge: Cambridge University Press, 1977).

2. *La Révolution du langage poétique* (Paris: Seuil, 1974), 618.

3. Benedict Anderson reminds us that Hegel was already construing the daily reading of the newspaper as modernity's substitute for morning prayer. See Anderson, *Imagined Communities,* 2d ed. (London: Verso, 1991), 35.

4. See the classic essay by Paul de Man, "Literary History and Literary Modernity," in *Blindness and Insight,* 2d ed. (Minneapolis: University of Minnesota Press, 1983), 142–65.

5. See Steve Lohr, "The Future Came Faster in the Old Days," *New York Times,* 5 October 1997: 4, 1.

6. These commercials were to be the source of Whittle's profit, and according to one report, the company sold $600,000 of commercial time per day. The service began

(and the flap occurred) in 1989, and although some states or municipalities prohibited the service, this did not stop the venture. In 1993 twelve thousand schools and 8.1 million children in forty-five states were receiving Channel One. See the World-Wide-Web page of the Producers, Writers, and Directors Caucus, "Whittle's Channel One: What Is It?" (http://pweb1.ni.net/caucus.org/what/quindexes/sum93/whittles. html); and Ann Devany, ed., *Watching Channel One: The Convergence of Students, Technology, and Private Business* (Albany: State University of New York Press, 1994).

7. I examined this ambiguity in the "Newspaper Culture" chapter of *Discourse/Counter-Discourse* (Ithaca, N.Y.: Cornell University Press, 1985), chapter 2. Dean de la Motte expands upon it in his interesting piece in the current volume.

8. Dean de la Motte's essay earlier in the current volume gives a revealing account of the development of Girardin's ideas prior to his founding of *La Presse*. Girardin's logic, and the process it determines, uncannily repeats itself today. Upon assuming office earlier this year, Mark Willes, the new publisher of the *Los Angeles Times*, declared that his objective was to strengthen the paper financially. Toward this end he announced two significant moves. In the first he cut the daily price of the paper by half. In the second he promulgated a plan to reorganize its production by associating with each editorial department an executive from the business side of the paper. The objective was to foster a better climate for advertising and to increase revenue from that source. Willes almost certainly made these decisions without any reference to (or knowledge of) the history of nineteenth-century French journalism. But his moves eerily recall Giradin's famous price cut, and Villemessant's declaration that his paper, *Le Figaro*, would only satisfy him when every line in it had been bought and paid for (see Terdiman, *Discourse/Counter-Discourse*, 125). On the *Times* controversy, see Ken Auletta, "Demolition Man," *The New Yorker*, 17 November 1997, 40–45; and Iver Peterson, "At Los Angeles Times, a Debate on News-Ad Interaction," *New York Times*, National edition, 17 November 1997, Business section, C1.

9. Like many other writers, I have also reproduced this often-told story of Girardin and Millaud. See Terdiman, *Discourse/Counter-Discourse*, chapter 2, from which these details are drawn.

10. See, for example, Charles Morazé, *Les Bourgeois conquérants: XIXe* (Paris: A. Colin, 1957), 264 [*The Triumph of the Middle Classes* (Garden City, N.Y.: Anchor, 1968), 341]. In the decade from 1870 to 1880, real wages in France rose by 10.7 percent, the highest figure for the century; see François Caron, *An Economic History of Modern France* (New York: Columbia University Press, 1979), 88. Caron's chapter 5 on the development of trade is a convenient source for data about the remarkable growth during this period. It should be noted, however, that a cyclical depression, which lasted from 1882 to 1897, made the economic conclusion of the century more somber than the previous decade had been; see Rondo Cameron, *France and the Economic Development of Europe 1800–1914*, 2d ed. (Chicago: Rand McNally, 1961), 132.

11. Between 1830 and 1880, total newspaper circulation in France increased by a factor of forty—by *four thousand* percent (see Terdiman, *Discourse/Counter-Discourse*, 118). It is easy to conceive that the character of a party paper selling five thousand copies will be quite different from a mass daily selling forty times that number. Around 1830, the mayor of Verrières in Stendhal's *Le rouge et le noir* complains bitterly to his wife about the "liberal papers," and particularly *Le Constitutionnel* (see part 1, chapters 2 and 5). But later in the century the criticism of newspapers tended to focus not only on their specific political opinions, but on the institution of journalism itself, which was seen as an increasingly pervasive and corrupting influence upon the form and conduct of daily life, whatever the flavor of an individual paper's politics might have been.

12. See Terdiman, *Present Past: Modernity and the Memory Crisis* (Ithaca, N.Y.: Cornell University Press, 1993), 11.

13. Paul Ricoeur has been the most prominent theoretician of what he termed the "school of suspicion." See his *Freud and Philosophy: An Essay on Interpretation,* Denis Savage, trans. (New Haven: Yale University Press, 1970), 32. See also my discussion in Terdiman, *Present Past,* 303–6.

14. As the epigraphs to my essay here remind us. For more detail concerning this critique, see Terdiman *Discourse/Counter-Discourse,* chapter 2 passim, and pages 190, 302–3, and 335.

15. I did attempt to give some notion of the complexity of the journalistic field during the period by examining, through the work of Daumier, the primary satirical newspapers that flourished at the time, particularly *Le Charivari* (see Terdiman, *Discourse/Counter-Discourse,* chapter 3).

16. The French title was *L'ordre du discours* (Paris: Gallimard, 1971). See Foucault, "Discourse on Language," in *The Archaeology of Knowledge* (New York: Pantheon, 1972), 215–37.

17. Nancy Armstrong's work helps considerably in formulating these issues. See *Desire and Domestic Fiction: A Political History of the Novel* (New York: Oxford University Press, 1987), "Introduction," esp. 23.

18. Accusations of such venality in the American university go back at least as far as Veblen. Thorstein Veblen, *Higher Learning in America* (New York: Huebsch, 1918), 222. Veblen originally intended to subtitle his volume on the university "A Study in Total Depravity."

19. I borrow the term "value accent" from Bakhtin's collaborator V. N. Vološinov. See *Marxism and the Philosophy of Language,* Ladislav Matejka and I. R. Titunik, trans. (New York: Seminar Press, 1973).

20. *Capital: A Critique of Political Economy.* Volume 3, David Fernbach, trans. (New York: Vintage, 1981), 956. Translation modified. I am conscious to what degree, despite their current lack of fashion, my analysis in this essay resurrects important elements in Marxist thinking about culture. It may be worth noting how appropriate

these Marxian analytical tools seem today for examining a primary social discourse in the very period of Marx's own analytical work, and at the height of capitalism's conquest of the social field.

21. Recall Hegel's image of the supersession of the church by journalism; see note 3 above.

22. It is worth noting that *Le Journal des femmes* dated from the early years of the July Monarchy, *La Fronde* from the fin de siècle. So, whatever characteristics they had in common proved quite durable over the course of the century.

23. David K. Shipler, *A Country of Strangers: Blacks and Whites in America* (New York: Knopf, 1997), quoted in K. Anthony Appiah's review, *New York Times Book Review*, 16 November 1997, 11.

24. The effect reminds me of the notion of "re/citation" that I sought to develop in *Discourse/Counter-Discourse* (chapter 4) concerning Marx's and Flaubert's corrosive politics of quoting—without comment or explicit critique—the idiocies of their contemporaries, confident that the imbecility of the utterances they reproduced would *deconstruct themselves* and collapse under their own weight of obtuseness.

25. Beyond these oblique effects, of course, *La Fronde* projected an image of women's effectiveness and capability in areas where women had not previously been much present. As Roberts persuasively puts it, "Durand's paper produced an image of women as knowledgeable about and involved in the conventionally masculine spheres of politics, jurisprudence, and high finance" (p. 320).

26. See Richard Rorty's polemic in favor of traditional mass politics and against what he sees as the hypertropic exaggeration of the transgressive potential of cultural politics: "Intellectuals in Politics," *Dissent* 38:4 (Fall 1991), 483–90. See also the commentary in Thomas Bender's *Intellect and Public Life* (Baltimore: Johns Hopkins University Press, 1993), 142–43.

27. In a paradigmatic figure apposite here, Michel de Certeau suggested thinking of these practices as *"perruque."* The French working-class slang term *"perruque"* refers to the stratagem by which factory workers appropriate a corporation's time and raw materials and, out of sight of management, refashion them to their own uses. See Certeau, *Practice of Everyday Life* (Berkeley: University of California Press, 1984), 24–28ff. Yet, realistically, we need to recall that the law and *the workers themselves* inevitably recognize that the time and the materials appropriated in *"perruque"* remain those of the corporation. And the victory won in diverting them is always constrained and modulated by the infrastructural reality of a management control that determines even the *thrill* accompanying such petty larcenies.

28. See Chambers, *Room for Maneuver: Reading (the) Oppositional (in) Narrative* (Chicago: University of Chicago Press, 1991). Such porousness has played a central role even in situations we would characterize as totalitarian. To take one example, a recent article in the *New Yorker* considered China's most popular novelist, Wang Shuo, whose

books are regularly seized by the regime. But repression is unable to stop their circulation. "[Wang] added . . . that he was unconcerned for his readers, who, by some estimates, number in the millions; after all, they could still get their hands on pirated editions." See "Bad Boy," *New Yorker,* 21 April 1997, 51. Another notorious example of this phenomenon was the inability of the Soviet authorities to cut off communication (both internal and international) via fax and the Internet at the time of the fall of their regime.

29. On these issues, see Herbert Marcuse, *One-Dimensional Man* (Boston: Beacon, 1964), and Louis Althusser, "Ideology and Ideological State Apparatuses," in *Lenin and Philosophy* (New York: Monthly Review Press, 1971), 127–86. These Marxist views coincide with Michel Foucault's poststructuralist analysis. See in particular his "Discourse on Language," in *The Archaeology of Knowledge.*

Selected Bibliography

Nineteenth-Century French Newspapers and Periodicals

La Caricature

Le Chambard socialiste

Le Charivari

Le Conseiller des femmes

Le Constitutionnel

Le XIXe Siècle

L'Echo de la fabrique

L'Echo des travailleurs

La Femme libre

Le Figaro

La Fronde

La Gazette des tribunaux

La Glaneuse

L'Illustration

L'Indépendance belge

Le Journal

Le Journal des connaissances utiles

Le Journal des femmes

Le Journal officiel

Le Journal pour rire

La Libre Parole

Le Matin

Le Monde illustré

Le Père Duchêne

Le Père Peinard

Le Petit Journal

La Petite République

La Plume

Le Précurseur

La Presse

Le Révolté

La Révolution socialiste

La Revue bleue

La Revue des revues

La Revue encyclopédique

Le Siècle

Le Temps

La Vie parisienne

Other Primary Sources

Avenel, Henry. *Le Monde des journaux en 1895*. Paris: L'Annuaire de la presse française, 1895.

——. *La Presse française au vingtième siècle*. Paris: Flammarion, 1901.

Balzac, Honoré de. *La Comedie humaine*. Edition de la Pleiade. Paris: Gallimard, 1977.

——. "De l'état actuel de la librairie" (*Feuilleton des journaux politiques*). *Œuvres complètes*, 28 vols. Paris: Club de l'honnête homme, 1956: 23, 547–50.

——. *Illusions perdues*. Paris: G-F, Ph. Berthier, ed. 1990.

——. "Lettre aux écrivains français" (*Revue de Paris*, 2 November 1834). *Œuvres complètes*, 28 vols. Paris: Club de l'honnête homme, 1956: 23, 223–38.

———. "Notes remises à Messieurs les Députés composant la commission de la loi sur la propriété littéraire." *Œuvres complètes,* 28 vols. Paris: Club de l'honnête homme, 1956: 23, 717–35.

———. "Sur les questions de la propriété littéraire et de la contrafaçon" (*Chronique de Paris,* 30 October 1836). *Œuvres complètes,* 28 vols. Paris: Club de l'honnête homme, 1956: 23, 298–306.

Baudelaire, Charles. "Le Peintre de la vie moderne" (1863). *Ecrits sur l'art.* Paris: Le Livre de poche classique, 1992, 369–414. Translated into English as "The Painter of Modern Life" in *The Painter of Modern Life and Other Essays.* Jonathan Mayne, trans. New York: Da Capo, 1964, 1–40.

Brazen, Jules, and Félix Ribeyre. *Grands journaux de France.* Paris: Jouast Père, 1862.

Brunet, Charles. *Le Père Duchêne d'Herbert.* Paris: Librairie de France, 1859.

Chambure, A. de. *A Travers la presse.* Paris: Th. Fert, Albouy et Cie, 1914.

Dubief, Eugène. *Le Journalisme.* Paris: Hachette, 1892.

Gautier, Théophile. *Correspondance générale.* Claudine Lacoste-Veysseyre, ed. Geneva: Droz, 1985.

Goncourt, Edmond, and Jules de Goncourt. *Journal: mémoires d'une vie littéraire.* 22 vols. Monaco: Imprimerie nationale, 1956–1958.

Hatin, Eugène. *Histoire politique et littéraire de la presse en France.* Paris: Poulet-Malassis, 1861.

Hugues, Clovis. *Paris vivant: Le Journal.* Paris: F. Sahure, 1890.

Jaouën, J. *Les Specialistes de la presse: Brillants pamphlétaires et fougueux polémistes.* Paris: Chamuel et Cie., 1901.

Leroy-Beaulieu, Anatole. *Les Responsabilités de la presse.* Paris: Comité de defense et de progrès social, 1898.

Mallat, Joseph. *La Presse et les lectures populaires.* Paris: Librairie de la société bibliographie, 1887.

Nettement, Alfred de. *Etudes critiques sur le feuilleton-roman.* 2 vols. Paris: Perrodil, 1845–46.

Pataud, Emile, and Emile Pouget. *Comment nous ferons la révolution.* Paris: J. Tallandier, 1909.

Pelaez, Antolin Lopez. *La Femme et la presse.* Poitiers: Société française d'imprimerie, 1902.

Physiologie de la presse. Paris: J. Laisne, 1841.

Pottier, Paul. *Professions et métiers. Les Journalistes.* Paris: Action populaire, 1907.

Pouget, Emile. *Le Père Peinard.* Roger Langlais, ed. Paris: Editions Galilée, 1976.

Rémusat, Charles de. *Mémoires de ma vie.* Charles Pouthas, ed. 5 vols. Paris: Plon, 1959.

Roure, Henry du. *La Presse d'aujourd'hui et la presse de demain.* Paris: Au Sillon, 1908.

Tavernier, Eugène. *Du Journalisme: Son Histoire, son rôle politique et religieux.* Paris: H. Oudin, 1902.

Secondary Sources

Adler, Laure. *A l'aube du féminisme: Les Premières journalistes, 1830–1850.* Paris: Payot, 1979.

Aguet, J.-P. "Le tirage des quotidiens de Paris sous la Monarchie de Juillet." *Revue Suisse d'histoire* 10 (1960): 216–86.

Albert, Pierre. *Histoire de la presse. Que sais-je?* Paris: Presses universitaires françaises, 1996.

Allen, James Smith. *In the Public Eye: A History of Reading in Modern France, 1800–1940.* Princeton, N.J.: Princeton University Press, 1991.

———. *Popular French Romanticism: Authors, Readers, and Books in the Nineteenth Century.* Syracuse: Syracuse University Press, 1981.

Ambroise-Rendu, Anne-Claude. "Du dessin de presse à la photographie (1878–1914): Histoire d'une mutation technique et culturelle." *Revue d'histoire moderne et contemporaine* 39 (January–March 1992): 6–28.

Anderson, Benedict. *Imagined Communities.* Rev. ed. London: Verso, 1991.

Angenot, Marc. *1889: Un état du discours social.* Montréal: Editions du préambule, 1989.

Auclair, Georges. *Le Mana quotidien. Structures et fonctions de la chronique des faits divers.* Paris: Anthropos, 1970.

Barthes, Roland. *Le Degré zéro de l'écriture.* Paris: Seuil, 1972. Translated as *Writing Degree Zero.* New York: Hill and Wang, 1968.

Bellanger, Claude et al., *Histoire générale de la presse française.* 3 vols. Paris: Presses universitaires de France, 1972.

Bell-Villada, Gene H. *Art for Art's Sake and Literary Life: How Politics and Markets Helped Shape the Ideology of Aestheticism, 1790–1990.* Lincoln and London: University of Nebraska Press, 1996.

Benjamin, Walter. *Charles Baudelaire: A Lyric Poet in the Era of High Capitalism.* Harry Zohn, trans. New York: Verso, 1983.

———. *Illuminations: Essays and Reflections.* New York: Schocken, 1969.

———. *Reflections: Essays, Aphorisms, Autobiographical Writings.* New York: Schocken, 1969.

Brantlinger, Patrick. "Mass Media and Culture in Fin-de-Siècle Europe." *Fin de siècle and Its Legacy,* Mikulás Teich and Roy Porter, eds. Cambridge: Cambridge University Press, 1990.

Certeau, Michel de. *The Practice of Everyday Life.* Berkeley: University of California Press, 1984.

Chambers, Ross. *Room for Maneuver: Reading (the) Oppositional (in) Narrative.* Chicago: University of Chicago Press, 1991.

Chandler, James et al., eds. *Questions of Evidence: Proof, Practice, and Persuasion across the Disciplines.* Chicago: University of Chicago Press, 1994.

Childs, Elizabeth C. "Big Trouble: Daumier, *Gargantua,* and the Censorship of Political Caricature," *Art Journal* 51, no. 1 (Spring 1992): 26–37.

———. "The Secret Agents of Satire: Daumier, *Censorship, and the Image of the Exotic* in Political Caricature, 1850–1860." *Proceedings of the Annual Meeting of the Western Society for French History,* 17 (1990): 334–45.

Chollet, Roland. *Balzac journaliste, le tournant de 1830.* Paris: Klincksieck, 1983.

Chu, Petra Ten-Doesschate, and Gabriel P. Weisberg, eds. *The Popularization of Images: Visual Culture under the July Monarchy.* Princeton: Princeton University Press, 1994.

Clark, T. J. *The Absolute Bourgeois: Artists and Politics in France, 1848–1851.* Princeton: Princeton University Press, 1973.

———. *The Painting of Modern Life: Paris in the Art of Manet and His Followers.* Princeton: Princeton University Press, 1984.

Collins, Irene. "The Government and the Press in France during the Reign of Louis-Philippe." *English Historical Review,* no. 271 (April 1954): 262–82.

Cuno, James. "Charles Philipon, La Maison Aubert, and the Business of Caricature in Paris, 1829–41." *Art Journal* 43, no. 4 (Winter 1983): 347–54.

Daudet, Ernest. *Bréviaire du journalisme.* Paris: Gallimard, 1936.

de la Motte, Dean. "Making News, Making Readers: The Creation of the Modern Newspaper Public in Nineteenth-Century France." Laurel Brake, Bill Bell, David Finkelstein, eds., *Defining Centres: Nineteenth-Century Media and the Construction of Identities.* London: Macmillan, 1999.

Delteil, Loys. *Le Peintre-Graveur illustré: Honoré Daumier,* 11 vols. Paris: Chez l'Auteur, 1925–30.

de Man, Paul. "Literary History and Literary Modernity." *Blindness and Insight,* 2d ed. Minneapolis: University of Minnesota Press, 1983, 142–65.

English, Donald. *The Political Uses of Photography in the Third French Republic, 1871–1914.* Ann Arbor: University of Michigan Research Press, 1984.

Ferenczi, Thomas. *L'Invention du journalisme en France. Naissance de la presse moderne à la fin de XIXe siècle.* Paris: Plon, 1993.

Foucault, Michel. *The Archaeology of Knowledge.* New York: Pantheon, 1972.

Furet, François, and Jacques Ozouf. *Lire et écrire. L'alphabétisation des français de Calvin à Jules Ferry.* 2 vols. Paris: Editions de Minuit, 1977. Translated as *Reading and Writing: Literacy in France from Calvin to Jules Ferry.* New York: Cambridge University Press, 1982.

Gelbart, Nina. *Feminine and Opposition Journalism in Old Regime France: Le Journal des dames.* Berkeley: University of California Press, 1987.

George, Albert Joseph. *The Development of French Romanticism: The Impact of the Industrial Revolution on Literature.* Syracuse: Syracuse University Press, 1955.

Goldstein, Robert Justin. *Censorship of Political Caricature in Nineteenth-Century France.* Kent, Ohio: Kent State University Press, 1989.

Guise, René. "Balzac et le roman feuilleton." *L'Année balzacienne* (1964): 283–338.

——. "Le roman-feuilleton et la vulgarisation des idées politiques et sociales sous la Monarchie de Juillet." *Romantisme et politique 1815–1851. Colloque de l'Ecole Normale Supérieure de Saint-Cloud (1966)*. Paris: Armand Colin, 1969: 316–28.

Habermas, Jürgen. *The Structural Transformation of the Public Sphere*. Thomas Burger and Frederick Lawrence, trans. Cambridge: MIT Press, 1989.

Hunt, H. J. *Le Socialisme et le romantisme en France: Etude de la presse socialiste de 1830 à 1848*. Oxford: Clarendon Press, 1935.

Huyssen, Andreas. *After the Great Divide: Modernism, Mass Culture, Postmodernism*. Bloomington: Indiana University Press, 1986.

Isser, Natalie. *The Second Empire and the Press: A Study of Government-Inspired Brochures in French Foreign Policy in Their Propaganda Milieu*. The Hague: Nijhoff, 1974.

Jameson, Fredric. *Marxism and Form: Twentieth Century Dialectical Theories of Literature*. Princeton: Princeton University Press, 1971.

——. *The Political Unconscious: Narrative as a Socially Symbolic Act*. Ithaca, N.Y.: Cornell University Press, 1981.

Kracauer, Siegfried. *The Mass Ornament: Weimar Essays*. Thomas Y. Levin, trans. Cambridge: Harvard University Press, 1995.

Langlois, Pamela. "The Feminine Press in England and France, 1875–1900." Ph.D. diss., University of Massachusetts, Boston. 1979.

Ledré, Charles. *La Presse à l'assaut de la monarchie. 1815–1848*. Paris: Armand Colin, 1960.

Lee, Charles. *The Hidden Public: The Story of the Book-of-the-Month Club*. New York: Doubleday, 1958.

Leith, James A., ed. *Images of the Commune—Images de la Commune*. Montreal: McGill-Queen's University Press, 1978.

Livois, René de. *Histoire de la presse française*. 2 vols. Lausanne: Editions SPES, 1965.

Maitron, Jean. *Le mouvement anarchiste en France*. 2 vols. Paris: Editions François Maspero, 1975.

Martin, Marc. *Trois siècles de publicité en France*. Paris: Odile Jacob, 1993.

Mazedier, René. *Historie de la presse parisienne*. Paris: Editions de pavois, 1945.

Melot, Michel. "Daumier and Art History: Aesthetic Judgement/Political Judgement," *Oxford Art Journal* 11, no. 1 (1988): 3–24.

Merriman, John M. *The Margins of City Life: Explorations on the French Urban Frontier, 1815–1851*. New York: Oxford University Press, 1991.

Milner, Max and Claude Pichois. *Histoire de la littérature française, de Chateaubriand à Baudelaire: 1820–1869*. Paris: G-F, 1996.

Morgan, Cheryl A. "Les Chiffons de la M(éd)use: Delphine Gay de Girardin, journaliste." *Romantisme* 85, no. 3 (1994): 57–66.

Morienval, Jean. *Les Créateurs de la grande presse: Emile Girardin, II, de Villemessant, Moïse Millaud.* Paris: Editions Spes, 1934.

Musée national des arts et traditions populaires. *Le Fait divers.* Paris: Editions de la réunion des musées nationaux, 1982.

Palmer, Michel. *Des Petits Journaux aux grandes agences.* Paris: Aubier, 1983.

Parent-Lardeur, Françoise. *Lire à Paris au temps de Balzac: Les Cabinets de lecture à Paris, 1815–1830.* Paris: Editions des hautes etudes en sciences sociales, 1981.

Pelissier, Pierre. *Emile de Girardin: Le Créateur de la presse moderne.* Paris: Denoël, 1985.

Petrey, Sandy. "Pears in History." *Representations,* no. 35 (Summer 1991): 52–71.

Pichois, Claude. "Les cabinets de lecture à Paris durant la première moitié du XIXe siècle." *Annales,* no. 3 (1959): 521–34.

Pierrot, Roger. *Honoré de Balzac.* Paris: Fayard, 1994.

Popkin, Jeremy D. *Revolutionary News: The Press in France, 1789–1799.* Durham, N.C.: Duke University Press, 1990.

Przyblyski, Jeannene M. "Moving Pictures: Photography, Narrative, and the Paris Commune, 1871." *Cinema and the Invention of Modern Life.* Leo Charney and Vanessa R. Schwartz, eds. Berkeley: University of California Press, 1995, 253–78.

Queffélec, Lise. *Le Roman-feuilleton français au XIXe siècle. Que sais-je,* no. 2466. Paris: Presses universitaires françaises, 1989.

Rancière, Jacques. "The Archeomodern Turn." In Michael P. Steinberg, ed., *Walter Benjamin and the Demands of History.* Ithaca, N.Y.: Cornell University Press, 1996, 24–40.

Reclus, Maurice. *Emile de Girardin: Le Créateur de la presse moderne.* Paris: Hachette, 1934.

Reddy, William, "Condottieri of the Pen: Journalists and the Public Sphere in Postrevolutionary France." *American Historical Review* 99 (December 1994): 1546–70.

Riley, Denise. *"Am I That Name?" The Category of "Woman" in History.* Minneapolis: University of Minnesota Press, 1988.

Roberts, Mary Louise. "Acting Up: The Feminist Theatrics of Marguerite Durand." *French Historical Studies* 19 (Fall 1996): 1103–38.

Rubin, Joan Shelley. *The Making of Middlebrow Culture.* Chapel Hill: University of North Carolina Press, 1992.

Sainéan, Lazare. *Le Langage parisien au XIXe siècle.* Paris: E. de Bocard, 1920.

Schwartz, Vanessa R. *Spectacular Realities: Early Mass Culture in Fin-de-Siècle Paris.* Berkeley: University of California Press, 1998.

Scott, Joan. *Only Paradoxes to Offer: French Feminists and the Rights of Man.* Cambridge: Harvard University Press, 1996.

Séguin, Jean-Pierre. *Les Canards illustrés du 19e siècle: Fascination du fait divers.* Paris: Musée-galerie de la seita, 1982.

Seigel, Jerrold. *Bohemian Paris: Culture, Politics, and the Boundaries of Bourgeois Life.* New York: Viking Penguin, 1986.

Silverman, Debora L. *Art Nouveau in Fin-de-Siècle France: Politics, Psychology, and Style.* Berkeley: University of California Press, 1989.

Sonn, Richard. *Anarchism and Cultural Politics in Fin-de-Siècle France.* Lincoln: University of Nebraska Press, 1989.

Strumingher, Laura. "Mythes et réalités de la condition féminine à travers la presse féministe lyonnaise des années 1830." *Cahiers d'histoire* 21 (1976): 409–24.

Sullerot, Evelyn. *Histoire de la presse féminine en France des origines à 1848.* Paris: Armand Colin, 1966.

Teich, Mikulás, and Roy Porter, eds. *Fin de Siècle and Its Legacy.* Cambridge: Cambridge University Press, 1990.

Terdiman, Richard. *Discourse / Counter-Discourse: The Theory and Practice of Symbolic Resistance in Nineteenth-Century France.* Ithaca, N.Y.: Cornell University Press, 1985.

——. *Present Past: Modernity and the Memory Crisis.* Ithaca, N.Y.: Cornell University Press, 1993.

Tournier, Maurice. "*Le Père Peinard* et le burlesque populaire" and "Subversion des valeurs sociales et subversion des valeurs de langue. L'Exemple du *Père Peinard.*" *Des Mots sur la grève: propos d'etymologie sociale.* Vol. 1. Paris: Klincksieck, 1992. 1:237–52; 1:253–64.

Tulard, Jean. *Les Révolutions de 1789 à 1851.* Paris: Fayard, 1985.

Van Dijk, Suzanna. *Traces de femmes: Présence féminine dans le journalisme français du XVIIIe siècle.* Amsterdam: APA Holland University Press, 1988.

Voyenne, Bernard. *Les Journalistes français.* Paris: CFPJ-Retz, 1985.

Wolgensinger, Jacques. *La Grande aventure de la presse.* Paris: Gallimard [Découvertes], 1989.

Zeldin, Theodore. *France 1848–1945.* 4 vols. Oxford: Oxford University Press, 1980.

Notes on Contributors

Maria Adamowicz-Hariasz is assistant professor at the University of Akron where she teaches courses in French language and literature. She has published articles on Eugène Sue and is currently revising her dissertation, " 'Le Juif errant' d'Eugène Sue. Poétique et politique d'un roman populaire," for publication.

James Smith Allen is professor of modern European history at Southern Illinois University, Carbondale. The author of two books and various articles on French history, he has just completed a book-length manuscript entitled, "The Poignant Relations of Three Modern French Women." He is currently working on the subject of women in freemasonry.

John R. Barberet is assistant professor of French and comparative literature at Case Western Reserve University and visiting assistant professor of French at Oberlin College. He has written on Sade, Marxism, and Baudelaire and is completing a book on the diffusion and reception of literature from Balzac to Baudelaire.

Elizabeth C. Childs teaches art history at Washington University. Her publications on the caricature of Daumier include the exhibition catalogue (with Kirsten Powell) *Femmes d'esprit: Women in Daumier's Caricature* (Middlebury College, 1990) and an essay in her anthology, *Suspended License: Censorship and the Visual Arts* (University of Washington Press, 1997). Her next book, forthcoming with University of California Press, is *In Search of Paradise: Painting and Photography in Colonial Tahiti*.

Dean de la Motte is assistant professor of French at Guilford College in Greensboro, North Carolina. He is the author of several articles on nineteenth-century French literature and culture, and he is coeditor of *Approaches to Teaching Stendhal's "The Red and the Black"* (MLA, 1999). He is at work on a book-length study of narratives of progress in nineteenth-century France.

Howard G. Lay is assistant professor of the history of art at the University of Michigan. He is nearing completion of a book that focuses on avant-garde and bohemian culture in fin-de-siècle Paris and the production of popular mythologies in and around Montmartre's notorious entertainment industry.

Cheryl Morgan is associate professor of French at Hamilton College. She coedited *Contre-courants: Les Femmes s'écrivent à travers les siècles* and has published on nineteenth-century French women writers. She is currently working on a critical biography of Delphine Gay de Girardin.

Jeremy D. Popkin, professor of history at the University of Kentucky, has published several books on the history of the French press, including *News and Politics in the Age of Revolution* (Cornell University Press, 1989) and *Revolutionary News: The Press in France, 1789–1799* (Duke University Press, 1990). He has also published *A History of Modern France* and *A Short History of the French Revolution,* both with Prentice Hall. He is currently working on a book about the press and the revolution of 1830.

Jeannene M. Przyblyski received her Ph.D. in art history from the University of California, Berkeley. She has published essays on Courbet's still lifes and on the precinematic conditions of photography during the Paris Commune. Her book entitled *The Paris Commune Between History and Memory: Photography, Revolution, and Repression in 1871* is forthcoming.

Mary Louise Roberts is associate professor of history at Stanford University. Her first book, *Civilization without Sexes: Reconstructing Gender in Postwar France, 1917–1927,* won the American Historical Association's Joan Kelly Award for the Best Book in Women's History 1994. She is currently working on a book manuscript titled "Great Performers: The New Woman, Journalism, and Theater at the Fin de Siècle."

Richard Terdiman is professor of French literature and the history of consciousness at the University of California, Santa Cruz. He has published on nineteenth- and twentieth-century French literature and culture. Among his books are *Discourse/Counter-Discourse* and *Present Past.* He is working on the cultural theory and experience of time in the modern period.